THE ORGANIZATION OF

INDUSTRY

THE ORGANIZATION OF
INDUSTRY

GEORGE J. STIGLER

The University of Chicago Press
Chicago and London

The University of Chicago Press, Chicago 60637
The University of Chicago Press, Ltd., London

00 99 98 97 96 95 94 93   5 6 7 8 9 10

Library of Congress Cataloging in Publication Data

Stigler, George Joseph, 1911–
  The organization of industry.

  Reprint. Originally published: Homewood, Ill.:
R.D. Irwin, 1968.
  Includes bibliographies and index.
  1. Industrial organization (Economic theory)
2. Industry. 3. Antitrust law—Economic aspects.
I. Title.
HD2326.S78   1983   338.7   82-20013
ISBN 0-226-77432-5 (pbk.)

PREFACE

The main content of this book is a reprinting of 17 articles I have written over the past two decades in the area of industrial organization. I have reprinted the articles as they appeared, and added commentaries in numerous cases; this seemed more appropriate than seeking to graft present views, where they differ, on an earlier position. There is also a substantial amount of previously unpublished material, some written years ago and some prepared especially for this volume.

Although the main topics in industrial organization are touched upon, the touch is often light. The ratio of hypothesis to reasonably persuasive confirmation is distressingly high in all economic literature, and it must be my chief if meager defense that I am not the worst sinner in the congregation.

June, 1968   GEORGE J. STIGLER

TABLE OF CONTENTS

APPENDIX

INDEX

Chapter 1

WHAT IS INDUSTRIAL ORGANIZATION?

Let us start this volume on a higher plane of candor than it will always maintain: there is no such subject as industrial organization. The courses taught under this heading have for their purpose the understanding of the structure and behavior of the industries (goods and service producers) of an economy. These courses deal with the size structure of firms (one or many, "concentrated" or not), the causes (above all the economies of scale) of this size structure, the effects of concentration on competition, the effects of competition upon prices, investment, innovation, and so on. But this is precisely the content of economic theory—price or resource allocation theory, now often given the unfelicitous name of microeconomics.

The reasons that courses emerge in industrial organization separate from those in economic theory are nevertheless mostly honorable:

1. Economic theory is sufficiently formal, and contains sufficient apparatus, so that a course in theory cannot go into detailed studies of empirical measurement of cost curves, concentration, etc.—so a course in industrial organization does go into these matters.
2. A course in theory, for the same reason, cannot go into public policy questions—in particular, those proposed by antitrust laws and public regulation—and so the course in industrial organization takes on these chores.

(There is also a less honorable reason for the separate field of industrial organization: much of its literature has been so nontheoretical, or even antitheoretical, that few economic theorists were attracted to it.) Neither policy nor empirical measurement provides a clean distinction between industrial organization and economic theory, however, and numerous chapters in my *Theory of Price* could perfectly well have come here.

By tradition only a portion of the economic system is included in industrial organization: one excludes labor markets, agricultural industries, retail markets, financial markets, and foreign trade. Each of these

1

fields contains enough materials and problems to fuel its own specialists and courses. The tradition will not stop us from making several reconnaissances in force.

PART I

What Is Competition? And Monopoly?

The nature of competition and monopoly, and their relationship to the number of firms in an industry and their comparative sizes, is our first problem. Skipping the history of the competitive concept,[1] the materials are:

CHAPTER 2

Competition (*International Encyclopedia of the Social Sciences*),[2] with three new addenda.

CHAPTER 3

Price and Non-Price Competition (*Journal of Political Economy*, 1968), a comparison of the two types of competition.

CHAPTER 4

The Measurement of Concentration, with addenda on oligopoly theory.

CHAPTER 5

A Theory of Oligopoly (*Journal of Political Economy*, 1964), an attempt to deal with the most difficult problem in price theory, with an amendment.

[1] It is given in "Perfect Competition, Historically Contemplated," *Journal of Political Economy*, February 1957.

[2] Reprinted by permission of Crowell-Collier and Macmillan, Inc. No part of this chapter may be reproduced without their written permission.

COMPETITION

Competition may be the spice of life, but in economics it has been more nearly the main dish. Competition has been a major force in the organization of production and the determination of prices and incomes, and economic theory has accorded commensurate importance to the concept.

Competition enters all major areas of man's life, and generally connotes rivalry between two or more men or groups for a given prize. Competition is often an end in itself. Sporting events are clear illustrations: we should be shocked if two teams called off the event or arranged a tie, and divided the prize. Indeed the prize is a minor goal in a true sporting event.

In economic life competition is not a goal: it is a means of organizing economic activity to achieve a goal. The economic role of competition is to discipline the various participants in economic life to provide their goods and services skilfully and cheaply.

I. PERFECT COMPETITION

Market Competition

When one asks (as Cournot was the first to do in a precise way, in 1838) whether the competition of three merchants will serve better than two, or why two (or three) do not combine into a monopoly, the answers prove to be elusive. But one can partially evade such questions by posing a very extreme degree of competition, which the economist calls perfect competition.

A main requirement of perfect competition is that the largest firm in an industry makes a trifling fraction of the industry's sales (or purchases), from which it follows that there be many firms in the industry. No definite number has been found for the maximum share of one firm compatible with competition; presumably the largest firm in a competitive industry can be larger, the more elastic the industry demand and the easier the conditions of entry by new firms.

These many firms, no one or few of which account for an appreciable share of the industry's output, are assumed to act independently. This can be viewed as a second condition for perfect competition, or as an inevitable corollary of the large numbers in the absence of legal controls over the industry. For it is a fact that there are insuperable difficulties in organizing an effective combination of many persons, when it is profitable for each person secretly to depart from the agreement (as is generally the case in economic life).

Such large numbers suggest, what is true, that (perfect) economic competition is *impersonal*. In the economic race, there are 1,000 or 100,000 runners, and each gets a prize proportional to his efforts. The fortunes of any one firm are independent of what happens to any other firm: one farmer is not benefited if his neighbor's crop is destroyed. The essence of perfect competition, therefore, is not strong rivalry but rather the utter dispersion of power to influence market behavior. The power, for example, to restrict quantities sold and raise prices is effectively annihilated when it is divided among a thousand men, just as a gallon of water is effectively annihilated if it is spread over a thousand acres.

A third condition of perfect competition is complete knowledge of offers to buy and sell by the participants in the market. This condition serves just the opposite purpose of the preceding condition. The assumption that traders act independently serves to keep them apart, and hence numerous; the assumption that each seller knows what various buyers will pay, and vice versa, is necessary to keep the parties together—in the same market. If seller A and buyer B dealt only with one another in ignorance of all other traders, and similarly for every other pair of buyers and sellers, each transaction would represent an exchange under bilateral monopoly.

These conditions of perfect competition are enough to insure that a single price will rule in a market—in fact perfect knowledge is enough for this purpose—and that this price is affected only negligibly by the actions of any one or few buyers or sellers. (It is sometimes additionally assumed that the product of all sellers be homogeneous, but this can also be viewed as part of the definition of the market or industry.) The definition of perfect competition is therefore sometimes expressed in the equivalent form: the demand curve facing any one seller is infinitely elastic; and the supply curve facing any buyer is infinitely elastic.

To these basic conditions of perfect competition—numerous traders on each side of the market, independence of action, and perfect knowledge—it is necessary to add *divisibility* of the commodity or service being traded. If the units are lumpy, it is possible that minor discontinuities will emerge that allow some small market power to individuals.[1]

These conditions of perfect competition pertain to a single market, whether of shoes or bonds or carpenter's services. So far as the presence or absence of monopoly power is concerned, it is not necessary to look at any other market. For this reason these conditions pertain to what may be called *market* competition.

It is traditional, however, to enlarge the conditions of competition so that they will insure an optimal allocation of resources, by specifying the nature of the movement of resources among markets and industries. This enlarged concept, which may be termed *industrial* competition, is our next subject.

The Mobility of Resources (Industrial Competition)

If a productive resource is to be utilized efficiently, it must be equally productive in all of its uses—clearly if its (marginal) product is less in one use than another, output is not being maximized. Hence two additional conditions have commonly been made a part of perfect competition: resources are mobile among uses; and their owners are informed as to yields in these various uses.

First, the mobility of resources. A vast galaxy of private and public barriers to the mobility of resources has been erected in various times and places: boycotts; certificates of convenience and necessity; patent licenses; settlements laws; franchises; licensing of occupations; etc. Such barriers are all actually or potentially incompatible with competition. But it is not necessary for competition that the movement of resources be

---

[1] The need for divisibility was demonstrated by Edgeworth with the following example. Let each servant work for only one master, and each master employ only one servant. Let each servant demand at least $50 per unit of time, and each master offer at most $100. If the number of servants and masters is large and equal, the wage rate will be indeterminate between $50 and $100. More important; one servant can drive the wage rate to $100 by withdrawing from the market (and similarly a master could drive the rate to $50), so even one of a thousand servants or masters can affect the rate. See Edgeworth, 1881, p. 46; Stigler, 1957, pp. 8–9. (A Bibliography for this chapter appears on p. 16.)

free: the retraining of a worker, or the transportation of a tool, may be costly without interfering with competition.

Second, the adequacy of information. We must enlarge our earlier condition of full information to include knowledge of the yields on resources in alternative employments. From another viewpoint, we may say that ignorance is a barrier to profitable movement of resources.

If these conditions are fulfilled, the maximum possible output (measured by value) will be obtained from a productive resource. If this be true for each resource, the output of the economy is at a maximum. This famous theorem (labeled "on maximum satisfaction" by Walras and Marshall) is subject to a qualification, as all interesting propositions are: the *private* marginal product of a productive resource (the amount its owner receives and hence what governs its allocation) must equal the *social* marginal product (private marginal product plus or minus the effects on others). Of course, the maximum value output is dependent upon the distribution of income (which affects the demands for goods and hence their prices).

Time and Competition

What we have termed *industrial* competition—competition including mobility of resources—obviously has an implicit time dimension. It takes time to move resources out of unprofitable fields, especially if the resources are specialized and durable so that only through disentangling depreciation funds can the resources be withdrawn. It takes time, too, to construct a new factory or shop if one wishes to enter an industry. Comparable statements can be made about the geographical and occupational mobility of labor. Similarly, time is a factor in the completeness of knowledge. It takes time to learn which industries or jobs are most remunerative, or to learn the prices quoted by various sellers (or the quality of service and product), and one's knowledge is more complete and reliable, the more thorough the search for information and the larger the experience on which it is based.

Capital embodied in specialized and durable equipment will not be transferred to other uses except at extreme price differentials in the short run, even though in the long run the slightest differential in returns may be sufficient to move capital funds. Conversely, only under extreme incentives will new establishments be created virtually overnight, as we sometimes observe in wartime.

This fact that it is more expensive to do things very quickly than at slower pace does not qualify the proposition that resources will tend to be put where they earn the most, but we are reminded of the implicit proviso: allowance being made for the cost of moving the resources.

The differences in returns to a resource in various uses can be very great in the short run, but will decline to a minimum level set by the cost of the most efficient method of moving resources. There is implicit in economic literature a widespread belief that these minimum costs of movement of resources are very small relative to their returns, so little imprecision arises from neglecting them entirely. This may be true, but it has not been demonstrated. The belief nevertheless led economists (for example, J. B. Clark) to postulate instantaneous and costless mobility as the pure case of perfect industrial competition. It seems preferable to say that minimum differentials in returns to resources are achieved only in the long run. Market competition is not so intimately related to time. One's information about price bids and offers improves somewhat as he searches the market more thoroughly—itself a time-consuming process— but the changing conditions of supply and demand lead to changes in prices which make the old information obsolete.

II. THE THEORY OF COMPETITIVE PRICES

The competitive structure of industry will lead to the establishment of competitive prices. Competitive prices are characterized by two main properties. The property of clearing markets is that of distributing existing supplies efficiently; the property of equalizing returns to resources is that of directing production efficiently.

The Clearing of Markets

A competitive price is one which is not perceptibly influenced by any one buyer or seller. When we say that such prices are fixed by "supply and demand" what we mean is that the ensemble of all buyers and sellers determine price.

Since every buyer can purchase all he wishes of the good or service at the market price, there are no queues or unsatisfied demands (given the price). Since every seller can sell all he wishes at this market price, there are no undisposable stocks, other than inventories which are voluntarily held for future periods. The competitive price, then, clears the market—it equates the quantities offered by sellers and sought by buyers.

Whenever we find a persistent queue among buyers, we know that the price is being held *below* the level which clears the market, and which we naturally call an equilibrium price. For example, when housing is unavailable under rent controls, we know that rents are below the equilibrium level. Whenever we find stocks held by sellers to be in excess of inventory needs, we know price is *above* the equilibrium level. The vast stocks of agricultural products held by the U.S. government are evidence that the prices of these products (more precisely, the amounts the government will lend on the products) are above the equilibrium level.

The importance of prices that clear markets is that this is the method by which goods and services are put in the hands of the people who most urgently wish them. If a price is held too low, some buyers who set a lower value on the commodity will get it while others in the queue who set a higher value get none. If the price is set too high, goods that buyers would be glad to purchase at a lower price go unsold even though (if a minimum price is imposed on a competitive industry) sellers would prefer to sell at this lower price.

The Equalization of Returns

It is part of the definition of industrial competition that every resource in an industry earns as much, but no more than, it would earn in other industries. The self-interest of the owners of productive resources (including, of course, that most important resource, the laborer) leads them to apply their resources where they yield the most, and thus to enter unusually attractive fields and abandon unattractive fields.

This equalization of returns, however, can be shown to imply that the prices of goods and services equal their (marginal) costs of production. The cost of a productive service to an industry is the amount that must be paid to attract it away from other uses—its foregone alternatives (which has given this most basic concept of cost the label of the alternative or opportunity cost theory). If the amount the productive resource earns in an industry is in excess of this cost, clearly other units of the resource presently outside the industry could earn more if they enter. Conversely, if the productive resource is earning less than its cost or alternative product, it will leave the industry. Hence if price exceeds cost, resources will flow in and lower price (and perhaps raise cost by raising the prices of the resources), and if price is less than cost, resources will flow out of the industry and increase price (and perhaps reduce costs).

The equality of the *marginal* products of a resource in all its uses is the condition for efficient production, as we have remarked. The equality of *average* products has often been substituted, with a regrettable loss of logic: consider the catastrophic waste (of capital) in having equal output per worker in two industries when the capital equipment per worker is 10 times as large in one industry as in the other. But if the *marginal product* of a resource is equal in its various uses, it follows that *marginal cost* must equal price. The resources necessary to produce one more unit of product A could produce an equal value of B, so the marginal cost of A—which is the foregone alternative of producing B—is equal to the value of A that it produces. Marginal cost, formally defined as an increment of cost divided by the increment of product associated with the increment of cost, and not the more easily measured average cost (total cost divided by output) is the economist's fundamental criterion of competitive price—and of optimum price.

Marshall's Period Analysis

The alternative uses open to a resource depend upon the time available for its redeployment (or, more fundamentally, how much one is willing to spend on its movement). This principle, joined to an empirical observation that one can alter the rate of operation of a plant much sooner than one can build a new plant or wear out an existing one, provide the bases for the standard (Marshallian) theory of long- and short-run competitive prices.

In the short run, defined as the period within which one cannot appreciably alter the number of plants (physical production units), the only method of varying output is to work a given plant more or less intensively. The so-called variable productive factors (labor, materials, fuel, etc.) are the only resources with effective alternative uses in this period, and therefore the only services whose returns enter into marginal costs. The returns to the productive factors embodied in the plant are called quasi-rents. So long as quasi-rents are greater than zero, it will be more profitable to operate a plant than to close it down.

The long run is defined as the period within which the entrepreneur can make any desired decision—including the decision to leave one industry and enter another. In this period all resources are variable in quantity,- and therefore the returns to all factors enter into marginal cost.

The Marshallian apparatus permits very useful simplifications in price theory, but only if its underlying empirical assumption is fulfilled: the long-run adjustments of the firm are of negligible magnitude in the short run (and hence can be neglected) and the short-run adjustments do not appreciably affect the long-run costs. When these conditions are not met—they fail, for example, if discharge of workers this period will lead to higher wage rates next period—the full analysis of the short run will still require explicit analysis of the long-run repercussions of the short-run decisions.

III. ALTERNATIVE CONCEPTS AND POLICIES

Less Stringent Concepts of Competition

The austerity and abstractness of the concept of perfect competition have led many economists to seek a more "realistic" concept, and this search has been reinforced by the need for a concept of competition in the enforcement of the American antitrust statutes. A variety of concepts have accordingly been proposed, but since they were deliberately contrived to fit the infinitely varied circumstances of a vast economy, they lack the analytical clarity of perfect competition.

The most popular of these variant concepts has been that of J. M. Clark, which he labeled *workable competition*. The philosophy of this concept is clear enough: real industries will seldom have thousands of independent firms, and never will the entrepreneurs have complete knowledge. It is not useful to characterize all of these industries as imperfectly competitive, for some will be near-monopolies and other will have prices, outputs, and rates of progress that deviate in only minor respects from what perfectly competitive industries would experience. In particular, many industries do not depart sufficiently from perfect competition (which is of course unattainable) to create any need for antitrust actions or public regulation.

Workable competition has been a very popular concept since its formalization in 1940, but its serious ambiguity has not been reduced during this period. How close an industry should be to competition (using observable criteria we shall discuss below) to be workably competitive has never been settled. Indeed the criteria (prices, service, product innovation, rates of return, etc.) which deserve most weight in any application of the concept have not been agreed upon. Two competent persons who study a particular industry can disagree on its workable competitiveness, and there exists no analytical basis for eliminating the disagreement.

Monopolistic competition, the other leading concept, is due to E. H. Chamberlin, and is directed to a different purpose. He emphasized the diversity in the products of firms which are normally considered members of a single industry—they differ in details of quality, in repute, in locational convenience, in the religion of their producer, and a hundred other details which may influence their desirability to various buyers. Chamberlin emphasized also the similarity of products made by what are viewed as different industries: one may use aluminum or steel or wood to build a chair. A person may ostentatiously display his wealth with jewels, servants, or trips abroad. Each firm, in this view, has some elements of uniqueness (monopoly power) and yet many rivals, and the admixture gives rise to the title of the concept. The theory of monopolistic competition has led to a much more thorough examination of the problems of defining commodities and industries. It has not been found useful in the analysis of concrete economic problems.[2]

Competitive Equilibrium

The lack of conscious coordination of the behavior of individuals in a competitive market has led many writers to assert the impossibility of any stable equilibrium. Some have denied that any order is observable: the continental cartel literature usually uses the word "chaotic" as a prefix to competition, and most proposals for an "orderly" policy assume that a competitive system is disorderly. Others have found cumulative tendencies in competition: for example, W. H. Thornton said that "if a single employer succeed in screwing down wages . . . his fellow-employers may have no alternative but to follow suit,"[3] and Sidney and Beatrice Webb elaborated this view into their famous theory of "higgling in the market."[4]

Modern economic analysis, on the other hand, makes competitive equilibrium the central part of the theory of prices and allocation of resources. The presence of order and continuity in markets composed of many independently acting buyers and sellers has been established beyond serious question, on both theoretical and empirical grounds.

The main stumbling block in the layman's acceptance of competitive equilibrium is the belief that many individuals acting independently will necessarily either undershoot or overshoot every appropriate change in output, prices, investment, etc. If, for example, increasing demand calls for a 10 percent increase in industry capacity, how can this precise total be achieved when a vast number of firms are individually and independently changing their plants in a hundred different proportions? In a sense this is a false question: no one can know that next year's demand will be exactly 10 percent larger, and neither a public body nor a private

---

[2] A fuller discussion of monopolistic competition is given in the Appendix, "Monopolistic Competition in Retrospect," at the end of this book.

[3] *On Labour* (1869), p. 81.

[4] *Industrial Democracy* (1897), Part III, chap. ii.

monopolist can guarantee to have the "right" amount of capacity next year. But let us put this complication aside.

The answer, then, is that there is much information available to guide the decisions of the numerous independent firms. Partly this is current information—every trade is abreast of the investment decisions of its various firms, of the developments in products and production methods, etc. This information comes from salesmen, trade journals, customers and suppliers, and a host of other sources. And lastly, the firm is guided by past behavior in the industry: if previous increases of output were supplied in some part by new firms, this becomes a factor in current decisions.

Empirical Evidence of Competition

A variety of statistical tests of the existence of competition have been proposed at various times, and at least three deserve some attention.

The presence of numerous firms, none dominant in size, is directly observable and is usually described by a low concentration ratio. The main difficulty with this structural test of competition is that the maximum concentration compatible with competition has not been determined, so the test is clear only when concentration is low. The problem is complicated by the fact that we have had no theoretical guide in the summarizing frequency distribution of firm sizes, which can, of course, be done in many ways.

Since a single price will rule under *perfect* competition, price homogeneity has often been proposed as a test of competition. We have already remarked that perfect knowledge is enough to insure a single price, whether the market is competitive or monopolistic. Indeed, in a market of numerous sellers and buyers it is impossible that all prices in a given short interval of time will be uniform. It is improbable for two reinforcing reasons: the transactions will seldom be in completely homogeneous goods (quantity discounts, promptness of payment, and a dozen other characteristics vary almost infinitely among transactions); and the cost of learning market prices is such that complete information is not worth its cost (with numerous traders). As a result, strict uniformity of prices has properly been viewed by the courts as a phenomenon more suggestive of collusion than of competition.

A related evidence of competition is more powerful: the absence of systematic price discrimination. If sellers are persistently obtaining higher net receipts (which need not be the same as prices) from some buyers than from others, we may be confident that they are acting in concert—a truly independent firm would concentrate its sales on the buyers who yielded higher net receipts.

Perhaps the most traditional test of the absence of competition is a high rate of return on investment. It has lost much popularity because of the difficulty of measuring profitability (in particular, the valuation of durable assets can conceal monopoly profits or create fictitiously high rates of return) and because an absence of high profits is compatible with various cartel arrangements. Yet it is true that unusually high or low rates of return will not persist for long periods in a competitive industry. More specifically, a recent study suggests that in unconcentrated manufacturing industries the rates of return of one year will provide no useful clue to the rates earned say five years hence (Stigler, 1963, chap. iii).

Public Policies

Laws, both statutory and common, have sought for centuries to protect competition. The Statute of Monopolies (1623), which was passed to restrain the Crown's use of grants of monopoly for revenue, was a famous example, as were also the statutes (which Adam Smith compared in rationality to laws against witchcraft) against forestalling, engrossing, and regrating grain.

The Sherman Act (1890) was path-breaking, therefore, not in its prohibition of restraints of trade but in the implementation of this policy by an administrative force charged with ferreting out and prosecuting such acts. This most basic of all antimonopoly laws forbad not only conspiracies in restraint of trade but also attempts to monopolize, and in such broad terms as almost to defy conflicts of spirit and letter. Criminal penalties were supplemented by the incentive of triple damages to private parties who were injured by the forbidden acts.

The complaint that the Sherman Act came into force only after competitive markets had been destroyed (which was not true, nor wholly false), and the belief that a group of specialists could deal with industrial problems more effectively than the judiciary had, and the general impatience of reformers, all combined to bring about (in 1914) the Clayton Act, which prohibited a set of practices which (it was believed) often led to monopoly, and the act creating the Federal Trade Commission to enforce the Clayton Act. With amendments—the most important being the Robinson-Patman Act (1936) and the Celler-Kefauver Merger Act (1950)—the legislative basis of American policy had been developed. This policy includes certain discordant anticompetitive elements (the Robinson-Patman Act, with its goal of rigid uniformity of prices, and the legalization of resale price maintenance), as general policies have a habit of doing.

That this policy has contributed to the competitiveness of the American economy is difficult to deny or to document. Yet international comparisons—in particular, of the same industry (often constituted of the same firms) in Canada and the United States—suggest that the policy has had substantial effects. So too does the fact that the favorite practices of the formal cartel—a joint sales agency or division of customers—are quite uncommon in the United States.

The policy of restricting agreements among competitors (but not the policy of seeking to prevent monopolies) has spread to numerous other nations since its introduction in the United States. The most common form is to require registration of agreements among firms in an industry, and the approval or disapproval of the agreement by a specially constituted body. This is the practice of England, Germany, and several other nations, as well as the European Common Market.

BIBLIOGRAPHY

CHAMBERLIN, E. H. *The Theory of Monopolistic Competition*. Cambridge, Mass.: Harvard University Press, 1933.

CLARK, J. M. "Toward a Concept of Workable Competition," *American Economic Review*, Vol. XXX (1940), pp. 241–56.

EDGEWORTH, F. Y. *Mathematical Psychics*. 1881. London School Reprints of Scarce Works in Economics, 1932.

KNIGHT, F. H. *Risk, Uncertainty and Profit*. New York: Houghton Mifflin Co., 1921. London School Reprints of Scarce Works in Economics, 1933.

MARSHALL, A. *Principles of Economics*. 8th ed. New York: Macmillan Co., 1922.

STIGLER, G. J. "Perfect Competition, Historically Contemplated," *Journal of Political Economy*, Vol. LXV (1957), pp. 1–17.

———. *Capital and Rates of Return in Manufacturing*. Princeton, N.J.: Princeton University Press, 1963.

Addendum 1: The Minimum Necessary Condition for Competition

The *sufficient* conditions for competition are listed above: unlimited numbers and perfect knowledge and divisibility, for market competition; and absence of all barriers to entry for industrial competition. These conditions are much stronger than we need, however, and this note will argue (but not rigorously prove) that a large number of rivals is sufficient to achieve competition.

In the case of market competition, the reason for believing adequate numbers of rivals is enough is simple: that number acting with the intelligence and thirst for profits of ordinary men will provide the other attributes.

1. We now know that knowledge collection is an ordinary economic activity, and it will be engaged in up to the point where increments of information yield no more than their cost. We do not specify, when we say that a master hires a servant for eight hours, that he will invest in supervision to guarantee that work is actually done during this time, up to where the increment of supervision remunerates its cost. But he will. Is not information on prices comparable? Indeed, often specialists in the provision of information will appear, simply because there are economies in its production (just as specialists will build clocks for workers to punch their work records).

2. Divisibility and continuity are more exotic properties of commodities and economic relationships.[5] Edgeworth's example of the difficulty created by indivisibility, let us recall, was: one servant could work for one, and only one, master, for a fixed-length working day, and the servant would not work for less than $50, the master would not employ him for more than $100. With an equal number of servants and masters (even if there were a thousand or million of each), wages would be indeterminate between these limits, and the addition or withdrawal of a single servant or master would now move the market wage to one of the limiting wage rates.

Again there are economic incentives to the traders to overcome the indivisibility. Consider Edgeworth's example. If a group of masters join, perhaps as a firm, perhaps simply by moving into an apartment house, the fixed proportion between master and servant can be eliminated, and the withdrawal of one worker will now make a small reduction in the amount (and hence only slightly raise the marginal significance) of domestic service to each master. Conversely, a firm hiring many servants and selling their services would find the withdrawal of one master to

---

[5] Divisibility and continuity are both involved in the problem. Unless the variables of economics are divisible (= continuously variable in quantity), the functions of these variables cannot be continuous. But, of course, it is possible for functions of continuous variables to be discontinuous, although no interesting economic examples have ever been suggested. The basic element from the economist's viewpoint is clearly divisibility.

entail only a small reduction—say, a day in a year or decade—in the amount of work available for each member of its labor force.

The argument generalizes. It is purely an article of faith that *natura non facit saltum*, and one for which I suspect that the physical basis is uncertain. But economic agents will profit by the elimination of discontinuities and hence seek to eliminate them. The immense variety of devices employed to reduce the impact of indivisibility range from partnership and rental to living in a large city in order to have opera facilities.

Numerous traders will then reduce both ignorance and indivisibility to such magnitudes that no further gain will be obtained by a marginal improvement. Furthermore, the information- and divisibility-producing activities can themselves be competitive in the sense that there are many producers of each. We shall then achieve not perfect competition but the socially optimum amount of competition.

When we turn to *industrial* competition, there is an obvious analogy. If the entrepreneurs in a field are enjoying unusual returns on resources, we must examine the basis of their position. If it is ignorance, we should again expect profit-seeking entrepreneurs elsewhere to invest in the search for profitable alternatives—the argument is identical with that on information and market competition. If the basis of unusually high rates of return is a state grant of exclusive rights, however, competition will not emerge; we argue, not that competition must exist everywhere, but that where numbers of rivals are adequate, it will exist. Still, we should expect competition to emerge in the industry of obtaining state grants of monopoly power.

Addendum 2: Natural Monopoly

Economists have accepted the conclusion that if the economies of scale are so large relative to the possible size of the industry that only one firm can exist, then only one firm (a monopoly) will exist. They (we) have also gone on to assert that this monopoly is able to set a monopoly price under these conditions. This assertion is not necessarily true, as Harold Demsetz has shown.[6]

Suppose that (1) a town can support only one electrical generating and distribution system, but (2) there is no legal barrier (such as a required certificate of convenience and necessity) to the entry of any person into this market. If, in addition, (3) there were only moderate costs

---

[6] H. Demsetz, "Why Regulate Utilities?" *Journal of Law and Economics*, April 1968.

in forming contracts with every potential buyer of electricity, Demsetz shows that the price of electricity will be set at the competitive level. For assume that company A, already in the field, sets a price of 5 cents per kwh when costs are only 4 cents. Potential rival B will make contracts with all customers to sell electricity for 4.9 cents, and similar competition by many other potential rivals will drive the price down to 4 cents. The condition for competition is many potential rivals, not necessarily many existing rivals. (The "many" rivals are necessary to exclude collusive oligopoly solutions.)

Rather than have A in the field, to be followed by tardy rivals, it would be more appropriate to illustrate the process by the simultaneous bidding of all potential rivals for the privilege of supplying electricity. This formulation avoids minor problems of the transition from monopoly to competitive price.

The role of low or zero transaction costs in dealing with customers deserves emphasis. If a potential rival has to seek out and contract with each potential customer, he must obviously be reimbursed for these transaction costs as well as for the costs of producing and distributing electricity. It may well be that the most efficient way to contract with customers is to offer to sell the product, allowing the customers to identify themselves and come forward with contracts to purchase. If a potential rival must resort to the more costly procedure of canvassing all possible customers and arranging contracts, he will not be tempted to enter unless the price exceeds the monopolist's costs by the potential rival's additional costs of transactions. Economists generally shy away from such asymmetrical situations, but in the absence of higher costs for potential entrants, the unentrenched monopolist must charge a competitive price.

Natural monopolies are often regulated by the state. We note that customers can auction off the right to sell electricity, using the state as the instrument to conduct the auction, and thus economize on transaction costs. The auction now consists of a promise to sell cheaply; it could, of course, consist of a sum of money paid in order to be an undisturbed monopolist. In this latter event the monopolist would earn a competitive rate of return on his investment and become a tax collector for the state.

Addendum 3: A Note on Potential Competition

The leading exponent of the importance of potential competition in protecting the community from exploitation by trusts was J. B. Clark. In a characteristic passage, he wrote:

When prices are unduly high, owing to the grasping policy of some trust, what happens? New competition usually appears in the field. Capital is seeking outlets, but it has become hard to find them. Readily, and sometimes almost recklessly, does it build new mills and begin to compete with trusts, when these consolidated companies do not know enough to proceed on a conservative plan. Let any combination of producers raise the prices beyond a certain limit, and it will encounter this difficulty. The new mills that will spring into existence will break down prices; and the fear of these new mills, without their actual coming, is often enough to keep prices from rising to an extortionate height. The mill that has never been built is already a power in the market: for if it will surely be built under certain conditions, the effect of this certainty is to keep prices down.[7]

Clark's only fear was that unfair tactics (selective price cutting, preemption of dealers, and railroad rebates) would stop potential competition, and he wished to restrict public policy to eliminating such tactics. He believed trusts were efficient and inevitable and also that potential rivals were an efficient check upon trusts—and made no effort to reconcile these views.

The "limit-price" theory of Bain,[8] subsequently elaborated by Modigliani,[9] is essentially a refurnished theory of potential competition. It differs from the traditional versions chiefly in being more precise.

In Modigliani's restatement, the analysis turns on economies of scale (although it could be adapted to a true barrier to entry). In Figure 2–1, let D be the industry demand curve, C the average cost curve of a potential entrant, and P_c the level of minimum costs for the existing firms (of optimum size). Shift the cost curve C to the right until no part of it lies below the demand curve, and the axis of ordinates with respect to which it is drawn shifts to T. The demand curve $P_m D$ is that which faces the new entrant if the existing firms (1) sell output OT at price P_m, and (2) they will persist in selling this amount if the potential entrant actually enters. The price P_m, so determined, is then the maximum price which, on these assumptions, will exclude entry.

Bain believes that such a price will tend to exclude new entrants for two reasons. The lower profits are less likely to be detected and invite entry. And the price so arrived at will be interpreted as evidence that the existing firms do not welcome new rivals and may possibly combat them

[7] *The Control of Trusts* (1901), p. 13.
[8] "A Note on Pricing in Monopoly and Oligopoly," reprinted in *Readings in Industrial Organization and Public Policy*, edited by Richard B. Heflebower and George W. Stocking (1958); *Barriers to New Competition* (1956).
[9] "New Developments on the Oligopoly Front," *Journal of Political Economy*, June 1958.

FIGURE 2-1

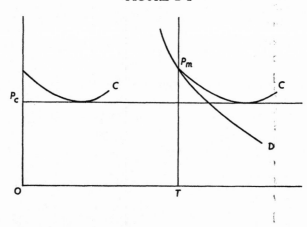

by active price competition.[10] The analysis does not guarantee low profits to existing firms, but presumably they are lower than they would be without regard to entry.

This theory raises questions faster than it answers them. Four are particularly troublesome:

1. Why should it be more profitable to exclude all entrants than merely to retard their rate of entry? Suppose at a price 10 percent above P_m (Figure 2-1), a new entrant will appear in seven years—may this not be more profitable?[11]
2. Why should a prospective entrant believe that after his entry a colluding group will not revise its policy so that all will earn returns above the competitive level? (The theory predicts the disappearance of more than competitive returns after a single firm enters.)
3. If the industry's demand is growing over time, how is the prospective entrant to be persuaded that he can have no share of the increments of demand?
4. Industry structure is irrelevant. The ability of the oligopolists to agree upon and police the limit price is apparently independent of the sizes and numbers of oligopolists. The theory of oligopoly is solved by murder.

No empirical evidence has been offered for the theory, which is not surprising.

The interesting question, from the viewpoint of both the theory of

[10] I so interpret the sentence: "[the potential entrant] may view the price which the established firm(s) currently charge as a partial indicator of the rival price policy he will face after entry." "A Note on Pricing in Monopoly and Oligopoly," p. 225.

[11] Bain notes the possibility, p. 230.

oligopoly and the measurement of concentration, is: How does one measure potential competition? The number of potential entrants is necessarily greater than the number of actual entrants (per unit of time); indeed the number of potential entrants is perhaps at a maximum in a *declining* industry such as agriculture.

The answer can be given at two levels. If we are asked, in an antitrust case, to determine whether Procter & Gamble was likely to enter the household bleach industry, we shall proceed by examining (1) the entry of other soap companies into bleaches, and (2) the similarity of bleaches to the other products (industries) into which soap companies enter. One can form a defensible estimate, and one which can be improved as our understanding of firm product structures develops.[12]

But if we are asked to identify the number of potential entrants of an industry, we must ultimately resort to the actual rate of entry when the industry was an attractive field for investment. Only when an industry has had substantial profits in excess of the competitive level and for a substantial period can we assume that potential entrants would seek to become more than potential. But then we are in effect using the magnitude and duration of monopoly profits as our main (inverse) measure of the number of potential entrants. Unless this measure can be replaced by another, potential competition has no *explanatory* value in dealing with monopoly price or monopoly profit.

[12] The Federal Trade Commission and the Supreme Court found entry to be likely, but on the basis only of casual intuition.

Chapter

3

PRICE AND NONPRICE

COMPETITION*

When a uniform price is imposed upon, or agreed to by, an industry, some or all of the other terms of sale are left unregulated. The setting of taxi-meter rates still allows competition in the quality of the automobile. The fixing of commission rates by the New York Stock Exchange still allows brokerage houses to compete in services such as providing investment information.

If additional firms may enter such a price-regulated field at no cost disadvantage, profits resulting from the price regulation will be eliminated in long-run equilibrium. But in the absence of free entry—and both the medallions required of taxis and the seats of New York Stock Exchange members are fixed in number—the question arises: Will any monopoly profit achieved by suppressing price competition be eliminated by nonprice competition?

We may emphasize that a symmetrical question arises if the firms are required to sell the same product (that is, have the same nonprice variable) but are allowed to compete freely in prices. For example, let every seller of gasoline provide the identical product. Will free price competition eliminate any monopoly profits arising from agreement not to compete in the quality of gasoline? Economists generally attribute much more efficacy to price than to nonprice competition without giving any clear explanation of the asymmetry of the two kinds of competition.

Let us take advertising as the prototype of nonprice variables. A previously competitive industry may form a cartel and (1) fix advertising jointly and allow competition in price or (2) fix price jointly and allow competition in advertising. We examine the two cases in turn.

Let each firm be operating, under competition, at output Q_o and price P_o (Fig. 3–1). Upon colluding on advertising, marginal costs—which

* By George J. Stigler. Reprinted from *Journal of Political Economy*, Vol. LXXII, No. 1 (February 1968). Copyright 1968 by the University of Chicago.

FIGURE 3–1

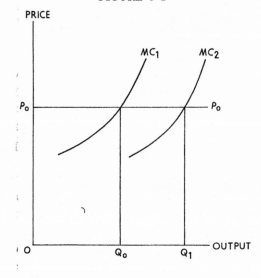

FIGURE 3–2

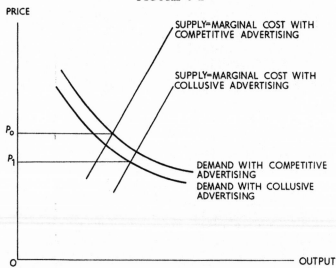

include the costs of advertising—are reduced at every output for each firm.[1] The firm expands its output to Q_1 by price competition. (It might be a heuristic improvement if a tiny price reduction were shown beyond

[1] Economists who find it uncomfortable to discuss advertising in a competitive industry can substitute another nonprice variable (such as durability of product, investment advice, or warranties of free repairs) with only terminological effects.

FIGURE 3–3

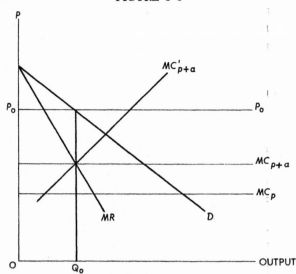

Q_o.) If marginal cost is rising, output will not increase sufficiently to lower price as much as marginal costs have fallen (see Fig. 3–2). The condition for elimination of profits is therefore constant marginal cost— which is, of course, equivalent to free entry, since existing firms can then expand to any extent without increasing marginal cost.[2]

Now consider the situation in which the cartel fixes the price and allows competition in advertising. Each firm now has a fixed share of total output at the common price (given the level of advertising expenditures), so it has a negatively sloping demand curve, D (Fig. 3–3). We present marginal costs (MC_{a+p}) as the sum of production costs plus the amount of advertising costs necessary for one firm to sell each quantity at the price set by the cartel, the other firms advertising a fixed amount. Two possibilities arise:

Marginal cost (MC_{p+a}) may be constant or fall. If marginal production cost (MC_p) is constant, MC_{p+a} will not rise if there are constant or increasing returns to advertising. If marginal production costs are increasing, then the rise must be offset by increasing returns to advertising.

Marginal cost (MC_{p+a}) may rise. With constant marginal production costs, this condition requires diminishing returns to advertising.

[2] If the demand of the firm had only finite elasticity because of differentiation, output would not increase indefinitely even with constant marginal production costs.

In the former case, each firm will seek to expand output by increasing advertising, without limit. The competitive advertising will be partially self-defeating, and marginal costs of advertising will shift upward until profits vanish (MC_{p+a} shifts up to P_o). In the latter case, the firm will expand to where marginal cost (of production plus advertising) will equal price.

The common belief of economists that price competition is much more effective in increasing output and reducing profits than non-price competition is now seen to rest upon an empirical judgment: Marginal costs of production do not rise so rapidly as marginal costs of advertising, quality competition, and other nonprice variables. Perhaps the following reformulation is more suggestive. An increment of output has a given marginal production cost. If the increment of output is sold by a price reduction, there is also the cost of reducing price on the units already being sold. If the increment of output is sold by increasing a nonprice variable (advertising, durability, etc.), there is also the cost of the additional amount of the nonprice variable. The common view, which is very plausible, is that the marginal nonprice variable cost is larger than the marginal price-reduction cost, if one starts from a monopoly position.

MATHEMATICAL NOTE

Let an industry consist of m firms. The industry demand curve is $Qp^n = c(mA)^\beta$, where Q = industry output, p = price, and A = advertising expenditures of a firm. When a cartel is formed, the demand of each firm will be $1/m$ of Q, or

$$q = \frac{Q}{m} = \frac{cp^{-n}(mA)^\beta}{m}. \tag{1}$$

The profits per firm in the cartel will be

$$\pi = pq - q^r - A, \tag{2}$$

where production costs are q^r. For maximum profits, after substituting (1) into (2) we have

$$\frac{\partial \pi}{\partial q} = \left[\frac{c(mA)^\beta}{mq} \right]^{1/n} - \frac{q}{n} \left[\frac{c(mA)^\beta}{mq} \right]^{(1/n)-1} \frac{c(mA)^\beta}{mq^2} - rq^{r-1} = 0 \tag{3.1}$$

and

$$\frac{\partial \pi}{\partial A} = \frac{q}{n} \left[\frac{c(mA)^\beta}{mq} \right]^{(1/n)-1} \frac{\beta c(mA)^{\beta-1}}{mq} m - 1 = 0. \tag{3.2}$$

These equations simplify to

$$p\left(1 - \frac{1}{n}\right) = rq^{r-1} \tag{3.11}$$

$$A = \frac{\beta q p}{n}. \tag{3.21}$$

These equations determine a p_o and A_o such that profits are at a maximum.

For an individual firm which will sell or advertise competitively, given that the cartel has fixed advertising or price (but not both), there exists a demand curve

$$qp^k = aA^a. \tag{4}$$

This demand function differs from that of the obedient cartel member (1) in representing demand if only this firm prices competitively $(k > n)$ *or* if only this firm advertises competitively $(a > \beta)$.

If the cartel fixes the amount of advertising at the profit-maximizing level, A_o, as determined by (3.11) and (3.21), the firm will set price competitively (or, perhaps better said, if k is infinite, the firm will set output competitively). Profits are

$$\pi = q\left(\frac{a}{q}\right)^{1/k} (A^a)^{1/k} - q^r - A_o, \tag{5}$$

and for maximum profits

$$\frac{d\pi}{dq} = A^{a/k}\left[\left(\frac{a}{q}\right)^{1/k} - \frac{q}{k}\left[\frac{a}{q}\right]^{(1/k)-1} \frac{a}{q^2}\right] - rq^{r-1} = 0$$

or

$$p\left(1 - \frac{1}{k}\right) = rq^{r-1}. \tag{6}$$

If k is infinite (homogeneous products), this equation has a solution only if $r > 1$. If $r = 1$ (constant marginal costs) and k is infinite, the quantity produced and sold by the firm will increase without limit and the market price must fall to marginal cost.

Similarly, when the cartel fixes price at the profit-maximizing level determined by (3.11) and (3.21), say at p_o, the firm maximizes profits by setting advertising competitively. Since

$$\pi = p_o q - q^r - A,$$
$$\pi = p_o a p_0^{-n} A^a - (a p_0^{-n} A^a)^r - A$$

and

$$\frac{d\pi}{dA} = \alpha p_o a p_0^{-n} A^{a-1} - r(a p_0^{-n} A^a)^{r-1} a p_0^{-n} \alpha A^{a-1} - 1. \qquad (7)$$

This expression may be written

$$\alpha a A^{a-1} p_0^{-n} [p_o - r(a p_0^{-n} A^a)^{r-1}] - 1$$

or

$$\alpha a A^{a-1} p_0^{-n} (p_o - MC_p) - 1, \qquad (7.1)$$

where MC_p is marginal production cost. This expression increases without limit as A increases (1) unless MC_p increases with output or (2) unless if MC_p is constant, $\alpha < 1$ (diminishing returns to advertising).

When every firm engages in competitive advertising, the effects are partly offsetting. Now let the demand function be

$$q p^n = a \left(\frac{A_i}{A_o}\right)^a A_0^\beta \qquad (4.1)$$

where A_i is the advertising expenditure of firm i and A_o is the average advertising of the other firms. (If A_o is constant, this formulation reduces to [4] with a suitable constant.) Then

$$\frac{d\pi}{dA_i} = \alpha a \left(\frac{A_i}{A_o}\right)^{a-1} p_0^{-n} A_0^{\beta-1} (p_o - MC_p) - 1. \qquad (7.2)$$

In the constant-returns case illustrated in Figure 3–3 with $\alpha = r = 1$ and $A_i = A_o$, (7.2) defines maximum profits when

$$A_i^{\beta-1} = \frac{p_o^n}{a(p_o - MC_p)},$$

at which value $\pi = 0$ (total and marginal profits are zero).

Chapter 4

THE MEASUREMENT OF CONCENTRATION

We begin with a distribution of the firms in an industry by size. The unit in which we measure size has been debated: some prefer output (physical or revenue); some prefer assets; still others take labor force or value-added. The unit of time over which size is measured has deserved, but not received, equal debate: should it be a day or a year or a decade? And, of course, the industry—the collection of firms which we bring together—is capable of various enumerations. We postpone these issues until we are better equipped to answer them.

The classical theory of oligopoly has nothing to say about the sizes of firms, so the firms are naturally assumed to be of equal size. Then the number of firms completely describes the industry structure as of any time, and if entry of additional firms is excluded, this number also describes the industry structure for all time. Then, by one of two routes, most economists reached the conclusion that the degree of competition (measured, say, by the reciprocal of the excess of price over marginal cost) increased with the number of firms.

> Route 1: One firm *is* monopoly by definition; many firms produce competition by observation (and perhaps by demonstration). No one could (or did, anyway) argue that the degree of competition should fluctuate down and up as the number of firms increased—surely the relationship was monotonic.
>
> Route 2: Cournot's theory of oligopoly made price fall (given costs) as the number of firms increased.

Neither route was thoroughly constructed: the observation that competition in price increases with number of rivals was not established statistically; and Cournot's theory had serious deficiencies.[1] In the light of our remarks on natural monopoly (p. 18), it is also clear that the degree of competition would vary more closely with the number of potential rivals than with the number of actual rivals.

[1] On the latter, see Addendum 1 to this chapter.

The *purpose* of a measure of concentration is to predict the extent of the departure of price (or, alternatively, of rate of return) from the competitive level. This purpose supplies an answer to our earlier question of how to measure the size of firm: two firms are equal in a market if they sell or buy equal quantities in that market. Hence measure a firm's size by sales, in a product market; by employees, in a labor market; by materials, in a material market; by assets, in a capital market. This purpose also answers our earlier question about the time period. The excess of price over short-run marginal cost is likely to be small because a high current price will adversely affect future demand. In any event, economic importance of monopoly is measured by the present value of all the future losses it imposes on society, and this present value will normally be dominated by long-run prices and costs. Moreover, a society will seldom be able to take any corrective action against a short-lived monopoly.

Even if one accepted as true the positive relationship between number of firms and degree of competition, there was no guidance in comparing the effects on competition of increasing the number of firms from three to four versus four to six. There was also no basis for saying that two firms of equal size would be more or less competitive than two firms, one of which was double the size of the other.

We should not be surprised, therefore, that when concentration began to be measured for many industries in industrial censuses—and this began as late as 1935 in the United States—wholly arbitrary measures of concentration were chosen. The United States took the share of output coming from the four largest firms; Great Britain the three largest firms; Canada the number of firms necessary to account for 80 percent of industry output. The apparently close correlation between such measures —which was spurious—seemed to make the precise choice unimportant.[2]

There are, in fact, two converging routes by which a measure of concentration may usefully be developed. The first route is to develop a theory which relates the probability of competitive behavior to measurable aspects of the firm structure, and the second route is to choose a measure which correlates well with observable indexes of competitive behavior. Remarkably little has been done along either route.

Few theories of oligopoly provide any guidance in devising a mea-

---

[2] Let $s_i =$ share of firm i, with the firms ranked by size (so $s_1 > s_2 > s_3 \ldots$). Then the correlations were made between (say)

$$C_1 = \sum_1^3 s_i \quad \text{and} \quad C_2 = \sum_1^4 s_i$$

and the elements common to both measures guarantee a large correlation. The proper correlation should have been between C_1 and s_4, which is vastly lower.

sure of concentration. To be sure, this is largely due to the failure of theorists to derive measures. Consider Cournot's theory:

1. Each firm faces the demand function,

$$p = f(q_1 + q_2 + \ldots + q_n)$$

were q_i is the output of firm i.

2. The marginal revenue of a firm is

$$\frac{d(q_i p)}{dq_i} = q_i \frac{dp}{dq} + p,$$

if—with Cournot—we assume that oligopolist i assumes that changes in his output have no influence up his rivals' outputs (so $\frac{dq}{dq_i} = 1$).

3. This marginal revenue is equated to marginal cost. If we introduce marginal cost functions such that the firms will be of various sizes, we can deduce a measure of concentration. A brief discussion of this approach is given in Addendum 2.

One measure of concentration has been derived from a theory of oligopoly. This theory asserts that the oligopolists wish to set a monopoly price, but they are limited by the difficulty of detecting secret competitive maneuvers by individual firms. The chief method of detecting such competitive price cutting is by watching the shares of each firm. Unfortunately, the share of a firm in industry sales fluctuates also for other ("random") reasons, and the more the random fluctuation, the greater the possibility of undetected price cutting.[3] This theory suggests that a measure of the fluctuation of shares (in the absence of secret price cutting) of individual firms should be used, and such a measure can be approximated by the Herfindahl measure (H) of concentration. If s_i is the share of firm i,

$$H = \Sigma s_i^2.$$

Three illustrative calculations are given in Table 4–1. The minimum value of H is $1/n$ if there are n firms of equal size; the maximum value is 1 (monopoly). If we take the reciprocal of H, therefore, we get the equivalent number of firms of equal size. In our example in Table 4–1:

Industry 1: $N_H = 1/H = 5$.

Industry 2: $N_H = 1/H = 4.44$.

Industry 3: $N_H = 1/H = 2.82$.

The index handles mergers very neatly, as we shall see later.

[3] An elaboration of the argument is given in Chapter 5.

TABLE 4–1
ILLUSTRATIVE HERFINDAHL MEASURES

Rank of Firm	Industry 1		Industry 2		Industry 3	
	Share	s^2	Share	s^2	Share	s^2
1	.2	.04	.30	.09	16/31 = .5161	.2663
2	.2	.04	.25	.0625	8/31 = .2581	.0666
3	.2	.04	.20	.04	4/31 = .1290	.0166
4	.2	.04	.15	.0125	2/31 = .0645	.0042
5	.2	.04	.10	.01	1/31 = .0323	.0010
Sum = H		.20		.2250		.3547
$N_H = \dfrac{1}{H} =$		5		4.44		2.82

A second general measure has been taken over from physics, namely, the measure of entropy. The index itself (E) is defined as the reciprocal of

$$N_E = \left(\frac{1}{s_1}\right)^{s_1} \left(\frac{1}{s_2}\right)^{s_2} \left(\frac{1}{s_3}\right)^{s_3} \cdots \left(\frac{1}{s_n}\right)^{s_n} = \frac{1}{E}$$

or

$$-\log E = \Sigma\, s_i \log\left(\frac{1}{s_i}\right)$$

and is readily calculated. The N_E index of the three distributions used to illustrate the Herfindahl index are given in Table 4–2.

TABLE 4–2
ILLUSTRATIVE ENTROPY MEASURES

	Industry 1			Industry 2			Industry 3	
s	$\log\dfrac{1}{s}$	$s\log\dfrac{1}{s}$	s	$\log\dfrac{1}{s}$	$s\log\dfrac{1}{s}$	s	$\log\dfrac{1}{s}$	$s\log\dfrac{1}{s}$
.2	.6990	.1398	.30	.5229	.1569	.5161	.2872	.1482
.2	.6990	.1398	.25	.6021	.1505	.2581	.5882	.1518
.2	.6990	.1398	.20	.6990	.1398	.1290	.8894	.1147
.2	.6990	.1398	.15	.8239	.1236	.0645	1.1904	.0768
.2	.6990	.1398	.10	1.0000	.1000	.0323	1.4908	.0415
Sum = log E =		.6990			.6708			.5330
$N_E = 5$				4.69			3.41	
$E = \dfrac{1}{N_E} = .2$				.213			.293	

The various proponents of the entropy measure have not yet given an explicit theory of the relationship of the measure to competitive behavior.[4] No doubt such a derivation will come sooner or later, and at present there is little reason to prefer either index over the other. Indeed, for ordinary distributions they will yield fairly similar results. They differ chiefly in the weight assigned to small firms. The Herfindahl index is essentially unaffected by the number of firms with shares smaller than 1 percent ($s^2 < .0001$), whereas the Entropy measure will give a competitive structure if there are immensely many firms. For example, if one firm has 90 percent of the industry output, and the remainder is divided equally among 10,000 firms, the two measures are:

1. Herfindahl

$$H = .9^2 + 10,000 \left(\frac{1}{100,000} \right)^2 = .8100001$$

$$N_H = 1.23$$

2. Entropy

$$N_E = \left(\frac{1}{.9} \right)^{.9} \left(\frac{1}{1/100,000} \right)^{.1} = 3.48 = \frac{1}{E} = \frac{1}{.287}$$

This sort of comparison indicates that the role of small firms is not very different in the two measures: neither nature nor public policy can produce the number of small firms necessary to increase the entropy measure appreciably if one or a few dominant firms are left undisturbed. The comparison also increases slightly one's preference for the Herfindahl measure: if the distribution of firm sizes is reasonably stable (that is, if the small firms survive in tiny corners of the market), an industry such as the example portrays will behave monopolistically.

The alternate route to develop a measure of concentration was the one actually chosen. Beginning with the study produced under the direction of Gardiner Means, *The Structure of the American Economy* (National Resources Planning Board, 1939), the census has supplied concentration measures of growing comprehensiveness, but basically wedded to the share of the output produced by the 4 (and later 8 and 20) largest firms.[5] A considerable history could be written on the search for high

[4] See M. O. Finkelstein and R. M. Friedberg, "The Application of an Entropy Theory of Concentration to the Clayton Act," *Yale Law Journal*, March 1967; Henri Theil, *Economics and Information Theory* (Amsterdam, 1967), chap. viii; A. and I. Horowitz, "Entropy, Markov Processes, and Competition in the Brewing Industry," to appear.

[5] However, Herfindahl measures are given in Ralph L. Nelson, *Concentration in the Manufacturing Industries of the United States* (New Haven, Conn., 1963).

correlations between these concentration ratios and (1) output and price changes in business cycles,[6] (2) price movements during inflations,[7] (3) rates of return on investment (which is discussed in Chapter 13), and (4) miscellaneous variables such as wage rates.[8] The main finding has been disappointment: seldom have good relationships been found between the concentration ratio and these potential indexes of monopoly power. For example, the Selden-dePodwin comparison of wholesale price movements from 1953 to 1959 and concentration ratios in 1954 yielded a correlation coefficient of .12 with the shares of the four largest firms and .02 with the Herfindahl index—although in candor one must add that many of us economists would expect this relationship to be negligible.[9]

What is unequivocally true, in any event, is that the process of improving concentration measures by examining empirical relationships to indices of monopoly behavior has been slow, unsystematic, and almost accidental. The process has been burdened by the large difficulty of obtaining good indices of monopoly behavior, but the burden is not unsupportable. It has been, and is now, possible both to refine the measures of monopoly power, such as rates of return, and to experiment with a variety of aspects of concentration such as:

1. Summary measures of the distribution of firm size (Herfindahl, log normal, entropy, etc.).
2. The stability of the shares of the leading firms over time.[10]
3. The influence of alternate measures of market size (including attention to imports and exports).

The Herfindahl and Entropy measures of the effect of a merger upon the level of concentration are easily derived.

1. The Herfindahl measure rises, when firms with shares s_1 and s_2 merge, by $(s_1 + s_2)^2 - s_1{}^2 - s_2{}^2 = 2s_1 s_2$.

---

[6] For example, W. F. Crowder, *The Concentration of Production in Manufacturing* (Temporary National Economic Committee Monograph No. 27 [Washington, D.C., 1941]), Part V.

[7] For example, H. J. dePodwin and R. T. Selden, "Business Pricing Policies and Inflation," *Journal of Political Economy*, April 1963.

[8] For example, J. W. Garbarino, "A Theory of Interindustry Wage Structure Variation," *Quarterly Journal of Economics*, May 1950.

[9] See Chapter 19, following.

[10] See I. M. Grossack, "Towards the Integration of Static and Dynamic Measures of Industrial Concentration," *Review of Economics and Statistics*, August 1965; and M. Gort, "Analysis of Stability and Change in Market Shares," *Journal of Political Economy*, February 1963.

2. The Entropy measure is additive in logarithmic form. Let $\log\left(\frac{1}{E}\right)$

$= \Sigma \, s_i \log \frac{1}{s_i}$, so the merger reduces $\log\left(\frac{1}{E}\right)$ by $s_1 \log \frac{1}{s_1}$

$+ \, s_2 \log\left(\frac{1}{s_2}\right) - (s_1 + s_2) \log \frac{1}{s_1 + s_2}.$

Both measures reflect the level of the acquiring firm as well as the acquired firm. Thus if a firm with 5 percent of output is acquired, the Herfindahl index rises by the following amounts:

Share of Acquiring Firm	Rise in H
0.05	0.005
.10	.01
.25	.025
.50	.05
.75	.075
.95	.095

The conventional four-firm concentration ratio would show one of three effects:

1. No rise if the merged firm was not one of the leading four.
2. A rise of .05 if the acquiring firm was one of the leading four, and the acquired firm was not.
3. A rise of a variable amount (but less than .05) if:
   a) The acquired firm was also one of the leading four (the concentration ratio would rise by the size of the previously fifth firm (which by hypothesis is less than .05).
   b) The acquiring firm became one of the leading four as a result of the merger (the concentration ratio would rise by the excess of its share over that of the previous fourth firm).

If the oligopoly theory presented in the next chapter has collided with truth, the concentration of buyers is also a major determinant of the degree of competition in an industry. The fewer (or larger) the buyers, the harder it is to distinguish a large shift in patronage due to price cutting from one due to chance, and hence the higher the probability of price cutting. We may, of course, measure concentration of buyers symmetrically to that of sellers—subject to the major proviso that data on the sizes of buyers is seldom reported. One can construct a combined measure of concentration of buyers (H_b) and sellers (H_s), such as H_s/H_b, and subject it to the same tests as a concentration measure of sellers.

Herfindahl indexes are used in empirical studies in later chapters, and in Chapter 21 a history of Herfindahl measures is given for seven industries in the United States and Great Britain.

Addendum 1: Cournot's Theory

Cournot begins his theory with the industry containing one firm (monopoly) and then proceeds to two or more rivals.[11] He begins by stating an assumption on their behavior:

. . . . *each of them* [the duopolists] *independently* will seek to make [his] income as large as possible.
We say *each independently*, and this restriction is very essential, as will soon appear; for if they should come to an agreement so as to obtain for each the greatest possible income, the results would be entirely different, and would not differ, so far as consumers are concerned, from those obtained in treating of a monopoly.[12]

Cournot assumes that each firm will treat the output of the other as fixed.

I once considered it a crucial objection to this theory that even if firm A changes his output 40 times, and each time B changes his output in response, A will continue to treat B's output as independent of his own. Such inability to learn from experience seemed incredible. I still believe that this is a weighty objection, but there is a more basic difficulty, one which would not be escaped if Cournot had assumed behavior which experience confirmed.[13]

This difficulty is that the behavior of the duopolists is being postulated rather than deduced. By assumption the duopolists are seeking to maximize profits. Then profit maximizing must imply the form of behavior—economic behavior is a means to achieve this end, not a separate part of man to be supplied by a psychiatrist or a sociologist. Collusion is *not* the only conceivable form of behavior, even if there are only two firms and collusion is legally permissible. In fact, collusion has costs, and the

[11] *Mathematical Principles of the Theory of Wealth* (New York, 1927), chap. vii.
[12] *Ibid.*, pp. 79–80.
[13] For example, firm A matches the price or output of firm B.

amount of it which the oligopolists will buy should be analyzed, not postulated.

This complaint at Cournot's theory is of course applicable to all oligopoly theories (Bertrand, Edgeworth, Stackelberg, etc.) which *postulate* the behavior of the oligopolists.

Addendum 2: Concentration With Cournot Oligopoly

Cournot dealt with homogeneous products so the size of a firm depends only upon its costs of production. In his basic model,

$$q_i \frac{dp}{dq} + p = \text{Marginal Cost} = \text{MC} \tag{1}$$

for each firm, and adding n such equations,

$$n q_i \frac{dp}{dq} + np = n\text{MC}$$

or

$$p = \text{MC} - \frac{p}{n\eta}, \tag{2}$$

where η is the elasticity of demand. Here price exceeds marginal cost (the competitive level) by an amount that varies inversely with the number of rivals. If we wish our concentration measure to portray this relationship, we could take

$$C = 1/n,$$

so concentration is reduced equally much by increasing the number of firms from (1) three to four (C falls from .33 to .25), (2) four to six (C falls from .25 to .17), (3) six to nine, and (4) nine to thirty-three.

The extension of Cournot's theory to firms of different sizes could be made by introducing a frequency distribution of marginal cost functions, but a simpler illustration will suffice for our purpose—which is to show that a theory of oligopoly will in general imply a theory of the measurement of concentration. Let the marginal revenue of each of two firms be

$$q_i \frac{dp}{dq} + p$$

and let the two marginal cost functions be

$$(q_1 + \lambda) \text{ and } (q_2 - \lambda)$$

then

$$q_1 \frac{dp}{dq} + p = q_1 + \lambda$$

$$q_2 \frac{dp}{dq} + p = q_2 - \lambda.$$

(3)

If we add these equations, we get

$$q \frac{dp}{dq} + 2p = q$$

(4)

so the combined output of the duopolists is independent of λ. Yet the difference between the outputs of the duopolists [found by equating the p's in equations in (3)] is:

$$q_2 - q_1 = \frac{2\lambda}{1 - \dfrac{dp}{dq}}.$$

(5)

Of course, this result depends upon the special cost functions.

We shall not pursue this analysis beyond noticing a problem in the formulation. In general, one cannot vary the costs and sizes of the firms and hold the monopoly, the oligopoly, and the competitive prices constant. In the above example, however, all three prices are independent of λ providing marginal costs are positive. It seems most natural to hold the monopoly price constant, which can be done by holding the *sum* of the marginal costs of the firms constant. Thus two eligible marginal cost functions would be

$$\frac{b}{a} q_1 \text{ and } \frac{b}{b-a} q_2 \qquad (b > a)$$

with firm 1 approaching monopoly as a approaches b. Here the monopolist's marginal cost of operating the two plants is $(q_1 + q_2)$.

Chapter

5

A THEORY OF OLIGOPOLY*[1]

No one has the right, and few the ability, to lure economists into reading another article on oligopoly theory without some advance indication of its alleged contribution. The present paper accepts the hypothesis that oligopolists wish to collude to maximize joint profits. It seeks to reconcile this wish with facts, such as that collusion is impossible for many firms and collusion is much more effective in some circumstances than in others. The reconciliation is found in the problem of policing a collusive agreement, which proves to be a problem in the theory of information. A considerable number of implications of the theory are discussed, and a modest amount of empirical evidence is presented.

I. THE TASK OF COLLUSION

A satisfactory theory of oligopoly cannot begin with assumptions concerning the way in which each firm views its interdependence with its rivals. If we adhere to the traditional theory of profit-maximizing enterprises, then behavior is no longer something to be assumed but rather something to be deduced. The firms in an industry will behave in such a way, given the demand-and-supply functions (including those of rivals), that their profits will be maximized.

The combined profits of the entire set of firms in an industry are maximized when they act together as a monopolist. At least in the traditional formulation of the oligopoly problem, in which there are no major uncertainties as to the profit-maximizing output and price at any time,

* By George J. Stigler. Reprinted from *Journal of Political Economy*, Vol. LXXII, No. 1 (February 1964). Copyright 1964 by the University of Chicago.
[1] I am indebted to Claire Friedland for the statistical work and to Harry Johnson for helpful criticisms.

this familiar conclusion seems inescapable. Moreover, the result holds for any number of firms.

Our modification of this theory consists simply in presenting a systematic account of the factors governing the feasibility of collusion, which like most things in this world is not free. Before we do so, it is desirable to look somewhat critically at the concept of homogeneity of products, and what it implies for profit-maximizing. We shall show that collusion normally involves much more than "the" price.

Homogeneity is commonly defined in terms of identity of products or of (what is presumed to be equivalent) pairs of products between which the elasticity of substitution is infinite. On either definition it is the behavior of buyers that is decisive. Yet it should be obvious that products may be identical to any or every buyer while buyers may be quite different from the viewpoint of sellers.

This fact that every transaction involves two parties is something that economists do not easily forget. One would therefore expect a definition of homogeneity also to be two-sided: if the products are what sellers offer, and the purchase commitments are what the buyers offer, full homogeneity clearly involves infinite elasticities of substitution between both products and purchase commitments. In other words, two products are homogeneous to a buyer if he is indifferent between all combinations of x of one and (say) $20 - x$ of the other, at a common price. Two purchase commitments are homogeneous to a seller if he is indifferent between all combinations of y of one and (say) $20 - y$ of the other, at a common price. Full homogeneity is then defined as homogeneity both in products (sellers) and purchase commitments (buyers).

The heterogeneity of purchase commitments (buyers), however, is surely often at least as large as that of products within an industry, and sometimes vastly larger. There is the same sort of personal differentia of buyers as of sellers—ease in making sales, promptness of payment, penchant for returning goods, likelihood of buying again (or buying other products). In addition there are two differences among buyers which are pervasive and well recognized in economics:

1. The size of purchase, with large differences in costs of providing lots of different size.
2. The urgency of purchase, with possibly sufficient differences in elasticity of demand to invite price discrimination.

It is one thing to assert that no important market has homogeneous transactions, and quite another to measure the extent of the heterogeneity.

In a regime of perfect knowledge, it would be possible to measure heterogeneity by the variance of prices in transactions; in a regime of imperfect knowledge, there will be dispersion of prices even with transaction homogeneity.[2]

The relevance of heterogeneity to collusion is this: It is part of the task of maximizing industry profits to employ a price structure that takes account of the larger differences in the costs of various classes of transactions. Even with a single, physically homogeneous product the profits will be reduced if differences among buyers are ignored. A simple illustration of this fact is given in the Appendix; disregard of differences among buyers proves to be equivalent to imposing an excise tax upon them, but one which is not collected by the monopolist. A price structure of some complexity will usually be the goal of collusive oligopolists.

II. THE METHODS OF COLLUSION

Collusion of firms can take many forms, of which the most comprehensive is outright merger. Often merger will be inappropriate, however, because of diseconomies of scale,[3] and at certain times and places it may be forbidden by law. Only less comprehensive is the cartel with a joint sales agency, which again has economic limitations—it is ill suited to custom work and creates serious administrative costs in achieving quality standards, cost reductions, product innovations, etc. In deference to American antitrust policy, we shall assume that the collusion takes the form of joint determination of outputs and prices by ostensibly independent firms, but we shall not take account of the effects of the legal prohibitions until later. Oligopoly existed before 1890, and has existed in countries that have never had an antitrust policy.

The colluding firms must agree upon the price structure appropriate to the transaction classes which they are prepared to recognize. A complete profit-maximizing price structure may have almost infinitely numerous price classes: the firms will have to decide upon the number of price classes in the light of the costs and returns from tailoring prices to the diversity of transactions. We have already indicated by hypothetical example (see Appendix) that there are net profits to be obtained by

---

[2] Unless one defines heterogeneity of transactions to include also differences in luck in finding low price sellers; see my "Economics of Information," *Journal of Political Economy*, June 1961 (below, Chapter 16).

[3] If the firms are multiproduct, with different product structures, the diseconomies of merger are not strictly those of scale (in any output) but of firm size measured either absolutely or in terms of variety of products.

catering to differences in transactions. The level of collusive prices will also depend upon the conditions of entry into the industry as well as upon the elasticities of demand.

Let us assume that the collusion has been effected, and a price structure agreed upon. It is a well-established proposition that if any member of the agreement can secretly violate it, he will gain larger profits than by conforming to it.[4] It is, moreover, surely one of the axioms of human behavior that all agreements whose violation would be profitable to the violator must be enforced. The literature of collusive agreements, ranging from the pools of the 1880's to the electrical conspiracies of recent times, is replete with instances of the collapse of conspiracies because of "secret" price cutting. This literature is biased: conspiracies that are successful in avoiding an amount of price cutting which leads to collapse of the agreement are less likely to be reported or detected. But no conspiracy can neglect the problem of enforcement.

Enforcement consists basically of detecting significant deviations from the agreed-upon prices. Once detected, the deviations will tend to disappear because they are no longer secret and will be matched by fellow conspirators if they are not withdrawn. If the enforcement is weak, however—if price cutting is detected only slowly and incompletely —the conspiracy must recognize its weakness: it must set prices not much above the competitive level so the inducements to price cutting are small, or it must restrict the conspiracy to areas in which enforcement can be made efficient.

Fixing market shares is probably the most efficient of all methods of combating secret price reductions. No one can profit from price cutting if he is moving along the industry demand curve,[5] once a maximum profit price has been chosen. With inspection of output and an appropriate formula for redistribution of gains and losses from departures from quotas, the incentive to secret price cutting is eliminated. Unless inspection of output is costly or ineffective (as with services), this is the ideal method of enforcement, and is widely used by legal cartels. Unfortunately for oligopolists, it is usually an easy form of collusion to detect, for it may require side payments among firms and it leaves indelible traces in the output records.

Almost as efficient a method of eliminating secret price cutting is to

---

[4] If price is above marginal cost, marginal revenue will be only slightly less than price (and hence above marginal cost) for price cuts by this one seller.

[5] More precisely, he is moving along a demand curve which is a fixed share of the industry demand, and hence has the same elasticity as the industry curve at every price.

assign each buyer to a single seller. If this can be done for all buyers, short-run price cutting no longer has any purpose. Long-run price cutting will still be a serious possibility if the buyers are in competition: lower prices to one's own customers can then lead to an expansion of their share of their market, so the price cutter's long-run demand curve will be more elastic than that of the industry. Long-run price cutting is likely to be important, however, only where sellers are providing a major cost component to the buyer.

There are real difficulties of other sorts to the sellers in the assignment of buyers. In general the fortunes of the various sellers will differ greatly over time: one seller's customers may grow threefold, while another seller's customers shrink by half. If the customers have uncorrelated fluctuations in demand, the various sellers will experience large changes in relative outputs in the short run.[6] Where the turnover of buyers is large, the method is simply impracticable.

Nevertheless, the conditions appropriate to the assignment of customers will exist in certain industries, and in particular the geographical division of the market has often been employed. Since an allocation of buyers is an obvious and easily detectible violation of the Sherman Act, we may again infer that an efficient method of enforcing a price agreement is excluded by the antitrust laws. We therefore turn to other techniques of enforcement, but we shall find that the analysis returns to allocation of buyers.

In general the policing of a price agreement involves an audit of the transactions prices. In the absence or violation of antitrust laws, actual inspection of the accounting records of sellers has been employed by some colluding groups, but even this inspection gives only limited assurance that the price agreement is adhered to.[7] Ultimately there is no substitute for obtaining the transaction prices from the buyers.

An oligopolist will not consider making secret price cuts to buyers whose purchases fall below a certain size relative to his aggregate sales. The ease with which price cutting is detected by rivals is decisive in this case. If p is the probability that some rival will hear of one such price reduction, $1 - (1 - p)^n$ is the probability that a rival will learn of at least one reduction if it is given to n customers. Even if p is as small as

---

[6] When the relative outputs of the firms change, the minimum cost condition of equal marginal costs for all sellers is likely to be violated. Hence industry profits are not maximized.

[7] The literature and cases on "open-price associations" contain numerous references to the collection of prices from sellers (see Federal Trade Commission, *Open-Price Trade Associations* [Washington, 1929], and cases cited).

0.01, when n equals 100 the probability of detection is .634, and when n equals 1000 it is .99996. No one has yet invented a way to advertise price reductions which brings them to the attention of numerous customers but not to that of any rival.[8]

It follows that oligopolistic collusion will often be effective against small buyers even when it is ineffective against large buyers. When the oligopolists sell to numerous small retailers, for example, they will adhere to the agreed-upon price, even though they are cutting prices to larger chain stores and industrial buyers. This is a first empirical implication of our theory. Let us henceforth exclude small buyers from consideration.

The detection of secret price cutting will of course be as difficult as interested people can make it. The price cutter will certainly protest his innocence, or, if this would tax credulity beyond its taxable capacity, blame a disobedient subordinate. The price cut will often take the indirect form of modifying some nonprice dimension of the transaction. The customer may, and often will, divulge price reductions, in order to have them matched by others, but he will learn from experience if each disclosure is followed by the withdrawal of the lower price offer. Indeed the buyer will frequently fabricate wholly fictitious price offers to test the rivals. Policing the collusion sounds very much like the subtle and complex problem presented in a good detective story.

There is a difference: In our case the man who murders the collusive price will receive the bequest of patronage. The basic method of detection of a price cutter must be the fact that he is getting business he would otherwise not obtain. No promises of lower prices that fail to shift some business can be really effective—either the promised price is still too high or it is simply not believed.

Our definition of perfect collusion, indeed, must be that no buyer changes sellers voluntarily. There is no competitive price cutting if there are no shifts of buyers among sellers.

To this rule that price cutting must be inferred from shifts of buyers there is one partial exception, but that an important one. There is one type of buyer who usually reveals the price he pays, and does not accept secret benefices: the government. The system of sealed bids, publicly opened with full identification of each bidder's price and specifications, is the ideal instrument for the detection of price cutting. There exists no

---

[8] This argument applies to size of buyer relative to the individual seller. One can also explain the absence of higgling in small transactions because of the costs of bargaining, but this latter argument turns on the absolute size of the typical transaction, not its size relative to the seller.

alternative method of secretly cutting prices (bribery of purchasing agents aside). Our second empirical prediction, then, is that collusion will always be more effective against buyers who report correctly and fully the prices tendered to them.[9]

It follows from the test of the absence of price competition by buyer loyalty—and this is our third major empirical prediction—that collusion is severely limited (under present assumptions excluding market sharing) when the significant buyers constantly change identity. There exist important markets in which the (substantial) buyers do change identity continuously, namely, in the construction industries. The building of a plant or an office building, for example, is an essentially nonrepetitive event, and rivals cannot determine whether the successful bidder has been a price cutter unless there is open bidding to specification.

The normal market, however, contains both stability and change. There may be a small rate of entry of new buyers. There will be some shifting of customers even in a regime of effective collusion, for a variety of minor reasons we can lump together as "random factors." There will often be some sharing of buyers by several sellers—a device commending itself to buyers to increase the difficulty of policing price agreements. We move then to the world of circumstantial evidence, or, as it is sometimes called, of probability.

III. THE CONDITIONS FOR DETECTING SECRET PRICE REDUCTIONS

We shall investigate the problem of detecting secret price cutting with a simplified model, in which all buyers and all sellers are initially of equal size. The number of buyers per seller—recalling that we exclude from consideration all buyers who take less than (say) 0.33 percent of a seller's output—will range from 300 down to perhaps 10 or 20 (since we wish to avoid the horrors of full bilateral oligopoly). A few of these buyers are new, but over moderate periods of time most are "old," although some of these old customers will shift among suppliers. A potential secret price cutter has then three groups of customers who would increase their patronage if given secret price cuts: the old customers of rivals; the old customers who would normally leave him; and new customers.

[9] The problem implicitly raised by these remarks is why all sales to the government are not at collusive prices. Part of the answer is that the government is usually not a sufficiently large buyer of a commodity to remunerate the costs of collusion.

Most old buyers will deal regularly with one or a few sellers, in the absence of secret price cutting. There may be no secret price cutting because a collusive price is adhered to, or because only an essentially competitive price can be obtained. We shall show that the loyalty of customers is a crucial variable in determining which price is approached. We need to know the probability that an old customer will buy again from his regular supplier at the collusive price, in the absence of secret price cutting.

The buyer will set the economies of repetitive purchase (which include smaller transaction costs and less product testing) against the increased probability of secret price cutting that comes from shifting among suppliers. From the viewpoint of any one buyer, this gain will be larger the larger the number of sellers and the smaller the number of buyers, as we shall show below. The costs of shifting among suppliers will be smaller the more homogeneous the goods and the larger the purchases of the buyer (again an inverse function of his size). Let us label this probability of repeat purchases p. We shall indicate later how this probability could be determined in a more general approach.

The second component of sales of a firm will be its sales to new buyers and to the floating old customers of rivals. Here we assume that each seller is equally likely to make a sale, in the absence of price competition.

Let us proceed to the analysis. There are n_0 "old" buyers and n_n new customers, with $n_n = \lambda n_0$ and n_s sellers. A firm may look to three kinds of evidence on secret price cutting, and therefore by symmetry to three potential areas to practice secret price cutting.

1. *The behavior of its own old customers.* It has, on average, n_0/n_s such customers, and expects to sell to $m_1 = pn_0/n_s$ of them in a given round of transactions, in the absence of price cutting. The variance of this number of customers is

$$\sigma_1{}^2 = \frac{(1-p)pn_0}{n_s}.$$

The probability of the firm losing more old customers than

$$\frac{(1-p)n_0}{n_s} + k\sigma_1$$

is given by the probability of values greater than k. The expected number of these old customers who will shift to any one rival is, say,

$$m_2 = \frac{1}{n_s - 1}\left[\frac{(1-p)n_0}{n_s} + k\sigma_1\right],$$

with a variance

$$\sigma_2{}^2 = \frac{n_s - 2}{(n_s - 1)^2}\left[\frac{(1-p)n_0}{n_s} + k\sigma_1\right].$$

The probability that any rival will obtain more than $m_2 + r\sigma_2$ of these customers is determined by r. We could now choose those combinations of k and r that fix a level of probability for the loss of a given number of old customers to any one rival beyond which secret price cutting by this rival will be inferred. This is heavy arithmetic, however, so we proceed along a less elegant route.

Let us assume that the firm's critical value for the loss of old customers, beyond which it infers secret price cutting, is

$$\frac{(1-p)n_0}{n_s} + \sigma_1 = \frac{(1-p)n_0}{n_s}\left[1 + \sqrt{\left(\frac{p}{1-p}\frac{n_s}{n_0}\right)}\right]$$
$$= \frac{(1-p)n_0}{n_s}(1+\theta),$$

that is, one standard deviation above the mean. Any one rival will on average attract

$$m_2 = \frac{1}{n_s - 1}\left[\frac{(1-p)n_0}{n_s} + \sigma_1\right]$$

of these customers, with a variance of

$$\sigma_2{}^2 = \frac{n_s - 2}{(n_s - 1)^2}\left[\frac{(1-p)n_0}{n_s} + \sigma_1\right].$$

Let the rival be suspected of price cutting if he obtains more than $(m_2 + \sigma_2)$ customers, that is, if the probability of any larger number is less than about 30 per cent. The joint probability of losing one standard deviation more than the average number of old customers and a rival obtaining one standard deviation more than his average share is about 10 percent. The average sales of a rival are n_0/n_s, ignoring new customers. The maximum number of buyers any seller can obtain from one rival without exciting suspicion, minus the number he will on average get without price cutting $([1-p]n_0/n_s[n_s-1])$, expressed as a ratio to his average sales, is

$$\frac{[\theta(1-p)n_0/(n_s-1)n_s+\sigma_2]}{n_0/n_s}$$

This criterion is tabulated in Table 5–1.

TABLE 5–1

PERCENTAGE GAINS IN SALES FROM UNDETECTED PRICE CUTTING BY A FIRM

Criterion I: $\dfrac{1}{(n_s-1)}\left[\theta(1-p)+\sqrt{\dfrac{n_s(n_s-2)\,(1-p)\,(1+\theta)}{n_0}}\right]$

$$\theta=\sqrt{\frac{p}{1-p}\frac{n_s}{n_0}}$$

Probability of Repeat Sales (p)	Number of Buyers (n_0)	Number of Sellers					
		2	3	4	5	10	20
p = 0.95	20	6.9	11.3	11.3	11.4	11.8	12.7
	30	5.6	8.9	8.8	8.8	9.0	9.6
	40	4.9	7.5	7.4	7.4	7.5	7.9
	50	4.4	6.6	6.5	6.4	6.5	6.8
	100	3.1	4.4	4.3	4.3	4.2	4.4
	200	2.2	3.0	2.9	2.8	2.8	2.8
	400	1.5	2.1	2.0	1.9	1.8	1.8
p = 0.90	20	9.5	14.8	14.7	14.6	14.8	15.7
	30	7.8	11.7	11.5	11.4	11.4	12.0
	40	6.7	10.0	9.7	9.6	9.5	9.9
	50	6.0	8.8	8.6	8.4	8.3	8.6
	100	4.2	6.0	5.8	5.6	5.4	5.5
	200	3.0	4.1	3.9	3.8	3.6	3.6
	400	2.1	2.8	2.7	2.6	2.4	2.4
p = 0.80	20	12.6	19.3	18.9	18.7	18.6	19.4
	30	10.3	15.4	15.0	14.7	14.5	15.0
	40	8.9	13.1	12.7	12.5	12.2	12.5
	50	8.0	11.6	11.2	11.0	10.6	10.8
	100	5.7	8.0	7.7	7.4	7.1	7.1
	200	4.0	5.5	5.3	5.1	4.8	4.7
	400	2.8	3.8	3.6	3.5	3.2	3.2
p = 0.70	20	14.5	22.3	21.8	21.5	21.2	21.9
	30	11.8	17.8	17.3	17.0	16.6	16.9
	40	10.2	15.2	14.8	14.5	14.0	14.2
	50	9.2	13.5	13.1	12.8	12.3	12.4
	100	6.5	9.3	9.0	8.7	8.2	8.2
	200	4.6	6.5	6.2	6.0	5.6	5.5
	400	3.2	4.5	4.3	4.2	3.8	3.7

The entries in Table 5–1 are measures of the maximum additional sales obtainable by secret price cutting (expressed as a percentage of average sales) from any one rival beyond which that rival will infer that the price cutting is taking place. Since the profitability of secret price cutting depends upon the amount of business one can obtain (as well as upon the excess of price over marginal cost), we may also view these numbers as the measures of the incentive to engage in secret price cutting. Three features of the tabulation are noteworthy:

a) The gain in sales from any one rival by secret price cutting is not very sensitive to the number of rivals, given the number of customers and the probability of repeat sales. The aggregate gain in sales of a firm from price cutting—its total incentive to secret price cutting—is the sum of the gains from each rival, and therefore increases roughly in proportion to the number of rivals.

b) The incentive to secret price cutting falls as the number of customers per seller increases—and falls roughly in inverse proportion to the square root of the number of buyers.

c) The incentive to secret price cutting rises as the probability of repeat purchases falls, but at a decreasing rate.

We have said that the gain to old buyers from shifting their patronage among sellers will be that it encourages secret price cutting by making it more difficult to detect. Table 5–1 indicates that there are diminishing returns to increased shifting: The entries increase at a decreasing rate as p falls. In a fuller model we could introduce the costs of shifting among suppliers and determine p to maximize expected buyer gains. The larger the purchases of a buyer, when buyers are of unequal size, however, the greater is the prospect that his shifts will induce price cutting.

In addition it is clear that, when the number of sellers exceeds two, it is possible for two or more firms to pool information and thus to detect less extreme cases of price cutting. For example, at the given probability levels, the number of old customers that any one rival should be able to take from a firm was shown to be at most

$$(1-p)\,\frac{n_0(1+\theta)}{n_s-1},$$

with variance

$$\frac{(n_s-2)\,(1-p)\,(1+\theta)}{(n_s-1)^2}\,n_0\,.$$

At the same probability level, the average number of old customers that one rival should be able to take from T firms is at most

$$\frac{T(1-p)n_0}{n_s-T}\left(1+\frac{\theta}{\sqrt{T}}\right)$$

with the variance

$$\frac{(n_s - T - 1)}{(n_s - T)^2} (1 - p) \left(1 + \frac{\theta}{\sqrt{T}}\right) n_0 T .$$

Each of these is smaller than the corresponding expression for one seller when expressed as a fraction of the customers lost by each of the firms pooling information.

There are, of course, limits to such pooling of information: not only does it become expensive as the number of firms increases, but also it produces less reliable information, since one of the members of the pool may himself be secretly cutting prices. Some numbers illustrative of the effect of pooling will be given at a later point.

2. *The attraction of old customers of other firms is a second source of evidence of price cutting.* If a given rival has not cut prices, he will on average lose $(1 - p)(n_0/n_s)$ customers, with a variance of σ_1^2. The number of customers he will retain with secret price cutting cannot exceed a level at which the rivals suspect the price cutting. Any one rival will have little basis for judging whether he is getting a fair share of this firm's old customers, but they can pool their information and then in the aggregate they will expect the firm to lose at least $(1 - p)(n_0/n_s) - 2\sigma_1$ customers, at the 5 percent probability level. Hence the secret price cutter can retain at most $2\sigma_1$ of his old customers (beyond his average number), which as a fraction of his average sales (ignoring new customers) is

$$\frac{2\sigma_1}{n_0/n_s} = 2 \sqrt{\frac{(1 - p)pn_s}{n_0}} .$$

This is tabulated as Table 5–2.

If the entries in Table 5–2 are compared with those in Table 5–1,[10] it is found that a price cutter is easier to detect by his gains at the expense of any one rival than by his unusual proportion of repeat sales. This second criterion will therefore seldom be useful.

3. *The behavior of new customers is a third source of information*

---

[10] For example, take $p = .95$. The entry for 10 customers per seller is 13.8 in Table 5–2—this is the maximum percentage of average sales that can be obtained by price reductions to old customers. The corresponding entries in Table 5–1 are 6.9 (2 sellers, 20 buyers), 8.9 (3 and 30), 7.4 (4 and 40), 6.4 (5 and 50), 4.2 (10 and 100), etc. Multiplying each entry in Table 5–1 by $(n_s - 1)$, we get the maximum gain in sales (without detection) by attracting customers of rivals, and beyond 2 sellers the gains are larger by this latter route. Since Table 5–1 is based upon a 10 percent probability level, strict comparability requires that we use 1.6 σ, instead of 2 σ, in Table 5–2, which would reduce the entries by one-fifth.

TABLE 5–2

OLD CUSTOMERS THAT A SECRET PRICE-CUTTER CAN RETAIN,
AS A PERCENTAGE OF AVERAGE SALES

$$\text{Criterion II: } 2\sqrt{\frac{p(1-p)}{2}\frac{n_s}{n_0}}$$

Probability That Old Customer Will Remain Loyal (p)	Number of Old Customers per Seller (n_0/n_s)			
	10	20	50	100
0.95.........	13.8	9.7	6.2	4.4
.90.........	19.0	13.4	8.5	6.0
.85.........	22.6	16.0	10.1	7.1
.80.........	25.3	17.9	11.3	8.0
.75.........	27.4	19.4	12.2	8.7
.70.........	29.0	20.5	13.0	9.2
.65.........	30.2	21.3	13.5	9.5
.60.........	31.0	21.9	13.9	9.8
.55.........	31.5	22.2	14.1	10.0
0.50.........	31.6	22.4	14.1	10.0

on price cutting. There are n_n new customers per period,[11] equal to λn_0. A firm expects, in the absence of price cutting, to sell to

$$m_3 = \frac{1}{n_s}\lambda n_0$$

of these customers, with a variance of

$$\sigma_3{}^2 = \left(1 - \frac{1}{n_s}\right)\frac{\lambda n_0}{n_s}.$$

If the rivals pool information (without pooling, this area could not be policed effectively), this firm cannot obtain more than $m_3 + 2\sigma_3$ customers without being deemed a price cutter, using again a 5 percent probability criterion. As a percentage of the firm's total sales, the maximum sales above the expected number in the absence of price cutting are then

$$\frac{2\sigma_3}{n_0(1+\lambda)/n_s} = \frac{2}{1+\lambda}\sqrt{\frac{(n_s - 1)\lambda}{n_0}}.$$

We tabulate this criterion as Table 5–3.

[11] Unlike old customers, whose behavior is better studied in a round of transactions, the new customers are a flow whose magnitude depends much more crucially on the time period considered. The annual flow of new customers is here taken (relative to the number of old customers) as the unit.

TABLE 5–3

MAXIMUM ADDITIONAL NEW CUSTOMERS (AS A PERCENTAGE OF AVERAGE SALES)
OBTAINABLE BY SECRET PRICE CUTTING

$$Criterion\ III: \frac{2}{1+\lambda} \sqrt{\frac{\lambda(n_s-1)}{n_0}}$$

Rate of Appearance of New Buyers (λ)	Number of Old Buyers (n_0)	Number of Sellers					
		2	3	4	5	10	20
1/100	20	4.4	6.3	7.7	8.9	13.3	19.3
	30	3.6	5.1	6.3	7.2	10.8	15.8
	40	3.1	4.4	5.4	6.3	9.4	13.6
	50	2.8	4.0	4.8	5.6	8.4	12.2
	100	2.0	2.8	3.4	4.0	5.9	8.6
	200	1.4	2.0	2.4	2.8	4.2	6.1
	400	1.0	1.4	1.7	2.0	3.0	4.3
1/10	20	12.9	18.2	22.3	25.7	38.6	56.0
	30	10.5	14.8	18.2	21.0	31.5	45.8
	40	9.1	12.9	15.8	18.2	27.3	39.6
	50	8.1	11.5	14.1	16.3	24.4	35.4
	100	5.8	8.1	10.0	11.5	17.2	25.1
	200	4.1	5.8	7.0	8.1	12.2	17.7
	400	2.9	4.1	5.0	5.8	8.6	12.5
1/5	20	16.7	23.6	28.9	33.3	50.0	72.6
	30	13.6	19.2	23.6	27.2	40.8	59.3
	40	11.8	16.7	20.4	23.6	35.4	51.4
	50	10.5	14.9	18.3	21.1	31.6	46.0
	100	7.4	10.5	12.9	14.9	22.4	32.5
	200	5.3	7.4	9.1	10.5	15.8	23.0
	400	3.7	5.3	6.4	7.4	11.2	16.2
1/4	20	17.9	25.3	31.0	35.8	53.7	78.0
	30	14.6	20.7	25.3	29.2	43.8	63.7
	40	12.6	17.9	21.9	25.3	38.0	55.1
	50	11.3	16.0	19.6	22.6	33.9	49.3
	100	8.0	11.3	13.9	16.0	24.0	34.9
	200	5.7	8.0	9.8	11.3	17.0	24.7
	400	4.0	5.7	6.9	8.0	12.0	17.4

Two aspects of the incentive to cut prices (or equivalently the difficulty of detecting price cuts) to new customers are apparent: the incentive increases rapidly with the number of sellers[12] and the incentive increases with the rate of entry of new customers. As usual the incentive falls as the absolute number of customers per seller rises. If the rate of entry of new buyers is 10 percent or more, price cutting to new customers

[12] And slowly with the number of sellers if customers per seller are held constant.

allows larger sales increases without detection that can be obtained by attracting customers of rivals (compare Tables 5–1 and 5–3).

Of the considerable number of directions in which this model could be enlarged, two will be presented briefly.

The first is inequality in the size of firms. In effect this complication has already been introduced by the equivalent device of pooling information. If we tabulate the effects of pooling of information by K firms, the results are equivalent to having a firm K times as large as the other firms. The number of old customers this large firm can lose to any one small rival (all of whom are equal in size) is given, in Table 5–4, as a percentage of the average number of old customers of the small firm; the column labeled $K = 1$ is of course the case analyzed in Table 5–1.

The effects of pooling on the detection of price cutting are best analyzed by comparing Table 5–4 with Table 5–1. If there are 100 customers and 10 firms (and $p = 0.9$), a single firm can increase sales by 5.4 percent by poaching on one rival, or about 50 percent against all rivals (Table 5–1). If 9 firms combine, the maximum amount the single firm can gain by secret price cutting is 28.9 percent (Table 5–4). With 20 firms and 200 customers, a single firm can gain 3.6 percent from each rival, or about 30 percent from 9 rivals; if these rivals merge, the corresponding figure falls to 14.0 percent. The pooling of information therefore reduces substantially the scope for secret price cutting.

This table exaggerates the effect of inequality of firm size because it fails to take account of the fact that the number of customers varies with firm size, on our argument that only customers above a certain size relative to the seller are a feasible group for secret price cutting. The small firm can find it attractive to cut prices to buyers which are not large enough to be potential customers by price cutting for the large seller.

The temporal pattern of buyers' behavior provides another kind of information: What is possibly due to random fluctuation in the short run cannot with equal probability be due to chance if repeated. Thus the maximum expected loss of old customers to a rival in one round of transactions is (at the 1σ level)

$$\frac{n_0}{(n_s - 1)n_s} (1 - p)(1 + \theta),$$

but for T consecutive periods the maximum expected loss is (over T periods)

$$\frac{T}{n_s - 1}(1 - p)\frac{n_0}{n_s}[1 + \theta \sqrt{T}],$$

TABLE 5-4

PERCENTAGE GAINS IN SALES FROM UNDETECTED PRICE CUTTING BY A SMALL FIRM

Criterion IV:

$$\frac{1}{n_s - K}\left[\theta(1 - p)\sqrt{K} + \sqrt{\frac{n_s K(1 - p)(n_s - K - 1)(1 + \theta/\sqrt{K})}{n_0}}\right]$$

$$\theta = \sqrt{\frac{p}{1 - p}\frac{n_s}{n_0}}$$

Probability of Repeat Sales (p)	Number of Firms ($n_s - K$ + 1)	Buyers per Small Seller (n_0/n_s)	Size of Large Firm (K)			
			1	2	5	9
p = 0.9	2	10	9.5	13.4	21.2	28.5
		30	5.5	7.7	12.2	16.4
		50	4.2	6.0	9.5	12.7
	3	10	11.7	15.8	23.9	31.4
		30	6.3	8.7	13.3	17.6
		50	4.8	6.6	10.2	13.5
	4	10	9.7	13.1	19.7	25.7
		30	5.2	7.1	10.9	14.4
		50	4.0	5.4	8.3	11.0
	10	10	5.4	7.2	10.7	14.0
		30	2.9	3.9	5.9	7.7
		50	2.2	2.9	4.5	5.9
p = 0.8	2	10	12.6	17.9	28.3	37.9
		30	7.3	10.3	16.3	21.9
		50	5.7	8.0	12.6	17.0
	3	10	15.4	21.0	32.1	42.3
		30	8.4	11.6	18.0	23.9
		50	6.4	8.9	13.8	18.4
	4	10	12.7	17.3	26.3	34.7
		30	6.9	9.5	14.7	19.5
		50	5.3	7.3	11.3	15.0
	10	10	7.1	9.5	14.4	18.9
		30	3.8	5.2	8.0	10.6
		50	2.9	4.0	6.1	8.1

with a variance of

$$\sigma_5^2 = \frac{(n_s - 2)}{(n_s - 1)^2} T(1 - p)\frac{n_0}{n_s}[1 + \theta\sqrt{T}].$$

This source of information is of minor efficacy in detecting price cutting unless the rounds of successive transactions are numerous—that is, unless buyers purchase (enter contracts) frequently.

Our approach has certain implications for the measurement of concentration, if we wish concentration to measure likelihood of effective collusion. In the case of new customers, for example, let the probability of attracting a customer be proportional to the firm's share of industry output (s). Then the variance of the firm's share of sales to new customers will be $n_n s(1-s)$, and the aggregate for the industry will be

$$C = n_n \sum_1^r s(1-s)$$

for r firms. This expression equals $n_n (1-H)$, where

$$H = \Sigma s^2$$

is the Herfindahl index of concentration. The same index holds, as an approximation, for potential price cutting to attract old customers.[13]

The foregoing analysis can be extended to nonprice variables, subject to two modifications. The first modification is that there be a definite joint profit-maximizing policy upon which the rivals can agree. Here we may expect to encounter a spectrum of possibilities, ranging from a clearly defined optimum policy (say, on favorable legislation) to a nebulous set of alternatives (say, directions of research).[14] Collusion is less feasible, the less clear the basis on which it should proceed. The second

---

[13] A similar argument leads to a measure of concentration appropriate to potential price cutting for old customers. Firm i will lose

$$(1-p)n_0 s_i$$

old customers, and firm j will gain

$$(1-p)n_0 \frac{s_i s_j}{1-s_i}$$

of them, with a variance

$$(1-p)n_0 \frac{s_i s_j}{1-s_i} \left(1 - \frac{s_j}{1-s_i}\right).$$

If we sum over all i $(\neq j)$, we obtain the variance of firm j's sales to old customers of rivals

$$(1-p)n_0 s_j(1+H-2s_j),$$

to an approximation, and summing over all j, we have the concentration measure,

$$(1-p)n_0 (1-H).$$

The agreement of this measure with that for new customers is superficial: that for new customers implicitly assumes pooling of information and that for old customers does not.

[14] Of course, price itself usually falls somewhere in this range rather than at the pole. The traditional assumption of stationary conditions conceals this fact.

modification is that the competitive moves of any one firm will differ widely among nonprice variables in their detectability by rivals. Some forms of nonprice competition will be easier to detect than price cutting because they leave visible traces (advertising, product quality, servicing, etc.) but some variants will be elusive (reciprocity in purchasing, patent licensing arrangements). The common belief that nonprice competition is more common than price competition is therefore not wholly in keeping with the present theory. Those forms that are suitable areas for collusion will have less competition; those which are not suitable will have more competition.

IV. SOME FRAGMENTS OF EVIDENCE

Before we seek empirical evidence on our theory, it is useful to report two investigations of the influence of numbers of sellers on price. These investigations have an intrinsic interest because, so far as I know, no systematic analysis of the effect of numbers has hitherto been made.

The first investigation was of newspaper advertising rates, as a function of the number of evening newspapers in a city. Advertising rates on a milline basis are closely (and negatively) related to circulation, so a regression of rates on circulation was made for fifty-three cities in 1939. The residuals (in logarithmic form) from this regression equation are tabulated in Table 5–5. It will be observed that rates are 5 percent above the average in one-newspaper towns and 5 percent below the average in two-newspaper towns, and the towns with one evening paper but also an independent morning paper fall nearly midway between these points. Unfortunately there were too few cities with more than two evening newspapers to yield results for larger numbers of firms.

TABLE 5–5

RESIDUALS FROM REGRESSION OF ADVERTISING RATES ON CIRCULATION[*]

Number of Evening Papers	n	Mean Residual (Logarithm)	Standard Deviation of Mean
One	23	0.0211	0.0210
With morning paper	10	− .0174	.0324
Without morning paper	13	.0507	.0233
Two	30	−0.0213	0.0135

[*] The regression equation is
$$\log R = 5.194 - 1.688 \log c + .139 (\log c)^2,$$
$$(.620) \qquad (.063)$$
where R is the 5 M milline rate and c is circulation.

Source: American Association of Advertising Agencies, *Market and Newspaper Statistics*, Vol. VIIIa (1939).

The second investigation is of spot commercial rates on AM radio stations in the four states of Ohio, Indiana, Michigan, and Illinois. The basic equation introduces, along with number of rivals, a series of other factors (power of station, population of the county in which the station is located, etc.). Unfortunately the number of stations is rather closely correlated with population ($r^2 = .796$ in the logarithms). The general result, shown in Table 5–6, is similar to that for newspapers: the elasticity of price with respect to numbers of rivals is quite small (— .07). Here the range of stations in a county was from 1 to 13.

TABLE 5–6
REGRESSION OF AM SPOT COMMERCIAL RATES (26 TIMES)
AND STATION CHARACTERISTICS, 1961
($n = 345$)

Independent Variables*	Regression Coefficient	Standard Error
1. Logarithm of population of county, 1960.......	.238	0.026
2. Logarithm of kilowatt power of station.........	.206	.015
3. Dummy variables of period of broadcasting:		
a) Sunrise to sunset..........................	−.114	.025
b) More than (a), less than 18 hours...........	−.086	.027
c) 18–21 hours..............................	−.053	.028
4. Logarithm of number of stations in county......	−.074	0.046
	$R^2 = .743$	

* Dependent variable: logarith of average rate, May 1, 1961 (dollars).

Source: "Spot Radio Rates and Data," *Standard Rate and Data Service, Inc.*, Vol. XLIII, No. 5 (May 1961).

Both studies suggest that the level of prices is not very responsive to the actual number of rivals. This is in keeping with the expectations based upon our model, for that model argues that the number of buyers, the proportion of new buyers, and the relative sizes of firms are as important as the number of rivals.

To turn to the present theory, the only test covering numerous industries so far devised has been one based upon profitability. This necessarily rests upon company data, and it has led to the exclusion of a large number of industries for which the companies do not operate in a well-defined industry. For example, the larger steel and chemical firms operate in a series of markets in which their position ranges from monopolistic to competitive. We have required of each industry that the earnings of a substantial fraction of the companies in the industry (measured by output) be determined by the profitability of that industry's products, that is, that we have a fair share of the industry and the industry's product is the dominant product of the firms.

Three measures of profitability are given in Table 5–7: (1) the rate of return on all capital (including debt), (2) the rate of return on net worth (stockholders' equity); (3) the ratio of market value to book value of the common stock.

TABLE 5–7
PROFITABILITY AND CONCENTRATION DATA

Industry*	Concentration (1954)		Average Rate of Return (1953–57)		Ratio of Market Value to Book Value (1953–57)
	Share of Top 4	H†	All Assets	Net Worth	
Sulfur mining (4)	98	0.407	19.03	23.85	3.02
Automobiles (3)	98	.369	11.71	20.26	2.30
Flat glass (3)	90	.296	11.79	16.17	2.22
Gypsum products (2)	90	.280	12.16	20.26	1.83
Primary aluminum (4)	98	.277	6.87	13.46	2.48
Metal cans (4)	80	.260	7.27	13.90	1.60
Chewing gum (2)	86	.254	13.50	17.06	2.46
Hard-surface floor coverings (3)	87	.233	6.56	7.59	0.98
Cigarettes (5)	83	.213	7.23	11.18	1.29
Industrial gases (3)	84	.202	8.25	11.53	1.33
Corn wet milling (3)	75	.201	9.17	11.55	1.48
Typewriters (3)	83	.198	3.55	5.39	0.84
Domestic laundry equipment (2)	68	.174	9.97	17.76	1.66
Rubber tires (9)	79	.171	7.86	14.02	1.70
Rayon fiber (4)	76	.169	5.64	6.62	0.84
Carbon black (2)	73	.152	8.29	9.97	1.40
Distilled liquors (6)	64	0.118	6.94	7.55	0.77

* The number of firms is given in parentheses after the industry title. Only those industries are included for which a substantial share (35 per cent or more) of the industry's sales is accounted for by the firms in the sample, and these firms derive their chief revenues (50 per cent or more) from the industry in question.

† H is Herfindahl index.

In addition, two measures of concentration are presented: (1) the conventional measure, the share of output produced by the four leading firms; and (2) the Herfindahl index, H.

The various rank correlations are given in Table 5–8. The various concentration measures, on the one hand, and the various measures of profitability, on the other hand, are tolerably well correlated.[15] All show

[15] The concentration measures have a rank correlation of .903. The profitability measures have the following rank correlations:

	Return on All Assets	Ratio of Market to Book Value
Return on net worth	.866	.872
Ratio of market to book value	.733	—

the expected positive relationship. In general the data suggest that there is no relationship between profitability and concentration if H is less than 0.250 or the share of the four largest firms is less than about 80 per cent. These data, like those on advertising rates, confirm our theory only in the sense that they support theories which assert that competition increases with number of firms.

TABLE 5–8
RANK CORRELATIONS OF MEASURES OF PROFITABILITY
AND MEASURES OF CONCENTRATION

	Measure of Profitability		
Measure of Concentration	Rate of Return on All Assets	Rate of Return on Net Worth	Ratio of Market Value to Book Value
Share of output produced by four largest firms..........	.322	.507	.642
Herfindahl index (H)..........	.524	.692	.730

Our last evidence is a study of the prices paid by buyers of steel products in 1939, measured relative to the quoted prices (Table 5–9). The figure of 8.3 for hot-rolled sheets, for example, represents an average of 8.3 percent reduction from quoted prices, *paid by buyers*, with a standard deviation of 7.3 percent of quoted prices. The rate of price cutting is almost perfectly correlated with the standard deviation of transaction prices, as we should expect: the less perfect the market knowledge, the more extensive the price cutting.

TABLE 5–9
PRICES OF STEEL PRODUCTS, 1939, AND INDUSTRY STRUCTURE, 1938

	Prices, 2d Quarter, 1939 (Percent)			
Product Class	Average Discount from List Price	Standard Deviation	Herfindahl Index	Output in 1939 Relative to 1937
Hot-rolled sheets.......	8.3	7.3	0.0902	1.14
Merchant bars.........	1.2	4.5	.1517	0.84
Hot-rolled strip........	8.5	8.3	.1069	0.56
Plates...............	2.6	4.8	.1740	0.85
Structural shapes.......	3.2	4.3	.3280	0.92
Cold-rolled strip.......	8.8	9.8	.0549	0.88
Cold-rolled sheets......	5.8	5.0	.0963	1.14
Cold-finished bars......	0.9	3.4	0.0964	0.83

Source: Prices: "Labor Department Examines Consumers' Prices of Steel Products," *Iron Age*, April 25, 1946; industry structure: 1938 capacity data from *Directory of Iron and Steel Works of the United States and Canada;* output: *Annual Statistical Report,* American Iron and Steel Institute (New York, 1938, 1942).

In general, the less concentrated the industry structure (measured by the Herfindahl index), the larger were the price reductions. Although there were no extreme departures from this relationship, structural shapes and hot-rolled strip had prices somewhat lower than the average relationship, and cold-finished bars prices somewhat higher than expected, and the deviations are not accounted for by the level of demand (measured by 1939 sales relative to 1937 sales). The number of buyers could not be taken into account, but the BLS study states:

> The extent of price concessions shown by this study is probably understated because certain very large consumers in the automobile and container industries were excluded from the survey. This omission was at the request of the OPA which contemplated obtaining this information in connection with other studies. Since a small percentage of steel consumers, including these companies, accounts for a large percentage of steel purchased, prices paid by a relatively few large consumers have an important influence upon the entire steel price structure. Very large steel consumers get greater reductions from published prices than smaller consumers, often the result of competitive bidding by the mills for the large volume of steel involved. One very large steel consumer, a firm that purchased over 2 pct of the total consumption of hot and cold-rolled sheets in 1940, refused to give purchase prices. This firm wished to protect its suppliers, fearing that "certain transactions might be revealed which would break confidence" with the steel mills. However, this company did furnish percent changes of prices paid for several steel products which showed that for some products prices advanced markedly, and in one case, nearly 50 pct. The great price advances for this company indicate that it was receiving much larger concessions than smaller buyers.[16]

These various bits of evidence are fairly favorable to the theory, but they do not constitute strong support. More powerful tests will be feasible when the electrical equipment triple-damage suits are tried.[17] The great merit of our theory, in fact, is that it has numerous testable hypotheses, unlike the immortal theories that have been traditional in this area.

Appendix

The importance of product heterogeneity for profit-maximizing behavior cannot well be established by an a priori argument. Nevertheless, the following simple exposition of the implications for profitability

[16] See "Labor Department Examines Consumers' Prices of Steel Products," *op. cit.*, p. 133.

[17] For example, it will be possible to test the prediction that prices will be higher and less dispersed in sales on public bids than in privately negotiated sales, and the prediction that price-cutting increases as the number of buyers diminishes.

of disregarding heterogeneity may have some heuristic value. The analysis, it will be observed, is formally equivalent to that of the effects of an excise tax on a monopolist.

Assume that a monopolist makes men's suits, and that he makes only one size of suit. This is absurd behavior, but the picture of the sadistic monopolist who disregards consumer desires has often made fugitive appearances in the literature so the problem has some interest of its own. The demand curve of a consumer for suits that fit, $f(p)$, would now be reduced because he would have to incur some alteration cost a in order to wear the suit. His effective demand would therefore decline to $f(p + a)$. Assume further that the marginal cost of suits is constant (m), and that it would be the same if the monopolist were to make suits of various sizes.

The effect on profits of a uniform product—uniform is an especially appropriate word here—can be shown graphically (Fig. 5–1). The decrease in quantity sold, with a linear demand curve, is

FIGURE 5–1

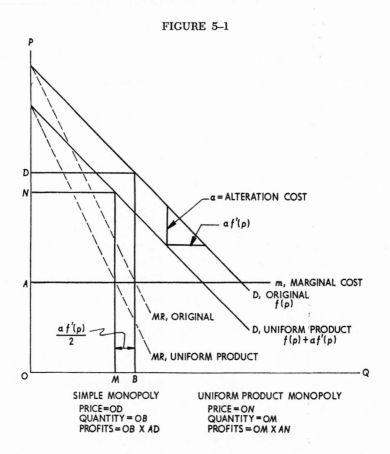

SIMPLE MONOPOLY
PRICE=OD
QUANTITY=OB
PROFITS=OB X AD

UNIFORM PRODUCT MONOPOLY
PRICE=ON
QUANTITY=OM
PROFITS=OM X AN

$$MB = \tfrac{1}{2}\, a f'(p) \,.$$

The decrease in the price received by the monopolist is

$$D\,N = \frac{MB}{f'(p)} - a = - \frac{a}{2} \,,$$

so if π is profit per unit, and q is output, the relative decline in total profit is approximately

$$\frac{\Delta\pi}{\pi} + \frac{\Delta q}{q} \,,$$

or

$$\frac{MB}{OB} + \frac{N\,D}{A\,D} \,.$$

Since

$$OB = \frac{f(m)}{2}$$

$$A\,D = - \frac{p}{\eta} \,,$$

where η is the elasticity of demand, the relative decline of profits with a uniform product is

$$\frac{af'(p)}{f(m)} + \frac{a\,\eta}{2p} = \frac{a\,\eta}{2p} + \frac{a\,\eta}{2p} = \frac{a\,\eta}{p} \,.$$

The loss from imposed uniformity is therefore proportional to the ratio of alteration costs to price.

Our example is sufficiently unrealistic to make any quantitative estimate uninteresting. In general one would expect an upper limit to the ratio a/p, because it becomes cheaper to resort to other goods (custom tailoring in our example), or to abandon the attempt to find appropriate goods. The loss of profits of the monopolist will be proportional to the average value of a/p, and this will be smaller, the smaller the variation in buyers' circumstances.

Still, monopolists are lucky if their long-run demand curves have an elasticity only as large as -5, and then even a ratio of a to p of 1/40 will reduce their profits by 12 percent. The general conclusion I wish to draw is that a monopolist who does not cater to the diversities of his buyers' desires will suffer a substantial decline in his profits.

Addendum: Revisions

Roland McKinnon in a comment upon the foregoing article makes two improvements (*Journal of Political Economy*, June 1966).

The first improvement is to introduce a more powerful test by comparing (1) the loss of customers by firm X to a suspected price cutter Y, with (2) the gain of customers by X from Y. When these types of information are available, they greatly increase the power of the tests in detecting price cutting.

The second improvement is more basic: McKinnon uses the Neyman-Pearson theory to create more systematic criteria of price cutting. Type I errors (an unjust accusation that Y is a price cutter) and Type II errors (failure to detect price cutting) are explicitly introduced, to get more rational criteria than the arbitrary choices in the article.

The qualitative rules of the article (such as that the probability of price cutting increases with the number of rivals) continue to hold.

PART II

The Determinants of Concentration

The forces which determine the size structure of industries are variously explained in the literature by barriers to entry, economies of scale, mergers, and a host of particular instances of these (such as patents). The materials presented include:

CHAPTER 6

Barriers to Entry, Economies of Scale, and Firm Size, a note on terminology.

CHAPTER 7

The Economies of Scale (*Journal of Law and Economics*, 1958), with an Addendum which possibly should precede the piece.

CHAPTER 8

Monopoly and Oligopoly by Merger (*Proceedings, American Economic Association*, 1950), with an Addendum.

CHAPTER 9

The Dominant Firm and the Inverted Umbrella (*Journal of Law and Economics*, 1964), a case study in mergers.

CHAPTER 10

Imperfections in the Capital Market (*Journal of Political Economy*, 1967).

CHAPTER 11

A Note on Patents.

Chapter 6

BARRIERS TO ENTRY, ECONOMIES OF SCALE, AND FIRM SIZE

Let us begin with definitions of the three concepts whose interrelations are the subject of this chapter:

1. Barriers to entry. A barrier to entry may be defined as a cost of producing (at some or every rate of output) which must be borne by a firm which seeks to enter an industry but is not borne by firms already in the industry.

2. Economies of scale. The economies of scale constitute the relationship between the size of a firm (or plant) and its costs of production in the broadest sense. The relationship may be symbolized by a long-run average cost curve representing the least possible cost of every output.

3. Firm size. Firm size can be measured by output. Multiple products are irrelevant to the subject of this note, so we shall assume that each firm has the identical product. Nevertheless, there may be product "differentiation" due to location, advertising, etc. Output is long-run equilibrium output.

Our problem is simply: on what does firm size depend—economies of scale, barriers to entry, or something else?

Two simple cases will suffice to demonstrate that the language of economists has been lax. The first case is a monopoly whose existence arises simply because only one firm can exist with the given industry demand (Fig. 6–1). Some economists will say that the economies of scale are a barrier to entry, meaning that such economies explain why no additional firms enter. It would be equally possible to say that inadequate demand is a barrier to entry. If we define a barrier as a differentially higher cost of new firms, there is no barrier and the firm size is governed by economies of scale and demand conditions.

Next, consider an industry with many independent firms but an absolute barrier to the entry of new firms. The New York City taxi business, with its limited license medallions, is an example. Let there also be diseconomies of scale beyond a given output (Fig. 6–2). With licensing,

FIGURE 6–1

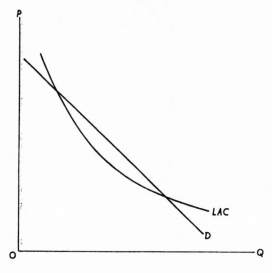

FIGURE 6–2

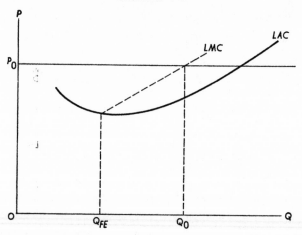

each firm operates at output Q_0, given the demand which yields a price P_0. With free entry, each firm would operate at output Q_{FE}.[1] The license-governed output of Q_0 is set by (dis)economies of scale *and* demand conditions *and* barriers to entry. In our unceasing search for more elegant formulations, however, we can get rid of barriers by stating that the firm

---

[1] If there are external economies or diseconomies (different costs for industry-wide output changes), the cost curve will shift, and its minimum at the simultaneously determined industry output will fix firm size.

size will be governed by economies of scale and the demand conditions *of the firm* (as well as of the industry)—which are influenced by barriers as well as by incomes, prices of other goods, etc.[2]

These examples suggest that we say that demand and cost (economies of scale) conditions govern the sizes of firms. The barriers to entry would then be restricted to differentially higher costs of new firms, which act as one force—others are location and advertising and product characteristics—which affects the demands of individual firms. This choice of language is consistent within itself, does no violence to our general understanding of these concepts, and begs no substantive issues.

FIGURE 6–3

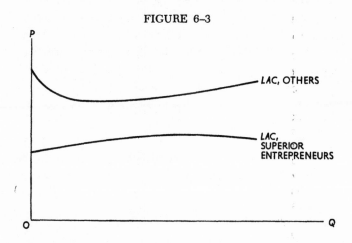

Several implications of this terminology may be commented upon briefly:

1. Entrepreneurs differ in abilities, so "the" long-run cost curve may differ among men. A superior entrepreneur operating with diseconomies of scale may monopolize an industry because his costs are below those of all potential rivals (Fig. 6–3). This offers no problems to our terminology because firm size is still governed by economies of scale (height and slope of cost curves) and demand, but it emphasizes the fact that the conventional language is directed to a situation in which curves depend only on factors (such as size) common to all firms. Of course, if the superior entrepreneur is also equally superior elsewhere, his alternative costs will be as high as those of other firms.

---

[2] If in this license case there were no diseconomies of scale, there might be only one firm (economies of scale) or an indeterminate number (constant returns to scale).

2. Capital requirements are often listed as a barrier to entry. Since existing firms also have to meet these requirements, they are not a barrier in our terminology. They are a determinant (if they are relevant at all) of the economies of scale—the shape of the long-run average cost curve.

3. Suppose, in an industry without economies of scale, a merger of firms lends to temporary monopoly profits. We would say that the (short-run) demand curve facing individual firms has been changed.

4. A firm sells its product at a higher price than rivals obtain. Again we say the size of the firm is governed by economies of scale and its demand curve. However, suppose that a given size of firm systematically gets higher prices because (for example) its product is more attractive to buyers. A small shoe manufacturer adapts to new fashions more quickly, or a large manufacturer of engines has a superior network of repair facilities. If the demand conditions of the firm vary with a characteristic associated with firm size, our language permits us to say that the characteristic is an element of demand or of economies of scale. In keeping with the general tradition of keeping out of demand as much of producer-controlled factors as one can, we would call these selling advantages economies of scale but no important principle is at stake.

5. "Free" entry, in our language, is entry by firms suffering no cost differentials relative to existing firms. Free entry is compatible with huge capital requirements (which are a source, perhaps, of economies of scale).

6. Product differentiation is often treated as a barrier to entry.[3] This is correct usage, on our approach, only if the costs of differentiation (design, advertising, etc.) are higher for a new firm than an existing firm. Otherwise differentiation is a (possible) source of economies of scale.

[3] See J. S. Bain, *Barriers to Entry* (Harvard University Press, 1956), chap. iv.

Chapter   THE ECONOMIES

7   OF SCALE*

The theory of the economies of scale is the theory of the relationship between the scale of use of a properly chosen combination of all productive services and the rate of output of the enterprise. In its broadest formulation this theory is a crucial element of the economic theory of social organization, for it underlies every question of market organization and the role (and locus) of governmental control over economic life. Let one ask himself how an economy would be organized if every economic activity were prohibitively inefficient upon alternately a small scale and a large scale, and the answer will convince him that here lies a basic element of the theory of economic organization.

The theory has limped along for a century, collecting large pieces of good reasoning and small chunks of empirical evidence but never achieving scientific prosperity. A large cause of its poverty is that the central concept of the theory—the firm of optimum size—has eluded confident measurement. We have been dangerously close to denying Lincoln, for all economists have been ignorant of the optimum size of firm in almost every industry all of the time, and this ignorance has been an insurmountable barrier between us and the understanding of the forces which govern optimum size. It is almost as if one were trying to measure the nutritive values of goods without knowing whether the consumers who ate them continued to live.

The central thesis of this paper is that the determination of the optimum size is not difficult if one formalizes the logic that sensible men have always employed to judge efficient size. This technique, which I am old-fashioned enough to call the survivor technique, reveals the optimum size in terms of private costs—that is, in terms of the environment in

* This paper was prepared at the National Bureau of Economic Research. I must thank Nestor Terleckyj for performing most of the statistical work. Reprinted from *Journal of Law and Economics*, Vol. I (October 1958). Copyright 1958 by the *Journal of Law and Economics*.

which the enterprise finds itself. After discussing the technique, we turn to the question of how the forces governing optimum size may be isolated.

I. THE SURVIVOR PRINCIPLE

The optimum size (or range of sizes) of enterprises in an industry is now ascertained empirically by one of three methods. The first is that of direct comparison of actual costs of firms of different sizes; the second is the comparison of rates of return on investment; and the third is the calculation of probable costs of enterprises of different sizes in the light of technological information. All three methods are practically objectionable in demanding data which are usually unobtainable and seldom up to date. But this cannot be the root of their difficulties, for there is up-to-date information on many economic concepts which are complex and even basically incapable of precise measurement (such as income). The plain fact is that we have not demanded the data because we have been unable to specify what we wanted.

The comparisons of both actual costs and rates of return are strongly influenced by the valuations which are put on productive services, so that an enterprise which over- or undervalues important productive services, will under- or overstate its efficiency. Historical cost valuations of resources, which are most commonly available, are in principle irrelevant under changed conditions. Valuations based upon expected earnings yield no information on the efficiency of an enterprise—in the limiting case where all resources are so valued, all firms would be of equal efficiency judged by either average costs or rates of return. The ascertainment on any scale of the maximum value of each resource in alternative uses is a task which only the unsophisticated would assume and only the omniscient would discharge. The host of valuation problems are accentuated by the variable role of the capital markets in effecting revaluations and the variable attitudes of the accountants toward the revaluations.[1]

The technological studies of costs of different sizes of plant encounter equally formidable obstacles. These studies are compounded of some fairly precise (although not necessarily very relevant) technical information and some crude guesses on nontechnological aspects such as marketing costs, transportation rate changes, labor relations, etc.—that is, much of the problem is solved only in the unhappy sense of being delegated to a technologist. Even ideal results, moreover, do not tell us the

---

[1] These problems are discussed by Milton Friedman in *Business Concentration and Price Policy*, pp. 230 ff. (1955).

optimum size of firm in industry A in 1958, but rather the optimum size of new plants in the industry, on the assumption that the industry starts *de novo* or that only a small increment of investment is being made.

The survivor technique avoids both the problems of valuation of resources and the hypothetical nature of the technological studies. Its fundamental postulate is that the competition of different sizes of firms sifts out the more efficient enterprises. In the words of Mill, who long ago proposed the technique:

> Whether or not the advantages obtained by operating on a large-scale preponderate in any particular case over the more watchful attention, and greater regard to minor gains and losses usually found in small establishments, can be ascertained, in a state of free competition, by an unfailing test. . . . Wherever there are lárge and small establishments in the same business, that one of the two which in existing circumstances carries on the production at the greater advantage will be able to undersell the other.[2]

Mill was wrong only in suggesting that the technique was inapplicable under oligopoly, for even under oligopoly the drive of maximum profits will lead to the disappearance of relatively inefficient sizes of firms.

The survivor technique proceeds to solve the problem of determining the optimum firm size as follows: Classify the firms in an industry by size, and calculate the share of industry output coming from each class over time. If the share of a given class falls, it is relatively inefficient, and in general is more inefficient the more rapidly the share falls.

An efficient size of firm, on this argument, is one that meets any and all problems the entrepreneur actually faces: strained labor relations, rapid innovation, government regulation, unstable foreign markets, and what not. This is, of course, the decisive meaning of efficiency from the viewpoint of the enterprise. Of course, social efficiency may be a very different thing: the most efficient firm size may arise from possession of monopoly power, undesirable labor practices, discriminatory legislation, etc. The survivor technique is not directly applicable to the determination of the socially optimum size of enterprise, and we do not enter into this question. The socially optimum firm is fundamentally an ethical concept, and we question neither its importance nor its elusiveness.

Not only is the survivor technique more direct and simpler than the

---

[2] *Principles of Political Economy*, p. 134 (Ashley ed.). Marshall states the same argument in Darwinian language: "For as a general rule the law of substitution —which is nothing more than a special and limited application of the law of survival of the fittest—tends to make one method of industrial organization supplant another when it offers a direct and immediate service at a lower price." *Principles of Economics*, p. 597 (8th ed., 1920).

alternative techniques for the determination of the optimum size of firm, it is also more authoritative. Suppose that the cost, rate of return, and technological studies all find that in a given industry the optimum size of firm is one which produces 500 to 600 units per day, and that costs per unit are much higher if one goes far outside this range. Suppose also that most of the firms in the industry are three times as large, and that those firms which are in the 500 to 600 unit class are rapidly failing or growing to a larger size. Would we believe that the optimum size was 500 to 600 units? Clearly not: an optimum size that cannot survive in rivalry with other sizes is a contradiction, and some error, we would all say, has been made in the traditional studies. Implicitly, all judgments on economies of scale have always been based directly upon, or at least verified by recourse to, the experience of survivorship.

This is not to say that the findings of the survivor technique are unequivocal. Entrepreneurs may make mistakes in their choice of firm size, and we must seek to eliminate the effects of such errors either by invoking large numbers of firms so errors tend to cancel or by utilizing time periods such that errors are revealed and corrected. Or the optimum size may be changing because of changes in factor prices or technology, so that perhaps the optimum size rises in one period and falls in another. This problem too calls for a close examination of the time periods which should be employed. We face these problems in our statistical work below.

We must also recognize that a single optimum size or firm will exist in an industry only if all firms have (access to) identical resources. Since various firms employ different kinds or qualities of resources, there will tend to develop a frequency distribution of optimum firm sizes. The survivor technique may allow us to estimate this distribution; in the application below we restrict ourselves to the range of optimum sizes.

The measure of the optimum size is only a first step toward the construction of a theory of economies of scale with substantive content, but it is the indispensable first step. We turn in later sections of this paper to the examination of the methods by which hypotheses concerning the determinants of optimum size may be tested.

II. ILLUSTRATIVE SURVIVORSHIP MEASURES

The survivor principle is very general in scope and very flexible in application, and these advantages can best be brought out by making concrete applications of the principle to individual industries. These applications will also serve to display a number of problems of data and interpretation which are encountered in the use of the survivor technique. We begin with the American steel industry.

In order that survivorship of firms of a given size be evidence of comparative efficiency, these firms must compete with firms of other sizes—all of the firms must sell in a common market. We have therefore restricted the analysis to firms making steel ingots by open-hearth or Bessemer processes.[3] Size has perforce been measured by capacity, for production is not reported by individual companies, and capacity is expressed as a percentage of the industry total to eliminate the influence of the secular growth of industry and company size.[4] The geographical extent of the market is especially difficult to determine in steel, for the shifting geographical pattern of consumption has created a linkage between the various regional markets. We treat the market as national, which exaggerates its extent, but probably does less violence to the facts than a sharp regional classification of firms. See data in Table 7–1.

Over two decades covered by Table 7–1 (and, for that matter, over the last half century) there has been a persistent and fairly rapid decline in the share of the industry's capacity in firms with less than half a percent of the total, so that we may infer that this size of firm is subject to substantial diseconomies of scale.[5] The firms with $\frac{1}{2}$ to $2\frac{1}{2}$ percent of industry capacity showed a moderate decline, and hence were subject to smaller diseconomies of scale. The one firm with more than one fourth of industry capacity declined moderately, so it too had diseconomies of scale. The intervening sizes, from $2\frac{1}{2}$ to 25 percent of industry capacity, grew or held their share so they constituted the range of optimum size.

The more rapid the rate at which a firm loses its share of the industry's output (or, here, capacity), the higher is its private cost of production relative to the cost of production of firms of the most efficient size.[6] This interpretation should not be reversed, however, to infer that the

[3] Crucible steel, which is made by smaller companies on average, is viewed as a separate, but closely related, industry.

[4] Capacity is least objectionable as a measure of firm size in an industry where production is continuous round the clock and the upward trend of output confers relevance on capacity. Both steel and our later example of petroleum refining meet these conditions.

[5] In 1930 the firm with $\frac{1}{2}$ percent of the industry capacity had a capacity of 364,000 net tons; in 1951, 485,000 net tons. Of course, we could have employed absolute firm size classes, but they are less appropriate to many uses.

[6] How shall we assess the efficiency of a size of firm which merely holds its share of industry output or capacity? Although more subtle interpretations are possible, it seems simplest to view this size class as one whose trend of industry share is imperfectly estimated from the data, and that with fuller data (i.e., for more firms or a longer period), all firm sizes would display rising or falling industry shares.

TABLE 7-1

DISTRIBUTION OF OUTPUT OF STEEL INGOT CAPACITY
BY RELATIVE SIZE OF COMPANY

Company Size (Percent of Industry Total)	Percent of Industry Capacity			Number of Companies		
	1930	1938	1951	1930	1938	1951
Under ½.........	7.16	6.11	4.65	39	29	22
½ to 1...........	5.94	5.08	5.37	9	7	7
1 to 2½..........	13.17	8.30	9.07	9	6	6
2½ to 5..........	10.64	16.59	22.21	3	4	5
5 to 10..........	11.18	14.03	8.12	2	2	1
10 to 25.........	13.24	13.99	16.10	1	1	1
25 and over......	38.67	35.91	34.50	1	1	1

Sources: *Directory of Iron and Steel Works of the United States and Canada,* 1930, 1938; *Iron Age,* January 3, 1952.

FIGURE 7-1

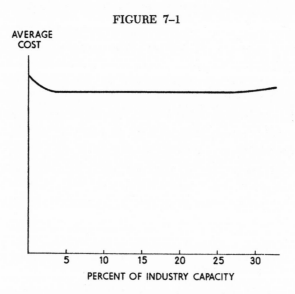

size class whose share is growing more rapidly is more efficient than other classes whose shares are growing more slowly; the difference can merely represent differences in the quantities of various qualities of resources.[7] In the light of these considerations we translate the data of Table 7-1 into a long run average cost curve for the production of steel ingots and display this curve in Figure 7-1. Over a wide range of outputs there is no evidence of net economies or diseconomies of scale.

[7] For example, one firm size within the optimum range may utilize superior salesmen, another firm size inferior salesmen (at suitably lower rates of pay), and the relative numbers of the two types will influence the relative growth in the industry shares of the two sizes.

Although the survivor test yields an estimate of the shape of the long-run cost curve, it does not allow an estimate of how much higher than the minimum are the costs of the firm sizes whose shares of industry output are declining. Costs are higher the more rapid the rate at which the firm size loses its share of industry output, but the rate at which a firm size loses a share of industry output will also vary with numerous other factors. This rate of loss of output will be larger, the less durable and specialized the productive resources of the firm, for then exit from the industry is easier. The rate of loss will also be larger, the more nearly perfect the capital and labor markets, so that resources can be obtained to grow quickly to more efficient size. The rate of loss will be smaller, given the degree of inefficiency, the more profitable the industry is, for then the rate of return of all sizes of firms is larger relative to other industries.

By a simple extension of this argument, we may also estimate the most efficient size of *plant* in the steel ingot industry during the same period (Table 7–2).

TABLE 7–2
DISTRIBUTION OF OUTPUT OF STEEL INGOT CAPACITY

Plant Size (Percent of Industry Total)	Percent of Industry Capacity			Number of Plants		
	1930	1938	1951	1930	1938	1951
Under ¼.........	3.74	3.81	3.25	40	29	23
¼ to ½..........	6.39	5.81	7.20	20	16	18
½ to ¾..........	6.39	4.18	3.82	11	7	6
¾ to 1..........	9.42	12.29	10.93	11	14	12
1 to 1¾.........	21.78	15.56	20.67	18	13	15
1¾ to 2½........	13.13	16.73	17.01	6	8	8
2½ to 3¾........	23.49	17.18	8.10	8	6	3
3¾ to 5.........	8.82	12.07	12.46	2	3	3
5 to 10.........	6.82	12.37	16.56	1	2	3

Sources: *Directory of Iron and Steel Works of the United States and Canada,* 1930, 1938; *Iron Age,* January 3, 1952.

Once again we will find that the smallest plants have a tendency to decline relative to the industry, and indeed this is implied by the company data. There is no systematic tendency toward decline in shares held by plants between ¾ percent and 10 percent of the industry size. We may therefore infer that the tendency of very small plants and companies to decline relative to the industry is due to the diseconomy of a small plant, and the tendency of the largest company (U. S. Steel) to decline has been due to diseconomies of multi-plant operation beyond a certain scale.

An equally important and interesting industry, passenger automobiles, uncovers different problems. Here we can use production data instead of capacity, and have no compunctions in treating the market as national in scope. The basic data for the individual firms are given in Table 7–3.

TABLE 7–3

PERCENTAGES OF PASSENGER AUTOMOBILES PRODUCED IN UNITED STATES BY VARIOUS COMPANIES, 1936–41 AND 1946–55

Year	General Motors	Chrysler	Ford	Hudson	Nash	Kaiser	Willys Overland	Packard	Studebaker	Other
1936.....	42.9	23.6	22.6	3.3	1.5	...	0.7	2.2	2.4	0.8
1937.....	40.9	24.2	22.6	2.7	2.2	...	2.0	2.8	2.1	0.5
1938.....	43.9	23.8	22.3	2.5	1.6	...	0.8	2.5	2.3	0.3
1939.....	43.0	22.7	21.8	2.8	2.3	...	0.9	2.6	3.7	0.3
1940.....	45.9	25.1	19.0	2.3	1.7	...	0.7	2.1	3.1	0.1
1941.....	48.3	23.3	18.3	2.1	2.1	....	0.8	1.8	3.2	0.1
1946.....	38.4	25.0	21.2	4.2	4.6	0.6	0.3	1.9	3.6	0.2
1947.....	40.4	21.7	21.3	2.8	3.2	4.1	0.9	1.6	3.5	0.5
1948.....	40.1	21.2	19.1	3.6	3.1	4.6	0.8	2.5	4.2	0.7
1949.....	43.0	21.9	21.0	2.8	2.8	1.2	0.6	2.0	4.5	0.2
1950.....	45.7	18.0	23.3	2.1	2.8	2.2	0.6	1.1	4.0	0.1
1951.....	42.2	23.1	21.8	1.8	3.0	1.9	0.5	1.4	4.2	0.1
1952.....	41.5	22.0	23.2	1.8	3.5	1.7	1.1	1.4	3.7	...
1953.....	45.7	20.3	25.2	1.2	2.2	1.0		1.3	3.0	...
1954.....	52.2	13.1	30.6	1.7		0.3		0.5	1.6	...
1955.....	50.2	17.2	28.2	2.0		0.1		2.3		...

Source: Hard's *Automotive Yearbook*, 1951, 1955, 1956.

A striking feature of the automobile industry is the small number of firms, and this poses a statistical problem we have glossed over in our discussion of steel: what confidence can be attached to changes in the share of industry output coming from a firm size when that size contains very few firms? For the automobile industry (unlike steel) we possess annual data, and can therefore take into account the steadiness of direction or magnitude of changes in shares of various firm sizes, and to this extent increase our confidence in the estimates. We may also extend the period which is surveyed, although at the risk of combining periods with different sizes of optimum firms. Aside from recourse to related data (the survivorship pattern of the industry in other countries, for example), there is no other method of reducing the uncertainty of findings for small-number industries.

The survivorship record in automobiles (summarized in Table 7–4) is more complicated than that for steel. In the immediate prewar years there was already a tendency for the largest company to produce a rising share and for the 2½ to 5 percent class to produce a sharply declining share; the smallest and next to largest sizes showed no clear tendency. In a longer span of time, however, the smallest companies reveal a fairly consistently declining share.[8] In the immediate postwar period, the 2½ to

TABLE 7–4

PERCENTAGE OF PASSENGER AUTOMOBILES PRODUCED BY
VARIOUS COMPANY-SIZES

	Company Size (as Percent of Industry)				Number of Companies	
Year	Over 35%	10–35%	2½–5%	Under 2½%	2½–5%	Under 2½%
1936........	42.9	46.2	3.3	7.6	1	5*
1937........	40.9	46.8	5.5	6.8	2	4*
1938........	43.9	46.1	5.0	5.0	2	4*
1939........	43.0	44.4	9.1	3.5	3	4*
1940........	45.9	44.1	3.1	6.9	1	6*
1941........	48.4	41.6	3.2	6.8	1	5
1946........	38.4	46.2	12.4	3.0	3	4
1947........	40.4	43.0	13.6	3.0	4	3
1948........	40.1	40.3	18.0	1.5	5	2
1949........	43.0	42.9	10.0	4.0	3	4
1950........	45.7	41.3	6.8	6.1	2	5
1951........	42.2	44.9	7.2	5.7	2	5
1952........	41.5	45.2	7.2	6.1	2	5
1953........	45.6	45.5	3.0	5.8	1	4
1954........	52.2	43.7	0	4.1	0	4
1955........	50.2	45.4	0	4.4	0	3

* Or more.
Source: Table 7–3.

5 percent size class was strongly favored by the larger companies' need to practice price control in a sensitive political atmosphere, and the same phenomenon reappeared less strongly in the first two years after the outbreak of Korean hostilities. From this record we would infer that there have been diseconomies of large size, at least for the largest size of firm, in inflationary periods with private or public price control, but substantial economies of large scale at other times. The long-run average cost curve is saucer-shaped in inflationary times, but shows no tendency to rise at the largest outputs in other times.

The automobile example suggests the method by which we deter-

[8] See Federal Trade Commission, *Report on Motor Vehicle Industry*, p. 29 (1939).

mine whether changing technology, factor prices, or consumer demands lead to a change in the optimum firm size. We infer an underlying stability in the optimum size in those periods in which the survivorship trends are stable. Indeed it is hard to conceive of an alternative test; one can judge the economic importance, in contrast to technological originality, of an innovation only by the impact it has upon the size distribution of firms.

Before we leave these applications of the survivorship technique we should indicate its flexibility in dealing with other problems which seem inappropriate to our particular examples. For example, a Marshallian may object that firms must begin small and grow to optimum size through time, so that the size structure of the industry in a given period will reflect this historical life pattern as well as the optimum size influences. In an industry such as retail trade this interpretation would be quite plausible. It can be met by studying the survivor experience of firm sizes in the light of the age or rate of growth of the firms. Again, one may argue that firms of different sizes have different comparative advantages at different stages of the business cycle. Such a hypothesis could be dealt with by comparing average survivorship patterns in given cycle stages with those calculated for full cycles.

Let us now turn to the methods by which one may test hypotheses on the determinants of optimum size.

III. INTER-INDUSTRY ANALYSES OF THE DETERMINANTS OF OPTIMUM SIZE

Once the optimum firm size has been ascertained for a variety of industries, the relationship between size and other variables can be explored. This is in fact the customary procedure for economists to employ, and the present investigation differs, aside from the method of determining optimum size, only in being more systematic than most such investigations. For example, numerous economists have asserted that advertising is a force making for large firms, and they usually illustrate this relationship by the cigarette industry. Will the relationship still hold when it is tested against a list of industries which has not been chosen to illustrate it? This is essentially the type of inquiry we make here.

Although the survivor method makes lesser demands of data than other methods to determine optimum firm size, it has equally exacting requirements of information on any other variable whose influence is to be studied. In the subsequent investigation of some 48 ("three-digit") manufacturing industries, whose optimum firm size is calculated from data in *Statistics of Income*, we have therefore been compelled to exclude some variables for lack of data and to measure others in a most imperfect manner. The industries we study, and the measures we contrive, are given in Table 7–5; we describe their derivation below.

1. *Size of firm.* The optimum size of firm in each industry is determined by comparing the percentage of the industry's assets possessed by firms in each asset class in 1948 and 1951.[9] Those classes in which the share of the industry's assets was stable or rising were identified, and the average assets of the firms within these sizes was calculated.[10] The range of optimum sizes is also given in Table 7–5. An industry was excluded if it had a very large noncorporate sector (for which we could not measure firm size) or gave strong evidence of heterogeneity by having two widely separated optimum sizes (as, for example, in "aircraft and parts").

2. *Advertising expenditures.* We have already remarked that extensive advertising is often mentioned as an explanation for the growth of large firms, especially in consumer goods industries such as cigarettes, liquor, and cosmetics. The argument supporting this view can take one of three directions. First, national advertising may be viewed as more efficient than local advertising, in terms of sales per dollar of advertising at a given price. Second, long continued advertising may have a cumulative impact. Finally, and closely related to the preceding point, the joint advertising of a series of related products may be more efficient than advertising them individually. We measure the variable by the ratio of advertising expenditures to sales, both taken from *Statistics of Income*.

3. *Technology and research.* A host of explanations of firm size are related to technological characteristics and research. Complicated production processes may require large companies, or at least large plants. The economies of research are held to be substantial; the outcome of individual projects is uncertain, so small programs are more risky; a balanced research team may be fairly large; and much capital may be required to bring a new process to a commercial stage and to wait for a return upon the outlay.

---

[9] These particular dates were dictated by the data; there were large changes in industry classification in 1948, and no minor industry data were tabulated for 1952. A better, but more laborious, determination of optimum size could have been made if the data for intervening years were utilized.

[10] A rough allowance for sampling fluctuations was made by comparing three-asset class moving averages.

TABLE 7-5
BASIC DATA ON 48 MANUFACTURING INDUSTRIES

Industry	Optimum Company Size (in $000 of Total Assets) (1948–51)	Optimum Range Class Limits (in $000) From	To	Average Establishment Size (in $000 of Value Added) (1947)	Number of Chemists and Engineers per 100 Employed (1950)	Advertising Expenditure as percent of Gross Sales (1950)
Motor vehicles, incl. bodies and truck trailers	827,828	100,000	open	3,715	1.5879	0.4395
Petroleum refining	765,716	100,000	open	3,420	6.9171	0.4562
Blast furnaces, steel works and rolling mills	525,485	100,000	open	8,310	2.0956	0.1321
Dairy products	446,483	100,000	open	110	0.7865	1.5221
Distilled, rectified and blended liquors	248,424	100,000	open	2,090	0.9041	1.3674
Pulp, paper, and paperboard	203,794	100,000	open	1,645	1.4927	0.3357
Paints, varnishes, lacquers, etc.	175,404	100,000	open	394	6.0431	1.3539
Railroad equipment, incl. locomotives and streetcars	150,217	100,000	open	3,407	2.7171	0.3611
Tires and tubes	141,600	10,000	open	11,406	2.0974*	0.9453
Grain mill products ex. cereals preparations	128,363	100,000	open	210	1.0344	1.2492
Drugs and medicines	123,662	100,000	open	552	6.2599	8.3858
Smelting, refining, rolling, drawing and alloying of nonferrous metals	100,398	10,000	open	1,658	2.9845†	0.4088
Office and store machines	65,914	10,000	open	1,411	2.5860	1.5812
Bakery products	58,960	50,000	100,000	192	0.2359	2.1335
Yarn and thread	44,375	10,000	open	687	0.4461	0.3238
Carpets and other floor coverings	37,337	10,000	100,000	1,119	1.2391	1.7295
Broadwoven fabrics (wool)	31,265	10,000	open	1,211	0.4461	0.3400
Watches, clocks, and clock work operated devices	31,025	10,000	50,000	705	1.2027	5.3238
Cement	29,554	10,000	100,000	1,600	2.1277‡	0.2726
Malt liquors and malt	28,922	10,000	open	1,750	0.9041	4.7962
Agricultural machinery and tractors	28,291	1,000	open	684	2.1816	0.8956
Structural clay products	24,001	10,000	100,000	253	1.6292	0.4552
Newspapers	23,428	10,000	100,000	168	0.1348§	0.1948
Knit goods	17,918	10,000	100,000	273	0.1244	0.8522
Confectionery	13,524	5,000	50,000	335	0.5950	2.6281
Commercial printing including lithographing	11,939	5,000	50,000	97	0.1348§	0.6474

TABLE 7-5 (Continued)

| Industry | Optimum Company Size (in $000 of Total Assets) (1948–51) | Optimum Range Class Limits (in $000) | | Average Establishment Size (in $000 of Value Added) (1947) | Number of Chemists and Engineers per 100 Employed (1950) | Advertising Expenditure as percent of Gross Sales (1950) |
		From	To			
Furniture—household, office, public building, and professional	11,378	5,000	50,000	209	0.3900‖	0.9125
Men's clothing	10,077	5,000	50,000	247	0.0456#	0.8795
Dyeing and finishing textiles, excl. knit goods	9,625	5,000	50,000	545	1.1223	0.3472
Canning fruit, vegetables and seafood	6,536	1,000	open	240	0.9144	1.8462
Broadwoven fabrics (cotton)	5,847	50	open	2,595	0.4461**	0.2822
Footwear, exc. rubber	4,359	1,000	100,000	524	0.1474	1.1619
Paperbags, and paperboard containers and boxes	4,127	1,000	100,000	428	0.6939	0.1854
Cigars	3,753	250	50,000	174	0.2274††	2.3188
Meat products	2,665	500	100,000	322	0.5983	0.4264
Nonferrous foundries	2,365	500	50,000	172	2.9845†	0.2793
Fur goods	1,966	1,000	5,000	55	0.0456#	0.4119
Partitions, shelving, lockers, etc.	1,545	500	50,000	121	0.3990‖	0.8678
Narrow fabrics and other small wares	1,382	500	5,000	226	0.4461**	0.3212
Wines	1,304	500	5,000	227	0.9041‡‡	3.5854
Women's clothing	1,304	500	50,000	150	0.0456#	0.9150
Books	1,137	50	50,000	399	0.1348§	2.8796
Periodicals	1,117	250	10,000	307	0.1348§	0.5245
Leather—tanning, curring and finishing	764	0	10,000	720	0.8140	0.1813
Concrete, gypsum and plaster products	762	250	10,000	53	2.1277‡	0.6855
Window and door screens, shades and venetian blinds	667	100	10,000	110	0.3990‖	1.0581
Non-alcoholic beverages	546	100	50,000	75	0.9041‡‡	4.0740
Millinery	468	250	5,000	108	0.0456#	0.4438

* Rubber products.
† Primary nonferrous.
‡ Cement, and concrete, gypsum and plaster products.
§ Printing, publishing and allied industries.
‖ Furniture and fixtures.
†† Tobacco manufactures.
‡‡ Beverage industries.
# Apparel and accessories.
** Yarn, thread, and fabric mills.

At present there is no direct measure available for either the importance of research or the intricacy of technology.[11] We use an index, chemists and engineers as a ratio to all employees, that may reflect both influences, but probably very imperfectly. When it becomes possible to make a division of these personnel between research and routine operation, a division which would be very valuable for other purposes also, the interpretation of an index of technical personnel will be less ambiguous.

4. *Plant size.* Plant size normally sets a minimum to company size, and therefore exerts an obvious influence on the differences among industries in company size. We are compelled to resort to a measure of plant size—value added per establishment in 1947—which is not directly comparable to company size because the 1947 Census of Manufactures did not report corporate establishments at the requisite level of detail.[12]

Preliminary analysis revealed that there is no significant relationship between firm size and advertising expenditures, so this variable was omitted from the statistical calculations. The average ratio of advertising expenditures to sales was 1.97 percent in consumer goods industries and 0.57 percent in producer goods industries, but in neither group was there a significant relationship between the ratio and firm size.[13]

A regression analysis confirms the impression one gets from Table 7–5 that the other variables we examine are positively related to optimum firm size:

$$X_1 = -5.092 + \underset{(10.8)}{34.6\,X_2} + \underset{(12.2)}{42.7\,X_3},$$

where

X_1 is firm size, in millions of dollars of assets,

X_2 is plant size, in millions of dollars of value added,

X_3 is engineers and chemists per 100 employees.

The standard errors of the regression coefficients are given below the coefficients.[14]

[11] In earlier experiments with two-digit manufacturing industries, capital-sales ratios were found to be uncorrelated with optimum firm size.

[12] But even if plants were measured by assets there would be some incomparability arising out of the fact that many large firms operate in many industries but are classified according to their dominant activity.

[13] The respective rank correlation coefficients were −.187 and −.059.

[14] The correlation coefficients are:

$$r_{12}=.460 \qquad r_{12.3}=.400$$
$$r_{13}=.471 \qquad r_{13.2}=.413$$
$$r_{23}=.252 \qquad r_{23.1}=.046$$

An examination of Table 7–5 suggests that the correlation would be higher if the data were somewhat more precise. The size of plant is unduly low in motor vehicles, because of the inclusion of suppliers of parts. Moreover the plant sizes have not been estimated by the survivor technique. Technological personnel are exaggerated in nonferrous foundries because we are compelled to use the ratio for a broader class, and the same is true of concrete products. The relatively small size of company in footwear, as compared to plant size, is at least partially due to the fact that the machinery was usually leased, and hence not included in assets. Industries which are "out of line" have not been omitted, however, for similar considerations may have caused other industries to be "in line." Yet the general impression is that the correlation would rise substantially with improved measurements of the variables.

The range of optimum sizes is generally wide, although the width is exaggerated, and our measurements impaired, because the largest asset class (over $100 million) embraces numerous firms of very different sizes—growth and inflation are outmoding the size classes used in *Statistics of Income*. In ten industries only this largest size has had a rising share of industry assets, and in another nine industries it is included in the range of sizes with rising shares. When the upper limit of optimum sizes is known, the range of optimum sizes is typically three or four times the average size of the firms in these sizes.

The results of this exploratory inter-industry study are at least suggestive—not only in their specific content but also in pointing out a line of attack on the economies of scale that escapes that confession of failure, the case method. The chief qualifications that attach to the findings are due to the imperfections of the data: the industry categories are rather wide; and the measure of technical personnel is seriously ambiguous. At least one finding—a wide range of optimum firm sizes in each industry— is so general as to deserve to be taken as the standard model in the theory of production.

IV. INTRA-INDUSTRY ANALYSIS OF THE DETERMINANTS OF OPTIMUM SIZE

One may also examine the varying fates of individual firms within an industry in the search for explanations of optimum size. If, for example, firms moving to optimum size were vertically integrated and those moving to or remaining in nonoptimum size were not so integrated, we could infer that vertical integration was a requisite of the optimum firm in the industry. This approach has the advantage over the inter-industry approach of not requiring the assumption that a determinant such as advertising or integration works similarly in all industries.

The intra-industry analysis, however, has a heavy disadvantage; it can be applied only to those variables for which we can obtain information on each firm, and in industries with numerous firms hardly any interesting variables survive this requirement. Because we could examine so few influences, and because the results were so consistently negative, we shall be very brief in describing our results in the industry—petroleum refining—in which this approach was tried.

TABLE 7–6

DISTRIBUTION OF PETROLEUM REFINING CAPACITY
BY RELATIVE SIZE OF COMPANY

Company Size (Percent of Industry Capacity)	Percent of Industry Capacity			Number of Companies		
	1947	1950	1954	1947	1950	1954
Under 0.1...........	5.30	4.57	3.89	130	108	92
0.1 to 0.2...........	4.86	3.57	3.00	34	24	22
0.2 to 0.3...........	2.67	2.16	2.74	11	9	11
0.3 to 0.4...........	2.95	2.92	1.65	8	8	5
0.4 to 0.5...........	2.20	0	.89	5	0	2
0.5 to 0.75.........	3.04	4.66	5.05	5	8	8
0.75 to 1.00........	.94	0	1.58	1	0	2
1.0 to 2.5..........	11.70	12.17	10.53	6	7	6
2.5 to 5............	9.57	16.70	14.26	3	5	5
5 to 10.............	45.11	42.15	45.69	7	6	7
10 to 15............	11.65	11.06	10.72	1	1	1
Total..............				211	176	161

Source: Bureau of Mines, Petroleum Refineries, including Cracking Plants in the United States, January 1, 1947, January 1, 1950, January 1, 1954, Information Circulars 7455 (March 1948), 7578 (August 1950), and 7963 (July 1954).

The basic survivor experience for companies and plants in petroleum refining is given in Tables 7–6 and 7–7, for the postwar period 1947–1954. In each case only operating plants are included, and asphalt plants and companies are excluded. Capacities are measured in terms of crude oil; as in the case of steel plants, actual outputs cannot be obtained for all companies.[15]

There is a family resemblance between the data for petroleum and steel companies: in each case there has been a substantial reduction in the share of the largest company. In the petroleum refining industry, the

[15] One percent of industry capacity was 52,508 barrels per day in 1947, and 76,811 barrels in 1954. Tentative calculations for regional markets indicate that the results are not greatly affected by using a national base.

size range from .5 percent to 10 percent has contained all the size classes which have stable or rising shares of industry capacity.

The plant survivor data suggest that the disappearance of the smaller companies has been due to the relative inefficiency of the smaller plants, for all plant size classes with less than .5 percent of the industry's capacity have also declined substantially. The sizes between .5 percent and 2.5 percent of industry capacity have all grown relatively, and the top plant size has declined moderately, so that the growth of company

TABLE 7–7
DISTRIBUTION OF PETROLEUM REFINING CAPACITY
BY RELATIVE SIZE OF PLANT

Plant Size	Percent of Industry Capacity			Number of Plants		
	1947	1950	1954	1947	1950	1954
Under 0.1...........	8.22	7.39	6.06	184	158	138
0.1 to 0.2...........	9.06	7.60	7.13	64	53	51
0.2 to 0.3...........	6.86	4.95	3.95	27	19	16
0.3 to 0.4...........	5.45	4.99	7.28	15	14	21
0.4 to 0.5...........	4.53	6.56	4.06	10	15	9
0.5 to 0.75.........	9.95	10.47	11.82	17	16	19
0.75 to 1.0.........	5.35	7.07	8.33	6	8	10
1.0 to 1.5..........	12.11	10.36	13.38	10	8	11
1.5 to 2.5..........	17.39	23.64	22.45	9	12	12
2.5 to 4.0..........	21.08	16.96	15.54	7	5	5
Total..............				349	308	292

Source: Same as Table 7–6.

sizes beyond 2.5 percent of industry capacity has presumably been due to the economies of multiple plant operation.

It has been claimed that backward integration into crude oil pipe lines was necessary to successful operation of a petroleum refinery. We tabulate some of the material bearing on this hypothesis in Table 7–8. There does not appear to be any large difference between the changes in market shares of firms with and without pipe lines. Since all firms with more than 0.75 percent of industry refining capacity have some pipe lines, a comparison (not reproduced here) was made between changes in their market shares and crude pipe line mileage per 1,000 barrels of daily refining capacity. There was no relationship between the two variables.[16]

[16] A corresponding investigation was made for research laboratories, which are reported in the Directory of Research Laboratories of the National Research Council. That the results showed no relationship between firm size and size of laboratories is not surprising, for the work of the research laboratories would influence only the firm's long-term growth.

The intra-industry analysis has its chief role, one may conjecture, in providing a systematic framework for the analysis of the data commonly employed in industry studies. A complete analysis of the plausible determinants of firm size requires such extensive information on the individual firms in the industry as to make this an unattractive method of attack on the general theory.

TABLE 7–8

INDUSTRY SHARES OF PETROLEUM REFINING COMPANIES WITH AND WITHOUT CRUDE PIPE LINES IN 1950

Company Size (Average of 1947, 1950, and 1954 Percentage of Industry Capacity)	Companies with Pipe Lines			Companies without Pipe Lines		
	Number 1950	Share 1947	Share 1954	Number 1950	Share 1947	Share 1954
Under 0.1	25	1.40	1.12	60	2.87	2.18
0.1 to 0.2	17	2.19	2.50	5	0.77	0.77
0.2 to 0.3	6	1.48	1.63	2	0.34	0.50
0.3 to 0.4	5	1.90	1.63	0	....	....
0.4 to 0.5	1	0.40	0.55	2	0.54	1.22
0.5 to 0.75	7	3.59	4.72	1	0.38	0.61
0.75 to 1.0	0	....	....	0	....	....
1.0 to 2.5	7	11.54	13.10	0	....	....
2.5 to 5.0	4	11.11	11.69	0	....	....
5.0 to 10.0	7	45.11	45.69	0	....	....
10.0 to 15.0	1	11.65	10.72	0	....	....
Not in existence all years	16	2.30	0.05	79	2.43	1.33
Total	96	92.67	93.40	149	7.33	6.60

Source: International Petroleum Register.

V. CONCLUSION

The survivor technique for determining the range of optimum sizes of a firm seems well adapted to lift the theory of economies of scale to a higher level of substantive content. Although it is prey to the usual frustrations of inadequate information, the determination of optimum sizes avoids the enormously difficult problem of valuing resources properly that is encountered by alternative methods.

Perhaps the most striking finding in our exploratory studies is that there is customarily a fairly wide range of optimum sizes—the long-run marginal and average cost curves of the firm are customarily horizontal over a long range of sizes. This finding could be corroborated, I suspect, by a related investigation: if there were a unique optimum size in an industry, increases in demand would normally be met primarily by near proportional increases in the number of firms, but it appears that much of the increase is usually met by expansion of the existing firms.

The survivor method can be used to test the numerous hypotheses on the factors determining the size of firm which abound in the literature. Our exploratory study suggests that advertising expenditures have no general tendency to lead to large firms, and another experiment (which is not reported above) indicates that fixed capital-sales ratios are also unrelated to the size of firms. The size of plant proves to be an important variable, as is to be expected, and the survivor method should be employed to determine the factors governing plant size. A rather ambiguous variable, the relative share of engineers and chemists in the labor force, also proves to be fairly important, and further data and work is necessary to disentangle research and routine technical operations. The determination of optimum size permits the investigator to examine any possible determinants which his imagination nominates and his data illuminate.

Addendum: Drawing Inferences from Firm Size on the Economies of Scale

1. In these notes I shall reexamine some of the analytical and procedural problems encountered in the empirical determination of economies of scale.

2. Suppose the economic conditions of an industry had been stable for a very long period, so the industry, and every firm in it, had achieved long-run equilibrium. Then there would exist a stable distribution of firm sizes. Statistical observation of this distribution over time would reveal only random fluctuations in the number of firms of any size.

3. If all the firms employed the same types and qualities of resources, and if over a given range there was constant returns to scale, the observed distribution of firms would be rectangular. For no firm could survive outside this range (by hypothesis), and there would be no reason for bunching of sizes.

4. If the market is not homogeneous, but has distinguishable geographical or quality components, even under the conditions just stated there will be a distribution of firms by size governed by the distribution of market components by size—provided a firm cannot operate (without cost disadvantage) in more than one component area.

5. If the firms used differing types and qualities of resources (fertile versus unfertile land, etc.), there would still be a range of uniform long-

run average costs, but the firms could have almost any frequency distribution of sizes within this range, depending upon the distribution of resources (by type). Note that now two firms could be of equal size, and yet one might be nonoptimum because of an inappropriate selection of resources.

6. With heterogeneous qualities of inputs, a quasi–long-run cost curve (including rents) is defined for each collection of resource types. If the distribution of firms is stable, all firm sizes will be equally efficient. Whether one of these quasi–long-run curves has a flat bottom or a single minimum can only be inferred from the stable distribution of firm sizes if one has a workable definition of resource types. Then one can see if

FIGURE 7–2

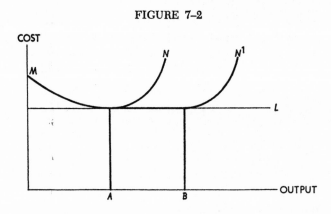

outputs A and B (in Figure 7–2), for example, are produced by the same types of resources (skilled versus unskilled labor, labor versus machines, etc.). If they are, there is a range of constant returns on the quasi–long-run cost curve (MN^1). Otherwise there is a single minimum cost output (A on MN). In the true long run, a firm may vary the type as well as amount of resources, so its effective cost curve is the envelope of the quasi–long-run curves, and by definition this curve is horizontal over the observed range of firm sizes.

7. The average optimum size of firms in an industry would simply be the weighted mean of the frequency distribution, but there would be no maximum optimum size and a zero minimum size if the distribution of firms was (for example) log normal. The extremes of the observed sizes could be designated as the limits of the optimum size range, but this would be unhappy terminology. Economically viewed, the possibility of a few firms entering at a very small scale would have no important effect upon the industry's output or behavior. Statistically viewed, the extreme

observations in an industry with only a modest number of firms would be very unstable.

8. It therefore seems desirable to define the minimum optimum size as the first class size which accounts for some arbitrary but significant fraction of the industry's output, say 10 percent. The reason the fraction is arbitrary is that we do not know how big a share of output a set of new entrants must have in order to exert a significant effect upon the industry's behavior. (This arbitrariness is intimately related to the arbitrariness of any measure of concentration.)

9. The difficulties we encounter in defining a minimum optimum size arise, not from the survivor principle, but from the fact that a frequency distribution of resources (and possibly of markets) underlies the argument. The conventional cost theory, with its single minimum long-run average cost, must assume resources which are identical for every firm. Where this is true, there will of course be either a single observable size of firm or (with constant returns to scale) a rectangular distribution of sizes.

10. Partly to give weight to significance of output, in the normal case, and even more to provide a natural "deflator" of data on size for different industries or times, the distribution of firm sizes will be expressed in terms of share of the industry's output.

11. Let a new equilibrium distribution of firm sizes in an industry be effected (by a change in technology, or factor prices, say). The original distribution O, a transitional distribution T, and the new equilibrium distribution, N, are illustrated in Figure 7–3. Our task is to determine whether we can deduce N from a knowledge of O and T.

FIGURE 7–3

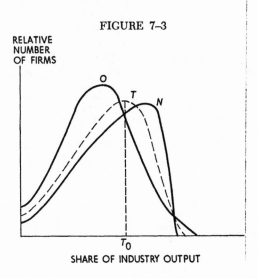

RELATIVE
NUMBER
OF FIRMS

SHARE OF INDUSTRY OUTPUT

12. The survivor method, as I employ it in the present chapter, assumes that any class size that is declining will ultimately vanish. It is usually adequate for the rectangular distributions mentioned in 9 above. But it seems clearly inadequate for the distributions usually observed.

13. Given the data for distributions O and T, we can calculate the empirical relative frequencies of a firm of any size in O moving to any size (including zero) in T. For example, we may observe the following facts:

	Period T		
Period O	Size 0	Size 1	Size 2
Size 0	0.98	0.02	0
Size 1	.05	.94	0.01
Size 2	0	.03	.97

We read these numbers as estimates of probabilities: 94 percent of size 1 firms in period O will be in the same size class in T. Of a large, arbitrarily chosen number of potential entrants (size 0 in period O), 2 percent enter size 1.

14. Suppose these probabilities are stable through time—then we can calculate the number of firms of each size in each succeeding period. It will be found that the distribution which is finally attained, if there are 1,000 firms in the three classes, is

Size 0.........652
Size 1.........261
Size 2......... 87

for the probabilities constitute a transition matrix of a Markov process, and one property of such processes is that their final state is independent of the original distribution.[17]

15. This method of estimating distribution N has the weakness that it requires a degree of knowledge (i.e., the transition matrix) which is often unavailable, but this difficulty is evident. The more interesting question is whether one can assume that the transition probabilities are stable.

[17] For an actual application of the technique to the steel industry, with implausible results, see Irma C. Adelman, "A Stochastic Analysis of the Size Distribution of Firms," *Journal of the American Statistical Association,* December 1958.

16. One would expect certain kinds of movements to be relatively more frequent in bad times, for example, plants closing. Conversely, one would expect other movements to be more common in good times (entry or extensive expansion, including merger). But this difficulty could be handled, at least in principle, by employing different transition matrices for the two kinds of periods.

17. The more basic difficulty is that one should expect the probabilities to have longer histories than a single time period (such as a year). Differently stated, some firm-size movements will be effected much more rapidly than others. Suppose large sizes suddenly become more efficient relative to small sizes (our Fig. 7–3 illustration). Since expansion often can be much more rapid than contraction, the growth of large firms will be more rapid than the decline of small firms (if mergers are not the method used to achieve the economies of size) so two years after the introduction of (for example) the new technique, the larger firms may have moved one half of the way to the new equilibrium while only one tenth of those small firms which will ultimately disappear have done so. These are generalized stochastic processes which deal with this problem, at a commensurate cost in complexity and demands for data.

18. A variety of stochastic models of firm growth are being developed to explain firm size distributions. An important example is contained in the study by Simon and Bonini.[18] They assume (1) a constant rate of entry of new firms into an industry, and (2) a "law of proportionate effect," that firms of every size class have the same (log normal) distribution of expected movements of size—that (for example) the same fraction of large as of small firms will grow (and decline) 20 or more percent a year. They claim good fits both to existing distributions of size of plant or firm and to transition matrices for the 500 largest industrial corporations.

19. Their economic explanation, parsimoniously given, is that there is constant returns to scale above a given size, and "it is natural to expect the firms in each size class to have the same chance on the average of increasing or decreasing in size in proportion to their present size."[19] On the contrary, it is unnatural to expect this: (1) The distribution of resources will by type seldom allow equi-proportional growth of all firm sizes. (2) Much more important, they assume that the industry is in long-run equilibrium. But in a changing world with imperfect foresight, this is

[18] H. Simon and C. Bonini, "The Size Distribution of Business Firms," *American Economic Review,* September 1958.
[19] *Ibid.,* p. 609.

hardly ever even approximately true, and firms of a size inappropriate to the new equilibrium will decrease in size relatively much more often than firms of appropriate size. Their only persuasive empirical test (the transition matrix for the 500 largest corporations) requires critical examination in an application to individual industries.[20]

20. Pending the development of appropriate stochastic models, one approach is to find empirical relationships between the rate of movement of firm sizes to equilibrium and observable firm characteristics. Thus the pattern of rates of convergence to equilibrium of firms might be a function of (1) their relative use of fixed capital, (2) their deviation from the new unambiguously optimum sizes (region to the right of T_0 in Fig. 7–3), (3) their relative ease of exit (frequency of conversion to other industries). If stable relationships are found, they will permit better predictions of the final distribution of firms by size than the simple assumption (used above) that declining class sizes will go to zero.

21. The determination of optimum sizes is, as a matter of experience, relatively insensitive to the precise way in which the survivor method is employed. The *mean* optimum size is especially insensitive to the particular assumption which is made about declining class sizes (for example, whether they go to zero, or to half their present size).

[20] *Ibid.*, p. 612.

Chapter 8

MONOPOLY AND OLIGOPOLY BY MERGER*

The growth of individual firms to great size through merger with rivals is an outstanding development of modern economic history. As late as 1890, Marshall could view the life history of the firm as a silhouette of that of man in an age of high infant mortality: the firm began as a small venture; if it survived the early years, it straggled along or grew at a rate governed by the entrepreneur's ability—occasionally reaching large size if his ability was extraordinary or his children's abilities great—but eventually it languished into obscurity and then into oblivion.[1] The whole process usually took place, one infers, in one or two generations. I have no reason to question the realism of this picture in the age of noncorporate enterprise; and there are reasons for not wholly abandoning it even today. An anthropomorphic theory of the growth of the firm, however, scarcely fits our modern giants. There are no large American companies that have not grown somewhat by merger, and probably very few that have grown much by the alternative method of internal expansion.[2]

The present paper seeks to summarize some of the major episodes in the development of the merger movement, with special reference to the question of monopoly. The discussion is restricted to so-called "horizontal" combinations, which are quantitatively much the most important form of merger.[3]

* Reprinted from *Papers and Proceedings, American Economic Review,* Vol. XL, No. 2 (May 1950).

[1] *Principles of Economics* (8th ed.; London, 1920), Bk. IV, chaps. xi, xii.

[2] Unless otherwise indicated, size of the firm is to be measured relative to the size of the industry.

[3] In 1937, 85.7 percent of the manufacturing establishments belonging to "central offices" (i.e., multiple-plant firms) were engaged in "uniform" activities. Of course many of these plants were constructed by the parent concern, and there are other deficiencies in the data, but it is probable that horizontal mergers are more important than all other forms of interplant relationship combined (see TNEC Monograph No. 27, *The Structure of Industry,* p. 164).

I. SOME GENERAL THEORETICAL CONSIDERATIONS

We wish to examine the conditions under which it is profitable for competing firms to merge for monopoly. It is expedient to begin with four unpromising assumptions, all of which will be relaxed or defended subsequently: (1) long-run average and marginal cost of production are equal for firms of all relevant sizes;[4] (2) entry of new firms is free, although not necessarily inexpensive; (3) the demand for the output of the industry is stable; (4) the specialized resources ("fixed factors") employed in the industry are indestructible.

Under these conditions, will mergers for monopoly occur? The tempting offhand reply is in the negative, because under these conditions there can be no monopoly profits in the long run; the first two conditions are sufficient to insure this. This offhand reply, however, is to the question: will mergers for monopoly exist? It is not an answer to our question: will mergers for monopoly occur? They may occur.

The argument that monopolies may be profitable even under these unfavorable conditions will be developed with a partial geometrical illustration. Consider an industry meeting the four conditions listed above and consisting of numerous identical firms which are in long-run competitive equilibrium. Each firm will have the short-run cost curves displayed in Figure 8–1, and it will be operating at output OA, price OB, and making no profits. All the firms are now merged into a monopoly, and each plant ($=$ former firm) now has a pro rata share of aggregate demand, AR, with corresponding marginal revenue, MR. Accordingly it operates at output OC and makes profits of OC times DE. Entry of new firms therefore takes place, and the pro rata demand curve of each plant in the merger now shifts to the left, price falls, and profits diminish.[5] Eventually the number of rivals will grow until the merger is reduced to the long-run equilibrium level of permanent loss, since neither the merger nor the new rivals can withdraw from the industry.

---

[4] This assumption will be discussed below, but perhaps a remark is called for on the indeterminacy of the output of the firm under competition when its long-run average cost curve is horizontal. The simplest way to eliminate the indeterminacy is to sacrifice the perfection of competition (but nothing else) by having each firm have a demand curve with an elasticity of (say) -100.

[5] The explicit analysis can be carried through by a conventional application of the dominant-firm analysis; that is, by constructing the demand curve for the monopoly by subtracting from the aggregate quantity demanded at each price the amount that the new firms (acting competitively) will sell (see my *Theory of Price* [New York, 1946], p. 227).

The simple but important conclusion to be drawn from this argument is that a merger for monopoly may be profitable, in the sense that the present value of the monopoly profits and (so to speak) monopoly losses is positive. If the entry of new firms is not too rapid, the merger may make monopoly profits for a considerable period; and, even though thereafter the losses are permanent, their discounted value need not be

FIGURE 8-1

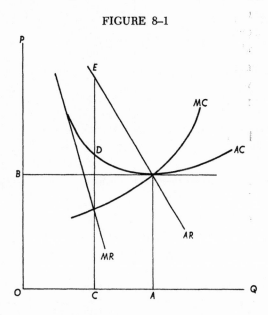

so large as to wipe out the initial gains. The essence of the explanation of mergers under these conditions therefore lies in the time required to achieve long-run equilibrium; and this essence lingers in the more general case.

If we relax our assumptions (2), (3), and (4), the prospects of net gain from merger for monopoly are increased in frequently encountered circumstances. If the specialized resources of the merger are not indestructible, investment can be withdrawn from the industry so that, after the initial period of gain and a subsequent period of loss, the long-run equilibrium will be attained, with the merger receiving a competitive rate of return on its investment in the industry.[6] If the industry's demand is growing, the amount of resources the merger must withdraw will be reduced; and, if the demand is growing sufficiently rapidly, no investment

[6] The period of loss arises because in general it requires less time to increase than to withdraw investment.

need be withdrawn: the merger can maintain its absolute size but decline in relative size.[7] If the entry of new firms and the expansion of rivals can be hindered or prevented, of course the monopoly profits will accrue for a longer period. If the rate of entry is a function of price and profits, the merger can reduce or retard entry by a lower price policy; in effect it buys a longer period of monopoly at the price of a lower rate of monopoly profits.

Let us consider now the mechanics of mergers for monopoly. (We defer the question of why mergers occur when they do.) If there are relatively few firms in the industry, the major difficulty in forming a merger is that it is more profitable to be outside a merger than to be a participant. The outsider sells at the same price but at the much larger output at which marginal cost equals price. Hence the promoter of a merger is likely to receive much encouragement from each firm—almost every encouragement, in fact, except participation. In order to overcome this difficulty, it will often be necessary to make the participation of each firm contingent on that of other firms and execute the merger in a single act. We know too little of the theory of coalitions to be able to predict the percentage of the industry that will be merged, but of course it must be fairly high if it is to have any purpose.

If there are relatively many firms in the industry, no one firm plays an important role in the formation of the merger; and it is possible for the merger to expand in a more gradual process and acquire firms on less exacting terms. In fact, several firms may enter upon programs of growth by merger.

Let us return to our first two assumptions. Our first assumption— that there are neither economies nor diseconomies of scale—will please few beside Euler. Two widely accepted, and somewhat inconsistent, beliefs clash with this assumption: (1) mergers are effected to obtain the economies of large-scale production and (2) the diseconomies of scale are the chief bulwark of competition. Both these beliefs will be discussed below; here we shall enter briefly into discussion of the validity of the assumption of constant returns to scale.

The comparative private costs of firms of various sizes can be measured in only one way: by ascertaining whether firms of the various sizes are able to survive in the industry. Survival is the only test of a firm's

---

[7] This assumes (with what validity I do not know) that the rate of entry of new firms will not be increased by the existence of the merger; but see the last point in the paragraph.

ability to cope with all the problems: buying inputs, soothing laborers, finding customers, introducing new products and techniques, coping with fluctuations, evading regulations, etc. A cross-sectional study of the costs of inputs per unit of output in a given period measures only one facet of the firm's efficiency and yields no conclusion on efficiency in the large.[8] Conversely, if a firm of a given size survives, we may infer that its costs are equal to those of other sizes of firm, being neither less (or firms of this size would grow in number relative to the industry) nor more (or firms of this size would decline in number relative to the industry).

A combination of this argument and casual observation suggests that the economies of scale are unimportant over a wide range of sizes in most American industries, for we commonly find both small and large firms persisting. We shall recur to this matter, but two observations should be made now. The first is that our analysis of mergers still holds if there are minor economies or diseconomies of scale, but fails if they are large. With large diseconomies, mergers are unprofitable; with large economies, monopoly or oligopoly is inevitable, and there will not be many rivals to merge. The second point is that the equality of private costs carries no implication that social costs of firms of different sizes are equal.[9]

Free entry—our second assumption—may be defined as the condition that long-run costs of new firms if they enter the industry will be equal to those of firms already in the industry. This does not mean, as many infer, that a new firm can enter and immediately be as profitable as an established firm. We do not begrudge the new firm a decent interval in which to build its factory; we should be equally willing to concede a period during which production is put on a smooth-running schedule, trade connections are developed, labor is recruited and trained, and the like. These costs of building up a going business are legitimate invest-

---

[8] As commonly conducted, statistical comparisons of costs or rates of return are not even conclusive on the "static" problem. They demand arbitrary asset valuations to avoid the tautological result that differences in costs measure returns on differences in capital values; and they usually cover too short a period to avoid the regression problem (on which, see M. Friedman and S. Kuznets, *Incomes from Independent Professional Practice* [New York, 1945], chap. vii).

[9] A comparison of the social costs of firms of different sizes would require, for example, the elimination of differences in private costs arising out of differences in "bargaining power" in purchasing inputs. It is tempting to argue that if the large firm is not more efficient than the small firm in private terms, it is less efficient in social terms (for then its monopolistic advantages are eliminated). I am inclined to yield to the temptation, although small firms have some private advantages (chain-store taxes) and large firms have private disadvantages (maintaining good public relations).

ment expenses, and, unless historical changes take place in the market, they must be equal for both established and new firms.[10]

With this understanding, free entry seems a valid characterization of most American industries. One may concede this and still argue that, because of the large capital requirements necessary to establish a new company of minimum efficient size, free entry is often difficult, and firms in industries with (absolutely) large capital requirements have a sheltered position. I have as little basis for my skepticism of this argument as its many adherents have given for supporting it.

This brief discussion leaves many questions about mergers unanswered. We shall attempt to answer some of them—and in the process discover new questions—by an examination of the merger movement in America. We shall find it useful to divide this history into two periods, in which monopoly and oligopoly, respectively, were the primary goals.

II. MERGER FOR MONOPOLY

The era of merger for monopoly ended in this country roughly in 1904, when the *Northern Securities* decision made it clear that this avenue to monopoly was also closed by the antitrust laws. The transition was abrupt in a historical sense. It is revealed by the fact that the United States Steel Corporation, which had quietly picked up in 1902-04 a few steel firms overlooked in the haste of organization, felt it necessary to obtain permission from President Theodore Roosevelt to acquire the Tennessee Coal and Iron Company in 1907.[11]

When and why did the merger movement begin? Sporadic mergers, often founded on marriage, are no doubt as ancient as man; probably for long they were occasional and relatively small in scale, and they were offset by the divestitures necessary to endow sons in a more fertile age. In this country mergers for monopoly began on a large scale only in the eighties, they reached a minor peak at the beginning of the nineties, and they attained their pinnacle at the end of the century.[12]

---

[10] On this view, the infant-industry argument for tariffs is mistaken (at least when external economies do not enter).

[11] Union Steel (1902), Troy Steel Products (1903), and Clairton Steel (1904) together had twice the ingot capacity of Tennessee Coal and Iron. On the last merger, see the hearings of the Stanley Committee, *Hearings before the Committee [of the House] on Investigation of United States Steel Corporation* (Washington, 1911), Parts 1–6.

[12] The number of combinations with capitalization of 1 million dollars or more,

Our theory is that mergers for monopoly are profitable under easy assumptions that were surely fulfilled in many industries well before the mergers occurred. The only persuasive reason I have found for their late occurrence is the development of the modern corporation and the modern capital market. In a regime of individual proprietorships and partnerships, the capital requirements were a major obstacle to buying up the firms in an industry, and unlimited liability was a major obstacle to the formation of partnerships.

General incorporation laws antedate the Civil War,[13] but the powers of these early corporations were severely limited. They could not hold stock in other corporations; they could not merge with another corporation; limits were placed on their capitalization; often they could not do business outside the state of incorporation; exchange of capital assets for stock required the unanimous consent of the stockholders; etc. Only in the eighties did New Jersey initiate the competition among states for corporations, which in twenty years eliminated almost every restriction on mergers.[14] In this same period the New York Stock Exchange developed into an effective market for industrial securities. These institutional changes seem to be the proximate causes for the development of the merger movement in the last two decades of the nineteenth century.

Almost invariably the leading firms joined together simultaneously, as our theory leads us to expect.[15] The combinations frequently attained high percentages of national output but seldom became strict monopolies. The contemporary estimates of their shares of the market are rough, and

---

as compiled by Luther Conant, varied as follows:

1887............... 8	1892...............10	1897............... 4
1888............... 3	1893...... 6	1898...............20
1889...............12	1894............... 2	1899...............87
1890...............13	1895............... 6	1900...............42
1891...............17	1896............... 5	

(Eliot Jones, *The Trust Problem in the United States* [New York, 1921], p. 39.) There was an earlier era of railroad consolidations (see, e.g., George P. Baker, *The Formation of the New England Railroad Systems* [Cambridge, 1937], especially chap. xi).

[13] See G. H. Evans, *Business Incorporations in the United States, 1800–1943* (New York, 1948).

[14] See E. Q. Keasbey, "New Jersey and the Great Corporations," *Harvard Law Review,* 1899–1900, pp. 198–212, 264–78; W. C. Noyes, *A Treatise on the Law of Intercorporate Relations* (Boston, 1902), and, especially, R. C. Larcom, *The Delaware Corporation* (Baltimore, 1937).

[15] [Standard Oil of New Jersey, once believed to be an exception, was shown by John McGee not to be one, in "Predatory Competition," *Journal of Law and Economics,* 1958.]

little attention was paid by the estimators to the shares of the firm in particular geographical and product markets. With these provisos, we may note that the mean share of the market controlled by the mergers studied by the Industrial Commission was 71 percent.[16] In the ninety-two large mergers studied by Moody, the distribution by share of market was similar: seventy-eight controlled 50 percent or more of the output of the industry; fifty-seven controlled 60 percent or more; and twenty-six controlled 80 percent or more.[17] Even in Dewing's fourteen industries in which the mergers failed, the mean percentage was 54.[18]

Almost invariably the share of the merger in the market declined substantially as time went on. Sometimes the entry of new firms was successfully prevented or delayed by ruthless warfare (National Cash Register), patents (Eastman, United Shoe Machinery), or coercion of suppliers or buyers (American Tobacco). These instances are not numerous, however, and such tactics were successful chiefly in small industries; in steel, sugar refining, agricultural implements, leather, rubber, distilleries, cans, etc., the dominant company lost ground relative to the industry.[19]

Why was merger preferred to collusion? Part of the answer lies in the prima facie illegality of collusion after 1890. This point should not be pressed, however. The effectiveness of the Sherman Law in dealing with conspiracies was not clear until 1899, when the *Addyston Pipe* case was decided;[20] and there was a contemporaneous wave of amalgamations in England, where conspiracies were unenforcible but not actionable.[21] Mention should also be made of the conflicting tendencies of the greater durability of mergers and the ability to avoid diseconomies of scale through collusion. I am inclined to place considerable weight upon one other advantage of merger: it permitted a capitalization of prospective monopoly profits and a distribution of a portion of these capitalized

---

[16] The distribution was:

Percent	Companies
25– 50	1
50– 75	11
75–100	10

(United States Industrial Commission, *Report,* Vol. XIII, *passim.*)

[17] John Moody, *The Truth about the Trusts* (New York, 1904), p. 487.

[18] A. S. Dewing, *Corporate Promotions and Reorganizations* (Cambridge, 1914), p. 526.

[19] For some instances see my *Five Lectures on Economic Problems* (London, 1949), Lecture 5.

[20] See W. H. Taft, *The Anti-Trust Act and the Supreme Court,* and J. D. Clark, *The Federal Trust Policy.*

[21] J. H. Clapham, *An Economic History of Modern Britain* (Cambridge, 1938), Vol. III, chap. iv.

profits to the professional promoter. The merger enabled a Morgan or a Moore to enter a new and lucrative industry: the production of monopolies.

It is sobering to reflect on the attitudes of professional economists of the period toward the merger movement. Economists as wise as Taussig, as incisive as Fisher, as fond of competition as Clark and Fetter, insisted upon discussing the movement largely or exclusively in terms of industrial evolution and the economies of scale. They found no difficulty in treating the unregulated corporation as a natural phenomenon, nor were they bothered that the economies of scale should spring forth suddenly and simultaneously in an enormous variety of industries—and yet pass over the minor firms that characteristically persisted and indeed flourished in these industries. One must regretfully record that in this period Ida Tarbell and Henry Demarest Lloyd did more than the American Economic Association to foster the policy of competition.

III. MERGER FOR OLIGOPOLY

One great change has taken place in the merger movement since the *Northern Securities* decision: the share of the industry merged into one firm has fallen sharply. In the early period, as we have seen, the leading firm seldom merged less than 50 percent of the industry's output; in the later period the percentage has hardly ever risen this high. The new goal of mergers is oligopoly.

The change has been most striking in the industries which were merged for monopoly at the beginning of the century. The merger firm has declined continuously and substantially relative to the industry in almost every case. The dominant firm did not embark on a new program of merger to regain its monopolistic position, however; the new mergers were undertaken by firms of the second class. The industry was transformed from near-monopoly to oligopoly. Cement, cans, petroleum, automobiles, agricultural implements, and glass are examples. We may illustrate the development by the steel industry (Table 8–1): United States Steel's share of ingot production dropped sharply, but the company absorbed only two small rivals (Columbia Steel, 1930; Geneva plant, 1945), and the chief mergers have been Bethlehem and Republic. Even if one lumps together the (say) four largest firms in the industry, in general there has been a decline in the concentration of production.[22]

The merger movement has also reached the many-firm industries in

[22] See my *Five Lectures,* pp. 63ff.

TABLE 8–1

MERGERS BY LEADING STEEL FIRMS MEASURED BY PERCENTAGE
OF INDUSTRY INGOT CAPACITY

| Company | Initial Year | Percent of Industry's Capacity | | | Percent of Industry's Capacity Acquired by Merger | |
		Initial Year	1908	1948	Initial Year— 1908	1908–48
U.S. Steel..........	1892	14.49	50.14	33.14	33.75	1.00
Bethlehem	1892	3.29	0.56	14.64	.....	12.66
Republic	1896	2.08	1.46	9.13	1.08	7.23
Jones and Laughlin	1898	4.59	4.17	5.03	0.18	2.05
National	1920	.....	.....	4.30	.....	0.90
Youngstown Sheet ..	1908	.....	1.76	4.25	.....	2.01
Inland	1904	0.50	0.59	3.61	.....	.....
American Rolling...	1901	0.07	0.15	3.57	0.05	2.28
Sharon	1904	0.28	0.26	1.67	.....	1.34
Colorado	1901	0.96	2.93	1.54	.....	0.19
Wheeling	1901	0.73	0.56	1.50	.....	1.41
Crucible	1898	0.71	1.01	1.33	1.06	1.49

Source: Compiled from directories of iron and steel works. The data presented by United States Steel Corporation indicate a much larger control in the first decade, presumably because the industry's capacity was overstated in the directories (see TNEC, *Hearings*, Part 26, pp. 13, 852).

the later period. We may measure mergers between 1919 and 1937 in a rough fashion by comparing the number of manufacturing establishments belonging to central offices at the two dates (Table 8–2); it appears

TABLE 8–2

MANUFACTURING ESTABLISHMENTS IN CENTRAL OFFICES, 1919 AND 1937

Industry	1919	1937
Food and kindred products........................	4,544	8,529
Textiles and their products........................	2,832	2,703
Iron and steel and their products...................	1,602	2,420
Lumber and its remanufactures....................	2,829	2,390
Leather and its finished products..................	495	503
Paper and printing...............................	918	1,865
Liquors and beverages............................	268	738
Chemicals and allied products.....................	2,409	2,800
Stone, clay, and glass products....................	1,100	1,325
Metal and metal products other than iron and steel....	445	530
Tobacco manufactures............................	533	124
Vehicles for land transportation...................	287	390
Miscellaneous industries..........................	1,362	1,382
Total......................................	19,624	25,665

Source: 1919 data from W. L. Thorp, *The Integration of Industrial Operations* (Washington, 1924), p. 113; 1937 data, which are only roughly comparable, from TNEC Monograph No. 27, *The Structure of Industry*, p. 211.

that the food industry was the chief center of merger activity, although the paper and printing and iron and steel industries also saw much merger activity. National Dairy is perhaps the most striking example of merger in the food industries—it acquired 331 firms in the decade ending in 1933[23]—but Borden, General Foods, General Mills, and the bakery chains also date from this period.[24] In general, such mergers led to local oligopoly in the primary products (fluid milk, bread, etc.) and to national oligopoly in lesser products such as cheese.

The Sherman Law seems to have been the fundamental cause for the shift from merger for monopoly to merger for oligopoly. Sometimes its workings were obvious, as when Standard Oil was dismembered and when the leading baking mergers were prevented from combining.[25] More often, however, its workings have been more subtle: the ghost of Senator Sherman is an ex officio member of the board of directors of every large company. This explanation for the new direction of mergers is vulnerable to the criticisms that it is simple and obvious, but no plausible alternative explanation is available.[26]

It is my impression—based chiefly upon the more modest issuance of securities of mergers and the apparent ease of entry into the new merging industries—that the mergers for oligopoly in the later period have been less effective in restraining or postponing competition than the earlier mergers for monopoly. This is not to argue, however, that they left competition as they found it; indeed, the one important weakness in the Sherman Act as it is sometimes interpreted is the belief that oligopoly affords a satisfactory form of organization of our economy. This belief is apparently held, as it was certainly fostered, by one of the greatest of contemporary judges, Learned Hand, the author of the famous dictum that control by one firm of 64 percent of an industry may not be monopoly and that 33 percent surely is not.[27] It is true, no doubt, that oligopoly is a weaker form of monopolization than the single firm, but it is not so weak a form that it can be left to its own devices. If this view—which is

[23] Federal Trade Commission, *Agricultural Income Inquiry* (Washington, 1938), I, p. 237.

[24] There was also much merging in fuel and ice; City Ice and Fuel is perhaps the largest merger, but several others, such as American Ice and Atlantic Company, were very active.

[25] *Agricultural Income Inquiry*, I, p. 308.

[26] Is is suggestive that mergers for monopoly continued to be typical in England in the twenties (see Patrick Fitzgerald, *Industrial Combination in England* [London, 1927]).

[27] ". . . it is doubtful whether sixty or sixty-four percent would be enough [to constitute monopoly]; and certainly thirty-three per cent is not" (*United States* v. *Aluminum Co. of America*, 148 F. [2d] 424).

almost universally held by modern economists—is correct, then our chief task in the field of antitrust policy is to demonstrate beyond judicial doubt the social undesirability of permitting oligopoly by merger (or by other methods) in large American industries.

IV. CONCLUSIONS

The foregoing survey of the merger movement raises a set of inter-related questions; they concern the economies of scale, the capital market, and the entry of firms into an industry.

The broad sweep of our discussion would suggest that the private diseconomies of large-scale production are only an occasional and minor barrier to merger for monopoly. The chief barriers to monopoly, in addition to the Sherman Act, have been the capital requirements of mergers and the tendency of rivals to grow in number and size.

To find in an imperfect capital market a bulwark of competition seems paradoxical, but the paradox is not deep. Until recent times the personal distribution of wealth set a limit upon the size of firms, and modern economic societies have been sufficiently egalitarian to make personal monopolization of large industries impossible. The corporation and the securities markets have severed the connection between personal wealth and industrial size and thus weakened the institutional basis of competitive enterprise.

The diseconomies of scale offer a weak supplement to the limitations once provided by personal wealth. Properly interpreted, conventional theory does not contradict this tentative finding. We customarily find in entrepreneurship the limitation to the size of firm, and we find the chief tasks of the entrepreneur arising out of uncertainty. Much, although of course not all, uncertainly stems from the competitive behavior of rivals, so that entrepreneurship may well be subject to increasing returns to relative size as well as to decreasing returns to absolute size, with no clear verdict for either force over a wide range of sizes.

We are thus led to "new entry" as the chief defense of competition—a most unseemly reversion to the ruling economic theory of 1900. It is now popular to deprecate the importance of new entry because few firms can accumulate the capital necessary to produce efficiently in the great industries. To the extent that the criticism rests on the alleged economies of scale, I have argued that it is mistaken; to the extent that it rests on imperfections of the capital market it runs contrary to (but is not necessarily inconsistent with) the argument we have advanced that the capital market has been improving—in certain directions, at least—too much! Yet there is support for the skeptics of easy entry in the fact that the mergers for monopoly have frequently been very profitable.

Such inconclusive conclusions are not too troublesome. This paper is designed to be only an introduction to the merger problem. To this end, it is sufficient if I emphasize again the significance of the movement. To the theorist it offers a stimulating challenge: the merger movement does not fit too well into the received categories of stable competition and irresistible monopoly. To the student of social policy it offers the promising hypothesis: it is possible to change the trend of industrial organization by the lackadaisical enforcement of an antitrust law. And to the student of social sciences it offers the supremely optimistic—and pessimistic—suggestion: when economists agree that a movement is inevitable, it is not.

Addendum

The period before 1950 has been reworked in two studies. Ralph L. Nelson, in *Merger Movements in American Industry, 1895–1956* (Princeton, 1959), reconstructs a basic new merger series for the period, 1895–1919, and tests various hypotheses for the earlier merger movement. J. F. Weston, in *The Role of Mergers in the Growth of Large Firms* (Berkeley, 1953), provides estimates of the role of mergers in concentration, but with an unsatisfactory statistical procedure; see my "The Statistics of Monopoly and Merger," *Journal of Political Economy*, February 1956. On mergers after 1950, an encyclopedic survey is given by Betty Bock, *Mergers and Markets* (3d ed.; New York, 1964); see also Chapter 21 below.

THE DOMINANT FIRM AND THE INVERTED UMBRELLA*

Chapter

9

When United States Steel Corporation was founded in 1901, it contained plants producing a large share of the nation's output of basic steel and fabricated steel products. The share of output of steel ingots was 66 percent in 1901. During the next two decades the firm's share of output fell gradually, reaching 46 percent in 1920 and 42 percent in 1925. Declines (usually of lesser magnitude) took place in the company's share of other products. These facts are not in serious dispute.

The interpretation of the facts enjoys no such unanimity. Two rival hypotheses for the formation of the combine will be tested in this note.

The first hypothesis is that a large, perhaps primary, purpose of the merger was to sell securities to untutored investors. The book value of assets of the constituent firms was written up from some $700 million to $1.4 billion when the new corporation was formed, and the common stock then issued is a classic example of watered stocks in the literature of corporation finance.

On this view it was incidental to the motives for the merger whether any important economies in production or any important monopoly power in the market was achieved. If U.S. Steel was not more efficient, or if it could not control entry, its share would decline with time, and the higher prices it may have set would provide an umbrella under which more efficient rivals would flourish and their shares would gradually increase. This aspect of the theory was not elaborated, because the focus was on the promotional profits in the original stock sales.[1]

---

* Aaron Director proposed the study, and Richard West, then a graduate student, performed the work under my negligent eye. Director refuses co-authorship, on grounds I find unconvincing; West has been given no chance to do so, on the ground that he has since become a professor and will now hire research assistants. As the middleman in this venture, I assume no credit and all blame. Reprinted from *Journal of Law and Economics*, Vol. VIII. Copyright 1965 by the *Journal of Law and Economics*.

[1] Perhaps the most influential statement of this hypothesis was made by Dewing, *Financial Policy of Corporations*, Bk. IV, chap. iv, 924-26 (4th ed. 1941).

The second hypothesis is that provided by the theory of the dominant firm. This theory assumes that U.S. Steel was formed for the monopoly power it achieved. The dominant firm will set a profit-maximizing price such that its marginal cost equals marginal revenue based upon *its* demand curve (the industry demand curve minus the amount supplied by others). The profit to be maximized is long run (actually, the sum of discounted future profits) so account will be taken of the rate at which rivals enter and expand. Nevertheless, the dominant firm will find, usually, that it is profitable to yield up some share of the industry, for higher prices may more than offset the decline in share.[2]

Neither theory denies the decline in share, which after all is a well-known historical fact. They differ on the wisdom of purchasing the stock of U.S. Steel when it was first offered: the former theory says this was an unwise purchase; the latter does not.

The purpose of this note is to investigate the financial returns to investors in U.S. Steel common stock and in that of other steel companies. On the former theory, the investors should have purchased stock in other steel companies; on the latter theory, U.S. Steel should have done as well as other steel companies.[3]

The financial returns of an investor are in principle easily determined:

1. Buy a block of stock in a company at a given date,—say $10,000 worth.
2. Reinvest all cash dividends in the stock.
3. Calculate the market value of the stock (including stock dividends) at any desired subsequent date.

This is in effect our procedure,[4] and it yields the returns reported in Table 9–1.

The experience of investors in the various companies whose stocks

[2] This version is explicit in Stigler, Monopoly and Oligopoly by Merger, in Papers and Proceedings of the Sixty-second Annual Meeting of the American Economic Association, 40 Am. Econ. Rev., 23 (May 1950). [Ch. 8 above]

[3] It is not certain as to whether U.S. Steel stock should have done precisely as well, or better or worse. This depends fundamentally on whether the costs of U.S. Steel were greater or less than those of other companies.

[4] The calculations depart in one respect from this description. The mean July price of the stock is used in calculating the number of shares purchased by reinvestment of dividends during a year, except when stock rights are issued. In this latter case the rights are valued as of the time they were exercisable, and reinvested at current prices.

The stocks whose quotations begin in later years are brought into the average in the first available year, with an investment equal to the average value of the current investments in other companies (excluding U.S. Steel).

TABLE 9–1. **MARKET VALUE OF INVESTMENT OF $10,000[a] PLUS REINVESTED DIVIDENDS FROM JULY, 1901[b]**

Year	U.S. Steel	Bethlehem	Colorado	Crucible	Lackawanna	Republic	Sloss-Sheffield	Average excluding U.S. Steel
1901	$ 10,672		$10,000	$ 10,000		$10,000	$10,000	$10,000
1902	9,606		9,427	10,383		9,240	9,905	9,739
1903	7,814		5,813	5,761		6,756	10,952	7,320
1904	3,599		3,199	2,139		3,678	10,994	5,002
1905	9,529	$ 13,851a	4,544	4,683		10,347	35,832	13,851
1906	10,707	13,102	4,884	4,839		13,595	28,184	12,920
1907	11,839	7,196	3,226	3,365	$12,920a	14,697	29,432	11,458
1908	13,890	9,503	2,930	2,652	10,835	9,948	28,054	10,043
1909	24,801	17,405	4,398	4,335	7,172	16,699	49,518	17,080
1910	26,688	11,945	3,166	4,900	10,123	15,949	38,343	13,796
1911	32,020	15,364	3,436	5,574	8,470	15,587	29,163	12,835
1912	31,374	16,648	3,037	7,331	7,884	13,921	32,789	13,568
1913	25,924	13,956	2,876	5,904	7,681	10,673	14,837	9,258
1914	29,990	18,817	2,532	6,857	7,300	11,195	16,190	10,380
1915	31,062	83,187	3,254	15,978	6,691	16,177	21,305	24,916
1916	47,455	209,845	4,324	29,865	9,594	23,363	28,302	51,908
1917	78,599	215,746d	5,144	37,195	15,750	49,767	35,684	61,198
1918	76,881	154,121	5,189	29,043	23,649	54,020	46,601	52,119
1919	84,081	193,172	6,028	56,543	23,740	60,497	58,411	66,867
1920	73,490	185,991	4,247	146,756e	26,552	61,714	62,892	80,950
1921	60,148	114,594	3,511	56,206	24,100	31,741	29,955	41,583
1922	84,009	185,844	3,124	84,936	13,493	49,501	39,919	65,059
1923	90,150	125,899	3,712	70,833	27,032c	30,204	38,904	53,910
1924	101,039	115,453	6,234	61,158		31,686	53,041	53,514

[a] For firms entering after 1901 (Bethlehem and Lackawanna) the average market value, excluding U.S. Steel, was employed as the amount of initial investment.

[b] Prices used in calculating values of stock are the averages of the high-lows for the first four Fridays in the month of July of each year, unless otherwise stated.

[c] Lackawanna merged with Bethlehem.

[d] In 1917 Bethlehem declared a 200% stock dividend in "Common B." All values between 1917–1922 were calculated on the basis of two types of Common—"old Common" and "Common B." In 1922 the two types were merged.

[e] During 1920 Crucible declared three stock dividends: 50% (April 30), 16-2/3% (July 31), 14-2/7% (August 31). In order to take account of the last two stock dividends the price used in calculating the 1920 value was an average of the high-lows of March 30, June 30, September 30 and December 30.

SOURCES: Stock quotations from *Financial and Commercial Chronicle*, 1901–1924. Dividends and splits from *Poor's Manual of Industrials* 1920, 1924.

were traded is presented graphically in Figure 9-1. The current market value of the shares obtained with an initial investment of $10,000, and with reinvestment of all earnings, is given for each year from 1901 to 1925. Since the figure is semi-logarithmic in scale, rates of increase can

FIGURE 9-1
MARKET VALUE OF INVESTMENT OF $10,000 PLUS REINVESTED
DIVIDENDS FROM JULY 1901

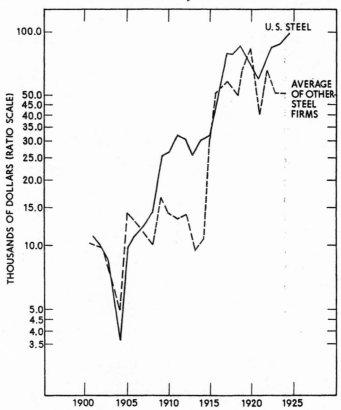

be read directly. The figure is sufficient to reach the main conclusion: the stockholders of U.S. Steel did better than those of any of the other companies except Bethlehem Steel. The average value of the investments in the other companies was below that of U.S. Steel in 16 of the 18 years after 1905. At the end of the period the accumulated market value of United States Steel was twice that of the average of the other companies.

The evidence seems conclusive that the exploitation of stockholders by promoters did not take place. The formation of United States Steel

Corporation must therefore be viewed as a master stroke of monopoly promotion; and it is churlish of the literature to complain at the $62 million of stock given to the Morgan syndicate for bringing it about.

Chapter 10 IMPERFECTIONS IN THE CAPITAL MARKET*

The adult economist, once the subject is called to his attention, will recall the frequency and variety of contexts in which he has encountered "imperfections-in-the-capital-market."

The area of industrial organization teems with instances. A predatory price cutter drives his small rival to the (poorly attended!) auction block—a technique which is not profitable if the small rival can borrow and ride out the competitive storm (Jones, 1921, pp. 77 ff.). [See references at end of chapter.] In fact, all systems of disciplining rivals by imposing losses require that the rival have inferior access to capital (Jones, 1921, p. 83; also Machlup, 1949, pp. 160 ff; Loescher, 1959, pp. 125 ff.). The cigarette companies earned large rates of return because potential rivals could not "afford" to advertise lavishly for years and so to develop acceptance of new brands (Nicholls, 1951, pp. 201, 412). The integration of a firm forward or backward has been explained as a device to increase (to presumably unattainable levels) the *capital* requirements of potential new firms (Stigler, 1950, p. 33; Blake and Jones, 1965, p. 392).

The labor markets provide an equally generous supply of examples. All of us have said that rates of return on investment in education of men were higher than rates on (other?) investment goods because of "imperfections-in-the-capital-market" (see Friedman and Kuznets, 1945, pp. 89–92, 391–92; Stigler, 1966, pp. 266–67). The monopsonistic power of an employer arises because the laborer (lacking capital) cannot hold back his services in a bilateral monopoly setting (Marshall, 1920, p. 568).

Perhaps these samples are sufficient to remind the reader of the variety and frequency of appearance of imperfections-in-the-capital-market. If not, we may add the considerable literature on capital rationing, with special reference to agriculture (see Schultz, 1940). The opulent

* Reprinted from *Journal of Political Economy*, Vol. LXXV, No. 3, June 1967. Copyright 1967 by the University of Chicago.

literature of economic development would not fail to supply instances (Lewis, 1955, pp. 127 ff.). The problem of usury is at least by half a problem in capital market imperfections (Ryan, 1924). And, arbitrarily to close this listing, there are numerous examples of imperfections-in-the-capital-market in corporation finance (Buchanan, 1940, p. 315) and the literature of the economics of exhaustible resources (Pigou, 1932, pp. 27–29).

Not only is imperfections-in-the-capital-market a popular concept, but what is more important, it is a terminal concept. Once this phrase has been written or spoken, the economist has finished with *that* strand of analysis. In the list of closing phrases of economics, which includes "that is an index number problem," and "of course the second-best considerations still remain," surely imperfections-in-the-capital-market deserves pride of place. This Gabriel-horn phrase has accordingly received only negligible and negligent attention. The present essay seeks to make preliminary amends for this neglect.

I. THE BASIC IMPERFECTION: INABILITY TO BORROW —CHEAPLY?

The most pervasive imperfection-in-the-capital-market is the inability to borrow funds. We may illustrate the allegation with the popular example of capital investment in human beings. The young man is denied a college education because he cannot borrow sufficient funds to pay his expenses of education and living.

It is not enough that a young man who wishes to enter the professions have sufficient ability; he must also be able to command funds to pay the expenses of training and to support himself during the training period. Because of the peculiar character of the capital investment in training, these funds cannot be obtained in the open market as a purely "business loan," and hence are not freely available to all. . . . If, relatively to the demand for professional services, there are few young men interested in entering the professional services who can get the necessary funds, one would expect underinvestment; in the contrary case, overinvestment [Friedman and Kuznets, 1945, pp. 89–90].

Becker points out that the same difficulty in borrowing is encountered by the young man who wishes to establish a new enterprise rather than go to college (Becker, 1964, p. 57).

The demonstration of this imperfection invariably consists in the high rates of interest earned or paid by the investor. Yet, this is surely not sufficient evidence to allow us to conclude that capital is being allocated inefficiently—any more than the fact that some people walk is proof of an imperfection in the automobile market. Let the would-be college student expect 12 percent on his investment in a college education when "the" interest rate is 6 percent. Surely we have to know what lenders are realizing on loans to college students; if it is 6 percent, the marginal return on capital is equal in various investment, and the allocation of capital is efficient.

The main, unspoken reply to this comment would probably be: surely the difference of 6 percent between what the borrower pays and the lender receives is too large to be accounted for by the cost of loans; and remember that the 12 percent rate was actually realized, so risks have already been compensated. I try to state this reply convincingly, but it is not a convincing reply: an empirical question cannot be settled by non-empirical arguments. If there is evidence that one can lend to students at a realized rate of more than 6 percent, although costs of lending (including raising funds) are 6 percent, the capital market is indeed imperfect. But the whole argument now turns upon the cost of transactions which no one has measured.[1]

There is a second defense of the allegation of imperfections-in-the-capital-market which is more or less explicit in this literature. The laborer is not allowed to pledge his future labor services as security for a loan, so the legal prohibition of "involuntary" servitude (of course the contract could be voluntary) makes him an unattractive borrower. This in indeed true, and of course the prohibition of enforceable labor contracts reduces the laborer's disposable property rights. But if lenders were to disregard this legal fact, they would be acting with gross stupidity, and their realized rates of return would probably be negative. The limitations placed upon borrowers by law are hardly to be labeled imperfections-in-the-capital-market. With any reasonable use of language, this legal limitation on laborers' bargaining rights should be called an "imperfection-of-the-labor-market."[2]

A misallocation of capital is created, not eliminated, if interest rates are reduced to borrowers without a commensurate reduction in the costs

[1] It is not even a very plausible kind of arithmetic. The rate of default on loans is strongly dependent upon the method by which borrowers are selected. An across-the-board offer of loans to all students would greatly increase the default rate.

[2] Whether it is a wisely legislated imperfection is no present concern. The prohibition of enforceable contracts for labor services is presumably desirable if laborers would often make bad contracts because of ignorance, lack of foresight, monopoly, and so on, and undesirable if such bad contracts were infrequent. The issue has nothing to do with the phenomenon that gave rise to the laws, namely, hereditary slavery.

of transactions. The situation is exactly comparable to the elimination of geographical differences in the price of a commodity: if prices at two points differ by less than transportation costs, the movement of goods is uneconomic.[3]

Most allegations of imperfections-in-the-capital-market, we believe, are based upon the failure of capital to flow into fields in which higher rates would be returned than are obtainable elsewhere. Consider the example of cutthroat competition: a firm (Mr. J. D. Rockefeller's, in the folklore) sells at unremunerative prices in a particular area and "drives a rival to the wall." Thereafter it buys the defunct rival at a trivial price and pursues a remunerative monopoly price policy.

If the capital market were efficient, this lesser rival could go to a lender and say:

> There is a threat of a three-month price war, during which I will lose $10,000, which unfortunately I do not possess. If you lend me the $10,000, I can survive the price war—and once I show your certified check to Rockefeller the price war will probably never be embarked upon. Even if the price war should occur, we will earn more by co-operation afterward than the $10,000 loss, or Rockefeller would never embark upon the strategy.

This argument seems wholly convincing to me.[4]

Often the charge of imperfection reads differently but, nevertheless, rests ultimately upon the inability of borrowers to get cheap funds. Consider the following charge:

> Everything we know about business finance stresses the imperfections of the capital market. A commodity market is at least theoretically capable of "pure competition": the common fund of knowledge we have to attribute to dealers in assuming pure competition is all knowledge about the present. But the knowledge dealers must share to admit of pure competition in the capital market is knowledge about the future. Thus it is inherently uncertain, and the uncertainty extends to the proceeds of transactions currently engaged in. This uncertainty unavoidably makes competition in the capital market "imperfect" [Hart, 1949, p. 171].

As a matter of terminology, Hart is entitled to call imperfect foresight a market imperfection, just as I am entitled to say that it is an imperfection in a wheat seed that it does not grow into nicely baked bread. Nevertheless, the language does not seem useful. What is germane here

---

[3] Nevertheless, Lance Davis (1963) measures the approach to a national capital market by the decline of differences among regions in interest rates. No one would dream of using this criterion for wheat or automobiles.

[4] And to Rockefeller, who bought out his rivals on favorable terms. See J. McGee (1958).

is that Hart cites the difference between borrowing and lending rates of a firm as a consequence of this imperfect foresight (Hart, 1949, p. 172), so an important manifestation of his type of imperfection is that a firm cannot borrow freely at "the" market rate. Again there is no showing of evidence that lenders to business receive a higher (or lower) realized rate of return than business lenders receive on loans to non-business.

II. MONOPOLY AS AN IMPERFECTION

There is ample historical precedent for identifying a perfect market with a competitive market (see Stigler, 1957). I personally oppose the identification, on the ground that the essence of a market is the exchange of titles, whereas the essence of competition is the diffusion of economic power. No market can be perfectly competitive, it is quite true, if the traders are very ignorant of offers and bids because many cases of bilateral monopoly or oligopoly may survive. But a market may be remarkably efficient as a place in which to make transactions, even though one party is a monopolist.

Often the charge of imperfections-in-the-capital-market has been a charge of monopoly. Thus, W. Arthur Lewis writes,

> Small farmers have a very high propensity to get into burdensome debt. This is mainly due to the risks to which they are subject. . . . It is also partly due to their own improvidence, but it is often just as much due to the deliberate policy of the moneylender. If the farmer owes more than he can pay, he is ripe for exploitation: the moneylender may compel him to sell all his marketable produce through the moneylender's agents, or to buy all his requirements in the moneylender's shop, in either case at unfavorable prices. Or the moneylender may drive the farmers bankrupt, buy their land cheaply, and take extortionate rents [1955, p. 127].[5]

The lenders are presumably able to get extortionate returns from the natives because they are not limited by competitors.

Whether we label monopoly a market imperfection or not, the monopoly power could lead to serious inefficiencies in the allocation of capital. It is not probable, however, that the inefficiencies will be large: capital (or general credit) is the most fungible, the most divisible, the most mobile of all productive services. It stems from innumerable individual and corporate savers, and no one saver ever possesses even 1 per cent of the annual savings. It flows to innumerable borrowers, public and private; and, except in socialized economies and in private enterprise

---

[5] I note in passing that Lewis uses "theory" in a remarkable sense.

economies during major wars (when the national government no doubt acts monopsonistically), there is seldom a borrower who takes even 2 percent of the annual savings.

The general market for capital is of course composed of many parts: there are regional markets and markets for types of credit (agricultural, commercial trade, installment, auto), but all deal in the same basic good, and each presumably has a highly elastic supply of funds.

The financial markets through which these various markets mobilize savings and deal with borrowers are of course highly varied in industrial structure. In a large city there are a hundred retailers to provide retail credit for the purchaser of shoes or apparel, but in a small town there is only one commercial bank to make short-term business loans. This bank has to compete with trade credit or with borrowing against real estate or pledged securities, but it may well possess some monopoly power.[6] At the other extreme, there has been monopoly in the syndicates which float large state-bond issues (West, 1965). Yet it is surely correct to say that monopoly is not the typical organization among financial markets and that where monopoly occurs its quantitative strength is usually smaller than in most other markets.

Of course these sweeping remarks do not constitute any proof of the negligible importance of monopoly in capital markets. All that is intended is the assertion that there is no commonsense presumption that monopoly is a customary and important element of capital markets.

III. MARKET PERFECTION AND IMPERFECTION

The function of a market is to permit the exchange of goods, so an efficient market (clearly a normative concept) permits all exchange which the traders prefer to non-exchange. If we assume away all costs of trading, the efficient market will achieve every desired exchange for homogeneous goods when there is only one price. This condition is clearly necessary: with two (or more) prices, one seller is receiving less than some other buyer is paying, and both would prefer to trade with one another than with whomever they are trading. This condition is also sufficient if everyone is permitted to make all trades that he wishes to make. A uniform price with queues, however, obviously violates our condition for efficiency.

The careless and overpopular use of imperfections-in-the-capital-

---

[6] In fact, a recent study by Sam Peltzman (1965) shows that FDIC licensing policies restricted entry into commercial banking after 1935 to less than half the rate that would otherwise have occurred, and as a result bank stock prices are higher than they would otherwise be.

market stems from the application of this simple theory to inappropriate conditions.

One cost of trading has always been recognized by the literature, probably because this cost is explicit and substantial: the cost of moving goods when buyer and seller are at different points. Indeed the Cournot definition of a market is that it is the *area* within which price tends to uniformity, allowance being made for transportation costs (Cournot, 1927, p. 51, n.). The proviso is obviously necessary: if the price at A is $1.00 and at B is $1.25, no buyer at B wishes to buy at A if transportation costs exceed $0.25.

Under these conditions, if the flow of goods in one direction is invariable and literally mathematically continuous, there will still be only one price in the market after deducting transportation costs. But these are conditions of extreme rigor, and it will not be true that at all moments the price of wheat on the country depot will be equal to the prices at the milling center minus transportation costs.[7] If, for example, there are inventories at an "import" point, then (since inventories cannot be carried without cost) price will fluctuate when inventories fluctuate.

Transportation costs are the prototype of all trading costs: costs of acquiring knowledge of products and other traders, inspecting quality, collecting funds, etc. There is no "imperfection" in a market possessing incomplete knowledge if it would not be remunerative to acquire (produce) complete knowledge: information costs are the costs of transportation from ignorance to omniscience, and seldom can a trader afford to take the entire trip.

Thus, complete knowledge of prices would require the canvass of all traders. Optimum information would require the canvass of traders only up to the point where the expected marginal return from search equals its marginal costs (see Stigler, 1961). The acquisition of complete information would in general be as wasteful as the transportation of a house valued at $30,000 in New York to California where it would be valued at $30,200. Comparable things can be said about all other costs of transactions,[8] so the criterion of an efficient market becomes one with an appropriate frequency distribution of prices. A good deal of work is required on this problem, but none is required to reject the criterion of a single price for an efficient market.

The application of this argument to specific instances of alleged

---

[7] I ignore the fact that seldom will transportation costs be a single number independent of season, quantity, and velocity.

[8] See the article by H. Demsetz for a comprehensive analysis of the subject, "The Cost of Transacting," *Quarterly Journal of Economics,* February 1968.

imperfections-in-the-capital-market may be illustrated by a famous example, the difference between borrower's and lender's risk discussed by Keynes (1936, p. 144).

> Two types of risk affect the volume of investment. . . . The first is the entrepreneur's or borrower's risk and arises out of doubts in his own mind as to the probability of his actually earning the prospective yield for which he hopes. If a man is venturing his own money, this is the only kind of risk which is relevant.
> But where a system of borrowing and lending exists, by which I mean the granting of loans with a margin of real or personal security, a second type of risk is relevant which we may call lender's risk. This may be due either to moral hazard . . . or the possible insufficiency of the margin of security. . . .
> Now the first type of risk is, in a sense, a real social cost, though susceptible to diminution by averaging as well as by an increased accuracy of foresight. The second, however, is a pure addition to the cost of investment which would not exist if the borrower and lender were the same person.

Keynes's last sentence is not devoid of ambiguity: How does a borrower *know* he will be honest? Did the young bank teller know when he entered employment that he was going to abscond to Brazil in seven years? But let such things be known. Then the difference in risks is clearly due to information costs. The lender cannot afford to acquire the information to subclassify a given borrower into a more homogeneous risk class, and so this borrower is grouped with a higher-risk man. The lender may not be distinguishing sufficiently among borrowers—meaning that additional investment in collecting information would be profitable—but such mistakes aside, the difference between the lender's and the borrower's estimates of risk is strictly analogous to difference in price due to transportation costs.

IV. CONCLUSION

The efficiency of markets should be of great interest to the economist: Economic theory is concerned with markets much more than with factories or kitchens. It is, therefore, a source of embarrassment that so little attention has been paid to the theory of markets and that little chiefly to speculation. Our condemnation of the easy use of imperfections-in-the-capital-market is a plea for the study of markets, not a claim that capital markets are "perfect." We cannot possibly afford perfect markets, but we regulate real markets in many ways, and it would be desirable to know what these regulations are achieving.

The attribution of imperfections to markets has been an easy game because markets seldom have defenders. In fact, it is worse than that: the only markets with well-endowed defenders are those which are monopolistically organized and can afford the expense of a defender. I do not propose that economists appoint themselves defenders of markets, however; it is enough if they resign from the prosecution.

REFERENCES

BECKER, GARY. *Human Capital.* New York: National Bureau of Economic Research, 1964.

BLAKE, H. M., AND JONES, W. K. "In Defense of Antitrust," *Columbia Law Review,* Vol. LXV (1965), p. 392.

BUCHANAN, N. S. *The Economics of Corporate Enterprise.* New York: Henry Holt & Co., 1940.

COURNOT, A. A. *Mathematical Principles of the Theory of Wealth.* New York: Macmillan Co., 1927.

DAVIS, LANCE. "The Investment Market, 1870–1914: The Evolution of a National Market," *J. Econ. Hist.,* Vol. XXV (1963).

FRIEDMAN, MILTON, AND KUZNETS, S. *Income from Independent Professional Practice.* New York: National Bureau of Economic Research, 1945.

HART, A. G. "Assets, Liquidity, and Investment," *Proc. American Econ. Assoc.* (May, 1949), p. 171.

JONES, ELIOT. *The Trust Problem in the United States.* New York: Macmillan Co., 1921.

KEYNES, J. M. *The General Theory of Employment, Interest and Money.* London: Macmillan Co., 1936.

LEWIS, W. A. *The Theory of Economic Growth* (Homewood, Ill.: Richard D. Irwin, Inc., 1955).

LOESCHER, S. M. *Imperfect Collusion in the Cement Industry.* Cambridge, Mass.: Harvard University Press, 1959.

McGEE, J. "Predatory Price Cutting," *J. Law and Econ.* (October 1958).

MACHLUP, F. *The Basing-Point System.* Philadelphia: Blakiston Co., 1949.

MARSHALL, A. *Principles of Economics.* New York: Macmillan Co., 1920.

NICHOLLS, W. H. *Price Policies in the Cigarette Industry.* Nashville, Tenn.: Vanderbilt Univ. Press, 1951.

PELTZMAN, SAM. "Entry into Commercial Banking," *J. Law and Econ.* (October 1965).

PIGOU, A. C. *The Economics of Welfare.* London: Macmillan Co., 1932.

RYAN, F. W. *Usury and Usury Laws.* Boston: Houghton Mifflin Co., 1924.

SCHULTZ, T. W. "Capital Rationing, Uncertainty, and Farm-Tenancy Reform," *J. Political Economy* (June 1940).

STIGLER, G. J. "Monopoly and Oligopoly by Merger," *American Economic Rev.*, Vol. XL (May 1950).

———. "Economics of Information," *J. Political Economy* (June 1961).

———. "Perfect Competition, Historically Contemplated," *ibid.* (February 1957). Reprinted in *Essays in the History of Economics*. Chicago: University of Chicago Press, 1965.

———. *The Theory of Price*. 3d ed. New York: Macmillan Co., 1966.

WEST, R. "New Issue Concessions on Municipal Bonds," *J. Business*, Vol. XXXVIII (April 1965).

Chapter II

A NOTE ON PATENTS

The production of knowledge (a compact, high-power, long-life battery, say) differs from the production of a factory building or other common investment goods in three respects:

1. The (economic) outcome of research expenditures is more uncertain than the outcome of expenditures on a building.
2. The knowledge, once produced, is usually or at least often cheaply appropriable by any other enterprise which wishes to use it, in the absence of legal barriers to appropriation.
3. If the producer is given sole possession of the knowledge, a monopoly position is conferred. There may be 100 or 1,000 similar factories, but there are not (at one time) 1,000 discoverable different storage batteries, and possibly not two.

Of course, each of these differences between the production of knowledge and tangible capital goods is a matter of degree. The difference of degree may even be minor for the uncertainty of outcome, since much new knowledge is produced to order and many tangible investments have highly uncertain economic outcomes. The difference in appropriability is larger, and that in the prospects for monopoly larger still, and we concentrate upon these two differences.

The ease with which many pieces of new knowledge may be appropriated by others presents at times a severe challenge to the owner of the knowledge in enforcing his exclusive rights. If the product carries the knowledge to every buyer, or if the process is capable of clandestine use, the producer of the knowledge may get only a small portion of its yield. The costs of enforcing patent rights probably have a significant influence upon the directions and nature of research.

The small costs of dissemination of knowledge once it is produced likens the production of knowledge to that of bridges—with the difference that wide use of the knowledge does not lead to congestion. The economist who favors the free use of an uncongested bridge because the

123

marginal cost of another passenger is zero therefore favors also the free use of new knowledge. In one respect the case is even stronger for free use of knowledge: knowledge is probably even more lumpy than bridges —one can build a bridge that will handle only 1,000 persons a day, I suppose, so an uncongested bridge is usually an error in prediction. No such capacity limit resides in knowledge of the reduction of bauxite or the making of a storage battery.

One could therefore argue that inventors should be rewarded by lump-sum grants rather than by exclusive ownership in order to permit the socially desirable unlimited use of knowledge. If a viable system of lump-sum grants equal to the contribution of a piece of knowledge to the national income (or welfare) could be devised, there would be a good case for using that system rather than patents. The difficulties of devising even remotely objective estimates of the social value of pieces of knowledge are prodigious, however.

The main theoretical question posed in the production of knowledge, however, is how to bring about the correct amount of resources in the search for new knowledge. Does our present patent system with its 17-year grant of exclusive possession of the knowledge bring forth approximately the right amount of research effort?

We normally give perpetual possession of a piece of capital to its maker and his heirs. The reason is simple: the marginal social product is the sum of *all* future yields of the piece of capital, and if capital is to be produced privately to where its marginal social product equals its marginal cost, the owner must receive all future yields. Why not the same rule for the producer of new knowledge?

The traditional formal answer, I assume, is that the new knowledge is usually sold monopolistically rather than competitively. The inventor of the safety razor does not have to compete with 500 equally attractive other new ways to shave, so he may charge a monopoly price for his razor. Note at once that this does not imply that inventors will do better on their investments in producing knowledge than other entrepreneurs do in producing tangible assets. The prospects of monopoly pricing will lead to such a scale of investment in producing knowledge that it will return only the competitive rate of return on average. Thus with a perpetual patent system too many resources would go into research and innovation, in this sense: the monopolistic sale of new knowledge would yield the same rate of return on resources as the competitive sale of other investment goods. How much overinvestment perpetual patents would incite is a question of how much monopoly the patentee on average obtains.

The fixed term of 17 years, then, operates to reduce the rewards of a patent system more nearly to those of a competitive exploitation of new knowledge. If we use a 10 percent interest rate, a 17-year annuity is worth 80 percent of a perpetuity, so implicitly our patent system assesses the overstimulation of perpetual patents at about 25 percent (that is 2.5 percent on capital) above competitive rates of return.

The monopoly element in copyrights is no doubt smaller: only a really rare author will sell after 20 years. Our 56-year patent system, by the same annuity calculation, estimates the monopoly exploitation of a copyright to be about 0.5 percent above the competitive level. A reasonable figure.

PART III

Topics in Market Behavior

The shotgun pattern of the essays in this section cannot be concealed or even well disguised.

Chapter 12

THE DIVISION OF LABOR IS LIMITED BY THE EXTENT OF THE MARKET*

Economists have long labored with the rate of operation of firm and industry, but they have generally treated as a (technological?) datum the problem of what the firm does—what governs its range of range of activities or functions. It is the central thesis of this paper that the theorem of Adam Smith which has been appropriated as a title is the core of a theory of the functions of firm and industry, and a good deal more besides. I shall (1) make some brief historical remarks on the theorem, (2) sketch a theory of the functions of a firm, (3) apply this theory to vertical integration, and (4) suggest broader applications of the theorem.

I. HISTORICAL INTRODUCTION

When Adam Smith advanced his famous theorem that the division of labor is limited by the extent of the market, he created at least a superficial dilemma. If this proposition is generally applicable, should there not be monopolies in most industries? So long as the further division of labor (by which we may understand the further specialization of labor and machines) offers lower costs for larger outputs, entrepreneurs will gain by combining or expanding and driving out rivals. And here was the dilemma: Either the division of labor is limited by the extent of the market, and, characteristically, industries are monopolized; or industries are characteristically competitive, and the theorem is false or of little significance. Neither alternative is inviting. There were and are plenty of important competitive industries; yet Smith's argument that Highlanders would be more efficient if each did not have to do his own baking and brewing also seems convincing and capable of wide generalization.

In the pleasant century that followed on the *Wealth of Nations*,

* Reprinted from *Journal of Political Economy*, Vol. LIX, No. 3 (June 1951).

this conflict was temporarily resolved in favor of Smith's theorem by the simple expedient of ignoring the conditions for stable competitive equilibrium. Ricardo, Senior, and J. S. Mill—and their less famous confreres—announced the principle of increasing returns in manufacturing—for Senior it was even an axiom. The exclusion of agriculture was based on the empirical judgment, not that further division of labor was impossible, but that it was a weaker tendency than that of diminishing returns from more intensive cultivation of a relatively fixed supply of land.

This was hardly a satisfactory solution, and, when Marshall came to reformulate classical economics into a comprehensive and internally consistent system, the dilemma could no longer be ignored. He refused to give up either increasing returns or competition, and he created three theories (of course, not only for this purpose) which insured their compatibility. First, and perhaps most important, he developed the concept of external economies—economies outside the reach of the firm and dependent upon the size of the industry, the region, the economy, or even the whole economic world. Second, he emphasized the mortality of able entrepreneurs and the improbability that a single business would be managed superlatively for any length of time. Third, he argued that each firm might have a partial monopoly—a separate, elastic demand curve for its product—so that, with expansion of its output, the price would usually fall faster than average costs.

For a time this reconciliation of competition and increasing returns served its purpose, but, as the center of price theory moved toward the firm, Smith's theorem fell into the background. External economies were a rather nebulous category relative to anything so concrete and definite as economists for a time believed the costs of a firm to be. It was pointed out by Professor Knight, moreover, that economies external to one industry may (and perhaps must) be internal to another. The industries in which the economies are internal will tend to monopoly; and, incidentally, it is no longer a foregone conclusion that such economies will be shared with the buyers. Since external economies seemed a refractory material for the popular analytical techniques, they were increasingly neglected.

Marshall's theory of business mortality was also increasingly neglected, with even less explicit consideration. It was not an approach that harmonized well with the economics of a stationary economy, and again the theory was very inconvenient to incorporate into cost and demand curves (especially if one will not use the concept of a representative firm). If the economies of scale within the firm were as strong as Marshall pictured them, moreover, it was not clear that continuously high-quality entrepreneurship was necessary to achieve monopoly. And could the giant firm not grow quickly by merger as well as hesitantly by internal expansion?

Marshall's third theory, of the falling demand curve for the individual firm, lost popularity for a generation because it was incompatible with perfect competition rigorously defined, and this became increasingly the standard model of analysis. And, paradoxically, when the falling demand curve was rediscovered and popularized in the 1930's by the proponents of imperfect and monopolistic competition, they used it not to examine the broad movements of industries and of economies but to focus price theory on the physiology and pathology of the firm.

In 1928, to retrace a step, the neglect of increasing returns had gone so far that Allyn Young felt the need to restore perspective by an emphatic indorsement of the fundamental importance of Smith's theorem: "That theorem, I have always thought, is one of the most illuminating and fruitful generalizations which can be found anywhere in the whole literature of economics."[1] His position seemed persuasive, but he did not resolve the technical difficulties of incorporating the extent of the market into competitive price theory. Indeed, he openly avoided this problem, asserting that the firm and perhaps also the industry were too small to serve as units of analysis in this area. And so, although Young's and Marshall's and Smith's position is often given lip service to this day, the tributes are tokens of veneration, not evidences of active partnership with the theory of the firm and the competitive industry.

II. THE FUNCTIONS OF A FIRM

The firm is usually viewed as purchasing a series of inputs, from which it obtains one or more salable products, the quantities of which are related to the quantities of the inputs by a production function. For our purpose it is better to view the firm as engaging in a series of distinct operations: purchasing and storing materials; transforming materials into semifinished products and semifinished products into finished products; storing and selling the outputs; extending credit to buyers; etc. That is, we partition the firm not among the markets in which it buys inputs but among the functions or processes which constitute the scope of its activity.

The costs of these individual functions will be related by technology. The cost of one function may depend upon whether the preceding

[1] "Increasing Returns and Economic Progress," *Economic Journal*, XXXVIII (1928), 529.

function took place immediately before or in the immediate vicinity, as when hot ingots are processed with a saving of heat. Or the interrelationships among processes may be remote, as when the entrepreneur must neglect production in order to supervise marketing.

Let us ignore for a moment these interrelationships of costs of various functions, in order to achieve a simple geometrical picture of the firm's costs of production. If the cost of each function depends only on

FIGURE 12–1

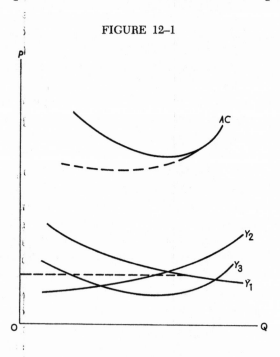

the rate of output of that function, we may draw a unique cost curve for it. Furthermore, if there is a constant proportion between the rate of output of each function and the rate of output of the final product (as when every 100 pounds of cement is bagged), we may draw the cost curves of all functions on one graph, and the (vertical) sum of these costs of various functions will be the conventional average-cost curve of the firm.

We should expect to find many different patterns of average costs of functions: some falling continuously (Y_1); some rising continuously (Y_2); some conventionally U-shaped (Y_3) (see Fig. 12–1). It is not impossible, of course, that the average cost of some operations first rises and then falls.

Now consider Smith's theorem. Certain processes are subject to increasing returns; why does the firm not exploit them further and in the process become a monopoly? Because there are other functions subject to diminishing returns, and these are, on balance, at least so costly that average cost of the final product does not diminish with output. Then why does the firm not abandon the functions subject to increasing returns, allowing another firm (and industry) to specialize in them to take full advantage of increasing returns? At a given time these functions may be too small to support a specialized firm or firms. The sales of the product may be too small to support a specialized merchant; the output of a by-product may be too small to support a specialized fabricator; the demand for market information may be too small to support a trade journal. The firm must then perform these functions for itself.

But, with the expansion of the industry, the magnitude of the function subject to increasing returns may become sufficient to permit a firm to specialize in performing it. The firms will then abandon the process (Y_1), and a new firm will take it over. This new firm will be a monopoly, but it will be confronted by elastic demands: it cannot charge a price for the process higher than the average cost of the process to the firms which are abandoning it. With the continued expansion of the industry, the number of firms supplying process Y_1 will increase, so that the new industry becomes competitive and the new industry may, in turn, abandon parts of process Y_1 to a new set of specialists.

The abandonment of function Y_1 by the original industry will alter each firm's cost curves: the curve Y_1 will be replaced by a horizontal line (ignoring quantity discounts) at a level lower than Y_1 in the effective region. The cost curve of the product (drawn with broken lines in Fig. 12–1) will be lower, and, on present assumptions, the output at which average costs are a minimum (if only one such output exists) becomes smaller.

Certain functions are also subject to increasing cost; why not abandon or at least restrict the scale of operation of these functions? The foregoing discussion is also applicable here, with one change. When the industry grows, the original firms need not wholly abandon the increasing-cost processes. Part of the required amount of the process (say, engine castings for automobiles) may be made within the firm without high average (or marginal) costs, and the remainder purchased from subsidiary industries.

In order to give a simple geometrical illustration, we have made two assumptions. The first is that the rate of output of the process and the rate of output of the final product are strictly proportional. This will be approximately true of some functions (such as making parts of a single final product), but it will also be untrue of other functions (such as advertising the product). If we drop the assumption, the substance of our argument will not be affected, but our geometrical picture becomes more complicated.[2]

Our second assumption, that the costs of the functions are independent, is more important. Actually, many processes will be rival: the greater the rate of output of one process, the higher the cost of a given rate of output of the other process or processes. Sometimes the rivalry will be technological (as in many multiple-product firms), but almost always it will also be managerial: the wider the range of functions the firm undertakes, the greater the tasks of coordination. Other processes will be complementary: the greater the rate of output of one process, the lower the cost of a given rate of output of the other processes. A most curious example of complementarity is the circular flow of materials within a plant; thus, in the course of making steel, steel plants supply a large part of their requirements for scrap.

If, on balance, the functions are rival, then usually the firm will increase its rate of output of the final product when it abandons a function; and I think that this is generally the case. For example, in the famous study of the Lancashire textile industry by Chapman and Ashton, it was found that firms engaged in both spinning and weaving in 1911 had, on average, 47,634 spindles, while those engaged only in spinning had, on average, 68,055 spindles.[3] But this is not necessary—indeed, they found the converse relationship in number of looms—and the effect of the range of functions on the size of the firm requires much study before we can reach safe generalizations.

III. VERTICAL INTEGRATION

Many economists believe that, with the growth of firms (and industries?), functions are usually taken over from previous independent industries. For example, United States Steel Corporation now mines its ores, operates its own ore-hauling railroads and ships, and, at the other

---

[2] We can either draw separate cost curves for the various functions or combine them on one chart, with the scales of the functions chosen so that the optimum amount of each function is shown for the given rate of final output.

[3] S. J. Chapman and T. S. Ashton, "The Sizes of Businesses, Mainly in the Textile Industries," *Journal of the Royal Statistical Society*, Vol. LXXVII (1914), p. 538.

end, fabricates barrels, oil-field equipment, and houses. (The number of economic views based chiefly on half-a-dozen giant corporations would repay morbid study.)

Broadly viewed, Smith's theorem suggests that vertical disintegration is the typical development in growing industries, vertical integration in declining industries.[4] The significance of the theorem can therefore be tested by an appeal to the facts on vertical integration.

Unfortunately, there are no wholly conclusive data on the trend of vertical integration. The only large-scale quantitative information at hand comes from a comparison of the 1919 study by Willard Thorp with the 1937 study by Walter Crowder of central offices (companies with two or more manufacturing establishments). In 1919, 602 manufacturing companies, or 13.0 percent of a moderately complete list of 4,635 companies, had two or more establishments making successive products, that is, the product of one establishment was the raw material of another establishment.[5] In 1937, successive functions were found in 565 companies (or 10.0 percent of a more complete list of 5,625 companies).[6] In 1919, successive functions were found in 34.4 percent of all complex central offices (companies with establishments in two or more industries); in 1937, in only 27.5 percent. Multiplant companies probably grew in relative importance during this period, so it is possible that a larger share of manufacturing output came from vertically integrated firms. But, so far as these multiplant companies are concerned, there seems to have been a tendency away from vertical integration.[7]

If one considers the full life of industries, the dominance of vertical disintegration is surely to be expected. Young industries are often strangers to the established economic system. They require new kinds or

[4] This is not a wholly rigorous implication, however. With the growth of industries, specialism of firms may take the form of dealing with a narrower range of products as well as performing fewer functions on the same range of products.

[5] W. Thorp, *The Integration of Industrial Operation* (Washington, D.C., 1924), p. 238. I have omitted railroad repair shops and also the 301 companies having establishments which made successive products, because mining establishments were included.

[6] W. F. Crowder, *The Integration of Manufacturing Operations* ("T.N.E.C. Monographs," No. 27 [Washington, D.C., 1941]), p. 197.

[7] The ratio of "value-added" to value of product is a crude index of the extent of vertical integration *within* establishments. It is interesting to note that in the 17 industries in which this ratio was highest in 1939 in manufacturing, the average number of wage-earners was 16,540. In the 17 industries in which the ratio was lowest, the average number of wage-earners was 44,449. Thus the vertically integrated establishments were in smaller industries than the vertically disintegrated establishments (see National Resources Planning Board, *Industrial Location and National Resources* [Washington, D.C., 1943], p. 270).

qualities of materials and hence make their own; they must overcome technical problems in the use of their products and cannot wait for potential users to overcome them; they must persuade customers to abandon other commodities and find no specialized merchants to undertake this task. These young industries must design their specialized equipment and often manufacture it, and they must undertake to recruit (historically, often to import) skilled labor. When the industry has attained a certain size and prospects, many of these tasks are sufficiently important to be turned over to specialists. It becomes profitable for other firms to supply equipment and raw materials, to undertake the marketing of the product and the utilization of by-products, and even to train skilled labor. And, finally, when the industry begins to decline these subsidiary, auxiliary, and complementary industries begin also to decline, and eventually the surviving firms must begin to reappropriate functions which are no longer carried on at a sufficient rate to support independent firms.

We may illustrate this general development from the cotton textile machinery industry, much of whose history has recently become available.[8] This industry began as a part of the textile industry: each mill built a machine shop to construct and repair its machines. The subsequent history is one of progressive specialism, horizontal as well as vertical: at various times locomotives, machine tools, the designing of cotton mills, and direct selling were abandoned. When the cotton textile market declined in the 1920's, the machinery firms added new products, such as paper machinery, textile machinery for other fabrics, and wholly novel products, such as oil burners and refrigerators. Indeed, one is impressed that even the longer cyclical fluctuations seem to have affected the extent of specialism in much the same way as have the secular trends.

Of course, this is not the whole story of vertical integration, and it may be useful to sketch some of the other forces at work. The most important of these other forces, I believe, is the failure of the price system (because of monopoly or public regulation) to clear markets at prices within the limits of the marginal cost of the product (to the buyer if he makes it) and its marginal-value product (to the seller if he further fabricates it). This phenomenon was strikingly illustrated by the spate of vertical mergers in the United States during and immediately after World War II, to circumvent public and private price control and allocations. A regulated price of OA was set (Fig. 12–2), at which an output

---

[8] G. S. Gibb, *The Saco-Lowell Shops* (Cambridge, Mass.: Harvard University Press, 1950); T. R. Navin, *The Whitin Machine Works since 1831* (Cambridge, Mass.: Harvard University Press, 1950).

of *OM* was produced. This quantity had a marginal value of *OB* to buyers, who were rationed on a nonprice basis. The gain to buyers and sellers combined from a free price of *NS* was the shaded area, *RST*, and vertical integration was the simple way of obtaining this gain. This was the rationale of the integration of radio manufacturers into cabinet manufacture, of steel firms into fabricated products, etc.

FIGURE 12–2

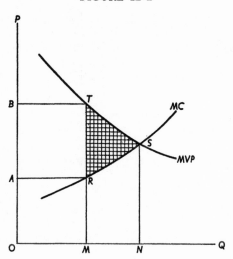

Although nonprice rationing provides the most striking examples of this force toward vertical integration, private monopolies normally supply the same incentive. Almost every raw-material cartel has had trouble with customers who wish to integrate backward, in order to negate the cartel prices. Since the cartel members are sharply limited in their output quotas, the discounted future profits of a cartel member need not be high, even with very high prices; so it is profitable for buyers to integrate backward by purchase (as well as by seeking noncartelized supply sources). The Rhenish-Westphalian Coal Cartel, for example, was constantly plagued by this problem:

> While a few of the members of the original syndicate agreement of 1893 had been steel companies which produced a part of their own coal and coke requirements, the steel industry, for the most part, had relied upon fuel purchased in the market. The stiffening of prices, coupled with the inelastic terms of sale resulting from the operation of the coal syndicate, now caused the steel companies to seek to free themselves from dependence upon the syndicate.
> . . . defensive measures were adopted by all classes of consumers. Some

of the large industrial consumers . . . acquired their own mines individually or in groups. Among these were such important companies as the Vereinigte Stahlwerke, Rhenische Stahlwerk-Admiral, Badische Anilin- und Sodafabrik, Norddeutsche Lloyd, Friedrich Krupp, and a number of others representing the electric, gas, railway equipment, rubber and other industries. Also some cities such as Cologne and Frankfurt were among them.[9]

Monopoly is a devious thing, and it leads to vertical integration for other reasons also. A firm cannot practice price discrimination in the stages in which it does not operate; only by fabricating cable could the Aluminum Company of America sell cable at less than the ingot price in competition with copper, while maintaining a higher price on less competitive products.[10] Again, it is possible that vertical integration increases the difficulty of entry by new firms, by increasing the capital and knowledge necessary to conduct several types of operation rather than depend on rivals for supplies or markets.

These remarks are not intended to constitute a theory of vertical integration. There is doubt, indeed, that we want a theory of vertical integration except as part of a theory of the functions of a firm. As soon as one tries to classify the variegated details of production, one finds how artificial and arbitrary "vertical" relationships are. Whether one wishes to treat vertical relationships separately or as part of a general theory, however, Smith's theorem promises to be a central part of the explanation.

IV. WIDER IMPLICATIONS

If Smith's theorem is less than a complete theory of the division of functions among industries, it is also something more than this: it sheds light on several aspects of the structure and workings of economies. A few of the implications of the principle of increasing specialization will be discussed very tentatively.

One expects to find some relationship between the functional structure of an industry and its geographical structure—after all, reductions of transportation costs are a major way of increasing the extent of the market. (A remainder is hardly necessary that we are dealing with highly interdependent forces and that unilateral causation is implicitly assumed for simplicity and emphasis.) Localization is one method of increasing the economic size of an industry and achieving the gains of specialization.

[9] A. H. Stockder, *Regulating an Industry* (New York, 1932), pp. 8, 11, and 36.

[10] D. H. Wallace, *Market Control in the Aluminum Industry* (Cambridge, Mass.: Harvard University Press, 1937), pp. 218–19, 380.

The auxiliary and complementary industries that must operate in intimate cooperation can seldom do so efficiently at a distance. I venture that, within a market area, geographical dispersion is a luxury that can be afforded by industries only after they have grown large (so that even the smaller production centers can reap the major gains of specialization) and that it must be sacrificed for geographical concentration, once the industry begins to shrink in size.

Closely related to this is the influence of localization upon the size of plant. The individual plants can specialize in smaller ranges of products and functions in highly localized industries (the size of the industry in some sense being held constant). In the United States geographically concentrated industries usually have fairly small plants,[11] There is also some evidence that the plants of an industry are smaller in the larger production centers. For example, in 1937 the average shoe factory in industrial areas had 137 employees, in other areas, 314 employees.[12] The dominance of medium-sized plants in highly localized industries has also been found in England.[13]

During the nineteenth century it was often said that England had the advantage of an "early start"; and this ambiguous statement had an element of truth which Smith's theorem more clearly expresses. As the largest economy in the world, it could carry specialism further than any other country, especially those "general" specialties (like railroads, shipping, banking, etc.) which are not closely attached to any one industry. England's advantage was a big start, as well as an early one.

Those too numerous people who believe that transactions between firms are expensive and those within firms are free will do well to study the organization of England during this period of eminence. In Birmingham, the center of the metal trades, specialism was carried out to an almost unbelievable extent. Consider the small-arms industry in 1860, when Birmingham was still the leading production center of the world:

Of the 5800 people engaged in this manufacture within the borough's boundaries in 1861 the majority worked within a small district round St Mary's Church. . . . The reason for the high degree of localization is not difficult to discover. The manufacture of guns, as of jewellery, was carried on by a large number of makers who specialized on particular processes, and this method of organization involved the frequent transport of parts from one workshop to another.

[11] National Resources Planning Board, *op. cit.*, pp. 250 ff.
[12] *Ibid.*, p. 257.
[13] P. S. Florence, *Investment, Location, and Size of Plant* (London: Cambridge University Press, 1948).

The master gun-maker—the entrepreneur—seldom possessed a factory or workshop. . . . Usually he owned merely a warehouse in the gun quarter, and his function was to acquire semi-finished parts and to give these out to specialized craftsmen, who undertook the assembly and finishing of the gun. He purchased materials from the barrel-makers, lock-makers, sight-stampers, trigger-makers, ramrod-forgers, gun-furniture makers, and, if he were engaged in the military branch, from bayonet-forgers. All of these were independent manufacturers executing the orders of several master gun-makers. . . . Once the parts had been purchased from the "material-makers," as they were called, the next task was to hand them out to a long succession of "setters-up," each of whom performed a specific operation in connection with the assembly and finishing of the gun. To name only a few, there were those who prepared the front sight and lump end of the barrels; the jiggers, who attended to the breech end; the stockers, who let in the barrel and lock and shaped the stock; the barrel-strippers, who prepared the gun for rifling and proof; the hardeners, polishers, borers and riflers, engravers, browners, and finally the lock-freers, who adjusted the working parts.[14]

At present there is widespread imitation of American production methods abroad, and "backward" countries are presumably being supplied with our latest machines and methods. By a now overly familiar argument, we shall often be a seriously inappropriate model for industrialization on a small scale. Our processes will be too specialized to be economical on this basis. The vast network of auxiliary industries which we can take for granted here will not be available in small economies. Their educational institutions will be unable to supply narrowly specialized personnel; they will lack the specialists who can improve raw materials and products. At best, the small economies that imitate us can follow our methods of doing things this year, not our methods of changing things next year; therefore, they will be very rigid. This position has been stated well by one observant citizen of a backward economy, Benjamin Franklin:

Manufactures, where they are in perfection, are carried on by a multiplicity of hands, each of which is expert only in his own part, no one of them a master of the whole; and if by any means spirited away to a foreign country, he is lost without his fellows. Then it is a matter of extremest difficulty to

---

[14] G. C. Allen, *The Industrial Development of Birmingham and the Black Country, 1860–1927* (London, 1929), pp. 56–57, 116–17. Commenting on a later period, Allen says: "On the whole, it can be said that specialization was most apparent in the engineering industries in which output was rapidly expanding; while the policy of broadening the basis [product line] was found, mainly, either in the very large concerns, or in industries in which the decline of the older markets had forced manufacturers to turn part of their productive capacity to serve new demands" (*ibid.*, pp. 335–36). The later history of the gun trade, in which American innovations in production techniques were revolutionary, suggest that the organization in Birmingham was defective in its provision for technical experimentation.

persuade a complete set of workmen, skilled in all parts of a manufactory, to leave their country together and settle in a foreign land. Some of the idle and drunken may be enticed away, but these only disappoint their employers, and serve to discourage the undertaking. If by royal munificence, and an expense that the profits of the trade alone would not bear, a complete set of good and skilful hands are collected and carried over, they find so much of the system imperfect, so many things wanting to carry on the trade to advantage, so many difficulties to overcome, and the knot of hands so easily broken by death, dissatisfaction, and desertion, that they and their employers are discouraged altogether, and the project vanishes into smoke.[15]

The division of labor is not a quaint practice of eighteenth-century pin factories; it is a fundamental principle of economic organization.

[Reference should have been, and now is, made to R. H. Coase, "The Nature of the Firm," *Economica*, 1937, reprinted in George J. Stigler and Kenneth E. Boulding (eds.), *Readings in Price Theory* (Homewood, Ill.: Richard D. Irwin, Inc., 1952).]

[15] "The Interest of Great Britain in America," cited by V. S. Clark, *History of Manufactures in the United States* (New York, 1949), I, 152. Clark adds: "In these words Franklin was but reciting the history of the more important colonial attempts to establish a new industry or to enlarge an old one with which he was personally familiar."

Chapter 13

A NOTE ON PROFITABILITY, COMPETITION, AND CONCENTRATION

The firms in a competitive industry expect to earn at least as much in the industry as they could earn elsewhere, or they would leave the industry. They will not expect to earn more because if earnings were higher their rivals would expand (if there were no diseconomies of scale) or new firms would enter. A monopolistic firm has the same minimum rate of earnings—it too can migrate to another industry.[1] If competition is leashed, however, the firm may earn a higher than competitive rate of return for a time or permanently. If investments are guided by reasonably good foresight, the average rate of return should be higher in monopolistic than in competitive industries.

Rates of return will also differ among industries for a second reason: industries are not always in equilibrium. Presumably, if our data on rates of return cover enough industries and time, the effects of disequilibrium (which can go in either direction) will become small, but the obscuring effect of such disturbances is usually substantial. If the impact of disequilibrium upon rates of return is as large as the impact of monopoly, the coefficient of correlation between rates of return and monopoly is reduced by 30 percent.[2]

All empirical studies are plagued also by imperfections in the data

---

[1] There are many nonexistent monopolies available for the asking—water companies in hamlets, for example.

[2] Let C_i be the true concentration level of industry i, and in equilibrium perfectly correlated with its monopoly power and monopoly profit. Let π_i, the actual rate of return, reflect also disequilibrium, so:

$$\pi_i = a + bc_i + u_i$$

where u_i is the disequilibrium effect. Then it can be shown that

$$r_{\pi c}^2 = \frac{b^2 \sigma_c^2}{b^2 \sigma_c^2 + \sigma_u^2}$$

and if $b^2 \sigma_c^2 = \sigma_u^2$, $r^2 = .5$ and $r = .707$.

If c and u are positively correlated, $r_{\pi c}$ is reduced all the more.

on rates of return. Three important examples will suffice to illustrate the limitations. Inflation makes historical costs, and depreciation based upon historical costs, obsolete. The returns in industries which have relatively durable assets, and in industries with relatively old assets, will be overstated relative to industries with the opposite characteristics. Again, certain expenditures—chiefly on research and advertising—yield returns over a period of years but are commonly charged off completely in the year in which they are made, so income and assets are both understated. If these expenditures are steady at a level just maintaining the assets (so expenditures equal depreciation), then assets are too small and reported rates of return too high. Finally, in small corporations which are owned by the officers, it is to their advantage to withdraw income as wages rather than as dividends because no corporation income tax need be paid on the wages (and the personal income tax is the same on wages and dividends). This third factor is associated with concentration (as the other imperfections may not be) because these small companies are important only in unconcentrated industries.[3]

On a different footing is the problem that the data on profits may be *too* good. If I create, by shrewdness or luck, a monopoly which yields 20 percent on my original investment, it is really worth twice its original cost if the appropriate rate of return is 10 percent. If I sell the monopoly, the buyer will earn only 10 percent upon *his* cost and there will appear to be no monopoly return. Accountants do not generally record such changes in valuation—they are opposed to including intangibles such as monopoly power and goodwill among the assets—but to the extent that they allow such perfectly valid market prices of assets, monopoly profits vanish.

The translation into numbers of the proposition that under competition there is a tendency for the rate of returns to approach equality is not a simple task. We have listed two reasons why, at any given time, rates of return may differ among competitive industries: the industries may be in disequilibrium (because it takes time to learn of rates of return and to leave one field and enter another), and the rates of return may be improperly reported. A third reason may be added: the rates of return that should approach equality allow for all advantages and dis-

---

[3] In my *Capital and Rates of Return in Manufacturing Industries* (New York, 1963), pp. 59–60, 67–69, an estimate is made of the effect of officer withdrawals in rates of return in concentrated and unconcentrated industries. Of the reported difference between concentrated and unconcentrated industries of 0.84 percent in 1949–54, about 0.8 percent was attributed to this factor.

advantages, so if industry A is much riskier than B, and men dislike risk, they must earn a higher average rate in A than B to compensate.

The average rates of return in unconcentrated manufacturing industries in 1955, 1956, and 1957 are tabulated in Table 13–1.[4] The average of the three years is of course more compact than that of any one year, but even if we lengthened the period to a hundred years the dispersion

TABLE 13–1

DISTRIBUTION OF RATES OF RETURN ON CAPITAL IN UNCONCENTRATED
MANUFACTURING INDUSTRIES, 1955–57*

($N = 55$)

Rate of Return (%)	Number of Industries			Average 1955–57
	1955	1956	1957	
−4 to −3			1	
−3 to −2			—	
−2 to −1	1	1	—	
−1 to 0	1	—	1	1
0 to 1	1	1	—	1
1 to 2	—	—	4	2
2 to 3	1	2	4	3
3 to 4	7	8	11	9
4 to 5	9	11	9	8
5 to 6	10	7	8	7
6 to 7	7	8	9	10
7 to 8	11	6	5	9
8 to 9	6	8	2	4
9 to 10	1	2	1	1
10 to 11			—	
11 to 12			1	
Mean	5.63	5.74	4.68	4.66
Standard deviation	2.24	2.35	2.32	2.02

* Data from George J. Stigler, *Capital and Rates of Return in Manufacturing Industries* (New York, 1963), Appendices B–1 and C–2.

among rates of return would not vanish. Quite aside from deficiencies in the data, there is no assurance that the entrepreneurs in each industry will on average predict correctly all the changes in supply and demand conditions. If the distribution were, say, bimodal (with two concentrations of industries around 5 or 10 percent) we would reject the classical proposition on rates of return approaching equality, but dispersion alone will not support a rejection.

A more illuminating way to look at the classical proposition is to ask: how long does it take, on average, for differences in rates of return

[4] An industry is defined as unconcentrated if it has a national market and a concentration ratio (for the four largest firms) under 50 percent, or a regional market and a concentration ratio under 20 percent.

among industries to vanish? Suppose we know the rates of return in the manufacturing industries of Table 13–1 in 1955. Will this pattern help to explain the pattern of rates among industries in 1956? Surely yes: differences in rates due to disequilibrium will not be removed immediately, it may require several years for firms in broad wool goods (who *lost* 1.51 percent on capital in 1955) to shift to dyeing and finishing of textiles (which earned 5.85 percent in 1955). In fact, the correlation of 1955 with 1956 rates was .80 and of 1956 with 1957 rates it was .78. But if competition is doing its work, on average these patterns will disappear after a time. The quicker the correlations go to zero, the greater the mobility of resources in response to differences in profitability. On average the correlations are close to zero after about five years: on average with a knowledge only of the rates of return in year t, one can explain more than half the variation in rates of return among industries in year $(t + 1)$ (i.e., $r^2 > .5$) but one can explain less than one-tenth of the variation in rates in year $(t + 5)$ (i.e., $r^2 < .1$). Hence the period within which given inequalities in rates of return among industries are essentially eliminated is perhaps five years—but of course varies with the cost of movement of capital.

A substantial number of investigations have been made of the relationship between concentration and rates of return.[5] The results are surprisingly consistent in two respects: a positive relationship is always found, and it is usually weak: not more than one half, and often less than one fifth, of the variance of rates of return among industries is accounted for by differences in concentration. The similarity of results is of course partly due to the use of the same or closely related data in the various studies. The disquieting feature is the fact that profitability is better

---

[5] The main studies are the following (in each case the number of industries and the correlation coefficient with a measure of profitability is given): J. S. Bain, "Relation of Profit Rate to Industry Competition", *Quarterly Journal of Economics*, August 1951 ($n = 42$, $r = .28$); N. R. Collins and L. E. Preston, *Concentration and Price-Cost Margins in Manufacturing Industries*—forthcoming ($N = 20$, $r = .42$ to .70); V. Fuchs, "Integration, Concentration, and Profits in Manufacturing Industries," *Quarterly Journal of Economics*, May 1961 ($n = 38$, $r = .28$ to .42); F. Kottke, "The Relationship of Measurable Characteristics of Industry Structure and Experience to the Profitability of the Industry Leaders," unpublished ($n = 38$, $r = .46$); H. Levinson, "Postwar Movements of Prices and Wages in Manufacturing Industries" (Joint Economic Committee, 1960), ($n = 19$, $r = .37$ to .76); R. Miller, "Marginal Concentration Ratios and Industrial Profit Rates," *Southern Economic Journal*, October 1967 ($n = 106$, $r = .28$ to .34); G. Stigler, (1) *Capital and Rates of Return in Manufacturing Industries* (New York, 1963), pp. 67–69 ($n = 99$, $r = .19$ to .23); (2) "A Theory of Oligopoly," Chapter 5, above ($n = 17$, $r = .52$ to .73); L. W. Weiss, "Average Concentration Ratios and Industrial Performance," *Journal of Industrial Economics*, July 1963 ($n = 22$, $r = .73$).

correlated with crude industry measures (food) than with more sharply defined industries (canned fruits and vegetables).

Our theory of oligopoly suggests that for a given level of concentration, the probability of successful collusion is smaller, the fewer the buyers. A loose test of this is provided for manufacturing industries in Table 13–2. The industries had national markets, and their 1954 concen-

TABLE 13–2
PERCENTAGE RATES OF RETURN, 1953–55, AND NUMBER OF BUYERS

	Under 6	*6–8*	*Over 8*
Many buyers	Distilled liquor Sugar refining Carpets, yarn Agricultural machinery Motorcycles and bicycles	Tobacco except cigarettes Soaps and detergents Office machinery	Cereal preparations Motor vehicles Glass
Few buyers	Tires & tubes Smelting nonferrous metals Railroad equipment Miscellaneous electric goods	Tin cans Automotive electric equipment Industrial chemicals Engines and turbines	

Source: George J. Stigler, *Capital and Rates of Return in Manufacturing Industries* (New York, 1963).

tration ratios (4 leading firms) were over 50 percent. The number of buyers was generally determined by whether the commodity was a producer or consumer good (automobile tires were one exception: the automobile manufacturers and major retailers [such as mail order businesses] are major customers). The results are timidly helpful (although they do not meet the usual tests of significance): no high rate of return industries dealt with few buyers.

Chapter

14

A THEORY OF DELIVERED

PRICE SYSTEMS*

The debate over the merits and legality of basing point price systems began in the early 1920's and followed a leisurely course until April 26, 1948. On that day the Supreme Court outlawed the multiple basing point price system in cement, and the debate now became continuous and urgent, and sometimes disingenuous. The debate has been unusual in that the participants have commonly used the same, relatively undisputed facts to support opposite contentions. The crosshauling of products has been interpreted by one party as a by-product of innocent competition, by the other party as evidence of collusion. The absorption of freight has been used by one party as evidence of the desire of firms to compete, by the other party as evidence of price discrimination.

If it is true that controversy over basing point prices has sometimes manufactured uncertainty, it is also true that uncertainty among economists has encouraged the controversy. No economist, so far as I know, has yet offered a satisfactory explanation for the appearance of delivered price systems. One important branch of the literature, associated with the names of Fetter and Mund and with the Federal Trade Commission, argues that basing point prices are simply a device hit upon by conspiring oligopolists.[1] The other important branch of the literature, in which de Chazeau and J. M. Clark are prominent names, argues that the basing point price system is an inevitable or highly probable development in industries characterized by heavy fixed costs, cyclically unstable demands, and oligopoly. Neither group has explained why this particular system of marketing evolved (rather than possible alternative systems such as division of territory) nor has either group explained why other

* Reprinted from *American Economic Review,* Vol. XXXIX, No. 6 (December 1949).
[1] Professor F. Machlup's *The Basing-Point System* (Philadelphia: Blakiston, 1949) is also in this tradition. At several points he also touches on the fundamental element of the theory to be presented in this paper (pp. 165–66, 197, 211–12), as, indeed, do most of the writers on the subject.

industries which share the characteristics they stress have adopted f.o.b. and other pricing systems.[2]

If the explanation to be given here is correct, basing point prices represent a collusive oligopolistic policy which maximizes the oligopolists' profits under particular but not uncommon economic and legal conditions. I, therefore, accept the positive contentions of both groups and seek to reconcile them through a study of the detailed rationale of delivered price systems. After a preliminary discussion of terminology, the theory of uniform delivered prices will be sketched, tests of the theory will then be examined, and finally the major implications of the theory for economic policy will be drawn.

I. TYPES OF GEOGRAPHICAL PRICE SYSTEMS

The price a buyer pays for a delivered commodity may vary continuously with the distance of the point of delivery from the point of production, or it may vary discretely or not at all (zone price systems). The chief forms of price quotation that lead to continuously variable delivered prices are:

a) F.o.b. mill prices. The delivered price at any point equals the price at the production center at which the purchase is made plus the actual transportation charge to the point of delivery.

b) Freight equalization. The delivered price at any point equals the lowest sum of factory price plus transportation charges from any production center, even though the purchase is made at another production center.

c) Basing point. This system differs from freight equalization in that not all production centers quote mill prices.[3]

These distinctions are quantitative, and not generic. If transportation costs are a trifling fraction of delivered prices, all systems of variable delivered and zone prices merge.[4] If there are mill price quotations

---

[2] Professor A. Smithies, who falls in neither group, concluded that the basing point price system did not in general maximize profits and, indeed, that it was comprehensible only under special assumptions whose relevance to the basing point industries was not demonstrated and is not obvious. See "Aspects of the Basing Point Price System," *American Economic Review*, Vol. XXXII, No. 4 (December 1942), pp. 705–26.

[3] If one does not wish to treat importation points as production centers, a second general difference is that not all points of mill price quotation are production centers.

[4] Zone prices will also emerge in a continuously variable delivered price system if transportation costs do not vary continuously with distance: for example, in the late 'thirties Douglas fir had the same transportation cost from the Pacific Northwest to all points north of the Ohio River and east of Chicago, so equality of price in this

(basing points) at all important production centers, the distinction between freight equalization and basing point prices is unimportant. If the price at one mill is equal to that at the nearest mill plus transportation cost, the former price is noneffective and a basing point system is achieved. The fundamental distinction is between f.o.b. mill and delivered price systems when freight costs are an appreciable fraction of price, and we proceed now to establish analytical criteria for this distinction.[5]

Consider first the common situation in which there are two or more firms at a production center. A firm at this center can increase its sales, relative to what they would be if the firm adhered to the same f.o.b. mill price as its rivals, by two types of price reductions: first, by price reductions within the natural territory of the center (say, that defined by stable f.o.b. mill prices); and second, by absorbing freight in order to enter other production centers' territories. If the firm makes price reductions (reductions in mill-net prices) only or chiefly by absorbing freight, and never or seldom by reducing prices to customers in its natural territory, it is practicing what I shall term systematic freight absorption. If the firm frequently uses both price reductions within its territory and freight absorption, I shall term its behavior competitive.[6] If the firm seldom makes either form of price reduction, it is presumably a participant in an agreement to divide the market and fix the price.

If there is only one firm at a production center, it can take sales from other firms only by invading their natural territories. The preceding argument still applies, but it must be restricted to the sales in areas where two or more firms are selling: it is difficult to define competitive behavior in areas where there are no competitors. The hypothetical example in Table 14–1 will illustrate this case. If firm I practices systematic freight absorption, its mill-net price declines as it makes sales beyond its natural market limit (F); in the area of overlapping sales (say D to H) the only form of (mill-net) price reduction is through freight absorption. If the firm behaves competitively, it will reduce the delivered price at points where its mill-net price is highest (D to F in our example) in order to

---

region was consistent with f.o.b. mill pricing. Such exceptions are eliminated if we define distance as economic distance.

[5] Zone price systems will not be discussed; see, however, note 15, below.

[6] It would be inexplicable if the firm reduced its price (relative to that of its rivals) within its territory and yet failed to absorb freight on some sales.

If the firm behaves competitively, on the above definition, its prices are indistinguishable from f.o.b. mill prices. This definition of competition is identical with that of the neoclassical theory if the latter is amended (as it should be) to incorporate the fact that on all except completely centralized exchanges the competitive firm sells at different prices to different customers in a period of price change.

take sales away from Firm II, before it begins absorbing freight to enter H's natural territory; so in the area of overlapping sales, I's mill-net price will not vary systematically with the point of sale.

Both situations—one and several firms at a production center—can be summarized in one definition of systematic freight absorption. A firm is practising systematic freight absorption if, at the consuming points where it and one or more rivals are making sales, its mill-net price varies with the distance of the consuming point.

TABLE 14–1
NUMERICAL EXAMPLE OF SYSTEMATIC FREIGHT ABSORPTION
(Mill Prices: $50.00)

Consumption Point	Transportation Costs from		Delivered Price	Mill-Net Prices	
	Firm I	*Firm II*		*Firm I*	*Firm II*
A	$ 0	$10	$50	$50	$40
B	1	9	51	50	42
C	2	8	52	50	44
D	3	7	53	50	46
E	4	6	54	50	48
F	5	5	55	50	50
G	6	4	54	48	50
H	7	3	53	46	50
I	8	2	52	44	50
J	9	1	51	42	50
K	10	0	50	40	50

Systematic freight absorption occurs only under oligopoly. It involves price discrimination at the point of production and is therefore inconsistent with substantial competition: the mill-net price of a firm is less on sales made at delivered prices set by other mill prices (price bases) than on sales made on its own mill price, and under competition the firm would sell only or chiefly in the higher mill-net area.[7] Nor would a monopolist with spatially separated plants practice systematic freight absorption, for this would be irrational price discrimination. He would be

[7] This is seldom disputed except in partisan arguments, and then only with astonishing implicit definitions of competition. One all-too-common definition of competition in this context is the policy of maximizing profits! For example, "As has been pointed out, mills at a considerable distance from a basing point have a freight advantage over other mills in selling to buyers in the territory around their mills. They behave competitively and naturally when they charge their customers a price which realizes that advantage." (U.S. Steel Corporation, *The Basing Point Method of Quoting Delivered Prices in the Steel Industry*, T.N.E.C. Monograph No. 42, p. 66.)

varying his mill-net price, not in accordance with the elasticity of the buyer's demand, but on the basis of the selection of the plant from which to ship the order.

The desirability of this definition of systematic freight absorption (and the implicit definition of delivered price systems) must be judged by its usefulness. The definition clearly suggests that the formal method of price quotation is insufficient to classify an industry's geographical price system, and this is a source of difficulty in testing theories to which we shall return.

II. A THEORY OF. DELIVERED PRICES

The following analysis is restricted to industries in which (1) transportation costs are a substantial fraction of delivered price for many customers; (2) there are few firms (or few large firms) at a production center; and (3) these firms wish to (or are compelled to) collude. The firms in these industries must solve two problems: how to divide sales among the firms at each production center;[8] and how to divide sales among production centers—in such a way as to maximize the industry's profits.

The distribution of sales among firms at a production center must be on a nonprice basis if mutually unprofitable price rivalry is to be avoided: the simplest legal solution of this problem would be to use f.o.b. mill prices and rely upon nonprice competition to divide sales among firms.[9] Any delivered price system is slightly inferior for this purpose because it requires additional calculations and therefore gives rise to additional errors and sources of misunderstanding among the firms. There have been many quarrels in the basing point price industries over rounding off numbers at different decimal points, the uncertainties of land-grant freight rates on purchases by the federal government, trucking and water transportation, etc. But the inferiority of the delivered price system is only slight.

The second problem, the division of sales among production centers,

---

[8] Our primary interest is in the case where there are two or more firms at each of the important production centers because this appears to be more important empirically. It is one of the minor mysteries of the basing point literature that almost all the analysis has been devoted to the case where there is only one firm at each production center.

[9] Several illegal systems, such as quotas or a joint sales agency plus quotas, might be more efficient. In the markets for homogeneous raw materials, however, non-price competition is not likely to become very expensive.

could also be solved by f.o.b. mill prices,[10] were it not for one characteristic of demand, which on our theory is the fundamental requirement for
a uniform delivered price system. This characteristic of demand is that
it is geographically unstable, *i.e.*, the proportion of national or regional
sales made in each consumption center is subject to substantial fluctuations. If a production center were to make all its sales within a given area,
it would often be in a state of feast or famine relative to the industry.

With an unstable geographical pattern of demand, f.o.b. mill pricing
would have one of two consequences in industries making non-storeable
products. The firms at a production center might maintain stable prices
(relative to other production centers), and then fluctuations in their
rate of output would be large.[11] Not only would this unstable rate of
production raise the costs of producing given outputs, but it would put
a severe strain on the agreement among the firms: some firms would be
losing money while other firms (perhaps multiple-plant firms with a plant
in the same production center) were prospering. Or, alternatively, the
price at the production center would fluctuate in response to changes in
demand: rising high in feast periods to attract output from other production centers; falling low in famine periods to permit sales in other territories. This sort of unpredictable flexibility of mill prices would make it
extremely difficult to maintain collusion among firms at the production
center, and even more difficult to maintain collusion between firms at
different production centers.

These objections to f.o.b. mill pricing lose some weight if the product is storeable. Then stable rates of production may be reconciled with
unstable rates of sale, through inventory adjustments. Yet inventory
adjustments are not likely to eliminate the problem. If the product comes
in many sizes and qualities, inventories would have to be enormous: for
example, the specifications for steel products are so various that inventories do not provide a feasible method of meeting local fluctuations in
demand.[12] The method of inventory adjustment is completely satisfactory
only if fluctuations in the geographical pattern of demand cancel out
quickly.[13]

---

[10] Or by division of market areas—which indeed would be the effect of a
stable system of f.o.b. mill prices.

[11] At times the output of the production center would have to be impossibly
large: for example, some large Western construction projects simply could not have
been supplied within the permitted time by Western steel and cement capacity.

[12] It is interesting to notice that the cement industry considers its product to
be perishable; see *Argument of George S. Leisure* (New York: Grosby Press, 1942),
pp. 77–78.

[13] If the aggregate demand for the product of the industry is also cyclically

If collusion could be complete—if the practices of a monopolist could be adopted—f.o.b. mill pricing would still be possible. The oligopolists could establish a joint sales agency, which would refer each order to the firm whose rate of production and distance from the buyer made it the most profitable source from which to fill the order. The group could compensate firms whose outputs were small in a given period at the cost of firms whose outputs had been large. A joint sales agency, however, is as easily detected as it is illegal under our antitrust laws.

Systematic freight absorption provides a satisfactory solution to all these problems. There is a single price at each point in the market (if transportation charges are agreed upon), so price rivalry is eliminated. One production center can sell in the "natural" territories of other production centers when this is necessary to obtain its share of the industry's sales; these distant sales involve freight absorption, moreover, and are therefore partly self-limiting. The various prices need not change often, so collusion is possible. Given the unstable geographical pattern of demand and the antitrust laws, systematic freight absorption permitted efficient collusion.

Crosshauling (simultaneous and geographically overlapping shipments from various production centers) is commonly held to be an important by-product of systematic freight absorption. It is difficult to see why crosshauling should arise because of the inherent nature of the system: production center A will be selling in the area of production center B only when it cannot sell its share of the industry's sales in its own area, and, therefore, when B will not be selling in A's territory. Some crosshauling will occur because of the variable time interval between orders and deliveries; this type of crosshaul would also exist under competition and probably under monopoly. Some crosshauling will also occur because of the desire of firms to keep sales agencies in important markets, and this type of crosshaul (with more shipping of products and less of salesmen) is attributable to oligopoly. One would not expect crosshauling to be a major waste under systematic freight absorption, however, and there is no empirical evidence that contradicts this expectation.[14] This is not to

---

unstable, there is an additional objection to the method of inventory adjustment. Inventories will be accumulated in regions in which recession first occurs, in the belief that this recession is an instance of geographical instability.

[14] Some writers use "crosshauling" to describe all wastes in transportation (given the location of the mills); see Federal Trade Commission, *Price Bases Inquiry* (Washington, D.C., 1932), chap. viii. The issue is largely terminological, but the measures of the uneconomic movement of goods—it was assumed by the Federal Trade Commission that freight absorption measures this movement—are seriously deficient.

say that a system of distribution designed to insure a stable share of total sales for each production center will be efficient from the social viewpoint, for it will not be.

The choice by the industry between freight equalization and a basing point system will be determined primarily by the nature of the production centers. If the production centers are well separated, freight equalization is simple and satisfactory. If production centers are spread out, so the firms at a center are not equidistant (in terms of transportation costs) from the important consumption centers, a basing point system will eliminate numerous minor complexities that would arise under freight equalization. The distinction between the two systems, however, is less significant and durable than that between f.o.b. mill and delivered prices.[15]

III. TESTING THE THEORY

We shall briefly discuss tests of the foregoing theory that create some presumption for its validity and then suggest further tests which have not been carried out.

Industries providing materials for large construction projects are likely to have geographically unstable demands; indeed this expectation gave rise to the theory. A sample investigation of contract awards for reinforcing steel bars, summarized in Table 14–2, amply confirms the expectation.[16] The instability is more clearly brought out by the percentage distribution of contract awards among the important consuming states (Table 14–3).[17] The longer-term instability of demand is also im-

[15] The theory will not be elaborated to consider plant location, number of price bases, inter-base differentials, etc. In general, the more unstable the geographical pattern of demand the fewer will be the production centers (since each firm will locate where it can sell in many territories) and the fewer will be the base prices. Single base prices will be used when a single production center is so large that it must often sell in every territory and other production centers are accordingly so small that they seldom need to sell to or past the dominant production center. (Obviously, if almost all production takes place at one center, there can be no systematic freight absorption or, for that matter, a problem of geographical prices.) Geographically unstable demand may lead to zone prices if transportation costs are not uniquely determinable; some of the late nineteenth century pools may be examples.
    The system of formula differentials between prices of multiple products provides close analogies to systematic freight absorption.

[16] The data exaggerate the short-run geographical instability of demand because they include only contracts for 100 or more tons, which are no doubt less stable geographically than the smaller orders. The awards cannot be compared accurately with total production because of the unknown time lags in filling orders, but it appears that about 35 percent of total sales in this period are accounted for by these contracts.

[17] Monthly contract awards, of course, show much greater instability. The correct time period for our theory will vary with the industry (being longer if inven-

TABLE 14–2
CONTRACT AWARDS FOR REINFORCING STEEL BARS, 1936*
(In Tons)

Region and State	Quarter			
	First	Second	Third	Fourth
Northeastern States				
Connecticut	750	750	100	660
Maine	0	0	200	0
Massachusetts	1,276	2,005	2,908	3,315
New Hampshire.	0	0	100	0
New Jersey.	1,760	1,755	2,826	2,270
New York.	15,340	4,200	14,088	4,169
Pennsylvania	6,400	5,700	425	950
Rhode Island.	1,010	0	500	100
Vermont	0	0	150	240
North Central States				
Illinois	10,768	6,406	13,670	5,755
Indiana	700	920	1,325	800
Iowa	0	0	0	625
Kansas	1,700	350	0	0
Michigan	3,150	0	600	400
Missouri	2,855	925	1,375	750
Ohio	650	2,950	715	2,000
Wisconsin	945	1,550	985	653
Western States				
Arizona	525	528	0	0
California	43,874	31,901	30,185	20,039
Colorado	1,128	8,412	4,343	7,356
Idaho	122	0	125	518
Montana	15,891	726	3,575	152
Nevada	100	681	0	502
New Mexico.	197	697	0	1,255
Oregon	100	1,315	0	124
Utah	0	0	0	280
Washington	4,509	2,282	706	117
Wyoming	357	389	597	0
Southern States				
Delaware	0	250	0	0
Kentucky	0	750	500	0
Maryland	2,700	0	0	0
Tennessee	0	0	300	0
Washington, D.C.	2,500	0	1,365	0
West Virginia.	0	0	360	0

* Compiled from *Iron Age*, 1936.

plicitly illustrated by these tables: for example, California consumed almost four tenths of the bars but had less than one fifteenth of the indus-

tories are possible) and with the variance of the time interval between orders and deliveries. It is interesting to notice that the California tonnages become much more erratic if the quarters are shifted back one week: 41,351; 15,969; 46,360; and 21,804 respectively.

TABLE 14–3
PERCENTAGES OF UNITED STATES CONTRACT AWARDS FOR REINFORCING
STEEL BARS IN LEADING CONSUMING STATES, 1936

State	Quarter			
	First	Second	Third	Fourth
California	36.8	42.3	36.8	37.8
Colorado	0.9	11.2	5.3	13.9
Illinois	9.0	8.5	16.7	10.9
Massachusetts	1.1	2.7	3.5	6.3
Montana	13.3	1.0	4.4	0.3
New York..............	12.9	5.6	17.2	7.9
Pennsylvania	5.4	7.6	0.5	1.8

try's capacity to produce bars, while the chief producing states (Pennsylvania, Ohio, and Illinois) consumed relatively little.[18]

It was argued above that f.o.b. mill prices would have to be very flexible relative to one another in order to reflect the shifting locus of demand and thus permit the sales areas of production centers to expand and contract—so flexible, in fact, as to make collusion impracticable. We may test this view by a comparison of prices in a period of f.o.b. mill pricing with those under basing point pricing (Table 14–4). Unfortunately, the same commodities cannot readily be used for both periods, but

TABLE 14–4
COMPARISON OF STEEL PRICES IN THREE MARKETS
1898–99, 1939–40*

Market	1898–99 Steel Billets	Steel Bars 1939–40
Pittsburgh		
Possible price changes..............	51	103
Price changes.....................	27	1
Philadelphia		
Possible price changes..............	51	103
Price changes.....................	38	1
Chicago		
Possible price changes..............	48	103
Price changes.....................	21	1
Pittsburgh-Philadelphia Differential		
Possible changes in differential.......	51	103
Changes in differential.............	39	0
Pittsburgh-Chicago Differential		
Possible changes in differential.......	48	103
Changes in differential.............	34	0

*Based on Tables 14–A1 and 14–A2, appendix pp. 163–64.

[18] See *Directory of the Iron and Steel Works of the United States and Canada, 1938* (New York: American Iron and Steel Institute, 1938), p. 441.

each seems representative of its period for the question in hand;[19] in both periods the demand for steel was rising. The comparison is qualified by the unknown amount of collusion in the earlier period and by the uncertainty of the significance of quoted prices in both periods. Nevertheless, the prediction of the theory is dramatically confirmed as to both the frequency of price changes with f.o.b. mill and basing point prices and the stability of differences between prices at different production centers.[20]

Still another type of test of the theory is provided by changes in the behavior of basing point price industries in periods when the demand for their products is geographically stable: the theory predicts that systematic freight absorption will diminish. Steel has had such a demand stability in the postwar years because the industry has been practicing nonprice rationing of buyers: the individual plant can sell all it wishes at its mill-net price. The prediction of the theory is fully confirmed:

Since the war almost all mills have stopped selling some products in certain distant markets and some mills have withdrawn on all products from some areas. . . .

In today's seller's market it is actually possible for a steel company to reduce its freight bill in the face of rising freight rates by careful choice of customers and market areas. . . .

Other f.o.b. mill sales are less obvious but it is known that some customers have been able to buy on f.o.b. mill pricing where it was a case of no discrimination; where the customer realized he was outside a mill's present market area and specifically asked for an f.o.b. mill price so as to get steel. Not all mills will sell this way.[21]

The practice of quoting an arbitrary Detroit base was also abandoned.[22]

The instability of the geographical pattern of demand in cement has been emphasized by the industry,[23] and it is documented by the geo-

---

[19] Billets had a much broader market in the earlier period, when vertical integration had not progressed so far.

[20] The collusive character of inter-base price differentials in the later period is shown in detail by de Chazeau; see D. R. Daugherty, M. G. de Chazeau, and S. S. Stratton, *Economics of the Iron and Steel Industry* (New York: McGraw-Hill Book Co., 1937), Vol. II, chap. xiii.

[21] *Iron Age*, May 13, 1948, pp. 119–20; see also *New York Times*, December 6, 1947, p. 23.

[22] Jones and Laughlin withdrew sheets and strip, and Republic and Carnegie-Illinois withdrew alloy bars from the Detroit arbitrary base, *Iron Age*, May 13, 1948, p. 120.

[23] See *Aetna Portland Cement Company et al.* v. *Federal Trade Commission*, in the United States Circuit Court of Appeals of the Seventh Circuit, October Term, 1945, Appendix A to Brief of Respondents-Petitioners, pp. 80 ff.

graphical instability of concrete paving work and large construction projects.[24]

Our theory predicts that in industries with unstable geographical patterns of demand, the relative distribution of production among production centers will be more stable than the relative distribution of consumption under a basing point price system, whereas the two distributions would be about equally unstable with f.o.b. pricing.[25] Were it not for the merging of the market areas of individual mills in the reports of the Bureau of Mines (no doubt because of disclosure prohibitions), it would be possible to compare exactly the relative stability of consumption and production in each mill area. The best that can be done with the published data is to make such a comparison for certain adjoining states (Illinois, Iowa, Kansas, and Missouri).[26] The percentage of aggregate production and consumption (in the four states) has been calculated for each state for the period 1921 through 1940, and the coefficients of variation of these percentages are tabulated below:

| | Coefficient of Variation | |
State	Percent of Aggregate Production	Percent of Aggregate Consumption
Illinois	7.5	11.0
Iowa	12.2	19.6
Kansas ......'...........	12.7	20.4
Missouri ....,...........	5.9	15.1

In each state relative consumption was more variable than relative production, as the theory predicts.

Our theory makes collusion a requirement for a delivered price system. In industries where there are few large firms, collusion (whether tacit or overt) or coercion is usually more profitable to every large firm than price competition. Therefore, however proper the legal principle that the defendant is presumed to be innocent of conspiracy, it has no place in economics. Indeed the presumption is the opposite: it is more

---

[24] For data on city and state paving (in which one-fourth of all cement is normally used), see annual issues of *Cement and Concrete Reference Book.*

[25] Provided the inter-base price differentials were stable, as they appear to have been in cement; see Federal Trade Commission, *Cement Industry* (Washington, D.C., 1933), Exhibit Tables 9 and 10.

[26] Each of the states has four to six mills. Indiana is not reported separately; this distorts our analysis because it is the leading source of the Chicago market (indeed an Indiana mill is the base that sets the Chicago price). See annual issues of *Minerals Yearbook.*

appropriate for the economist to ask why oligopolists compete as often as they do.

In the cement and steel industries, the evidences of overt collusion are ample. The basing point price system was put on a firm basis in the steel industry under Judge Gary's iron-hand-in-velvet-glove regime, and it was greatly strengthened under the N.R.A. The testimony in the cement case contains many instances of overt collusion. Foreign experience in these industries reinforces the conclusion that collusion is necessary to delivered price systems. The German cement industry was on a f.o.b. mill price system until a cartel was formed, after which it used delivered prices.[27] The German steel cartel used a basing point system,[28] and the English steel industry abandoned f.o.b. mill pricing for a delivered price system in the 1920's, after amalgamation and federation had proceeded far.[29]

The bituminous coal industry supplies some excellent illustrations of the role of collusion.[30] In the United States, coal was sold f.o.b. mine when the industry was not regulated; under the National Bituminous Coal Act of 1937, delivered prices were set and limited freight absorption was permitted and in some circumstances phantom freight required.[31] In Great Britain the development was parallel: f.o.b. mine prices were used before the compulsory cartelization of 1930; thereafter the industry moved toward a delivered price system.[32] The highly developed Rhenish-Westphalian syndicate was able to act like a monopolist for it had control over the marketing of all coal in the "uncontested" areas, and it set f.o.b. mine prices.[33]

---

[27] K. Ehrke, *Übererzeugung in der Zement Industrie von 1858–1913* (Jena: Gustav Fischer, 1933), pp. 14–15, 161.

[28] See *Die Deutsche Eisenerzeugende Industrie,* in *Ausschusz zur Untersuchung der Erzeugungs—und Absatzbedingungen der deutschen Wirtschaft* (Berlin: E. S. Mittler, 1930). A joint sales agency was used, but the collusion was not complete. Each of the large firms maintained a sales organization because, in the words of F. Thyssen, "one fine day the cartel could go up in air . . ." (*ibid., p.* 315).

[29] See D. L. Burn, *The Economic History of Steelmaking, 1867–1939* (London: Cambridge University Press, 1940), p. 377.

[30] The geographical pattern of demand for coal is apparently much more stable than that of steel and cement, but this is offset by the greater density of producing centers. On the pattern in Germany, see Johannes Schröder, *Der Absatzraum der Ruhrkohle* (Gieszen: Otto Kindt, 1929).

[31] R. H. Baker, *The National Bituminous Coal Commission* (Baltimore: Johns Hopkins University Press, 1941), pp. 140–41, 157, 193–94.

[32] See the annual survey numbers of the *Iron and Coal Trades Review,* for example, January 15, 1937, pp. 90–91; January 21, 1938, pp. 82–83.

[33] See J. H. Jones, G. Cartwright, and P. H. Guenault, *The Coal-Mining Industry* (London: Pitman and Sons, 1939), pp. 274–75. The Belgian cartel used a multiple basing point price system (*ibid.,* pp. 227–28).

Delivered price systems have been alleged or shown to exist in cast iron pipe;[34] rigid steel conduit;[35] various kinds of lumber;[36] copper, lead, and zinc;[37] plaster and lime;[38] plate glass;[39] floor and wall tiles,[40] and numerous other industries.[41] Some of these industries very probably have unstable geographical patterns of demand, for example, cast iron pipe, rigid conduits, and building materials.[42] In other of these industries it is doubtful that freight absorption is systematic.[43] The one industry in which it seems probable that the geographical pattern of demand is stable and yet delivered prices are adhered to is beet sugar; I have not been able to establish definitely that it is an exception.[44]

Other tests of the theory, which have not been undertaken, can easily be suggested. Pig iron was sold f.o.b. mill before the N.R.A., thereafter, it was sold on a basing point system. According to our theory, this change is due to increasing oligopoly or increasing instability of demand.

[34] Clair Wilcox, Competition and Monopoly in American Industry, T.N.E.C. Monograph No. 21, p. 157.

[35] Triangle Conduit and Cable Co. v. Federal Trade Commission, 168 Fed. 2d 175 (1948).

[36] T.N.E.C. Monograph No. 33, Geographical Differentials in Prices of Building Materials, chap. xiii; A. R. Burns, The Decline of Competition (New York: McGraw-Hill Book Co., 1936), pp. 291 ff.

[37] F. A. Fetter, The Masquerade of Monopoly (New York: Harcourt, Brace, 1931), chap. xiv.

[38] T.N.E.C. Monograph No. 33, chaps. iv, vii.

[39] U.S. Tariff Commission, Plate Glass, Report 110, Second Series (Washington, D.C., 1936), p. 25.

[40] U.S. Tariff Commission, Earthen Floor and Wall Tiles, Report 141, Second Series (Washington, D.C., 1941), pp. 86ff.

[41] There is also some evidence of the equivalent of delivered price systems on the buying side in the cottonseed industry (Federal Trade Commission, Report on Cottonseed Industry [Senate Doc. 209, Part 13, 71st Cong. 2d Sess.], esp. pp. 15,823 ff.) and in the buying of crude petroleum and iron scrap.

[42] The wire rope industry also shares this demand characteristic; see Study of Pricing Methods (Hearings pursuant to S. Res. 241 [the so-called Capehart Committee], pp. 311–12).

[43] In copper, for example, the existence of a single basing point is doubtful. Most refineries are near New York, most consumers in New England. "The quotation is almost always on a delivered basis—that is, the seller pays the freight to the buyer's plant. Sellers are willing to sell f.o.b. refinery, however, should the buyer so desire." E. H. Robie, "The Marketing of Copper," Engineering and Mining Journal-Press, April 21, 1923, pp. 704–9, quotation at p. 707.

[44] Corn sirup is also mildly troublesome. It was long quoted on a single base (Chicago). The geographical pattern of demand appears to be stable, at least in the short run. One is tempted to explain the single base by the geographical concentration of production and consumption. Over half the corn sirup is made in Illinois and most of the remainder in neighboring states. The chief demand for corn sirup is in candy and confectionery, and 30.5 percent of the candy was made in Illinois in 1939 and only 8.2 percent in all the other states producing large amounts of corn sirup. (See Census of Manufactures, 1939.) The Chicago base price therefore involved only a small amount of irrational (profit-reducing) price discrimination, and simplified the price structure.

It is said that cement was sold f.o.b. mill on the Pacific Coast; if true, this case has similar implications to be tested.

The most general and satisfying test would be provided by a general measurement of the geographical instability of demand in oligopolistic industries, which could be compared with the pricing practices of these industries. If the industries with relatively unstable geographical demand patterns used chiefly delivered prices, and those with stable geographical demand patterns chiefly f.o.b. mill prices, it could not be doubted that the theory contains a large element of the correct solution.

This test does not seem feasible with the data now published. The most promising source of information on demand patterns is the quarterly reports on terminations of classes of railroad freight by states.[45] Unfortunately, this series does not extend back of 1940 (except by broad geographic areas); it lumps together wide classes of commodities; and often the state is too large a unit. The other serious problem, already referred to, is the inconclusiveness of the formal method of price quotation. The data necessary to measure the geographical instability of demand and the extent of systematic freight absorption exist in the sales ledgers of the firms, to which the academic investigator cannot always obtain access.

IV. CONCLUSION

If our theory of delivered prices is correct, we may easily dispose of the chief criticism that is made of the cement decision: that it will divide the nation into many local monopolies. Quite aside from the fact that this statement is wholly ambiguous (in that it tells us nothing of how strong these local monopolists will be), it is simply wrong because it overlooks the normal instability of demand in these industries. The individual plant cannot operate efficiently with an unstable demand in the area of its production and must therefore frequently invade other plants' areas.

The immediate effect of f.o.b. mill pricing in a period of non-price rationing is of course to increase the revenues of firms which have been absorbing freight.[46] With the restoration of price rationing and the customary geographical instability of demand, f.o.b. mill pricing will require a flexibility of prices that will often be beyond the reach of colluding

---

[45] Interstate Commerce Commission, Tons of Revenue Freight Originated and Tons Terminated in Carloads by Groups of Commodities and by Geographic Areas (Statement No. Q-550 [S.C.S.]).

[46] The steel industry also raised its mill prices at the time it shifted to f.o.b. mill pricing: semi-finished products rose 10 percent and finished products 20 percent from May to July, 1948 (Steel, January 3, 1949, p. 303).

oligopolists, so we may expect more frequent outbreaks of price competition. A period of increasing price competition may lead to either further mergers or alternative forms of collusive marketing, or to increasingly competitive behavior of these industries. The relative probabilities of these two outcomes depend chiefly on other and more fundamental elements of our antitrust policy than the prohibition of price discrimination.

Appendix

TABLE 14–A1
PRICE OF STEEL BILLETS AT PHILADELPHIA, PITTSBURGH,
AND CHICAGO, 1898–99*
(Per Ton)

Date		Price			Excess over Pittsburgh Price	
		Pitts-burgh	Phila-delphia	Chicago	Phila-delphia	Chicago
1898 July	6.......	$14.50	$16.50	$16.25	$2.00	$1.75
	13.......	14.50	16.50	16.25	2.00	1.75
	20.......	14.50	16.50	15.75	2.00	1.25
	27.......	14.50	16.50	15.75	2.00	1.25
August	3.......	14.50	16.25	15.75	1.75	1.25
	10.......	15.25	17.00	16.00	1.75	.75
	17.......	15.90	18.00	16.50	2.10	.60
	24.......	16.00	17.75	16.50	1.75	.50
	31.......	16.00	17.75	17.00	1.75	1.00
September	7.......	16.00	18.00	17.50	2.00	1.50
	14.......	16.00	17.75	17.50	1.75	1.50
	21.......	16.00	18.00	17.00	2.00	1.00
	28.......	16.00	17.75	17.00	1.75	1.00
October	5.......	15.75	17.75	17.00	2.00	1.25
	12.......	15.50	17.75	17.00	2.25	1.50
	19.......	15.50	18.00	17.00	2.50	1.50
	26.......	15.50	17.75	17.00	2.25	1.50
November	2.......	15.15	17.25	17.00	2.10	1.85
	9.......	15.00	17.25	17.00	2.25	2.00
	16.......	14.85	17.00	17.00	2.15	2.15
	23.......	15.25	17.00	17.00	1.75	1.75
	30.......	15.25	17.00	17.00	1.75	1.75
December	7.......	15.50	17.25	17.00	1.75	1.50
	14.......	16.00	17.25	17.50	1.25	1.50
	21.......	16.00	17.35		1.35	
	28.......	16.25	18.50	17.50	2.25	1.25
1899 January	5.......	16.25	18.55	17.50	2.30	1.25
	11.......	16.50	18.90	18.25	2.40	1.75
	18.......	16.50	19.50	18.50	3.00	2.00
	25.......	17.25	19.10	18.50	1.85	1.25
February	1.......	17.25	19.25	18.50	2.00	1.25
	8.......	17.25	19.50	18.50	2.25	1.25
	15.......	18.00	20.50	20.00	2.50	2.00
	22.......	19.50	22.00	21.00	2.50	1.50

TABLE 14–A1 (*Continued*)

Date		Price			Excess over Pittsburgh Price	
		Pitts-burgh	Phila-delphia	Chicago	Phila-delphia	Chicago
1899 March	1......	$22.00	$24.00	$23.00	$2.00	$1.00
	8......	23.50	25.50	23.50	2.00	0.
	15......	25.50	26.00	24.00	.50	−1.50
	22......	25.50	26.00	25.50	.50	0.
	29......	25.00	26.50	25.50	1.50	.50
April	5......	25.00	28.00	25.50	3.00	0.50
	12......	25.50	27.50	25.50	2.00	0.
	19......	25.50	27.50	25.50	2.00	0.
	26......	25.50	28.00	25.50	2.50	0.
May	3......	26.00	27.50	25.50	1.50	−0.50
	10......	26.00	28.50	27.50	2.50	1.50
	17......	27.00	29.00	28.00	2.00	1.00
	24......	28.00	29.75	28.50	1.75	.50
June	1......	29.00	30.50		1.50	
	8......	30.00	31.00	32.00	1.00	2.00
	14......	31.50	31.50	32.50	0.	1.00
	21......	31.50	34.00	34.00	2.50	2.50
	28......	31.50	34.00		2.50	

* Compiled from *Iron Age*.

TABLE 14–A2

PRICE OF STEEL BARS AT PITTSBURGH, PHILADELPHIA, AND CHICAGO, 1939–40*
(Per Pound)

Date		Price			Excess over Pittsburgh Price	
		Pitts-burgh	Phila-delphia	Chicago	Phila-delphia	Chicago
1939 January	7........	2.25	2.57	2.25	.32	0.
...						
...						
...						
May	13........	2.25	2.57	2.25	.32	0.
	20........	2.15	2.47	2.15	.32	0.
...						
...						
...						
December 23........		2.15	2.47	2.15	.32	0.
1940 ...						
...						
...						
December 28........		2.15	2.47	2.15	.32	0.

* Compiled from *Steel*; no price changes in unreported weeks.

Chapter   A NOTE ON

15   BLOCK BOOKING*

The phenomenon of block booking of movies—the offer of only a combined assortment of movies to an exhibitor—has been the subject of several antitrust cases. In the most recent case, *United States* v. *Loew's Inc.*,[1] Mr. Justice Goldberg, speaking for the Court, again struck down the practice, stating flatly: "The antitrust laws do not permit a compounding of the statutorily conferred monopoly."

The explanation of the practice of block booking is not explicit in the decision, but a fair interpretation is this: The owner of two films uses the popularity of one to compel the exhibitor to purchase the other as well. This is not a full explanation, however, for it does not explain why the seller should wish to sell the inferior film.

Consider the following simple example. One film, Justice Goldberg cited *Gone with the Wind*, is worth $10,000 to the buyer, while a second film, the Justice cited *Getting Gertie's Garter*, is worthless to him. The seller could sell the one for $10,000, and throw away the second, for no matter what its cost, bygones are forever bygones. Instead the seller compels the buyer to take both. But surely he can obtain no more than $10,000, since by hypothesis this is the value of both films to the buyer. Why not, in short, use his monopoly power directly on the desirable film? It seems no more sensible, on this logic, to block book the two films than it would be to compel the exhibitor to buy *Gone with the Wind* and seven Ouija boards, again for $10,000.

The explanation of the practice must lie elsewhere. The simplest plausible explanation is that some buyers would prize one film much more relative to the other. Consider the two buyers:

A would pay $8,000 for film X and $2,500 for film Y.
B would pay $7,000 for film X and $3,000 for film Y.

* Reprinted from Philip B. Kurland, *The Supreme Court Review* (1963). Copyright 1963 by the University of Chicago.
[1] 371 U.S. 38, 52 (1962).

165

If the seller were to price the two films separately, he would receive:

1. $5,000 for the sale of Y, at $2,500 per buyer. A higher price would exclude A and reduce receipts.
2. $14,000 for the sale of X, at $7,000 per buyer on the same logic.

The total received is $19,000. But with block booking, a single price of $10,000 can be set for the pair of films, and $20,000 will be received.[2]

On this approach, block booking is a method of selling calculated to extract larger sums than otherwise would be possible. The value of ten films will be the same for two TV stations with comparable markets and advertising rates, but the relative values of the individual films will vary from city to city. These differences cannot be gauged so closely by the seller as by the buyer, so a block price is used to capture a lafger return.[3]

This is a logical explanation for block booking, but is it the correct explanation? Several empirical tests may be specified:

1. From *Variety,* in olden days one could look up the receipts from the exhibition of movies in various cities. If the relative appeal of movies in different cities varied substantially, the theory is plausible; if the relative appeal is much the same in most cities, the theory is false.

2. Again from trade sources, one can determine whether the average receipts (per year) of a theater were determined by attendance, income, etc. If there was a good relationship, the block rate could be established with some precision and would not forfeit large gains from discriminating among individual theaters.

3. From the record, one can perhaps determine whether the sales prices of given blocks of films were closely related to objective criteria of

---

[2] Of course a price of $10,500 could have been set for buyer A, but this degree of precision of measurement of demand may be impossible. If it is possible, then clearly there is no need for block booking, on the present explanation.

[3] The formal theory may be sketched; it was suggested to me by Milton Friedman. Let p_{1a} be the maximum price buyer 1 would pay for film a, and similarly with other subscripts. With separate prices,

$$p_a = \min (p_{1a}, p_{2a}) ,$$
$$p_b = \min (p_{1b}, p_{2b}) .$$

With block-booking,

$$p = \min (p_{1a} + p_{1b}, p_{2a} + p_{2b}) .$$

The latter will be larger than the sum of the former if $p_{1a} > p_{2a}$, $p_{1b} < p_{2b}$ (or the converse). The argument is incomplete in that $2p_a$ may be less than p_{1a} or p_{2a}, but the argument could be extended to cover no sales to one buyer by using expressions such as max $(2 \min [p_{1a}, p_{2a}], p_{1a}, p_{2a})$, etc.

stations' ability to pay (chiefly advertising rates). If so, again the possibility of personal discrimination in price must be ruled out.

No systematic testing has been carried out, but a few suggestive, and supporting, pieces in evidence are given in the Appendix.

Whether this simple hypothesis survives or not, clearly the Court's assertion that monopoly must not be compounded is futile. Let a man own two patents on related products, say a gas turbine engine and a diesel engine, or two copyrights, on *Gone with the Wind* and *Leaving with the Gale.* They are substitutes and in setting the price of one, he must take account of its effect on the sales of the other: the monopolies will be compounded.

The decision to outlaw block booking is not objectionable because it rests on an incomplete analysis. The effect of the decision, if it is effective, is to reduce the receipts of the owners of the films, and to increase the receipts of another set of monopolists, the owners of TV licenses. If the TV licenses were sold by the government, the redistribution would be beneficial; as it stands, no clear judgment seems possible.

Appendix

Two separate studies shed some light on the plausibility of the hypothesis that block booking is essentially a price discrimination technique.

1. The first week, first-run attendance receipts of a series of movies in large American cities were tabulated. A period before the major onslaught of television was chosen. The underlying data are reported in Table 15–A1.

For each city a receipts figure (say, r_e) was calculated for each film on the assumption that this film had obtained the same share of receipts in this city as it did in all cities combined. The expected receipts (r_e) are compared with actual receipts (r_a), by the formula

$$\frac{|r_a - r_e|}{r_e},$$

taking absolute values since we are not interested in the sign of the relative deviation.

The mean absolute relative deviation, to give the average of this expression its formidable title, is 14.4 percent for 12 pictures in 7 cities, and 14.9 percent for 7 pictures in 13 cities. Thus if the seller (actually lessor) of a picture to the theater in a particular city assumed that it

TABLE 15–A1

RECEIPTS FROM FIRST-WEEK EXHIBITION OF MOVIES, 1946–47

(Thousands of Dollars)

City	Movie*											
	A	B	C	D	E	F	G	H	I	J	K	L
Washington, D.C.	31.0	28.0	33.0	25.0	24.0	26.0	29.0	20.0	25.0	26.0	23.0	29.0
Indianapolis	27.0	22.0	19.0	21.0	17.0	14.0	20.0	13.0	12.0	13.0	18.0	15.0
Los Angeles	62.5	65.7	111.0	75.6	80.0	66.0	23.0	74.9	65.2	67.0	73.8	62.0
Minneapolis	38.0	22.0	21.0	23.0	15.0	11.0	27.0	15.0	14.0	20.0	26.0	17.0
Montreal	17.0	22.5	16.0	16.0	14.5	13.0	18.0	14.2	14.0	15.0	13.0	14.5
Philadelphia	52.0	47.5	50.0	53.5	31.5	37.0	53.0	32.0	33.0	32.0	35.0	45.0
Pittsburgh	40.0	27.0	26.1	28.0	24.0	20.0	32.5	13.0	19.5	24.0	22.0	22.0
Buffalo	31.0	28.0	24.0	29.5	24.0	16.0	27.0	. . .	. . .	. . .	. . .	. . .
Cincinnati	36.0	30.5	29.5	18.0	16.0	13.0	26.0	. . .	. . .	. . .	. . .	. . .
Seattle	27.3	16.0	26.0	16.0	16.8	13.2	27.0	. . .	. . .	. . .	. . .	. . .
San Francisco	45.0	23.0	46.0	37.5	24.5	30.0	45.0	. . .	. . .	. . .	. . .	. . .
St. Louis	24.0	30.0	21.0	32.0	24.0	19.0	24.0	. . .	. . .	. . .	. . .	. . .
Omaha	23.0	9.3	18.0	15.3	12.2	8.5	17.2	. . .	. . .	. . .	. . .	. . .

* See opposite page for key to movie titles.

Source: *Variety*, Nov. 6, 1946, through May 7, 1947.

TABLE 15–A2

Number of Weeks of First Run of Movies, 1946–47

| City* | Movie† | | | | | | | | | | | |
---	A	B	C	D	E	F	G	H	I	J	K	L
Washington, D.C.	2	2	5	2	3	2	2	1	2	5	3	2
Indianapolis	3	4	2	2	2	2	3	3	1	1	2	2
Minneapolis	5	8	5	3	2	1	4	2	4	6	6	4
Montreal	4	7	2	1	2	1	2	2	2	1	2	2
Philadelphia	9	8	5	4	3	3	4	4	4	4	4	3
Pittsburgh	4	7	6	4	3	3	2	3	3	4	4	3
Buffalo	3	5	3	4	2	2	3	…	…	…	…	…
Cincinnati	4	6	4	4	3	3	3	…	…	…	…	…
Seattle	7	15	6	3	2	3	5	…	…	…	…	…
San Francisco	3	3	4	3	2	3	5	…	…	…	…	…
St. Louis	7	8	4	4	3	3	3	…	…	…	…	…
Omaha	2	3	3	2	1	1	2	…	…	…	…	…

* Los Angeles excluded from weeks of first-run analysis because of multiple first runs.
† See below for key to movie titles.

Source: same as Table 15–A1.

Key to Movie Titles

A. *Blue Skies*
B. *Jolson Story*
C. *Razor's Edge*
D. *Till the Clouds Roll By*
E. *Undercurrent*
F. *Humoresque*
G. *Two Years before the Mast*
H. *Dark Mirror*
I. *Deception*
J. *It's a Wonderful Life*
K. *Margie*
L. *The Time, the Place, and the Girl*

would have the same appeal (relative to other pictures) as in other cities, he would on average be making a 14 percent over- or underestimate. This is indeed an underestimate of the variation among cities, since our procedure excluded pictures appearing in certain cities in double features or with stage shows.

A related aspect of this difference among cities in tastes for particular shows is the length of the first run (Table 15–A2). A summary number corresponding to that used for Table 15–A1 would indicate a larger relative difference among cities, chiefly because the unit of time (a week) is rather lumpy.

2. The aggregate value of all films to a television station is, on our hypothesis, tolerably well explained by the power of the station, characteristics of the population it serves, etc. If this be true, block booking does not forego appreciable revenue relative to higgling over individual pictures.

An interesting study by Professor Harvey Levin[4] gives some support to this view. He made a statistical analysis of the excess of the sales price of thirty-one television stations over the replacement costs of their tangible assets in 1956-59, as a measure of their franchise values. The explanatory variables were:

Retail sales in the station's market
Buying income in the market
TV homes per TV station
Network hourly rate of the station
National minute spot rate of the station
Age of station
Network affiliation
Percentage of market population that is urbanized

He obtained a coefficient of multiple correlation of .935.

[4] "Economic Effects of Broadcast Licensing," *Journal of Political Economy,* April 1964. Most of the explanatory variables were not very helpful: buying income and national minute spot rate explained most of the franchise values.

Chapter 16
THE ECONOMICS OF INFORMATION*[1]

One should hardly have to tell academicians that information is a valuable resource: knowledge *is* power. And yet it occupies a slum dwelling in the town of economics. Mostly it is ignored: the best technology is assumed to be known; the relationship of commodities to consumer preferences is a datum. And one of the information-producing industries, advertising, is treated with a hostility that economists normally reserve for tariffs or monopolists.

There are a great many problems in economics for which this neglect of ignorance is no doubt permissible or even desirable. But there are some for which this is not true, and I hope to show that some important aspects of economic organization take on a new meaning when they are considered from the viewpoint of the search for information. In the present paper I shall attempt to analyze systematically one important problem of information—the ascertainment of market price.

I. THE NATURE OF SEARCH

Prices change with varying frequency in all markets, and, unless a market is completely centralized, no one will know all the prices which various sellers (or buyers) quote at any given time. A buyer (or seller) who wishes to ascertain the most favorable price must canvass various sellers (or buyers)—a phenomenon I shall term "search."

The amount of dispersion of asking prices of sellers is a problem to be discussed later, but it is important to emphasize immediately the fact that dispersion is ubiquitous even for homogeneous goods. Two examples of asking prices, of consumer and producer goods respectively, are dis-

* Reprinted from *Journal of Political Economy*, Vol. LXIX, No. 3 (June 1961). Copyright 1961 by the University of Chicago.
[1] I have benefited from comments of Gary Becker, Milton Friedman, Zvi Griliches, Harry Johnson, Robert Solow, and Lester Telser.

played in Table 16–1. The automobile prices (for an identical model) were those quoted with an average amount of "higgling": their average was $2,436, their range from $2,350 to $2,515, and their standard deviation $42. The prices for anthracite coal were bids for federal government purchases and had a mean of $16.90 per ton, a range from $15.46 to $18.92, and a standard deviation of $1.15. In both cases the range of prices was significant on almost any criterion.

TABLE 16–1
ASKING PRICES FOR TWO COMMODITIES

A. CHEVROLETS, CHICAGO, FEBRUARY, 1959*

Price (Dollars)	Number of Dealers
2,350–2,400	4
2,400–2,450	11
2,450–2,500	8
2,500–2,550	4

B. ANTHRACITE COAL, DELIVERED (WASHINGTON, D.C.), APRIL, 1953†

Price per Ton (Dollars)	Number of Bids
15.00–15.50	2
15.50–16.00	2
16.00–16.50	2
16.50–17.00	3
17.00–18.00	1
18.00–19.00	4

* Allen F. Jung, "Price Variations Among Automobile Dealers in Metropolitan Chicago," *Journal of Business*, pp. XXXIII (January 1960), 31–42.
† Supplied by John Flueck

Price dispersion is a manifestation—and, indeed, it is the measure—of ignorance in the market. Dispersion is a biased measure of ignorance because there is never absolute homogeneity in the commodity if we include the terms of sale within the concept of the commodity. Thus, some automobile dealers might perform more service, or carry a larger range of varieties in stock, and a portion of the observed dispersion is presumably attributable to such differences. But it would be metaphysical, and fruitless, to assert that all dispersion is due to heterogeneity.

At any time, then, there will be a frequency distribution of the prices quoted by sellers. Any buyer seeking the commodity would pay whatever price is asked by the seller whom he happened to canvass, if he were content to buy from the first seller. But, if the dispersion of price quotations of sellers is at all large (relative to the cost of search), it will pay, on average, to canvass several sellers. Consider the following primitive example: let sellers be equally divided between asking prices of $2 and $3. Then the distribution of minimum prices, as search is lengthened, is shown in Table 16–2. The buyer who canvasses two sellers instead of one has an expected saving of 25 cents per unit, etc.

TABLE 16–2
DISTRIBUTION OF HYPOTHETICAL MINIMUM PRICES BY
NUMBERS OF BIDS CANVASSED

No. of Prices Canvassed	Probability of Minimum Price of		Expected Minimum Price
	$2.00	$3.00	
1............	0.5	0.5	$2.50
2............	0.75	0.25	2.25
3............	0.875	0.125	2.125
4............	0.9375	0.0625	2.0625
∞	1.0	0	2.00

The frequency distributions of asking (and offering) prices have not been studied sufficiently to support any hypothesis as to their nature. Asking prices are probably skewed to the right, as a rule, because the seller of reproducible goods will have some minimum but no maximum limit on the price he can accept. If the distribution of asking prices is normal, the distributions of minimum prices encountered in searches of one, two, and three sellers will be those displayed in Figure 16–1. If the distribution is rectangular, the corresponding distributions would be those shown in Panel B. The latter assumption does not receive strong support from the evidence, but it will be used for a time because of its algebraic simplicity.

In fact, if sellers' asking prices (p) are uniformly distributed between zero and one, it can be shown that:[2] (1) The distribution of minimum prices with n searches is

$$n(1-p)^{n-1}, \tag{1}$$

(2) the average minimum price is

$$\frac{1}{n+1}$$

[2] If $F(p)$ is the cumulative-frequency function of p, the probability that the minimum of n observations will be greater than p is

$$[1 - F(p)]^n = \left[\int_p^1 d x \right]^n.$$

and (3) the variance of the average minimum price is

$$\frac{n}{(n+1)^2\,(n+2)}.$$

Whatever the precise distribution of prices, it is certain that increased search will yield diminishing returns as measured by the expected

FIGURE 16–1

A. NORMAL DISTRIBUTION

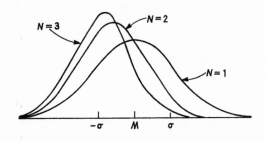

B. UNIFORM DISTRIBUTION

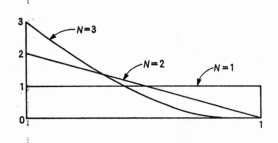

reduction in the minimum asking price. This is obviously true of the rectangular distribution, with an expected minimum price of $1/(n+1)$ with n searches, and also of the normal distributions.[3] In fact, if a distribu-

---

[3] The expected minimum prices with a normal distribution of mean M and standard deviation σ are

Search	Expected Minimum Price
1...................	M
2...................	$M - .564\sigma$
3...................	$M - .846\sigma$
4...................	$M - 1.029\sigma$
5...................	$M - 1.163\sigma$
6...................	$M - 1.267\sigma$
7...................	$M - 1.352\sigma$
8...................	$M - 1.423\sigma$
9...................	$M - 1.485\sigma$
10..................	$M - 1.539\sigma$

tion of asking prices did not display this property, it would be an unstable distribution for reasons that will soon be apparent.[4]

For any buyer the expected savings from an additional unit of search will be approximately the quantity (q) he wishes to purchase times the expected reduction in price as a result of the search,[5] or

$$q \left| \frac{\partial P_{\min}}{\partial n} \right|. \tag{2}$$

The expected saving from given search will be greater, the greater the dispersion of prices. The saving will also obviously be greater, the greater the expenditure on the commodity. Let us defer for a time the problem of the time period to which the expenditure refers, and hence the amount of expenditure, by considering the purchase of an indivisible, infrequently purchased good—say, a used automobile.

The cost of search, for a consumer, may be taken as approximately proportional to the number of (identified) sellers approached, for the chief cost is time. This cost need not be equal for all consumers, of course: aside from differences in tastes, time will be more valuable to a person with a larger income. If the cost of search is equated to its expected marginal return, the optimum amount of search will be found.[6]

Of course, the sellers can also engage in search and, in the case of unique items, will occasionally do so in the literal fashion that buyers do. In this—empirically unimportant—case, the optimum amount of search will be such that the marginal cost of search equals the expected increase in receipts, strictly parallel to the analysis for buyers.

---

[4] Robert Solow has pointed out that the expected value of the minimum of a random sample of n observations,

$$E(n) = n \int_0^\infty p(1 - F)^{n-1} F' dp,$$

is a decreasing function of n, and

$$[E(n + 2) - E(n + 1)] - [E(n + 1) - E(n)]$$

is positive so the minimum decreases at a decreasing rate. The proofs involve the fact that the density function for the rth observation from the maximum in a sample of n is

$$n \binom{n - 1}{r - 1} F^{n-r} (1 - F)^{r-1} F' dp.$$

[5] The precise savings will be (a) the reduction in price times the quantity which would be purchased at the higher price—the expression in the text—plus (b) the average saving on the additional purchases induced by the lower price. I neglect this quantity, which will generally be of a smaller order of magnitude.

[6] Buyers often pool their knowledge and thus reduce the effective cost of search; a few remarks are made on this method below.

With unique goods the efficiency of personal search for either buyers or sellers is extremely low, because the identity of potential sellers is not known—the cost of search must be divided by the fraction of potential buyers (or sellers) in the population which is being searched. If I plan to sell a used car and engage in personal search, less than one family in a random selection of one hundred families is a potential buyer of even a popular model within the next month. As a result, the cost of search is increased more than one hundredfold per price quotation.

The costs of search are so great under these conditions that there is powerful inducement to localize transactions as a device for identifying potential buyers and sellers. The medieval markets commonly increased their efficiency in this respect by prohibiting the purchase or sale of the designated commodities within a given radius of the market or on non-market days. The market tolls that were frequently levied on sellers (even in the absence of effective restrictions on non-market transactions) were clear evidence of the value of access to the localized markets.

Advertising is, of course, the obvious modern method of identifying buyers and sellers: the *classified* advertisements in particular form a meeting place for potential buyers and sellers. The identification of buyers and sellers reduces drastically the cost of search. But advertising has its own limitations: advertising itself is an expense, and one essentially independent of the value of the item advertised. The advertising of goods which have few potential buyers relative to the circulation of the advertising medium is especially expensive. We shall temporarily put advertising aside and consider an alternative.

The alternative solution is the development of specialized traders whose chief service, indeed, is implicitly to provide a meeting place for potential buyers and sellers. A used-car dealer, turning over a thousand cars a year, and presumably encountering three or five thousand each of buying and selling bids, provides a substantial centralization of trading activity. Let us consider these dealer markets, which we shall assume to be competitive in the sense of there being many independent dealers.

Each dealer faces a distribution of (for example) buyers' bids and can vary his selling prices with a corresponding effect upon purchases. Even in the markets for divisible (and hence non-unique) goods there will be some scope for higgling (discrimination) in each individual transaction: the buyer has a maximum price given by the lowest price he encounters among the dealers he has searched (or plans to search), but no minimum price. But let us put this range of indeterminacy aside, perhaps by assuming that the dealer finds discrimination too expensive,[7] and inquire how the demand curve facing a dealer is determined.

Each dealer sets a selling price, p, and makes sales to all buyers for whom this is the minimum price. With a uniform distribution of asking prices by dealers, the number of buyers of a total of N_b possible buyers who will purchase from him is

$$N_i = KN_b n(1-p)^{n-1}, \tag{3}$$

where K is a constant.[8] The number of buyers from a dealer increases as his price is reduced, and at an increasing rate.[9] Moreover, with the uniform distribution of asking prices, the number of buyers increases with increased search if the price is below the reciprocal of the amount of search.[10] We should generally expect the high-price sellers to be small-volume sellers.

The stability of any distribution of asking prices of dealers will depend upon the costs of dealers. If there are constant returns to scale, the condition of equal rates of return dictates that the difference between a dealer's buying and selling prices be a constant. This condition cannot in general be met: any dealer can buy low, and sell high, provided he is

---

[7] This is the typical state of affairs in retailing except for consumer durable goods.

[8] Since $n(1-p)^{n-1}$ is a density function, we must multiply it by a dp which represents the range of prices between adjacent price quotations. In addition, if two or more sellers quote an identical price, they will share the sales, so $K = dp/r$, where r is the number of firms quoting price p.

[9] For

$$\frac{\partial N_i}{\partial p} = -\frac{(n-1)N_i}{(1-p)} < 0,$$

and

$$\frac{\partial^2 N_i}{\partial p^2} = \frac{(n-1)(n-2)N_i}{(1-p)^2} > 0$$

if $n > 2$.

[10] Let

$$\log N_i = \log K + \log N_b + \log n + (n-1)\log(1-p).$$

Then

$$\frac{1}{N_i}\frac{\partial N_i}{\partial n} = \frac{1}{n} + \log(1-p)$$

$$= \frac{1}{n} - p,$$

approximately.

content with a small volume of transactions, and he will then be earning more than costs (including a competitive rate of return). No other dealer can eliminate this noncompetitive rate of profit, although by making the same price bids he can share the volume of business, or by asking lower prices he can increase the rewards to search and hence increase the amount of search.

With economies of scale, the competition of dealers will eliminate the profitability of quoting very high selling and very low buying prices and will render impossible some of the extreme price bids. On this score, the greater the decrease in average cost with volume, the smaller will be the dispersion of prices.[11] Many distributions of prices will be inconsistent with any possible cost conditions of dealers,[12] and it is not evident that strict equalities of rates of return for dealers are generally possible.

If economies of scale in dealing lead to a smaller dispersion of asking prices than do constant costs of dealing, similarly greater amounts of search will lead to a smaller dispersion of observed selling prices by reducing the number of purchasers who will pay high prices. Let us consider more closely the determinants of search.

Determinants of Search

The equation defining optimum search is unambiguous only if a unique purchase is being made—a house, a particular used book, etc. If purchases are repetitive, the volume of purchases based upon the search must be considered.

If the correlation of asking prices of dealers in successive time periods is perfect (and positive!), the initial search is the only one that need be undertaken. In this case the expected savings of search will be the present value of the discounted savings on all future purchases, the future savings extending over the life of the buyer or seller (whichever is shorter).[13] On the other hand, if asking prices are uncorrelated in successive time periods, the savings from search will pertain only to that

---

[11] This argument assumes that dealers will discover unusually profitable bids, given the buyers' search, which is, of course, only partly true: there is also a problem of dealers' search with respect to prices.

[12] With the rectangular distribution of asking prices, if each buyer purchases the same number of units, the elasticity of demand falls continuously with price, so that, if average cost equaled price at every rate of sales (with one seller at each price), marginal costs would have to be negative at large outputs. But, of course, the number of sellers can be less at lower prices.

[13] Let the expected minimum price be $p_1 = f(n)_1$ in period 1 (with $f' < 0$) and let the expected minimum price in period 2, with r a measure of the correlation

period,[14] and search in each period is independent of previous experience. If the correlation of successive prices is positive, customer search will be larger in the initial period than in subsequent periods.[15]

The correlation of successive asking prices of sellers is usually positive in the handful of cases I have examined. The rank correlation of anthracite price bids (Table 16–1) in 1953 with those in 1954 was .68 for eight bidders; that for Chevrolet dealers in Chicago February and August of 1959 was .33 for twenty-nine dealers—but, on the other hand, it was zero for Ford dealers for the same dates. Most observed correlations will, of course, be positive because of stable differences in the products or services, but our analysis is restricted to conditions of homogeneity.

As a rule, positive correlations should exist with homogeneous products. The amount of search will vary among individuals because of differences in their expenditures on a commodity or differences in cost of search. A seller who wishes to obtain the continued patronage of those buyers who value the gains of search more highly or have lower costs of search must see to it that he is quoting relatively low prices. In fact, goodwill may be defined as continued patronage by customers without continued search (that is, no more than occasional verification).

A positive correlation of successive asking prices justifies the widely

---

between sellers' successive prices, be

$$p_2 = \left(\frac{p_1}{f(n)_2} \right)^r f(n_2) .$$

If the cost of search is λ per unit, total expenditures for a fixed quantity of purchases (Q) per unit of time are, neglecting interest,

$$E = Q(p_1 + p_2) + \lambda(n_1 + n_2) .$$

Expenditures are a minimum when

$$\frac{\partial E}{\partial n_1} = Qf'(n_1) + Qr[f(n_1)]^{r-1} \times [f(n_2)]^{1-r} f'(n_1) + \lambda = 0.$$

and

$$\frac{\partial E}{\partial n_2} = (1-r)Q[f(n_1)]^r \times [f(n_2)]^{-r} f'(n_2) + \lambda = 0.$$

If $r = 1$, $n_2 = 0$, and n_1 is determined by $Qf'(n_1) = -\lambda/2$, the cost of search is effectively halved.

[14] See n. 13; if $r = 0$, $n_1 = n_2$.

[15] Let $f(n) = e^{-n}$. Then, in the notation of our previous footnotes,

$$n_1 - n_2 = \frac{2r}{1-r} ,$$

approximately.

held view that inexperienced buyers (tourists) pay higher prices in a market than do experienced buyers.[16] The former have no accumulated knowledge of asking prices, and even with an optimum amount of search they will pay higher prices on average. Since the variance of the expected minimum price decreases with additional search, the prices paid by inexperienced buyers will also have a larger variance.

If a buyer enters a wholly new market, he will have no idea of the dispersion of prices and hence no idea of the rational amount of search he should make. In such cases the dispersion will presumably be estimated by some sort of sequential process, and this approach would open up a set of problems I must leave for others to explore. But, in general, one approaches a market with some general knowledge of the amount of dispersion, for dispersion itself is a function of the average amount of search, and this in turn is a function of the nature of the commodity:

1. The larger the fraction of the buyer's expenditures on the commodity, the greater the savings from search and hence the greater the amount of search.
2. The larger the fraction of repetitive (experienced) buyers in the market, the greater the effective amount of search (with positive correlation of successive prices).
3. The larger the fraction of repetitive sellers, the higher the correlation between successive prices, and hence, by condition (2), the larger the amount of accumulated search.[17]
4. The cost of search will be larger, the larger the geographical size of the market.

An increase in the number of buyers has an uncertain effect upon the dispersion of asking prices. The sheer increase in numbers will lead to an increase in the number of dealers and, *ceteris paribus*, to a larger range of asking prices. But, quite aside from advertising, the phenomenon of pooling information will increase. Information is pooled when two buyers compare prices: if each buyer canvasses s sellers, by combining they effectively canvass $2s$ sellers, duplications aside.[18] Consumers compare prices of some commodities (for example, liquor) much more often than of others (for example, chewing gum)—in fact, pooling can be looked upon as a cheaper (and less reliable) form of search.

---

[16] For that matter, a negative correlation would have the same effects.

[17] If the number of sellers (s) and the asking-price distributions are the same in two periods, but k are new sellers, the average period-1 buyer will have lost proportion k/s of his period-1 search.

[18] Duplications will occur more often than random processes would suggest, because pooling is more likely between buyers of similar location, tastes, etc.

Sources of Dispersion

One source of dispersion is simply the cost to dealers of ascertaining rivals' asking prices, but even if this cost were zero the dispersion of prices would not vanish. The more important limitation is provided by buyers' search, and, if the conditions and participants in the market were fixed in perpetuity, prices would immediately approach uniformity. Only those differences could persist which did not remunerate additional search. The condition for optimum search would be (with perfect correlation of successive prices):

$$q\left|\frac{\partial p}{\partial n}\right| = i \times \text{marginal cost of search} ,$$

where i is the interest rate. If an additional search costs $1, and the interest rate is 5·percent, the expected reduction in price with one more search would at equilibrium be equal to $0.05/q$—a quantity which would often be smaller than the smallest unit of currency. But, indivisibilities aside, it would normally be unprofitable for buyers or sellers to eliminate all dispersion.

The maintenance of appreciable dispersion of prices arises chiefly out of the fact that knowledge becomes obsolete. The conditions of supply and demand, and therefore the distribution of asking prices, change over time. There is no method by which buyers or sellers can ascertain the new average price in the market appropriate to the new conditions except by search. Sellers cannot maintain perfect correlation of successive prices, even if they wish to do so, because of the costs of search. Buyers accordingly cannot make the amount of investment in search that perfect correlation of prices would justify. The greater the instability of supply and/or demand conditions, therefore, the greater the dispersion of prices will be.

In addition, there is a component of ignorance due to the changing identity of buyers and sellers. There is a flow of new buyers and sellers in every market, and they are at least initially uninformed on prices and by their presence make the information of experienced buyers and sellers somewhat obsolete.

The amount of dispersion will also vary with one other characteristic which is of special interest: the size.(in terms of both dollars and number of traders) of the market. As the market grows in these dimensions, there will appear a set of firms which specialize in collecting and selling information. They may take the form of trade journals or specialized brokers. Since the cost of collection of information is (approximately) independent of its use (although the cost of dissemination is not), there is a strong tendency toward monopoly in the provision of information: in general, there will be a "standard" source for trade information.

II. ADVERTISING

Advertising is, among other things, a method of providing potential buyers with knowledge of the identity of sellers. It is clearly an immensely powerful instrument for the elimination of ignorance—comparable in force to the use of the book instead of the oral discourse to communicate knowledge. A small $5 advertisement in a metropolitan newspaper reaches (in the sense of being read) perhaps 25,000 readers, or fifty readers per penny, and, even if only a tiny fraction are potential buyers (or sellers), the economy they achieve in search, as compared with uninstructed solicitation, may be overwhelming.

Let us begin with advertisements designed only to identify sellers; the identification of buyers will not be treated explicitly, and the advertising of price will be discussed later. The identification of sellers is necessary because the identity of sellers changes over time, but much more because of the turnover of buyers. In every consumer market there will be a stream of new buyers (resulting from immigration or the attainment of financial maturity) requiring knowledge of sellers, and, in addition, it will be necessary to refresh the knowledge of infrequent buyers.

Suppose, what is no doubt too simple, that a given advertisement of size a will inform c percent of the potential buyers in a given period, so $c = g(a)$.[19] This contact function will presumably show diminishing returns, at least beyond a certain size of advertisement. A certain fraction, b, of potential customers will be "born" (and "die") in a stable population, where "death" includes not only departure from the market but forgetting the seller. The value of b will obviously vary with the nature of the commodity; for example, it will be large for commodities which are seldom purchased (like a house). In a first period of advertising (at a given rate) the number of potential customers reached will be cN, if N is the total number of potential customers. In the second period $cN(1 - b)$

---

[19] The effectiveness of the advertisement is also a function of the skill with which it is done and of the fraction of potential buyers who read the medium, but such elaborations are put aside.

of these potential customers will still be informed, cbN new potential customers will be informed, and

$$c[(1 - b) \, n - cN(1 - b)]$$

old potential customers will be reached for the first time, or a total of

$$cN[1 + (1 - b)(1 - c)] \, .$$

This generalizes, for k periods, to

$$cN[1 + (1 - b)(1 - c) + \ldots + (1 - b)^{k-1}(1 - c)^{k-1}] \, ,$$

and, if k is large, this approaches

$$\frac{cN}{1 - (1 - c)(1 - b)} = \lambda N \, . \tag{4}$$

The proportion (λ) of potential buyers informed of the advertiser's identity thus depends upon c and b.

If each of r sellers advertises the same amount, λ is the probability that any one seller will inform any buyer. The distribution of N potential buyers by the number of contacts achieved by r sellers is given by the binomial distribution:

$$N(\lambda + [1 - \lambda])^r \, ,$$

with, for example,

$$\frac{Nr!}{m!(r - m)!} \lambda^m (1 - \lambda)^{r-m}$$

buyers being informed of exactly m sellers' identities. The number of sellers known to a buyer ranges from zero to r, with an average of $r\lambda$ sellers and a variance of $r\lambda(1 - \lambda)$.[20]

The amount of relevant information in the market, even in this simple model, is not easy to summarize in a single measure—a difficulty common to frequency distributions. If all buyers wished to search s sellers, all buyers knowing less than s sellers would have inadequate information, and all who knew more than s sellers would have redundant information, although the redundant information would not be worthless.[21] Since the value of information is the amount by which it reduces

[20] This approach has both similarities and contrasts to that published by S. A. Ozga, "Imperfect Markets through Lack of Knowledge," *Quarterly Journal of Economics*, Vol. LXXIV (February 1960), pp. 29–52.

[21] The larger the number of sellers known, the larger is the range of prices among the sellers and the lower the expected minimum price after s searches. But this effect will normally be small.

the expected cost to the buyer of his purchases, if these expected reductions are ΔC_1, ΔC_2, . . . , for searches of 1, 2, . . . , the value of the information to buyers is approximately

$$\sum_{m=1}^{r} \frac{r!}{m!(r-m)!} \lambda^m (1-\lambda)^{r-m} \Delta C_m .$$

The information possessed by buyers, however, is not simply a matter of chance; those buyers who spend more on the commodity, or who search more for a given expenditure, will also search more for advertisements. The buyers with more information will, on average, make more extensive searches, so the value of information will be greater than this last formula indicates.

We may pause to discuss the fact that advertising in, say, a newspaper is normally "paid" for by the seller. On our analysis, the advertising is valuable to the buyer, and he would be willing to pay more for a paper with advertisements than for one without. The difficulty with having the sellers insert advertisements "free" and having the buyer pay for them directly is that it would be difficult to ration space on this basis: the seller would have an incentive to supply an amount of information (or information of a type) the buyer did not wish, and, since numerous advertisements are supplied jointly, the buyer could not register clearly his preferences regarding advertising. (Catalogues, however, are often sold to buyers.) Charging the seller for the advertisements creates an incentive for him to supply to the buyer only the information which is desired.

It is commonly complained that advertising is jointly supplied with the commodity in the sense that the buyer must pay for both even though he wishes only the latter. The alternative of selling the advertising separately from the commodity, however, would require that the advertising of various sellers (of various commodities) would be supplied jointly: the economies of disseminating information in a general-purpose periodical are so great that some form of jointness is inescapable. But the common complaint is much exaggerated: the buyer who wishes can search out the seller who advertises little (but, of course, enough to be discoverable), and the latter can sell at prices lower by the savings on advertising.

These remarks seem most appropriate to newspaper advertisements of the "classified" variety; what of the spectacular television show or the weekly comedian? We are not equipped to discuss advertising in general because the problem of quality has been (and will continue to be) evaded by the assumption of homogeneous goods. Even within our narrower framework, however, the use of entertainment to attract buyers to information is a comprehensible phenomenon. The assimilation of information is not an easy or pleasant task for most people, and they may well be willing to pay more for the information when supplied in an enjoyable form. In principle, this complementary demand for information and entertainment is exactly analogous to the complementary demand of consumers for commodities and delivery service or air-conditioned stores. One might find a paradox in the simultaneous complaints of some people that advertising is too elaborate and school *houses* too shoddy.

A monopolist will advertise (and price the product) so as to maximize his profits,

$$\pi = Npq\lambda - \phi(N\lambda q) - ap_a ,$$

where $p = f(q)$ is the demand curve of the individual buyer, $\phi(N\lambda q)$ is production costs other than advertising, and ap_a is advertising expenditures. The maximum profit conditions are

$$\frac{\partial \pi}{\partial q} = N\lambda \left(p + q\frac{\partial p}{\partial q} \right) - \phi'N\lambda = 0 \qquad (5)$$

and

$$\frac{\partial \pi}{\partial a} = Npq\frac{\partial \lambda}{\partial a} - \phi'Nq\frac{\partial \lambda}{\partial a} - p_a = 0 . \qquad (6)$$

Equation (5) states the usual marginal cost–marginal revenue equality, and equation (6) states the equality of (price — marginal cost) with the marginal cost $[p_a/Nq(\partial\lambda/\partial a)]$ of advertising.[22]

With the Cournot spring (where production costs $\phi = 0$) the monopolist advertises up to the point where price equals the marginal cost of informing a buyer: the monopolist will not (cannot) exploit ignorance as he exploits desire. The monopolist will advertise more, the higher the "death" rate (b), unless it is very high relative to the "contact" rate

[22] The marginal revenue from advertising expenditure,

$$\frac{Npq}{p_a} \frac{\partial \lambda}{\partial a}$$

equals the absolute value of the elasticity of demand by equations (5) and (6); see R. Dorfman and P. O. Steiner, "Optimal Advertising and Optimal Quality," *American Economic Review*, Vol. XLIV (1954), p. 826.

(c).[23] The monopolistic situation does not invite comparison with competition because an essential feature—the value of search in the face of price dispersion—is absent.

A highly simplified analysis of advertising by the competitive firm is presented in the Appendix. On the assumption that all firms are identical and that all buyers have identical demand curves and search equal amounts, we obtain the maximum-profit equation:

$$\text{Marginal production cost} = p\left(1 + \frac{1}{\eta_{qp} + \eta_{Kp}}\right), \tag{7}$$

where η_{qp} is the elasticity of a buyer's demand curve and η_{Kp} is the elasticity of the fraction of buyers purchasing from the seller with respect to his price. The latter elasticity will be of the order of magnitude of the number of searches made by a buyer. With a uniform distribution of asking prices, increased search will lead to increased advertising by low-price sellers and reduced advertising by high-price sellers. The amount of advertising by a firm decreases as the number of firms increases.

Price advertising has a decisive influence on the dispersion of prices. Search now becomes extremely economical, and the question arises why, in the absence of differences in quality of products, the dispersion does not vanish. And the answer is simply that, if prices are advertised by a large portion of the sellers, the price differences diminish sharply. That they do not wholly vanish (in a given market) is due simply to the fact that no combination of advertising media reaches all potential buyers within the available time.

Assuming, as we do, that all sellers are equally convenient in location, must we say that some buyers are perverse in not reading the advertisements? Obviously not, for the cost of keeping currently informed about all articles which an individual purchases would be prohibitive. A typical household probably buys several hundred different items a month, and, if, on average, their prices change (in some outlets) only once a month, the number of advertisements (by at least several sellers) which must be read is forbiddingly large.

The seller's problem is even greater: he may sell two thousand items (a modest number for a grocery or hardware store), and to adver-

---

[23] Differentiating equation (6) with respect to b, we find that $\partial a/\partial b$ is positive or negative according as

$$b \lessgtr \frac{c}{1 - c}.$$

If $c \geq \frac{1}{2}$, the derivative must be positive.

tise each on the occasion of a price change—and frequently enough there-after to remind buyers of his price—would be impossibly expensive. To keep the buyers in a market informed on the current prices of all items of consumption would involve perhaps a thousandfold increase of news-paper advertising.

From the manufacturer's viewpoint, uncertainty concerning his price is clearly disadvantageous. The cost of search is a cost of purchase, and consumption will therefore be smaller, the greater the dispersion of prices and the greater the optimum amount of search. This is presumably one reason (but, I conjecture, a very minor one) why uniform prices are set by sellers of nationally advertised brands: if they have eliminated price variation, they have reduced the cost of the commodity (including search) to the buyer, even if the dealers' margins average somewhat more than they otherwise would.

The effect of advertising prices, then, is equivalent to that of the introduction of a very large amount of search by a large portion of the potential buyers. It follows from our discussion in Section I that the dispersion of asking prices will be much reduced. Since advertising of prices will be devoted to products for which the marginal value of search is high, it will tend to reduce dispersion most in commodities with large aggregate expenditures.

III. CONCLUSIONS

The identification of sellers and the discovery of their prices are only one sample of the vast role of the search for information in economic life. Similar problems exist in the detection of profitable fields for investment and in the worker's choice of industry, location, and job. The search for knowledge on the quality of goods, which has been studiously avoided in this paper, is perhaps no more important but, certainly, analytically more difficult. Quality has not yet been successfully specified by economics, and this elusiveness extends to all problems in which it enters.

Some forms of economic organization may be explicable chiefly as devices for eliminating uncertainties in quality. The department store, as Milton Friedman has suggested to me, may be viewed as an institution which searches for the superior qualities of goods and guarantees that they are good quality. "Reputation" is a word which denotes the persis-tence of quality, and reputation commands a price (or exacts a penalty) because it economizes on search. When economists deplore the reliance of the consumer on reputation—although they choose the articles they read (and their colleagues) in good part on this basis—they implicitly assume that the consumer has a large laboratory, ready to deliver current information quickly and gratuitously.

Ignorance is like subzero weather: by a sufficient expenditure its effects upon people can be kept within tolerable or even comfortable bounds, but it would be wholly uneconomic entirely to eliminate all its effects. And, just as an analysis of man's shelter and apparel would be somewhat incomplete if cold weather is ignored, so also our understanding of economic life will be incomplete if we do not systematically take account of the cold winds of ignorance.

Appendix

Under competition, the amount of advertising by any one seller (i) can be determined as follows. Each buyer will engage in an amount s of search, which is determined by the factors discussed above (Sec. 1). He will on average know

$$(r-1)\lambda + \lambda_i$$

sellers, where λ_i is defined by equation (4) for seller i. Hence,

$$\frac{\lambda_i}{(r-1)\lambda + \lambda_i}$$

percent of buyers who know seller i will canvass him on one search, and

$$\left(1 - \frac{\lambda_i}{(r-1)\lambda + \lambda_i}\right)^s$$

percent of the buyers who know i will not canvass him in s searches,

$$s \leqslant (r-1)\lambda + \lambda_i.$$

Therefore, of the buyers who know i, the proportion who will canvass him at least once is[24]

$$1 - \left(1 - \frac{\lambda_i}{(r-1)\lambda + \lambda_i}\right)^s.$$

If we approximate

$$\frac{\lambda_i}{(r-1)\lambda + \lambda_i}$$

by

$$\frac{\lambda_i}{r\lambda}$$

[24] The formula errs slightly in allowing the multiple canvass of one seller by a buyer.

and take only the first two terms of the binomial expansion, this becomes

$$\frac{s\lambda_i}{r\lambda}$$

The receipts of any seller then become the product of (1) the number of buyers canvassing him,

$$\frac{s\lambda_i}{r\lambda}\lambda_i N = T_i ,$$

(2) the fraction K of those canvassing him who buy from him, where K depends upon his relative price (and the amount of search and the number of rivals), and (3) sales to each customer, pq. If ϕ (T_iKq) is production costs and ap_a advertising costs, profits are

$$\pi = T_iKpq - \phi(T_iKq) - ap_a .$$

The conditions for maximum profits are

$$\frac{\partial \pi}{\partial p} = T_i\left(K\frac{\partial pq}{\partial p} + pq\frac{\partial K}{\partial p}\right) - T_i\phi'\left(K\frac{\partial q}{\partial p} + q\frac{\partial K}{\partial p}\right) = 0 \qquad (8)$$

and

$$\frac{\partial \pi}{\partial a} = Kpq\frac{\partial T_i}{\partial a} - \phi'Kq\frac{\partial T_i}{\partial a} - p_a = 0 . \qquad (9)$$

The former equation can be rewritten in elasticities as

$$\phi' = p\left(1 + \frac{1}{\eta_{qp} + \eta_{Kp}}\right) \qquad (8a)$$

Price exceeds marginal cost, not simply by $(-p/\eta_{qp})$ as with monopoly, but by the smaller amount

$$\frac{-p}{\eta_{qp} + \eta_{Kp}}$$

where η_{Kp} will generally be of the order of magnitude of the number of searches made by a buyer.[25] Equation (9) states the equality of the marginal revenue of advertising with its marginal cost. By differentiating equation (9) with respect to s and taking ϕ' as constant, it can be shown that increased search by buyers will lead to increased advertising by low-

---

[25] In the case of the uniform distribution, η_{Kp} is

$$\frac{-(s-1)p}{1-p} .$$

price sellers and reduced advertising by high-price sellers (with a uniform distribution of prices).[26]

By the same method it may be shown that the amount of advertising by the firm will decrease as the number of rivals increases.[27] The aggregate amount of advertising by the industry may either increase or decrease with an increase in the number of firms, s, depending on the relationship between λ and a.

[26] The derivative $\partial a / \partial s$ has the sign of $(1 + \eta_{Ks})$, and this elasticity equals

$$1 + s \log [1 - p]$$

with a uniform distribution of prices.

[27] By differentiation of equation (2) with respect to r one gets

$$r \frac{\partial a}{\partial r} \left\{ \lambda_i \frac{\partial^2 \lambda_i}{\partial a^2} + \left(\frac{\partial \lambda_i}{\partial a} \right)^2 \right\} = \lambda_i \frac{\partial \lambda_i}{\partial a} \left(1 - \frac{r}{K} \frac{\partial K}{\partial r} \right).$$

The term in brackets on the left side is negative by the stability condition; the right side is positive.

Chapter

17

INFORMATION IN THE
LABOR MARKET*[1]

The young person entering the labor market for the first time has an immense number of potential employers, scarce as they may seem the first day. If he is an unskilled or a semiskilled worker, the number of potential employers is strictly in the millions. Even if he has a specialized training, the number of potential employers will be in the thousands: the young Ph.D. in economics, for example, has scores of colleges and universities, dozens of governmental agencies, hundreds of business firms, and the Ford Foundation as potential employers. As the worker becomes older the number of potential employers may shrink more often than it grows, but the number will seldom fall to even a thousand.

No worker, unless his degree of specialization is pathological, will ever be able to become informed on the prospective earnings which would be obtained from every one of these potential employers at any given time, let alone keep this information up to date. He faces the problem of how to acquire information on the wage rates, stability of employment, conditions of employment, and other determinants of job choice, and how to keep this information current. I shall concentrate attention on the determination of wage rates.

I. THE DISPERSION OF WAGE RATES

Even with strict homogeneity of commodities, we usually find some dispersion in the prices which are offered by sellers or buyers. Only if either buyers have complete knowledge of all sellers' offers, or all sellers have complete knowledge of all buyers' offers, will there be a single price. Complete knowledge, however, is seldom possessed, simply be-

* Reprinted from *Journal of Political Economy*, Vol. LXX, No. 5 (October 1962), Part 2, Supplement. Copyright 1962 by the University of Chicago.

[1] I am deeply indebted to Claire Friedland for the statistical work in this paper. H. Gregg Lewis made very helpful comments on an earlier version.

cause it costs more to learn of alternative prices than (at the margin) this information yields.[2]

The labor markets display the same characteristics, but their analysis is much complicated by the lack of homogeneity of the workers (and, to a much lesser extent, of non-wage conditions of employment). In order to form some estimate of the nature of the "pure" dispersion of wages due to imperfect knowledge, we shall begin with a very special class of college graduates.

A tolerably pure estimate of the dispersion of wage offers to homogeneous labor is provided by the contemporary offers to the same person. For 44 graduates of the Graduate School of Business at the University of Chicago who received 144 offers (in 1960 and 1961) from corporations, the standard deviation of monthly rates was $43. The mean offer was $540.7, so the coefficient of variation was 7.9 percent.[3]

Since this job market was completely localized in one office, and there is considerable intercommunication among the national companies whose representatives solicit prospective employees (and among prospective employees), this appears to be a conservative estimate of the gross dispersion for given quality. The fact that each student on average solicited only 2.25 offers works in the same direction. The differences in the attractiveness of non-wage elements of the various jobs, however, are impossible to discover.[4] On balance it appears that the true dispersion is substantially underestimated, and later evidence suggests that it may be much larger in less organized markets.

Unfortunately, distributions of offers to given individuals are not available for any large occupational group or any extended geographical market. One must deal with offers (or wage rates paid) by individual

[2] The argument is elaborated in my "The Economics of Information," *Journal of Political Economy,* June 1961. [Chapter 16 above.]

[3] There was no systematic or significant difference in the standard deviations for those who received 2, 3, 4, or 5 or more offers:

| Number of | | Standard |
Offers	Students	Deviation
2...............	17	$46
3...............	13	35
4...............	7	49
5 or more........	7	43

The basic data were made available by courtesy of David Huntington of the Placement Bureau of the Graduate School of Business.

[4] The extent to which initial wage rates are reliable indexes of subsequent wage rates is investigated below.

employers or groups of employers, and the dispersion of such offers may be either larger or smaller than the true distribution we desire. The dispersion of distributions of company average offers will be larger insofar as they reflect differences in quality of workers (or of jobs),[5] or cover several labor markets; the dispersion will be smaller insofar as intracompany dispersion is eliminated. In our sample of business graduates, the standard deviation of the average offers of companies is $40, compared with that of $43 for given students. Although no unique relationship between these dispersions can be assumed, we can and will assume that for similar labor markets they are reasonably well correlated.

The dispersion of wage offers in the small Chicago sample is approximately equal to that of the national sample of wage offers made each year by Frank Endicott.[6] The coefficients of variation of groups other than engineers range from 6.4 percent to 9.1 percent (Table 17–1); the corresponding figure for our sample was 7.3 percent.

TABLE 17–1
MONTHLY HIRING RATES OF COLLEGE GRADUATES BY
LARGE CORPORATIONS, 1958–60

Occupation	Number of Companies	Mean Salaries			Coefficient of Variation (Percent)		
		1958	1959	1960	1958	1959	1960
Engineers	66	472	493	515	4.04	4.22	4.26
Accountants	40	421	435	457	6.45	6.93	6.42
Salesmen	29	410	426	447	8.78	8.18	9.11
General business....	41	403	416	431	8.60	8.96	8.64

Source: Endicott Survey worksheets. All companies here included reported in each of the three years.

If the expected period of employment exceeds one year (as it does), the worker must also make an estimate of future wage differences among employers. Endicott's data permit an estimate of the correlation of successive annual rates (Table 17–2). The correlations are high, and—what is more surprising—two of the four cases show no tendency to diminish when the time period is lengthened to two years. If the correlations were to remain high for long periods, the differences in wages would presumably reflect compensating differences in the non-wage terms of employment. But the normal pattern surely is one of declining correlation co-

[5] The variance of offers, within a given specialty, is usually much larger between than "within" individuals who have received multiple offers.

[6] We are indebted to Endicott for permission to examine the company reports for three years.

efficients as the period is lengthened, if only as a Galton regression phenomenon.

TABLE 17–2
CORRELATION COEFFICIENTS OF SALARY RATES IN 1958, 1959, AND 1960 FOR COLLEGE GRADUATES

		Correlation Coefficient		
Occupation	Number of Companies	1958 and 1959	1959 and 1960	1958 and 1960
Engineers	66	.660	.761	.577
Accountants	40	.723	.872	.720
Sales	29	.849	.885	.871
General business........	41	.853	.891	.873

Source: Same as Table 17–1.

Differences in initial wage rates would also be offset by different rates of increase in wages, so the present values of different jobs could still be equal. Endicott's survey for 1960 reported the average salary paid to college graduates after one year of service, and these salaries may be compared with those paid initially. The relationship for accountants was

$$W_2 = 24.71 + 1.039W_1, \qquad (N = 67),$$
$$(.062)$$

where W_2 was the wage in 1960 and W_1 the wage in 1959; the relationship is close ($r = .900$). So far as these data go, they suggest that initial wage rates are a good predictor of wage rates in the following year.

These fragments illustrate rather than prove the existence of substantial dispersion in hiring rates for homogeneous labor. This dispersion cannot be measured precisely, but is of the order of magnitude of 5–10 percent even in so well organized a market as that of college graduates at a single university.

II. THE PROBLEM OF INFORMATION

A worker will search for wage offers (and an employer will search for wage demands) until the expected marginal return equals the marginal cost of search. Under what conditions will this search eliminate all dispersion of wage rates for homogeneous labor?

The conditions are severe. It is not sufficient for demand and supply to have been stable indefinitely long, and hence "the" equilibrium wage not to have changed for an indefinitely long period, in order to eliminate all dispersion. If workers were to change employment (perhaps because of improving skills) or employers were to change identity (because of the turnover of firms), it still would not pay to search enough to eliminate all dispersion. But if these changes were infrequent—say, once every three years or more—the dispersion of wage rates would be fairly small, although not negligible.[7] Changes in jobs due to changes in workers' tastes and abilities and employers' identities therefore set some minimum on the dispersion of wage rates. If the market has appreciable geographical extent, transportation costs of workers (and plants) add to this minimum dispersion.

The fluctuations of supply-and-demand conditions add a new source of dispersion. The information of the worker (and employer) now becomes obsolete with time: there will be changes in the level of wages and in the relative wage rates of different employers (and workers) which call for additional search. The more rapidly "the" equilibrium wage rate changes, the smaller the returns from search and hence the smaller the amount of search that will be undertaken—and the larger the resulting wage dispersion.

The subsequent analysis is devoted to an application of this approach to the costs and returns from search for various types of workers. The unavailability of a temporal sequence of closely spaced wage distributions makes it impossible to explore the effects of rates of change of equilibrium prices on the amount of dispersion.

[7] With a rectangular wage offer distribution between 0 and 1, the average maximum wage encountered in n searches is $n/(n+1)$, so the expected marginal wage rate gain from $(n+1)$ searches is

$$\frac{n+1}{n+2} - \frac{n}{n+1} = \frac{1}{(n+1)(n+2)},$$

which, multiplied by the expected duration of employment, is the marginal income gain from search. If employment is expected to last m days, and the cost of search is k days, the amount of search will be given by

$$\frac{m}{(n+1)(n+2)} = \frac{kn}{n+1},$$

or n is approximately $\sqrt{m/k}$, or (say) 25 with three years of expected employment, and $k = 1$. The coefficient of variation of wages is

$$\sqrt{\frac{n}{(n+1)^2(n+2)}} \cdot \frac{n+1}{n} = \frac{1}{\sqrt{n(n+2)}} = \sqrt{\frac{k}{m}},$$

which would be 4 percent in our example. This argument is an adaptation of that in "The Economics of Information," *op. cit.*, p. 215.

The Returns from Search by Workers

We shall begin our analysis of the returns from search by forming some estimate of the magnitude of the return as a function of the amount of search. To this end, let us assume that the wage offers by all possible employers are normally distributed.[8] Then the expected maximum wage offer (w_m) a man will encounter in n searches is approximately[9]

$$w_m = .65 n^{.37} \sigma_w + \overline{w},$$

and the marginal wage rate increase from one additional search is

$$\frac{\partial w_n}{\partial n} = \frac{.24 \sigma_w}{n^{.63}}.$$

If $\sigma_w = \overline{w}/10$, the marginal wage rate gain from additional search is:

Search (n)	Marginal Wage Rate Gain
5	.0087 $\overline{w}$
10	.0056 $\overline{w}$
15	.0044 $\overline{w}$
20	.0036 $\overline{w}$

If the annual wage rate is $6,000, the marginal wage rate gain is therefore of the order of $20 to $50 in this range of search.

If the structure of employer wage offers were permanently fixed, and if the worker lived forever, the marginal income gain from additional search would be simply the capitalized value of the marginal *wage-rate* gain. If the structure were permanent and the duration of employment t_o years, the marginal *income* gain would be the value of the corresponding annuity, namely,

$$\frac{\partial w_n}{\partial n} \frac{(1+i)^{t_o} - 1}{i(1+i)^{t_o}}.$$

In this extreme case of a permanent wage structure, the order of magnitude of the marginal income gain from search is illustrated by the following table, where $\sigma_w = \overline{w}/10$ and $i = 6$ percent.

---

[8] The Chicago student wage offers are consistent with this assumption, and it seems intuitively more plausible than the rectangular distribution which was used (for algebraic convenience) in "The Economics of Information" and in n. 7.

[9] The expression is simply an approximation (for $3 < n < 20$) to the mean maximum observation from a normal population in random samples of size n; the precise values are given in W. J. Dixon and F. J. Massey, *Introduction to Statistical Analysis* (New York, 1957), p. 407.

Prospective Years of Employment	Amount of Search	
	5 Employers	15 Employers
3.............	.023 $\overline{w}$	.012 $\overline{w}$
5.............	.037 $\overline{w}$	.018 $\overline{w}$
10.............	.064 $\overline{w}$	.032 $\overline{w}$

For the $6,000 salary level, these marginal income gains run from $66 (fifteen employers, three years) to $384 (five employers, ten years).

But these gains are exaggerated because there is not a perfect correlation between the wage offers of employers in successive time periods. The employers themselves do not know wage offers sufficiently well to preserve a perfect correlation, even if they mysteriously wished it, and the appearance of new employers adds a further reason for continued search by the worker.

When the correlation of successive wage offers is positive but less than unity it will still pay the worker to search more intensively in the earlier periods because this search will have some value in subsequent periods. In a simple two-period model, the details of which are given in the appendix, the increased search in the first period due to correlation of wage rates will increase the expected maximum wage offer in the proportion $br^2/(1 - b)$, or approximately $r^2/2$. If $r = .5$, the amount of search in period 1 will be increased by 20 percent, with roughly a 12 percent increase in salary.

It would be possible to analyze a variety of phenomena in the light of the correlation of successive wage offers. For example, the higher the correlation, the longer the expected tenure of a worker with a company, and therefore the lower the quit rate. Unfortunately there are no published data, so far as I know, which allow calculation of the correlations, although of course these data dwell in the worksheets of numerous wage surveys.

As a poor substitute, one can examine the average wage rates (measured by earnings per worker) on a geographical basis. The average earnings per worker in a state will be an index of wage rates in the given industry, and it will be a better index the more similar the occupational and wage structures of the industry in various states. A sample of such calculations is reported in Table 17–3.

Several features of these geographical patterns are noteworthy. The dispersion of earnings among states is much smaller in the recent period, and the decline occurred in twenty-one of twenty-five industries. The inference is that the national market has become more perfect, and the inference is commended by the fact that costs of movement have fallen

TABLE 17–3

CHARACTERISTICS OF AVERAGE EARNINGS IN SELECTED MANUFACTURING INDUSTRIES, 1904–9 AND 1947–54
(Identical States)

Industry	Number of States	Correlation Coefficients		Average Coefficient of Variation (Percent)	
		1904 and 1909	1947 and 1954	1904 and 1909	1947 and 1954
Non-ferrous foundries..........	8	.895	.663	15.3	8.7
Motor vehicles and equipment...	9	.349	.106	8.9	4.9
Structural clay products........	23	.982	.938	29.4	19.3
Ship and boat building.........	9	.894	.703	17.6	10.6
Rubber products..............	8	.270	.672	8.1	6.4
Musical instruments and parts...	7	.953	.460	25.7	8.7
Confectionery products........	17	.819	.876	15.3	17.8
Beer and ale.................	12	.921	.834	15.4	10.8
Mattresses and bedsprings......	9	.830	.906	22.0	22.9
Furniture and fixtures, excluding mattresses and bedsprings....	33	.941	.912	26.2	17.0
Fertilizers	13	.905	.952	20.4	20.4
Meat products...............	29	.728	.922	18.5	15.8
Flour and meal..............	14	.935	.530	21.8	12.0
Bakery products.............	20	.952	.918	18.2	12.6
Bottled soft drinks...........	15	.954	.874	20.1	18.4
Manufactured ice.............	21	.926	.854	22.8	25.5
Woolen and worsted fabrics.....	8	.987	.844	17.6	8.7
Knitting mills................	17	.955	.774	23.5	11.2
Paperboard containers........	18	.906	.926	17.1	14.0
Printing and publishing........	47	.912	.906	21.3	11.8
Drugs and medicines..........	13	.725	.924	16.2	14.0
Soap and related products......	10	.950	.681	14.8	12.0
Paints and allied products......	15	.742	.870	18.4	11.2
Leather tanning and finishing....	9	.968	.906	19.0	13.8
Footwear (except rubber).......	12	.932	.703	13.1	9.2
Average......................		.853	.786	18.7	13.5

substantially relative to wage rates over the period. The correlation coefficients reveal a slight decline on average, although they are based upon a seven-year interval in the later period (including a year of turbulent demobilization) as against a five-year interval in the earlier period.[10] The

[10] The industries are also more homogeneous in the later period, and this serves to increase the correlation coefficients.

comparison timidly suggests that the difference in earnings increasingly represents differences in the quality of labor rather than in its compensation.

The most direct implication of the formal analysis is that the gains from search are larger the longer the prospective period of employment. When search is more extensive, however, the dispersion of maximum wage rates will be smaller—the lowest wage offers will more often be rejected for known better offers.[11] So the realized dispersion of wage rates should be smaller the longer the prospective period of employment. Several tests of this implication can be made.

Women generally expect to stay in the labor force a shorter period than men do, so among homogeneous groups of men and women we should expect that the latter have larger dispersions. The occupational wage surveys do reveal this expected difference.[12] The major difficulty in making extensive tests of this prediction is that the tabulated Census data on earnings (in 1940 and 1950) do not allow the removal of the effects of age (men have a much wider dispersion of ages) and of race (Negro women are a larger fraction of the female labor force than Negro men are of the male labor force).[13]

Similar comparisons can be made of younger and older workers.

---

[11] Or, more precisely, the distribution of maximum offers has a variance that decreases as the number of searches increases.

[12] For example, hourly earnings of shipping packers in manufacturing in Chicago have the following characteristics:

	1952	1957
Males:		
Interquartile range	23.4¢	43.8¢
Median rate	144.2	182.0
Interquartile ratio (percent)	16.2	24.1
Females:		
Interquartile range	28.4¢	45.8¢
Median rate	109.8	175.7
Interquartile ratio (percent)	25.9	26.1

Source: Bureau of Labor Statistics, Bulls. 1105 and 1202–15.

With normally distributed varieties, the interquartile ratio is 1.35 times the coefficient of variation.

[13] A moderately extensive analysis was made of dispersions of income in 1949 in large cities for selected occupations, and an analysis was made of earnings in 1939 for waiters and waitresses. The 1949 data showed larger dispersions for women than for men; the 1939 data for the one occupation showed the opposite. The heterogeneity of age and race (and in 1940 the inclusion of self-employed workers) are such that I believe the results are wholly inconclusive. For the same reason, the consistently smaller *average* wages of women (which are predicted by the theory) are not supporting evidence.

The coefficient of variation increases with age for engineers (see Table 17–4). The coefficient of variation of 1949 earnings of plumbers and pipe-fitters was 40.8 percent; that of apprentices was 32.9 percent.[14] The dis-

TABLE 17–4
MONTHLY ENGINEERING EARNINGS, BY AGE, 1929

Age	Mean Monthly Earnings	Standard Deviation	Coefficient of Variation (Percent)
23.................	161.0	85.1*	52.9*
24–25.............	189.5	58.2	30.7
26–27.............	230.1	86.4	37.6
28–31.............	282.8	117.5	41.6
32–35.............	349.9	175.7	50.2
36–39.............	400.0	221.6	55.4
40–47.............	464.1	294.5	63.5
48–55.............	510.0	346.0	67.8
56–63.............	544.3	399.8	73.4
64 or more........	487.6	356.3	73.1

* This class appears to be heterogeneous: two of the respondents had salaries 20 standard deviations above the mean.
Source: A. Fraser, Jr., "Employment and Earnings in the Engineering Profession, 1929 to 1934," Bureau of Labor Statistics, Bull. No. 682, 233, Table 2.

persion of salaries of college teachers is larger the higher the rank (and age) of the teacher.[15] A more powerful test would be provided by a comparison of wages of students in summer employment with young men of the same age who had permanently left school.

[14] On the other hand, the coefficients of variation for machinists and tool makers (30.1 percent) and apprentices (29.7 percent) were essentially identical. These are all United States data, influenced by extent of part-time work (which was much higher among apprentices than among machinists).

[15] The interquartile ratios $[(Q_3 - Q_1)/Q_2]$ of academic salaries in 1959–60 were:

Rank	Percent	
	Men	Women
Professor	33.0	31.8
Associate professor............	23.3	26.2
Assistant professor............	19.7	24.2
Instructor	19.3	21.7

These calculations are based upon National Education Association, Higher Education Series, Research Report, 1960–R3. See also my Trends in Employment in the Service Industries (New York: National Bureau of Economic Research, 1956), p. 128.

The smaller dispersion of salaries of women professors is found in every type of college and university reported. Women make up less than one-twelfth of the full professors and more than twice as large a fraction even of associate professors. The roles of ability and discrimination in producing this reversal of the basic pattern would be interesting to know.

Our original estimate of the coefficient of variation of earnings in section 1 was of the order of 10 percent. The differences cited above—for example, 60 percent versus 30 percent for engineers of fifty-five and twenty-five years of age—might suggest a much larger estimate of the effects of ignorance. These gross dispersions are due to at least three different components, however, only the first two of which involve information:

i. The dispersion of earnings of engineers increases with age because younger engineers make more extensive search than older engineers.
ii. The difference in ability of engineers becomes better known as they become older (and have worked longer for a given employer).[16]
iii. The older engineers have made different amounts of "on-the-job" investment in training, which serves to increase their dispersion of abilities.

The disentanglement of the second and third components of dispersion is especially difficult. We reach again the conclusion that the differences in quality of workers cast a deep shadow over all measures of pure dispersion due to differences in knowledge (or, for that matter, due to other forms of investment).

The effect of the absolute level of earnings, which may also enter into the determination of the gain from search, will be considered in the next section.

The Costs of Search

The larger the cost of search the less search will be undertaken by a worker at a given level of dispersion of employers' wage offers. These costs will vary systematically with various characteristics of occupations.

When prospective employers of a worker are readily identified—which is partly associated with how specialized a worker is—search for a job is more economical: one does not have to waste inquiries on wholly irrelevant possibilities. We should therefore expect the dispersion of actual wage rates to be less the more easily the employers are identified.

This prediction is supported by several analyses of earnings in the twenty metropolitan areas in 1950. Domestic servants have higher coefficients of variation than laundry operatives in nineteen of twenty areas (with means of 75.2 percent and 54.0 percent, respectively). The confirmation is less emphatic in the comparison of taxi drivers with truck

---

[16] This increased dispersion in earnings due to better recognition of differences in ability (the search for information on the quality of workers) is of course to be reckoned as a reduction in the dispersion of earnings of homogeneous workers.

drivers (the former have lower coefficients of variation in thirteen of twenty regions, but the means are virtually identical: 44.2 percent and 45.7 percent).[17]

The costs of search are also lower the higher the probability that a given, identified employer is taking on men. This would argue that in periods of expanding employment the dispersion of wages will be smaller. But unemployment among a class of workers also works in the opposite direction to reduce the cost of search. Within local markets the cost of search is primarily a cost in time, to be valued (at least approximately) by the mean wage rate, as a measure of the leisure value of time. But for the unemployed worker, this alternative cost of leisure is negligible. In the search in other labor markets, however, both transportation costs and foregone earnings must be incurred.[18]

The effects of the level of earnings on the amount of search are equally difficult to disentangle. If the absolute dispersion (σ_w) is proportional to the mean wage, the mean wage affects costs and returns from search proportionately, and there is no effect on the amount of search. On the other hand, it appears to have been the regular practice for employment agencies to charge a fee that is a higher percentage of larger initial salaries—the fee is progressive.[19] The simplest explanation would be that the expected duration of employment is greater the higher the initial wage rate. On the whole, this kind of evidence seems much more persuasive than that based on interoccupational comparisons.

The search for information may take forms other than direct solicitation: newspaper advertisements, employment agencies, employer search, and the myriad forms of pooling of information by workers. Some require little expenditure of time and—if used alone—would lead us to expect that the dispersion of wage rates should be equal in absolute terms (standard deviations, not coefficients of variation) for workers at different wage levels. Such information, however, is incomplete and limited, and if more is needed solicitation is eventually resorted to. The marginal cost of search may rise as search increases.

The private employment agencies offer a fertile field for investigation from this viewpoint. Their *raison d'être* is information, and they should have specialized in the occupations in which information is most

---

[17] These Census data are moderately more persuasive than those rejected earlier because differences due to race, part-time work, and age are smaller.

[18] Hence the mean wage rates for given work should vary more among establishments in an extensive area than within a single labor market.

[19] P. H. Douglas and A. Director, *The Problem of Unemployment* (1931), p. 267.

difficult for the employer or worker to obtain. Their fees, indeed, would provide a direct estimate of the marginal cost of information in these occupations.

III. THE EMPLOYERS' SEARCH

There is direct search by employers, wholly comparable to that of workers, in certain industries. College teaching is an obvious example: the employer canvasses graduate schools, professional journals, and the like for potential employees and invites them in to be looked over. This kind of direct solicitation is most probable when the workers are highly specialized, of course.

The main reason for workers undertaking the burden of solicitation is that it is cheaper for them than for employers. When an employer has numerous employees the probability that a given employer needs additional workers is much greater than the probability that a given worker will accept a job offer. The identification problem is usually also less for a worker than for an employer—the fraction of wasted search will be much smaller for a steelworker than for a steel company. But where the number of employees per employer approaches unity (domestic service, vice-presidents in charge of marketing), the employer usually takes on some or all of the task of search.

The employers' search involves more than the identification of potential workers: they must be "processed" to a degree set by the personnel practices, and there are training costs (including low productivity) for a time. Walter Oi estimates that the initial hiring and training cost per worker was (in 1951) about $382 for International Harvester, the cost rising rapidly with the level of skill.[20]

One way to reduce hiring costs is to pay higher relative wages. Not only is the quit rate of existing workers reduced by high wages, but on average, more obviously high-quality workers will accept offers. Wage rates and skilled search are substitutes for the employer: the more efficiently he detects workers of superior quality the less he need pay for such quality.

The small company has distinct advantages in the hiring process, so far as judging the quality of workers is concerned. The employer can directly observe the performance of the new worker and need not resort to expensive and uncertain rating practices to estimate the workers' per-

[20] "Labor as a Quasi-Fixed Factor," *Journal of Political Economy,* December 1962, p. 546.

formance. It is well known that wage rates are less in small plants than in large, and the difference reflects at least in part (and perhaps in whole) the lower costs to the small-scale employer of judging quality. A similar result obtains with respect to dispersion of wages: a sample of such data is given in Table 17–5. Men should in general enter smaller companies the greater their ability.

TABLE 17–5

COEFFICIENTS OF VARIATION OF HOURLY WAGE RATES OF MALE EMPLOYEES
IN SELECTED MANUFACTURING INDUSTRIES BY CLASS OF WORKER

Industry and Employer	Number of Plants	Coefficient of Variation (Percent)		
		Skilled	Semiskilled	Unskilled
Radios:				
Two largest companies........	2	12.8	16.7	13.8
Other companies.............	22	24.6	24.9	20.9
Soap:				
Large companies.............	13	15.1	16.8	17.2
Other companies.............	59	25.6	24.5	23.3
Explosives:				
Three largest companies.......	28	16.2	14.1	15.8
Other companies.............	23	19.8	17.4	19.5
Meatpacking:				
Four largest companies........	59	....	20.4	....
Small companies.............	182	....	28.1	....

Source: *Hourly Earnings of Employees in Large and Small Enterprises* ("Temporary National Economic Committee Monograph," No. 14, 1948), pp. 21, 54, 59, 66, 70. The same pattern holds without exception for female employees. The meatpacking data refer to the northern wage district, and to all employees.

These last remarks represent in a sense a contradiction to the main argument of this paper. For previously I have accepted wage dispersion as a measure of ignorance but now take it as a measure of ability (less dispersion implies greater ignorance). The contradiction is only superficial because the problem of information on quality has been replacing that of information on price, and heterogeneity of quality has replaced homogeneity. Yet this shift poses again the central difficulty with which we began: the entanglement of quality and price variation in labor markets.

IV. INFORMATION AS CAPITAL

The information a man possesses on the labor market is capital: it was produced at the cost of search, and it yields a higher wage rate than on average would be received in its absence.

From the viewpoint of the individual worker, the capital value of his knowledge can be calculated by the usual method of valuing an asset; that is, discounting its future revenue. In section 1, above, we gave the marginal income gain from search as

$$\frac{\partial w_m}{\partial n} \frac{(1 + i)^{t_o} - 1}{i(1 + i)^{t_o}}$$

that is, the marginal wage-rate gain times the present value of an annuity of duration t_o. The total income gained is the integral of this expression over the range of search, or

$$(w_m - \overline{w}) \frac{(1 + i)^{t_o} - 1}{i(1 + i)^{t_o}}.$$

This formula, as we observed, is an over-estimate to the extent that future wage rates paid by various employers are not perfectly correlated with present wage rates. Conversely, if the duration of work with one employer is t_o, there will be some value to the knowledge presently acquired, in the search for alternative employments after t_o. This offset will be larger the larger the correlation of wage offers over time.

The duration of given jobs varies systematically with age and skill. Gladys Palmer's study suggested an average duration of a job of about three years for men between the ages of twenty-five and thirty-four, rising to six years for men over sixty-five.[21] The turnover of jobs is higher among unskilled workers than among skilled workers. If the worker has a prospective job duration of three years, and the coefficient of variation of wage offers is 10 percent, the capital value of his knowledge, by the above formula (with $i = .06$), would be

$.32 \ \overline{w}$ if 5 wage offers are found,
$.47 \ \overline{w}$ if 15 wage offers are found.

If such numbers are applied to the entire labor force, one gets an aggregate of private capital in laborer's information on the order of $100 billion.

The employer has a corresponding capital value of information: it is equal to the present value of the savings in wage rates for given quality of workers (or the superior quality of workers at given wage rates). The larger the amount of search by workers, the less will be the opportunity (or the greater the cost) for the employer to achieve a given saving in

---

[21] *Labor Mobility in Six Cities* (New York, 1954), p. 53. The durations are biased downward for the younger men because not all were in the labor force for an entire decade.

wage rates. The division of the investment in information between employers and workers will be determined by institutional characteristics of the market: where it is more economical for one party to acquire the information, the other party will make relatively small investments.

From the social viewpoint, the return from investment in information consists in a more efficient allocation of the labor force: the better informed the labor market, the closer each worker's (marginal) product is to its maximum at any given time. From this viewpoint, the function of information is to prevent less efficient employers from obtaining labor, and inefficient workers from obtaining the better jobs. In a regime of ignorance, Enrico Fermi would have been a gardener, Von Neumann a checkout clerk at a drugstore.

The social capital is not necessarily equal to the sum of the private capitals. If most workers search intensively, employers who offer low wage rates will be unable to fill their jobs and will be forced either to close down or to raise wage rates—so if I enter the labor market and do not search, I nevertheless profit from others' knowledge of the market. This effect arises because of the existence of the economies of scale.

The amounts and kinds of information needed for the efficient allocation of labor, whether judged from the viewpoint of the laborer, the employer, or the community, extend far beyond the determination of wage rates. The kinds and amounts of skill men should acquire pose parallel informational problems, and so too do the nonmonetary conditions of employment. The traditional literature has not done these problems justice. It is doubtful that justice would be more closely approached by making exaggerated claims of the importance of the problem of information. There is no exaggeration however, in the suggestion that the analysis of the precise problems of information and of the methods an economy uses to deal with them appears to be a highly rewarding area for future research.

Appendix

Let n_1 and n_2 be the search in the two periods, λ the average cost of search. Then the "profit" of a worker from search, neglecting interest, is

$$\pi = w_1 + w_2 - \lambda(n_1 + n_2) \, ,$$

where

$$w_1 = an_1^{\,b} \, ,$$
$$w_2 = a(n_2 + r^2 n_1)^b \, .$$

For a maximum,

$$\frac{\partial \pi}{\partial n_1} = abn_1^{b-1} + ab(n_2 + r^2 n_1)^{b-1} r^2 - \lambda = 0. \tag{1}$$

$$\frac{\partial \pi}{\partial n_2} = ab(n_2 + r^2 n_1)^{b-1} - \lambda = 0. \tag{2}$$

Equating values of λ,

$$n_2 = n_1\{(1 - r^2)^{1/(1-b)} - r^2\}. \tag{3}$$

It follows from (3) that $n_2 = n_1$ when $r = 0$. It can be shown that if $r = 1$, $n_2 = 0$,[22] and

$$n_1 = \left(\frac{\lambda}{2ab}\right)^{1/(b-1)}.$$

Search in period 1 makes a marginal wage contribution of

$$\frac{\partial w_2}{\partial n_1} = ab(n_2 + r^2 n_1)^{b-1} r^2$$

in period 2. The optimum amount of search in period 1, from equations (1) and (2), is

$$n_1 = \left(\frac{\lambda}{ab}\right)^{1/(b-1)} (1 - r^2)^{1/(b-1)}. \tag{4}$$

The wage rate in period 1 with a correlation of r exceeds that with no correlation in the proportion

$$\frac{a(\lambda/ab)^{b/(b-1)} (1 - r^2)^{b/(b-1)} - a(\lambda/ab)^{b/(b-1)}}{a(\lambda/ab)^{b/(b-1)}}$$

or by $(1 - r^2)^{b/(b-1)} - 1$, or approximately by $br^2/(1 - b)$.

---

[22] If r approaches unity, equations (1) and (2) yield

$$\frac{ab}{n_1^{1-b}} = 0,$$

or n_1 becomes infinite, and by equation (2),

$$n_2 + r^2 n_1 = \left(\frac{\lambda}{ab}\right)^{1/(b-1)}$$

so n_2/n_1 approaches $-r^2$ as n_1 approaches infinity. Since n_2 has a minimum of zero, n_1 is fixed by (1) at the expression in the text.

Chapter 18

THE KINKY OLIGOPOLY

DEMAND CURVE AND

RIGID PRICES*

Just before World War II, the theory was advanced that there exists a kink in the demand curve for the product of an oligopolist and that this kink goes far to explain observed price rigidities in oligopolistic industries. The theory has rapidly gained wide acceptance: many economists give it some place in their theoretical system, and some economists make it *the* theory of oligopoly price.

The theory is an ingenious rationalization of the price rigidities that were reported in many statistical studies of prices during the thirties, and no doubt this explains its popularity. But no one, so far as I know, has examined in detail either the pure theory of the kinky demand curve or the degree of correspondence between the price patterns implied by the theory and the observed price patterns in oligopolistic industries. These two tasks will be undertaken in Part I and Part II, respectively, of this paper.

I. THE FORMAL THEORY

1. The Received Theory

The theory of the kinky demand curve was advanced independently and almost simultaneously by R. L. Hall and C. J. Hitch in England and Paul M. Sweezy in America.[1] The latter's version will be summarized first.

The Sweezy Version. The market situation contemplated by Sweezy is one in which rivals will quickly match price reductions but only hesitantly and incompletely (if at all) follow price increases. This pattern of expected behavior produces a kink at the existing price ($= p_0$

* Reprinted from *Journal of Political Economy*, Vol. LV, No. 5 (October 1947).
[1] Hall and Hitch, "Price Theory and Business Behavior," *Oxford Economic Papers*, No. 2 (May 1939), pp. 12–45; and Sweezy, "Demand under Conditions of Oligopoly," *Journal of Political Economy*, Vol. XLVII (August 1939), pp. 568–73.

in Fig. 18–1) in the demand curve for the product of an oligopolist,[2] and the corresponding marginal revenue curve will possess a discontinuity the length of which is proportional to the difference between the slopes of the upper and lower segments of the demand curve at the kink.[3] Sweezy assumes that "the marginal cost curve passes between the two

FIGURE 18–1

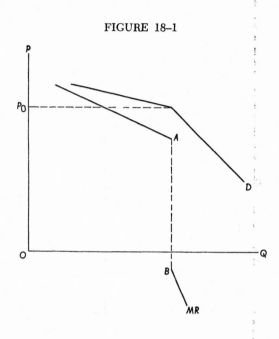

parts of the marginal revenue curve," so that fluctuations in marginal cost are not likely to affect output and price.

He considers also two other possibilities. An oligopolist may believe

[2] The demand curve for the product of an oligopolist can be defined only if the reactions of rivals to price changes are known. The upper branch of the demand curve in Fig. 18–1 represents the quantities that consumers will buy from one oligopolist at various prices if rival producers set a price of p_0; the lower branch represents the quantities that consumers will buy if the rivals charge identical prices. This demand curve is objective in the sense that it is consistent with the facts of the market if rivals behave in the specified manner. Sweezy appears to view it as subjective because it is based upon beliefs concerning rivals' price reactions which may have to be revised (although no occasions for revision of beliefs are treated in his article).

[3] With reference to Fig. 18–1, if $f(x)$ is the demand curve, x_0 the output at the kink, and subscripts 1 and 2 refer to the upper and lower segments of the demand curve respectively,

$$A - B = x_0[f'(x_0 - O) - f'(x_0 + O)] = p_0 \left(\frac{1}{\eta_1} - \frac{1}{\eta_2} \right).$$

that secret price cuts will remain secret, in which case the demand curve becomes elastic throughout and the kink disappears. Or the oligopolist may be a price leader, so that price increases will be followed and the kink again disappears.[4]

Sweezy assumes that shifts in demand will not affect the price at which the kink occurs and argues that the results of increases and decreases of demand are asymmetrical:

1. An increase of demand will make the demand curve less elastic in its upper branch, since rivals are operating closer to capacity,[5] and more elastic in the lower branch because rivals "are less worried about losses in [of?] business." If marginal costs are also shifting upward as demand increases, "an increase in demand is more likely to lead to a price increase than to a price cut."

2. A decrease in demand will have the converse effects—increased elasticity of the upper branch and decreased elasticity of the lower branch —so the discontinuity of marginal revenue will be increased and the oligopolists will be "more anxious than ever" to hold to the existing price.

Except where price leaders exist or secret price concessions are possible, therefore, oligopoly price may rise in good times and will not be reduced in bad times.[6]

The Oxford Version. Hall and Hitch conclude, after reporting interviews with some thirty-eight entrepreneurs on price policy, that businessmen seek prices that cover average cost, regardless of marginal revenue and marginal cost (which they seldom know).[7] This "full-cost" principle is apparently the result of tacit or open collusion, consideration

---

[4] These possibilities, which are obviously mutually exclusive, are illustrated in the same diagram (Sweezy, *op. cit.*, p. 571, Fig. 2). If the upper branch (for the price leader) and the lower branch (for the secret price cutter) were nevertheless joined, the resulting marginal revenue curve would again be discontinuous, but then maximum profits would never be secured at the price at which the kink arises.

[5] *Ibid.*, p. 571. Presumably the rivals' higher rates of production lead them to follow the price increase (although this reaction causes trouble; see below), or, if they maintain prices the buyers are rationed.

[6] The implications of Sweezy's theory for price rigidity were emphasized by M. Bronfenbrenner in "Applications of the Discontinuous Oligopoly Demand Curve," *Journal of Political Economy*, Vol. XLVIII (1940), pp. 420–27.

[7] The treatment of entrepreneurial knowledge is contradictory. On the one hand, Hall and Hitch state that "most of our informants were vague about anything so precise as elasticity. . . . . In addition, many, perhaps most, apparently made no effort, even implicitly, to estimate elasticities of demand . . . . and of those who do, the majority considered the information of little or no relevance to the pricing process save perhaps in very exceptional conditions" (Hall and Hitch, *op. cit.*, p. 18). But, on the other hand, a majority of the entrepreneurs believed that price cuts would be matched and price increases would not be matched by rivals (*ibid.*, p. 21, Tables 3 and 4) so they did act rationally on marginal principles (within a certain framework).

of long-run demand and costs, moral conviction of fairness, and uncertainty of effects of price increases and decreases.[8] The particular results of the interviews need not be discussed here.[9]

The entrepreneur therefore sets a price that covers average cost (including "profits") at the expected or some conventional output (see Fig. 18–2). Increases or decreases of demand will usually shift the kink

FIGURE 18–2

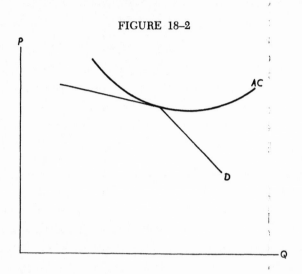

to the right or left and leave price unchanged, but there are two exceptions to this rule:

1. If the demand decreases greatly and remains small for some time, the price is likely to be cut in the hope of maintaining output. The chief explanation for this price cut is that one rival becomes panicky and his irrational behavior forces the others to cut prices.

2. If the average cost curves of all firms shift by similar amounts, due perhaps to changes in factor prices or technology, this is "likely to lead to a revaluation of the 'full cost' price" (*ibid.*, p. 25). However, ". . . . there will be no tendency for [prices] to fall or rise more than the wage and raw material costs" (*ibid.*, p. 32).

The full-cost principle would suggest also that prices will vary in-

---

[8] Several of these factors contradict the existence of a kink in the demand curve.

[9] The questioning was not persistent and resourceful, nor were ambiguous answers clarified; for example, three entrepreneurs did not charge more than average cost because "buyers technically informed about costs" (*ibid.*, p. 21). Does this mean that buyers would otherwise enter into production of the article? Why was the same answer not given for unwillingness to sell below cost?

versely with output, i.e., that high prices are necessary to cover the high average costs of small outputs. This price pattern is not followed, apparently, because the oligopolists (1) place a value on price stability, (2) are influenced by the kink, and (3) wish to "keep plant running as full as possible, giving rise to a general feeling in favour of price concessions."[10]

Comparison of the Versions. The Sweezy version is a consistent application of the kinky demand curve to price determination, without conflicting principles to modify its workings. The Oxford version embraces also the "full-cost" principle (and apparently also the "large-output" principle), although the possibilities of conflict between the two are manifold. Hall and Hitch resolve some of the conflicts by abandoning the kink (e.g., when prices follow production costs) and some by abandoning the "full-cost" principle (e.g., when entrepreneurs do not raise prices in depression). They take no account of the difficulties raised by differences among the average costs of various oligopolists or of many other troublesome features of the "full-cost" principle. Their thesis that the kink follows changes in wage rates and material prices implies a degree of collusion—or at least such beautiful rapport—among the oligopolists that it is hard to see why a kink should appear at all (see below). Their fluid version can explain any pattern of prices, and therefore forecast none, and accordingly I shall henceforth devote primary attention to the Sweezy version.

2. Elaboration of the Theory

The discussions of the kinky demand curve have been rather laconic. Certain implications of the theory must be elaborated in order to derive specific price patterns for the subsequent empirical tests.

The Length of the Discontinuity in Marginal Revenue. The length of the discontinuity in marginal revenue is proportional to the difference between the slopes of the demand curve on the two sides of the kink. The longer this discontinuity, the greater the fluctuations in marginal cost (and in demand, if the kink stays at the same price) that are compatible with price stability and therefore the greater the probability of rigid prices in any interval of time. Some of the factors that affect the length of this discontinuity are:

a) The number of rivals (of a given degree of closeness, measured by the cross-elasticity of demand). We should expect that a price in-

[10] *Ibid.*, p. 28.

crease is more likely to be followed if there are few rivals than if there are many, because the rivals will realize that the temporary gains from holding down their prices will soon be erased. If this is so, the discontinuity will be short (in time) or nonexistent when there are few rivals. The larger the number of rivals, the less likely are they to follow one oligopolist's price increases; on the other hand, the less likely are they also to match his price reductions, at least immediately. It seems probable, therefore, that the discontinuity is longest with an intermediate number of rivals, say, five to ten.

b) *The relative size of rivals* (*of a given degree of closeness*). When one firm (or an inner clique) is dominant in size, it will presumably be the price leader. When this firm increases its price, rivals are likely to follow (for individually they can sell as much as they wish at the ruling price); when the firm cuts prices the rivals must follow. Hence the dominant firm will have no kink in its demand curve. The smaller firms cannot raise their prices above the leader's unless he is rationing buyers but can shade prices without being followed immediately or perhaps at all.[11] Again there will be no kink.

c) *The differences among the rivals' products.* The discontinuity will be longer, the more homogeneous the products, because customers will shift more rapidly to the low-price firm.

d) *The extent of collusion.* Should explicit collusion replace the stand-offish attitude visualized by the theory, the kink will vanish; there is no kink in a monopolist's demand curve.

Other factors affecting the length of the discontinuity in marginal revenue could be mentioned, for example, the number of buyers.[12] But

[11] These conclusions can also be reached by a more mechanical application of kink theory. A rise of the dominant firm's price will so increase the demand of each small firm that marginal cost will intersect marginal revenue at an output less than that at which the kink occurs, so the small firm will also increase price. A reduction in price by a small firm will decrease the demand for the output of the dominant firm by so small an amount that probably no price change will be induced.

[12] Fewness of buyers is difficult to fit into the kink theory. If few buyers face a competitive supply, each will presumably believe that, if he raises his buying price, rivals will follow and the quantity supplied to him will not increase much; and, if he lowers his buying price, rivals will not follow and the quantity supplied to him will decrease greatly. Hence there will be a kink in the supply curve to the firm (which is illustrated by Bronfenbrenner, *op. cit.*). Combining this with oligopoly of sellers, presumably both supply and demand curves have a kink at the same price, which will be especially rigid.

But the whole argument is very elusive. If one buyer offered a higher price to a seller who assumed that his rivals would not follow a price increase, the seller would of course offer his entire output to the buyer, whose supply curve might therefore be extremely elastic for higher prices—the opposite of the above argument. And, conversely,. if one seller offered a lower price to one buyer, who assumed that his rivals these factors do not lend themselves to the type of empirical tests that will be employed in Part II and will not be discussed.

The Workings of the Kink. In order to study the workings of the kinky demand curve, let us consider two producers (of equal size) of similar, but not identical, commodities. The initial demand and marginal revenue curves of duopolist A are given in Figure 18–3; they are denoted

FIGURE 18–3

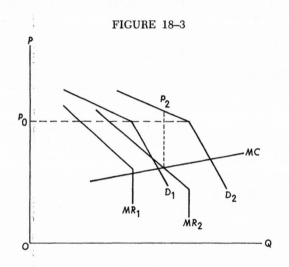

by the subscript 1. Assume now that the aggregate demand for the two commodities increases so that A's demand curve shifts to D_2, but marginal costs do not change. Then A will increase his price to p_2. What will duopolist B do?

If B's costs and demand are similar to A's, the former will simultaneously raise his price to p_2. But then D_2 must be redrawn above p_0 because this branch was drawn on the assumption that the rival's price was p_0. The situation becomes classical duopoly—with the usual wide range of possible patterns of behavior. It would be foolish to put a new kink in D_2 (as redrawn) at the level p_2. Experience has shown that the rival will follow a price increase, and businessmen will learn from this experience that there is no kink.

On the other hand, B may still find it profitable to stay at price p_0.

---

would be unwilling to reduce their buying prices, the buyer would snatch at the bargain so the seller's demand curve would be elastic for lower prices—again the opposite of the above argument. The difficulty is that the assumptions are inconsistent: if sellers believe that price reductions will be matched but price increases will not be matched and buyers believe the opposite, someone is likely to be wrong.

But then his demand curve must shift to the right, for it was drawn on the assumption that A set a price of p_0 or less. If this demand shift leads B to set a new price, then A's demand curve must be redrawn. Again the existence of the kink is contradicted by experience.

The theory of the kinky demand curve explains why prices that have been stable should continue to be stable despite certain changes in demand or costs. But the theory does not explain why prices that have once changed should settle down, again acquire stability, and gradually produce a new kink. One possible explanation might be that a period of stability of demand and costs has created a tradition of stable prices, so that, when demand or cost conditions change materially, the kink has emerged to preserve price stability.

Other Kinks and Discontinuities. For present purposes it is not necessary to discuss additional implications of the theory of kinky demand curves, but two are of sufficient interest to deserve brief mention.

The pattern of oligopolistic behavior underlying the kinky demand curve will also produce a discontinuous marginal cost curve. If one firm reduces its wage rate, for example, other firms will not follow, but these other firms will match wage increases. At the output corresponding to this input kink, there will be a discontinuity in marginal cost. A good part of the appeal of the kinky demand curve theory is that it is easy to draw demand and cost curves that lead to price stability. This appeal is definitely weakened if the marginal cost curve is also discontinuous, as the reader can readily verify.

The same general line of reasoning leads to kinks in the curves of other variables of policy—advertising, quality changes, etc. Indeed, the logic of the theory requires only that there be one variable—output—against which the discontinuities in the other variables may be displayed.

3.   Alternative Theories of Price Stability

Explanations of price stability are not common or prominent in the neoclassical price theory of Marshall's era. (Part II of this paper contains some evidence that bears on the question whether this is a cause for commendation or condemnation.) Of course it would be a grotesque caricature to describe this theory as requiring a change of price in response to every quiver of the demand or the cost curve. Three factors making for price stability were generally incorporated (without emphasis) into the neoclassical theory.

Long-Run Considerations. In the long run the demand curve is usually more elastic because buyers can make changes in technology, commitments, and habits that permit use of substitutes and because new rivals will be attracted at certain prices. Therefore an exorbitant current price may lose more (discounted) revenue in the future than it adds in the present. This type of consideration argues against raising prices greatly in short-run periods of inelastic demand but does not imply price rigidity.[13]

Administrative Weaknesses in Collusion. When a group of producers arrives at a mutually agreeable or tolerable price by collusion, this price will have a strong tendency to persist. When some of the firms will be injured by a price change (which must often occur when their costs, market areas, and product structures differ), they will naturally oppose change. When all will gain from a price change, they will usually wish different amounts of change. Opening the question of prices may therefore lead to a pitched battle, and one can seldom be sure that things will stay in hand. Frequent resort to this area of political-economic determination must be avoided, so changes are postponed as long as possible. If they are postponed long enough, the need for them will pass.

Cost of Price Changes. The nature of the product and market may be such that small or frequent price changes cost more than they yield. There are costs of informing buyers of price changes: new lists, advertising, etc. If long-term contracts contain provisions that the buyer will receive any price reductions during the life of the contract, the short-run marginal revenue from a price reduction may be small or negative. Even when there are no contracts, price reductions may incur the ill will of early buyers of a "style" good.

4. A Comparison of the Implications of the Theories of Price Stability

There is no reason why the kinky demand curve cannot be joined with the other explanations of price stability. But there is also no purpose in adding it to the neoclassical theory unless it explains price behavior in areas where the other explanation is silent or contradicts the implications of the neoclassical theory in areas where both apply. For the empirical tests in Part II, the following differences between the implications of the kinky demand curve and the neoclassical theory will be used:

a) The kinky demand curve theory is silent on monopolies, for the essential feature of retaliation by rivals is absent. Should monopoly prices

---

[13] Marshall also had the doctrine that prices will not fall to prime costs in depression because of a fear of "spoiling the market" (*Principles of Economics* [8th ed.; London: Macmillan & Co., 1920], pp. 374–76). He apparently assumed, in addition to oligopoly, that the long-run demand curve was inelastic for price reductions.

be rigid, the forces that explain this rigidity (say cost of price changes) may suffice to explain an equal amount of price rigidity under oligopoly. Unless the factors making for monopoly price rigidity do not operate under oligopoly, we can dispense with the kink unless greater rigidity is found in the oligopolistic industries.

b) The discontinuity in marginal revenue will disappear, and with it the reason for price rigidity, if formerly independent firms enter into collusion. The neoclassical theory emphasizes the administrative weaknesses in collusion, on the other hand, and this argues for greater price rigidity.

c) Prices will be relatively flexible with very few and with many firms in the industry, and relatively rigid with a moderate number of firms (say, five to ten), according to the kink theory. The neoclassical theories of oligopoly are neither outspoken nor unanimous on this question, but there is a general suggestion that price flexibility increases continuously with the number of firms.

d) When there is a dominant firm or set of firms (acting together) in the role of price leader, prices should be more flexible than if there is no price leader, on the kink theory. The neoclassical theory is silent on this point.

e) Given the number and size configuration of firms, prices should be more flexible the more heterogeneous the products, under the kinky demand curve theory. The neoclassical theory has no such implication.

II. EMPIRICAL TESTS OF THE THEORY

One may submit to empirical tests either the assumption of entrepreneurial behavior underlying the theory of the kinky demand curve or the implications of the kink for price behavior. The former alternative requires an analysis of the sequence of price changes made by oligopolists in an industry; the latter alternative can be developed by a comparison of observed price rigidity with that prophesied by the theory.

1. The Validity of the Assumption

If price increases of one firm are not followed by rivals, but price reductions are followed, the oligopolists have a basis in experience for believing that there is a kink in their demand curves. If price reductions are not followed by rivals, or price increases are as closely followed, no such objective basis for a kink exists.

The cigarette industry (with three large firms) offers a good example of the type of experience that would create a belief in the existence of a kink. On September 28, 1918, the American Tobacco Company raised the list price of Lucky Strikes from $6.00 to $7.50 per thousand, but the rivals continued to charge the lower price. The sales of Lucky Strikes fell 31 percent from September to November, when the price was reduced to $6.00, and continued to decline for several months.[14] The later price history in this industry, however, is not such as to create a belief in the existence of a kink:

> April 20, 1928: Reynolds (Camels) announced a reduction from $6.40 to $6 per thousand, effective April 21. American Tobacco followed on April 21 and Liggett and Myers on April 23.
>
> October 4, 1929: Reynolds announced an increase to $6.40, effective October 5, and both rivals followed on that day.
>
> June 23, 1931: Reynolds announced an increase to $6.85, effective June 24, and both rivals followed that day.
>
> January 1, 1933: American Tobacco reduced its price to $6, effective January 3, and both rivals followed that day.
>
> February 11, 1933: American Tobacco reduced its price to $5.50, and both rivals followed the same day.
>
> January 9, 1934: Reynolds increased its price to $6.10, and both rivals followed the same day.[15]

These price changes, incidentally, were relatively larger than they appear: the manufacturer's net was smaller by a three-dollar tax and trade discounts.

The more complicated pattern of price changes for automobiles is illustrated for two leading firms in Figure 18–4. The prices of the two firms changed at different dates and by different amounts, and price increases were more nearly simultaneous than price reductions. Price experience in this field should not lead a firm to believe that price reductions will be matched immediately or wholly nor that in a period of business recovery rivals will fail to increase prices.

Six anthracite companies produced 62.5 per cent of the aggregate output in 1930, and eight companies usually produce 70 to 80 percent of aggregate output.[16] The prices of seven companies, for each size of coal, are listed (in very large type) every week in the *Coal and Coal*

[14] This episode is reported by William H. Nicholls, *Price Policies in the Cigarette Industry* (Nashville, 1951), p. 50.

[15] Federal Trade Commission, *Agricultural Income Inquiry* (Washington, D.C., 1937), I, 448. The history of prices after 1934 follows essentially in the same pattern, although Nicholls reports an unmatched and unsuccessful price increase by Liggett and Myers on July 30, 1946—followed by a general increase on October 14, 1946, with American Tobacco the price leader.

[16] C. E. Fraser and G. F. Doriot, *Analysing Our Industries* (New York: McGraw-Hill Book Co., 1932), pp. 400, 401.

Trade Journal. These prices are identical and they almost invariably change on the same day.[17] There is no evidence of a kink: prices change often in a marked, but by no means rigid, seasonal pattern.

FIGURE 18–4
FACTORY PRICES OF PLYMOUTH AND FORD FOUR-DOOR SEDANS,
JUNE 1929—MAY 1937

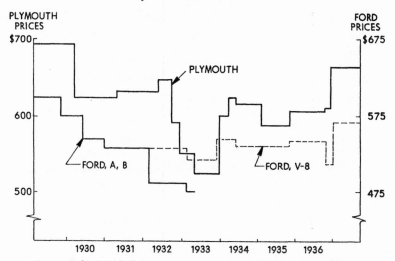

Source: Federal Trade Commission, *Report on Motor Vehicle Industry* (76th Cong., 1st sess., House Doc. 468 [Washington, D.C., 1940]), pp. 894–95, 896.

Some direct evidence argues against the existence of a kink in the demand curve for steel produced by United States Steel: Bethlehem, for example, has faithfully followed the price increases.[18] But the important evidence is indirect: there is no evidence of price rigidity within this industry. The official price lists and trade-journal quotations have been honored almost exclusively in the breach, and the transactions take place at prices that appear to be fairly sensitive to demand conditions.[19] It is

[17] Occasionally there is a temporary discrepancy. For example, six companies announced prices of $4.70 per ton for pea-size coal in the July 4, 1929, issue; one company retained the previous price of $4.60. A week later the exception disappeared.

[18] Temporary National Economic Committee, *Hearings,* Part 19: *Iron and Steel Industry* (Washington, D.C., 1940), pp. 10587 ff.

[19] See especially the study made by the Bureau of Labor Statistics, "Labor Department Examines Consumers' Prices of Steel Products," *Iron Age,* April 25, 1946. United States Steel officials testified before the T.N.E.C. that the Birmingham quotation had not been realized between 1932 and 1939 and that the general reduction in 1938 was merely a formal recognition of ruling prices (*Hearings,* Part 19, pp. 10546, 10505 ff.). See also *Hearings,* Part 27: *Iron and Steel Industry* (Washington, D.C., 1940), pp. 14141 f., 14172 f.

debatable whether the steel industry, with its price leader, should have rigid prices on the kinky demand curve theory, and it is also debatable whether the price leader often leads the industry in lowering prices.

Three firms produce most of the dynamite used in mining, quarrying, and construction in the United States. The wholesale prices for 40 percent ammonium dynamite, per 50-pound bag, moved as follows during the thirties:

> February 27, 1933: All firms reduced the price from $12.25 to $10.50.
> March 12, 1934: Du Pont and Hercules reduced the price to $10; Atlas followed 17 days later.
> January 14, 1935: All firms increased the price to $10.50.
> May 7, 1936: Du Pont and Hercules reduced the price to $9.50; Atlas followed the next day.
> May 8, 1937: Du Pont and Atlas increased the price to $10.50; Hercules followed 3 days later.[20]

Again there is no empirical basis for believing the kink exists.

Socony-Vacuum and Atlantic Refining are two important sellers of gasoline in the Boston area. Aside from three periods in 1934 and 1935 when Socony-Vacuum's price was less than Atlantic's, the prices of the two firms changed as shown in the accompanying list in the period 1929–37.

> Simultaneous price changes............................40
>   Increases 22
>   Opposite 1
>   Decreases 17
>
> Delay in following price increases........................12
>   Days
>   1 9
>   2 1
>   3 1
>   4 1
>
> Delay in following price decreases........................10
>   Days
>   1 1
>   2 3
>   3 1
>   10 1
>   21 1
>   23 1
>   28 1
>   47 1

[20] I am indebted to Mr. Edward W. Proctor of Brown University for the information in this paragraph, which was secured by correspondence with Du Pont, Atlas Powder, and Hercules Powder. The three companies have headquarters in Wilmington; the latter two were created in 1912 by an antitrust action.

It appears, then, that price increases are more nearly simultaneous than price decreases—the opposite of the kinky demand curve assumption.[21]

The most striking case of contradiction of the assumption of the theory, however, is provided by potash. On June 1, 1934, the American Potash and Chemical Corporation issued a price list that carried about 26 per cent reductions from the prices in the previous year. The other firms failed to follow. On June 26 the lower prices were withdrawn, and the company lamented: "It was expected that other potash producers would likewise announce their prices in accordance with long prevailing custom. No such announcements have been forthcoming. Under the circumstances this Company is compelled to withdraw the schedule of prices and terms referred to."[22]

In these seven industries there is little historical basis for a firm to believe that price increases will not be matched by rivals and that price decreases will be matched. This indicates only that not every oligopoly has reason to believe that it has a kinky demand curve, and most adherents of the theory would readily concede this.[23] On the other hand, here are seven industries in which the existence of the kinky demand curve is questionable—a list that is longer by seven than the list of industries for which a prima facie case has been made for the existence of the kink.[24]

2. The Validity of the Implications

The kinky demand curve would prove to be an incorrect or unimportant construction if oligopoly prices were as flexible as monopoly and/or competitive prices. It is not possible to make a direct test for price rigidity, in part, because the prices at which the products of oligopolists sell are not generally known. For the purpose of such a test we need transaction prices; instead, we have quoted prices on a temporal basis, and they are deficient in two respects.

[21] I am indebted to Mr. Melvin D. Sargent of Brown University for the information on gasoline prices. The price quotations are from *Oil Price Handbook, 1929–37* (Cleveland: National Petroleum News, 1938).

[22] *Chemical Industries* (July 1934), p. 49.

[23] But apparently not all. O. Lange treats only of kinky demand curves in his theory of oligopoly (see *Price Flexibility and Employment* [Bloomington: Principia Press, 1944], chap. vii); and L. Tarshis has recently done the same in his *The Elements of Economics* (New York: Houghton Mifflin Co., 1947), pp. 139 ff.

[24] In the Conference on Price Research study, *Cost Behavior and Price Policy* (New York: National Bureau of Economic Research, 1943), it is stated: "There is rather strong reason for believing that leading firms in the automobile, steel, agricultural implement, and many other industries act upon approximately this view of the situation [i.e., that there is a kink in the demand curve]" (*ibid.*, p. 278). The reason is not given. We have discussed automobiles and steel; agricultural implements will be taken up subsequently.

The first deficiency is notorious: Nominal price quotations may be stable although the prices at which sales are taking place fluctuate often and widely. The disparity may be due to a failure to take account of quality, "extras," freight, guaranties, discounts, etc.; or the price collector may be deceived merely to strengthen morale within the industry. The various studies of steel prices, already referred to, contain striking examples of this disparity, and others can be cited.[25] We cannot infer that all nominally rigid prices are really flexible, but there is also very little evidence that they are really rigid.

The second deficiency is that published prices are on a temporal basis. If nine-tenths of annual sales occur at fluctuating prices within a month (as is true of some types of tobacco), and the remainder at a fixed price during the rest of the year, the nominal price rigidity for eleven months is trivial. With each price we ought to have the corresponding quantities sold: for a study of price rigidity, "April" would better be the fourth one-twelfth of the year's sales than the fourth month of the year.

Despite these shortcomings, a comparison of the implications of the kinky demand curve for price behavior with observable behavior (even if observable only in bulletins of the Bureau of Labor Statistics) has some value. If the theory cannot explain the pattern of rigidity of quoted prices among industries, there is no presumption that it would explain the pattern of transaction price rigidity among industries.

Our tests are made by comparing observed price rigidity in a group of industries with the relative rigidities forecast by the theory for industries with these market structures. We choose the period, June, 1929, through May, 1937, which embraces both a complete business cycle and the periods used in most empirical studies of price rigidity. We require three types of information:

a) A list of oligopolistic industries. The two basic criteria are (1) a fairly precise knowledge of the industry structure, and (2) continuous price and output series. The industries are described briefly in the Appendix.[26]

b) Some measure of expected price changes in the absence of restrictions on price changes. Shifts in demand are of primary (although far from exclusive) importance, and we measure them roughly by the

[25] See the industry studies of the Division of Research of N.R.A.; the prices revealed in prosecutions under the Robinson-Patman Act; Saul Nelson, "A Consideration of the Validity of the Bureau of Labor Statistics Price Indexes," in *The Structure of the American Economy* (Washington, D.C.: National Resources Committee, 1939), pp. 173–84.

coefficient of variation of production (or some related series) in 1929, 1931, 1933, 1935, and 1937.

c) *A measure of price rigidity.* The basic test used is frequency of change in the monthly price quotations; for the theory under examination implies that there will be *no* changes—not merely that the price changes will be small. This test is supplemented by the coefficient of variation of monthly prices for two reasons. First, the price series have technical features that lead to more numerous price changes than actually occur. They are often averages of weekly quotations, and hence show two changes in the monthly averages when a price change occurs within a month.[27] They are often averages of prices of several firms, and if each firm makes one price change the average can display as many changes as there are firms. Second, it can be argued that the kink is an exaggeration —that actually there is a sharp bend in the demand curve of the firm so that small price changes are what the theory prophesies.[28] But frequent small price changes would still be improbable because of the cost of making price changes.

The basic data that are used in the tests are summarized in Table 18–1; fuller information is given in the Appendix. It will be observed that the two tests of price rigidity differ substantially: the coefficient of rank correlation between number of price changes and coefficient of variation of prices is +.69 for the nineteen oligopolies listed in Table 18–1.

Monopolies versus Oligopolies. The monopolies listed in Table 18–1 are unsurpassed for price rigidity, despite the fact that their outputs varied more than those of most oligopolistic industries. This finding, which could be supported by more cases,[29] suggests the possibility that the forces that make for price rigidity in monopolies are sufficiently strong

[26] More specifically, the oligopolies discussed by Clair Wilcox in *Competition and Monopoly in American Industry* ("T.N.E.C. Monographs," No. 21 [Washington, D.C., 1940]) formed the basic list. An industry was excluded if (1) necessary information was not available, (2) the industry was analyzed in the preceding section, or (3) the firms were in known collusion throughout the period. In addition, many chemicals were excluded because of ignorance of substitution relationships.

[27] Thus the B.L.S. reports as eight changes the six changes made by Pittsburgh Plate Glass during the period.

[28] To secure a sharp bend, we must assume that rivals will partly follow price increases and decreases that are small but fail to follow large increases and completely follow large decreases.

[29] Thus, the price of magnesium was very rigid; the rentals of the International Business Machines Corporation have not varied (Wilcox, *op. cit.,* p. 106); the retail price of incandescent lamps of common sizes changed once or twice (United States Tariff Commission, *Incandescent Electric Lamps* [Report No. 133 (2d ser., Washington, D.C., 1939)], p. 47); this was virtually a General Electric monopoly because of its licensing provisions.

to account for the lesser rigidity in oligopolies. One might argue that special factors are at work in monopoly, but the only two that come to mind are fear of governmental attention or action and the conservatism that comes with size. The former, however, is even more effective against

TABLE 18–1

MEASURES OF MARKET STRUCTURE FOR 21 PRODUCTS AND OF THEIR
PRICE FLEXIBILITY AND OUTPUT VARIABILITY, JUNE, 1929–MAY, 1937

	Num- ber of Firms in In- dustry	Price Leader	Price Flexibility		Coeffi- cient of Varia- tion of Output
			Num- ber of Price Changes	Coeffi- cient of Varia- tion	
Oligopolies:					
Bananas	2	Yes	46	16	17
Boric acid.........	3	No	7	17	16
Cans	4	Yes	6	5	27
Cement	12	No	14	11	41
Copper	4	No	63	37	43
Gasoline*	11	No	84	22	16
Grain-binder	2	Yes	5	3	63
Linoleum	2	No?	12	9	30
Newsprint	9	No	6	16	16
Plaster	3	Yes	4	5	29
Plate Glass........	2	No	8	13	34
Plows	6	No	25	6	50
Rayon	8	No	26	30	34
Soap	3	No	9	12	7
Starch	4	Yes	20	12	13
Sulphur	2	Yes	0	0	24
Tires	8	No	36	9	16
Tractors	4	Yes	6	6	76
Window glass......	3	No	20	21	24
Monopolies:					
Aluminum	1	...	2	6	47
Nickel	1	...	0	0	35

* In Pennsylvania and Delaware.

oligopolies because of the importance of conspiracy in the antitrust laws, and the latter is presumably also a function of absolute size. It should be added that the neoclassical theory does not provide a satisfactory explanation for this extraordinary rigidity of monopoly prices.

According to the kink theory, there will be no kink when the oligopolists enter into explicit collusion; and hence prices would be expected to become more flexible. All empirical evidence contradicts this implication. Of our industries, at least two had periods of collusion. There was a combination of rayon producers to fix prices between October 21, 1931, and May 23, 1932:[30] There were no price changes during this period, none in the preceding period of equal length, and four in the subsequent period of equal length. There are only two periods of protracted rigidity in the price series for copper: the first occurs under Copper Exporters (a Webb-Pomerene cartel), the second under N.R.A.

A number of examples are also provided by other industries. On August 30, 1932, the six important growers and canners of pineapple entered a ten-year agreement to restrict output and market through the Pineapple Producers Cooperative Association.[31] In the thirty-nine months preceding this date there were seventeen price changes in canned pineapples; in the subsequent fifty-seven months, eight changes. Prices of typewriters were very rigid during a period when the four important producers were charged with colluding.[32] During the period of operation of the midwestern oil pool (Madison Oil Case), prices "displayed a rigidity without parallel in the history of the industry."[33]

If the disappearance of the kink through collusion has a tendency to increase price flexibility, this tendency is completely submerged by the opposite effects of administrative limitations on cartel price policy.

The Number of Firms. The number of firms that enters into the formation of price policy is difficult to determine; a completely satisfactory determination would require knowledge of cross-elasticities of demand, the entrepreneur's knowledge and objectives, and similar data. As an unsatisfactory substitute for this information, we have been guided by two criteria: that sufficient firms be included to account for two-thirds to three-quarters of the output of the product and that the largest firm omitted from the count sell less than a tenth of the amount sold by the largest firm in the industry. Although these rules are arbitrary, they focus attention on relevant variables: if we do not include enough firms to account for a predominant share of output, the firms will not be able to control prices (attenuated oligopoly); and if we exclude firms large relative to those that are included, we may be omitting firms that are in the oligopolistic relationship. The precise number of firms, even by these arbitrary criteria, is in doubt in more than half the industries listed in

[30] "Viscose Company *et al.,*" *Federal Trade Commission Decisions,* Vol. XXV (Washington, D.C., 1939), p. 425.
[31] "The move brought all the island packers into complete accord and cooperation for the first time in history" (*New York Times,* August 31, 1932, p. 10); see also J. A. Shoemaker, "Labor Conditions in Hawaii," *Monthly Labor Review,* January 1941, pp. 30 ff.
[32] Wilcox, *op. cit.,* p. 140.
[33] *Ibid.,* p. 136.

Table 18–1, but it was thought better to give a single number than a range that invites mechanical averaging to secure a single number.

Our expectation, on the kink theory, is that a very few rivals will have relatively flexible prices because the impossibility of maintaining a price lower than a rival's will be evident. On the other hand, with many rivals the fear that price cuts will be matched is reduced, and again the kink disappears. We do not test this latter implication because it is identical with that of the neoclassical theory.

If the data in Table 18–1 are summarized by number of firms, we find a definite tendency for price flexibility to increase with the number of firms in the industry (Table 18–2). The coefficient of rank correlation

TABLE 18–2

| Number of Firms in Industry | Number of Industries in Sample | Price Flexibility | | Average of Coefficients of Variation of Outputs |
		Number of Price Changes	Coefficient of Variation	
2	5	14.2	8.2	33.6
3, 4	8	16.8	14.4	29.4
6, 8	3	29.0	15.0	33.3
9, 11, 12	3	34.7	16.3	24.3

between number of firms and number of price changes is $+.41$, that between number of firms and coefficient of variation of prices is $+.31$. There is virtually no relationship between fluctuations of output and number of firms, nor is the strength or direction of relationship between number of firms and price flexibility affected if industries with price leaders are segregated.[34] Thus there is a weak tendency for a greater number of firms to be associated with a greater frequency and amplitude of price changes, the contrary of the implications of the kinky demand curve.

Price Leadership. The term, "price leadership," is used in two very different senses in economic literature. In the one sense it refers to a dominant firm that sets the price, allows the minor firms to sell what they wish at this price (subject perhaps to nonprice competition), and supplies the remainder of the quantity demanded. In the other sense, price leadership refers to the existence of a firm that conventionally first announces price changes that are usually followed by the remainder of the industry,

[34] The coefficient of rank correlation between number of firms and number of price changes is .37 for seven products with price leaders and .39 for twelve products without price leaders.

even though this firm may not occupy a dominant position. For example, International Paper was for a long period the price leader in newsprint although it produced less than one-seventh of the output, and it was succeeded in this role by Great Northern, a smaller firm. This latter type of price leadership has been illuminatingly described by S. A. Swensrud of Standard Oil of Ohio:

> In any territory all suppliers are watching the same things. They watch the statistical position of the industry as a whole, that is, production of crude oil and gasoline, sales of petroleum products, and stocks of crude oil and gasoline. . . . They watch the ambitions of competitors to increase their share of the business in the territory. They gage these ambitions by reports of salesmen on price concessions to commercial customers, by observations of the amount of business done by trackside operators and sellers of unbranded and locally branded gasoline, by the reports of salesmen as to competitive offers being made to dealers, and by reports of salesmen as to the extent of secret price cuts, discounts, and the like being offered by retailers. All these facts are constantly before local managers and central organizations.
>
> Now suppose that secret price cutting by dealers in some particular area breaks out into the open in the form of a cut in the posted price because some dealer becomes disgusted with the uncertainty as to how much business he is losing to competitors granting secret discounts. As the openly admitted price reduction operates, the local officers of all suppliers are assailed with demands from dealers, relayed and in some instances emphasized by salesmen, for a reduction in the tank-wagon price. . . . The local manager of the leading marketer of course faces more demands than any other manager. He attempts to gage the permanence of the retail cut. Frequently local managers elect to make no change in the tank-wagon price. Ordinarily this decision springs from the conclusion that the local price war will soon run its course because it is not supported by weakness in basic markets. On other occasions the local manager concludes that the causes of the retail price cutting rest primarily on the availability of sufficient low-price gasoline so that the condition may be considered deep-seated, and he therefore authorizes or recommends a local reduction in the tank-wagon price. . . . Thus the particular local territory becomes a subnormal territory, that is, one in which prices are out of line with those generally prevailing in the marketing area.
>
> The major sales executives of all companies watch carefully the number and size of subnormal markets. . . . If the number of local price cuts increases, if the number and amount of secret concessions to commercial consumers increase, if the secret unpublicized concessions to dealers increase, it becomes more and more difficult to maintain the higher prices. . . . Finally, some company, usually the largest marketer in the territory, recognizes that the subnormal price has become the normal price and announces a general price reduction throughout the territory. . . .
>
> In summary, therefore, the so-called price leadership in the petroleum industry boils down to the fact that some company in each territory most of the

time bears the onus of formally recognizing current conditions. . . . In short, unless the so-called price leader accurately interprets basic conditions and local conditions, it soon will not be the leading marketer. Price leadership does not mean that the price leader can set prices to get the maximum profit and force other marketers to conform.[35]

The difference between these two types of price leadership from the viewpoint of the theory of kinky demand curves is basic. The dominant firm has no kink in its demand curve because rivals have no reason for charging a lower price: they are permitted to sell as much as they wish at the leader's price.[36] The second type of leader, the barometric firm, commands adherence of rivals to his price only because, and to the extent that, his price reflects market conditions with tolerable promptness. The widespread development of barometric firms is therefore explicitly a device to insure that there will be no kink, or that the kink will not prevent readjustment of price to important changes in cost or demand conditions.

Only the price leadership exercised by dominant firms, therefore, is relevant in testing the implication of the kinky demand curve theory that there will be no kink when there is price leadership. Accordingly, we classify as industries with price leaders only those in which there is a relatively large firm, producing, say, 40 per cent of the output of the industry at a minimum, and more if the second largest firm is large (because otherwise the situation approaches classical duopoly). On this basis there are seven leaders among our nineteen industries (see Table 18–1), and they are compared with the remaining twelve industries in Table 18–3. Except for the number of price changes of two-firm industries (where bananas dominates the result), the prices of industries with price leaders are less flexible than those of industries without price leaders, despite the larger fluctuations of output of the former group. This is contrary to Sweezy's conjecture and is in keeping with the price rigidity found in monopolistic industries.

Goodness of Substitutes. It is almost inherent in the methods of quotation of price statistics that most of the commodities examined in this article are nearly homogeneous. If products are rather heterogeneous, the significance of an average price becomes doubtful and the B.L.S. does not report it. Of our nineteen industries, only six have products whose prices appear to differ significantly and persistently among firms:

[35] W. S. Farish and J. H. Pew, *Review and Criticism . . . . of Monograph No. 39* ("T.N.E.C. Monographs," No. 39A [Washington, D.C., 1941]), pp. 47–49.

[36] For the details of price determination in this situation see my "Notes on the Theory of Duopoly," *Journal of Political Economy*, Vol. XLVIII (1940), pp. 523 ff.

TABLE 18–3

	Industries with Leader	Industries without Leader
Two-firm industries:		
Number in sample......................	3	2
Average number of price changes..........	17	10
Average coefficient of variation of prices....	6.3	11.0
Average coefficient of variation of outputs...	34.7	32.0
Three- and four-firm industries:		
Number in sample......................	4	4
Average number of price changes..........	9	24.8
Average coefficient of variation of prices....	7.0	21.8
Average coefficient of variation of outputs...	36.2	22.5

soap, tractors, grain-binders, plows, tires, and linoleum. Their prices appear to change less often and less widely, on average, than those of homogeneous products as shown in Table 18–4. It should be noted that we might, with some justification, have designated our monopolies (aluminum and nickel) as oligopolies with differentiated products.

3. Conclusion

The empirical evidence reveals neither price experiences that would lead oligopolists to believe in the existence of a kink nor the pattern of changes of price quotations that the theory leads us to expect. The industries included in these tests are not very numerous, but they are sufficiently varied and important to suggest that similar adverse results would be secured from a larger sample.

But is this adverse conclusion really surprising? The kink is a barrier to changes in prices that will increase profits, and business is the collection of devices for circumventing barriers to profits. That this barrier should thwart businessmen—especially when it is wholly of their own fabrication—is unbelievable. There are many ways in which it can be circumvented. We have had occasion to notice the development of price

TABLE 18–4

	Homogeneous Products	Heterogeneous Products
Number of products......................	13	6
Average number of price changes............	23.4	15.5
Average coefficient of variation of prices......	15.8	7.5
Average coefficient of variation of outputs.....	25.7	40.3

leadership of the barometric variety as one device, and the old-fashioned solution of collusion is not always overlooked. In addition there is the whole range of tactical maneuvers that Neumann and Morgenstern's theory of games has uncovered. In the multidimensional real world there are many ways to teach a lesson, especially when the pupil is eager to learn.

Appendix

The summary descriptions of the industries used in Part II are based upon indicated references and C. L. James, *Industrial Concentration and Tariffs*, T.N.E.C. Monograph No. 10 (Washington, 1940); *The Structure of Industry*, T.N.E.C. Monograph No. 27 (Washington, D.C., 1941); and C. Wilcox, *Competition and Monopoly in American Industry*, Monograph No. 21 (Washington, D.C., 1940), which may be referred to for information on imports, concentration ratios, and general market structures, respectively. Price quotations are from the Bureau of Labor Statistics bulletins, *Wholesale Prices*. In the few cases where price quotations begin in 1931, the number of price quotations reported in Table 1 is 96/77 of the actual number. Unless otherwise noted, quantity data are from S. Fabricant's *The Output of Manufacturing Industries, 1899–1937* (New York: National Bureau of Economic Research, 1940).

ALUMINUM:
>   The Aluminum Company of America produced all new aluminum during the period and also dominated the scrap market.
>   Quantity: production (*Minerals Yearbook*)
>   D. H. Wallace, *Market Control in the Aluminum Industry* (Cambridge: Harvard University Press, 1937)

BANANAS:
>   In 1936 United Fruit handled 60 per cent, and Standard Fruit and Steamship 30 per cent, of the bananas imported.
>   Prices: Jamaica 9's to July, 1931, then Honduras (spliced for continuity)
>   Quantities: imports (*Statistical Abstract*)

BORIC ACID:
>   In 1937 there were only three producers. Pacific Coast Borax produced half of the total, American Potash and Chemical about 40 percent, and Stauffer Chemical the remainder.
>   C. L. James, *op. cit.*, chap. v.

CANS:
>   In 1937 American Can produced about half, and Continental Can about one-quarter, of total output. The latter company also produced cans for Campbell Soup on a fixed-fee basis. McKeesport Tin Plate was third, with

about 10 percent of output, and Owens-Illinois Can was fourth, with less than 5 percent. There were also fourteen smaller companies.

Standard Statistics Company, *Standard Corporation Reports*

CEMENT:

In 1931 the leading companies in the northeastern section and their percentages of sales were Lehigh, 19.1; Universal Atlas, 15.2; International, 8.1; Penn-Dixie, 7.9; Alpha, 6.7; a total of 57.0 percent. The next seven mills (it is not clear that each was separately owned), with individual percentages ranging from 3.6 down to 2.4, totaled another 20.3 percent.

Prices: Northampton

Quantities: production, northeastern section (*Minerals Yearbook*)

Federal Trade Commission, *Cement Industry* (73d Cong., 1st sess., Senate Doc. 71 [Washington, D.C., 1933])

COPPER:

In 1947 the leading companies and their percentages of total production were Kennecott Copper, 35.9; Anaconda, 22.9; Phelps Dodge, 18.8; Calumet and Hecla, 4.5.

Quantities: production (*Minerals Yearbook*)

The Structure of Industry, pp. 248–49

GASOLINE:

In 1938 the leading companies in the Pennsylvania-Delaware area and their percentages of sales were Atlantic Refining, 21.9; Standard Oil of New Jersey, 14.5; Gulf Oil, 10.2; Sun Oil, 9.8; Standard Oil of Indiana, 8.5; Consolidated Oil, 7.6; Socony-Vacuum, 6.8; Texas, 4.8; Tide Water, 3.4; Pure Oil, 2.1; and Cities Service, 2.3. In 1926 Atlantic's percentage was 44.5 and Gulf Oil's, 20.8.

Prices: Pennsylvania

Quantities: consumption in Pennsylvania and Delaware (*Minerals Yearbook*)

Federal Trade Commission, *Report on Distribution Methods and Costs*, Part IV (Washington, D.C., 1944), p. 52

GRAIN-BINDER:

In 1935 the leading companies and their percentages of total sales were International Harvester, 67.2; Deere, 24.7; and there were also four other companies.

Quantities: production (1933 estimated from *Census of Manufactures*)

Federal Trade Commission, *Report on the Agricultural Implement and Machinery Business* (75th Cong., 3d sess., House Doc. 702 [Washington, D.C., 1938]), p. 153

LINOLEUM:

In 1937 there were only four producers of inlaid linoleum. Armstrong Cork and Congoleum Nairn supplied most of the output.

Prices: 1931 on

Quantities: production, 1931 on

Standard Statistics Company, *Standard Corporation Reports*

NEWSPRINT:

In 1928 the leading firms and their percentages of the total production in

Canada and the United States were International Paper, 14; Canadian Power and Paper, 12; Abitibi, 11; Great Northern, 9; Crown Zellerbach, 8; Minnesota and Ontario, 5; Price, 5; and Powell River, 4. Crown Zellerbach operated only on the Pacific Coast, where it supplied 70 percent of the total.

Quantities: domestic production plus imports (the latter from *Statistical Abstract*)

Federal Trade Commission, *Newsprint Paper Industry* (71st Cong., spec. sess., Senate Doc. 214 [Washington, D.C., 1930]), pp. 18 ff.

NICKEL:

The International Nickel Company produces about 90 per cent of the output of North America, and its leading rival, Falconbridge Nickel Mines, sells chiefly in Europe.

Quantities: domestic production plus imports minus exports (*Minerals Yearbook*)

A. Skelton in *International Control in the Non-ferrous Metals*, ed. W. Y. Elliott (New York: Macmillan Co., 1937), Part II, chap. v

Report of Commissioner, Combines Investigation Act, *Canada and International Cartels* (Ottawa, 1945), p. 31

PLASTER:

In 1937 United States Gypsum produced almost half the output. National Gypsum and Certain-teed Products and Celotex are other large producers of gypsum products and together account for almost 40 percent of 1937 output of plaster. The four firms produced 83.4 percent of total output.

Quantities: production (1933 estimated from *Minerals Yearbook*)

PLATE GLASS:

In 1935 Libby-Owens-Ford and Pittsburgh Plate Glass produced 95 percent of the output of plate glass; their outputs were about equal. The remainder of the industry consisted of three firms, of which one (Ford Motor) produced for its own use.

Prices: 3–5 square feet

Quantities: production (United States Tariff Commission study [cited below], p. 91; 1936 used in lieu of unknown 1937 data)

United States Tariff Commission, *Flat Glass and Related Glass Products* (2d ser.; Rept. No. 123 [Washington, D.C., 1937]), p. 24

"Life Goes On," *Fortune*, January, 1934, p. 43

PLOWS:

In 1936 the leading firms and their percentages of total sales were International Harvester, 17.5; Oliver, 16.7; Unknown, 15 to 20 (judging from the 1937 concentration ratio of 65.7); Deere, 12.2; Avery, 3.5; and Minneapolis-Moline, 2.5. It is not certain that the latter two are fifth and sixth in size.

Prices: walking, two-horse

Federal Trade Commission, *Agricultural Implements* (73d Cong., 1st sess., Senate Doc. 71 [Washington, D.C., 1933]), p. 151

RAYON:

In 1935 the capacities of the leading firms for producing yarn were American Viscose, 34.8; Du Pont Rayon, 17.6; Celanese, 12.8; North American, 7.3; Industrial Rayon, 6.1. Four smaller firms had an additional 14.9 percent of capacity. Output was fairly close to capacity in this year.

Prices: 300 denier, first quality

Quantities: production of yarn (*Chemical and Metallurgical Engineering*, February, 1943, p. 116)

The Structure of Industry, pp. 263–64

SOAP:

In 1931 Procter and Gamble sold about 40 percent, Colgate-Palmolive-Peet about 24 percent, and Lever Brothers about 14 percent of total soap. In 1935 the four largest firms produced 73.5 percent of all soap (which is believed to be less concentrated than hand soap) and the eight largest firms 83.1 percent.

Prices: 1931 on, toilet soap

Quantities: production, 1931 on

"Procter and Gamble," *Fortune*, December, 1931, p. 97

STARCH:

In 1937 Corn Products Refining Company made more than half of the total sales. The other large firms are A. E. Staley Manufacturing, Penick and Ford, and American Maize Products, with about one third of total sales. There were also seven smaller companies.

C. L. James, *op. cit.*, p. 15

SULPHUR:

In 1937 Texas Gulf Sulphur supplied 64 percent of total output, Freeport Sulphur, 26 percent, and two other companies another 9 percent.

Minerals Yearbook

TIRES:

In 1933 the leading companies and their percentages of the industry's capacity were Goodyear, 26.4; Firestone, 13.6; United States, 12.3; Goodrich, 12.0; Fisk, 9.1; Kelly-Springfield, 3.5; Mansfield, 2.8; General Tire, 2.6.

Prices: Balloon (spliced for continuity)

W. H. Gross, *Evidence Study No. 36 of the Rubber Tire Manufacturing Industry* (Washington, D.C., N.R.A. Division of Review [October, 1935]), p. 5

TRACTORS:

In 1935 the leading companies and their percentages of total sales were International Harvester, 49.5; Deere, 24.5; Allis-Chalmers, 9.5; J. I. Case, 7.1. In 1929 International Harvester's percentage was 59.9 and Deere's, 21.1.

Prices: 10-20 horse-power.

Federal Trade Commission, *Agricultural Implements*, p. 153.

WINDOW GLASS:

In 1935 the industry was composed of 12 companies with 21 plants, of which 13 were in operation. Libby-Owens-Ford, Pittsburgh Plate Glass, and American Window Glass produced more than 75 percent of total output. In 1936 four other companies organized a common sales company (Fourco Glass Company) which bought up several idle plants. These four companies comprised virtually the entire industry thereafter.

Price: Single B

United States Tariff Commission, *Flat Glass,* p. 24

Chapter

19

ADMINISTERED PRICES AND
OLIGOPOLISTIC INFLATION*

The Kefauver Committee launched its hearings on administered prices and their relationship to inflation in July, 1957, and for three years they were the dominant theme of the Committee's work. The Committee's interests have ranged beyond administered prices—and since 1960 this subject has been virtually ignored—but my discussion will be directed chiefly to the original theme of the investigation.

Cats may have nine lives, but economic theories are fortunate if they have one. Gardiner Means has therefore been doubly fortunate. The first life of his doctrine was a very vigorous one: during the 1930's the theory of administered prices incited much controversy and extensive empirical studies. The previously relatively unnoticed phenomenon of price rigidity was forcibly impressed on everyone, and the persistent economic malaise made everyone receptive to suggestions of deficiencies in the price system. If true, Means's suggestion—it was no more—that rigid prices led to large decreases in output and employment, whereas industries with flexible prices underwent small (if any) reductions in output, was of the highest importance. Unfortunately, the facts did not support this suggestion.[1] Toward the end of the decade the literature on rigid prices displayed growing anemia; it is fair to say that economists abandoned the close study of the subject, less because its lack of scientific import was established than because it had become boring.

The second life has enjoyed a much narrower participation by professional economists: an ambitious senator and his energetic and tena-

* This paper is one of several prepared by members of a study group which was formed by Professor Carl Auerbach, at the request of the Fund for the Republic, to appraise the work of the Kefauver Committee. Of course, the views here expressed do not necessarily represent those of Auerbach, the study group, the Fund for the Republic, or the majority of the Kefauver Committee. Reprinted from *Journal of Business of the University of Chicago*, Vol. XXXV, No. 1 (January 1962).

[1] The most extensive investigation was made in TNEC Monograph No. 27 (Washington, D.C.: U.S. Government Printing Office, 1941).

cious economist have provided the chief motive power of the revival. A few economists—notably Galbraith and Lerner—have embraced a position sympathetic to administered price inflations, but most economists have not given the theory serious attention, let alone support or criticism.

The doctrine that since 1955 the primary source of inflation has been the upward movement of administered prices was set forth at the outset of the hearings. Means' presentation was essentially empirical and, in the beginning, very weak. He presented a chart which showed that (with certain arbitrary exclusions) ninety-three wholesale prices (of the Bureau of Labor Statistics series) which changed seventy-seven or more times during 1926–33, did not on average rise from May, 1955, to May, 1957, whereas the eighty prices that changed less than eight times in the earlier period rose about 6 or 7 percent from 1955 to 1957.[2] This analysis of the behavior from May, 1955, to May, 1957, of prices classified by 1926–33 behavior was bizarre statistical play; it received much-needed reinforcement in a later appearance (January, 1959) before the Committee. On this occasion he presented the dramatic chart which I reproduce as Figure 19–1. Its structure was as follows:

1. Take the commodity classes of the BLS wholesale price index, and characterize each one as dominated by administered, market, or mixed prices (represented by solid rectangles, white rectangles, and dotted rectangles, respectively).
2. Let the base for the rectangle for a commodity class be proportional to its weight in the WPI index.
3. Let its height be proportional to the change in prices from 1953 to 1957.

Then he found that almost all price increases were in the administered-price industries, and every price decrease was in a nonadministered price area.[3] The beginning of the administered-price inflation, it may be noted, was now dated two years earlier than in the initial testimony.

A detailed criticism of this chart does not seem necessary, but three of its important weaknesses should be mentioned. First, the classification of price areas is highly subjective, not to say whimsical. Means's basic test of the presence of administered prices is the frequency of price changes. Yet he classifies—to give only one comparison—textiles and apparel as market-dominated and rubber products as administered, although both groups had on average nine price changes from December, 1953, to De-

---

[2] *Hearings before the Subcommittee on Antitrust and Monopoly of the Committee on the Judiciary, United States Senate, 1957* (Washington, D.C.: U.S. Government Printing Office, 1957), Part I, p. 90; also see pp. 124, 149.

[3] *Hearings,* Part IX, p. 4748; Part X, p. 4899.

cember, 1956.[4] Second, the criterion of frequency of price change is hopelessly ambiguous, as will be demonstrated below. And finally, even Means's purposeful procedure yields no pattern after 1957.[5]

FIGURE 19–1
WHOLESALE PRICE CHANGES, BY PRODUCT GROUPS, 1953–57
(Average Increase, 6.8 per cent)

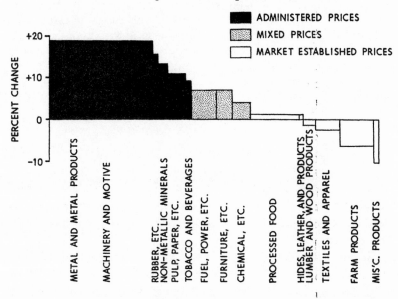

Means had absolutely no explanation for this phenomenon, not previously observed in "our history of prices."[6] He argued that many firms had a range of discretion in setting prices, but no hypothesis was presented as to why, in 1955 (or 1953) this discretion should for the first time be employed to raise prices persistently.

By a felicitous application of the division of labor, Galbraith supplied and presented to the Committee a theory, of sorts.[7] After a debonair selection of illustrative prices (with *1951* the beginning of the new era), he asserted a congruence between price movements and concentration of output. The oligopolists—Galbraith does not share Means's unwillingness

---

[4] *Hearings*, Part IX, p. 4756. I have recalculated these averages excluding commodities with a 1952–53 weight in the Wholesale Price Index of less than one thousand BLS units (roughly 0.04 percent of the aggregate index): the average number of price changes is then 10.0 for textiles and apparel, 14.9 for rubber products.

[5] From May, 1957, to March, 1961, the average increases in Means' categories are: administered prices, 2.64 percent; mixed prices, 0.34 percent; market-dominated prices, 3.19 percent.

[6] *Hearings*, Part I, p. 88; also see Part IX, p. 4752.

[7] *Hearings*, Part I, p. 88.

to identify administered prices and monopoly power—are held to lag in their price adjustments to increased demands:

> I come now to a central point. With inflation, the demand curves of the firm and industry are moving persistently to the right. Under these circumstances there will normally be an incomplete adaptation of oligopoly prices. Prices will not be at profit-maximizing levels in any given situation, for the situation is continually changing while the adaptation is by deliberate and discrete steps. This means that at any given time there will ordinarily be a quantum of what may be called unliquidated monopoly gains in the inflationary context. The shift in demand calls for a price increase for maximization; since the adaptation is currently incomplete, prices can at any time be raised and profits thereby enhanced. Absolute generality cannot be claimed for this proposition. There is an obvious, although I think outside, possibility that although adaptation is by discrete steps there will be anticipatory adaptation at each move.

This is, of course, a hypothesis—and one which does not answer the question of how an inflationary period gets under way. It was subjected to no tests in its original presentation, and in his first appearance before the Committee Galbraith continued to give only homely examples.[8] In the second appearance, Means's empirical findings are embraced and adduced as evidence.[9]

So much for the setting. A host of queries are raised by the facts and theories of these men and by the relevant Committee investigations; I shall discuss three: (1) The definition and existence of administered prices; (2) Oligopoly prices and inflation; and (3) The Committee hearings on monopoly pricing.

I. DEFINITION AND EXISTENCE OF ADMINISTERED PRICES

Means, the coiner of the phrase, defined an administered price as "a price set by someone, usually a producer or a seller, and kept constant for a period of time and for a series of transactions."[10] In contrast, a market price "fluctuates on the basis of supply and demand." These definitions are deplorably loose: no period of fixity of price is specified even in principle, and it is not obvious that price rigidity excludes adaptation to demand-and-supply changes. For example, a university changes tuition

---

[8] One corollary, the tendency of restrictive monetary policy to bear only on non-oligopolists, was cited (*Hearings*, Part I, p. 44); but it had no better empirical basis (see I. Schweiger, "Adequacy of Financing for Small Business since World War II," *Journal of Finance*, Vol. XIII [1958], Vol. pp. 323–47).

[9] *Hearings*, Part X, p. 4927.

[10] *Hearings*, Part I, p. 75.

fees only once a year, but transactions take place only once a year so supply-and-demand conditions effectively change only once a year at most.

In practice Means defined rigidity in terms of the frequency of changes in wholesale prices reported by the BLS.[11] The definition of administered prices as prices which are fixed over a significant period of time seemed to have empirical content—Means' studies in the 1930's displayed many industrial prices which change once a year or less. But the price rigidity was a gross statistical illusion, and it is a sad commentary on the quality of the literature on this subject that the illusion passed (and before the Kefauver Committee still passes) as truth.

TABLE 19-1
FREQUENCY OF PRICE CHANGE PER MONTH IN QUOTED WHOLESALE PRICES,
DECEMBER, 1953–DECEMBER, 1956

| | Number of Reporters | | | | |
Product Type	One	Two	Three	Four	Five or More
Average Price Changes per Month					
Materials, nonfood	0.103	0.143	0.206	0.207	0.392
Consumer goods, nonfood	.056	.101	.170	.200	.287
Producers goods	.088	.129	.208	.230	.288
Number of Commodities					
Materials, nonfood	44	47	88	52	41
Consumer goods, nonfood	43	51	74	30	34
Producers goods	34	41	78	33	18

Source: McAllister, op. cit., p. 390.

Of the some nineteen hundred prices presently in the wholesale price index, well over five hundred are based upon the reports of one or two sellers. The basic question was never raised: how do the quoted prices behave when the number of price reporters varies? Recently it has been raised and answered,[12] by analyzing the frequencies of price change for a random sample of one-third of the BLS wholesale prices. The results are given in Table 19-1.

The correlation of frequency of price change with the number of price reporters is very striking: it is roughly true of semi-manufacturers and finished goods (other than food) that the prices change in proportion

[11] In the 1930's the monthly prices were averages of weekly prices; now the BLS reports the price in the middle of the month. Hence a price change in the 1930's was reported as *two* changes if it did not take place at the beginning of a month.
[12] By Harry E. McAllister in Staff Paper No. 8 of the report, "Price Statistics of the Federal Government," printed as *Government Price Statistics* by the Joint Economic Committee (Washington, D.C.: U.S. Government Printing Office, January 21, 1961).

to the number of reporters.[13] With one reporter the prices of finished goods change about 0.07 times per month (or once every fourteen months); with two reporters, 0.11 times per month (or once every nine months); with three reporters, 0.19 times per month (or once every five months); etc.

Nor is this result due to the fact that the BLS collects fewer price quotations from industries that are highly concentrated. McAllister took random samples of 1, 2, 3, . . . reporters for the commodities with several reporters and calculated the frequency of price changes for these samples. The averages are substantially identical with those actually observed, so we can attribute the price change frequencies primarily to the number of reporters, not to their industry characteristics.[14]

[13] More precisely, the data are consistent with the hypothesis that the price quoted by one seller changes independently of the changes in the prices of the other sellers. Let p be the probability of a change in quoted price by one seller (per month). Then with unrelated price changes, (1) The probability of a price change with two reporters is $2p - p^2$, the sum of the probabilities minus the probability that both will change prices the same month; (2) The probability of a price change with three sellers is $3p - 3p^2 + p^3$, by a similar argument. In the case of finished consumer goods, the observed and calculated probabilities of a price change are:

Number of Reporters	Probability of Price Change per Month	
	Actual	Hypothetical
1	.056	.056
2	.101	.109
3	.170	.159

[14] The comparisons are as follows:

Number of Reporters	Probability of Price Change per Month	
	Actual	Random Sample
Consumer goods, nonfood:		
1	0.056	0.068
2	.101	.098
3	.170	.177
4	.200	.187
5	0.287	0.322
Producer goods:		
1	0.088	0.076
2	.129	.128
3	.208	.201
4	.230	.233
5	0.288	0.342

Source: McAllister, *op. cit.*, p. 391.

No investigation has yet been made into the minor related question: for a given number of reporters, does the frequency of change of quoted prices vary with the number of firms in the industry?

We emerge, then, with the finding that Means's tabulations of frequency of price change are unknown mixtures of the actual behavior of quoted prices and the number of firms reporting such prices. By increasing the number of price reporters, the BLS can reduce price inflexibility by the same order of magnitude as the increase in the number of reporters. The major development which Means believes to have outmoded neoclassical economic theory is the "development" of collecting a number of price quotations inappropriate to the measurement of short-run flexibility.

But the more important flaw in the doctrine of rigid prices is that it is concerned only with the behavior of *quoted* prices. Economists have always suspected that the nominally rigid quoted prices did not represent at all accurately the actual behavior of the prices at which important transactions take place. Two recent studies now offer persuasive support for the suspicion.

The first study, also by McAllister, makes comparisons of wholesale price quotations from January, 1957, through December, 1959, with prices paid by large private buyers. In each case the buying price is that of a single company and is therefore more rigid than it would be if several buyers were represented.[15]

A total of 30 comparisons is reported in Table 19–2. In only two cases (waste paper and mercury) did the BLS quotations change more frequently, and both were cases where the BLS price was not rigid. In the group as a whole, company prices changed 236 times compared with 127 changes in BLS prices, so even single-buyer quotations were almost twice as flexible. The company price quotations were 325 in number, and a biased estimate of the maximum number of price changes was 325 minus 30 or 295, and the actual number of changes was 236, or 80 per cent of this estimate of possible changes.[16] In addition, 12 prices which were rigid in the BLS quotations showed no change in the company quotations, but no frequency of purchase was reported for them, and they are suspect.[17] The general conclusion is clear: the BLS greatly underestimates

---

[15] Not only is the analysis of the number of reporters relevant here, but the buyers did not buy every month. The comparisons are made with BLS prices which were rigid for periods of three or more months.

[16] There is an ambiguity in the company quotations which must be noted. Some companies reported only months of price change, with no indication of whether purchases were made in other months. It is possible that some purchases were made in unreported months at unchanged prices, which, if reported, would lower the relative frequency of change.

[17] McAllister lists items such as flavoring syrup, typewriter ribbons, ethylene glycol, etc. Even here one may be entitled to reservations. For example, one of these commodities (hydrochloric acid) whose price was rigid at $30 per ton during the period had government bid prices ranging down to $18 per ton on July 31, 1950

TABLE 19–2
COMPARISON OF FREQUENCY OF CHANGE OF COMPANY
BUYING PRICES WITH BLS PRICES, 1956–59

Commodity	Number of Company Price Quotations	Number of Price Changes					
		Company			BLS		
		Rise	Fall	Total	Rise	Fall	Total
Coke, Milwaukee........	5	3	1	4	1	0	1
Coke, Indianapolis.......	11	5	4	9	1	1	2
Residual fuel oil, New York	18	1	8	9	1	8	9
Aluminum sulfate.........	4	1	1	2	1	0	1
Carbon dioxide..........	5	2	2	4	0	0	0
Salt	6	2	1	3	2	0	2
Silver nitrate............	14	6	6	12	4	1	5
Alcohol, ethyl...........	6	4	0	4	1	0	1
Carbon tetrachloride.....	11	9	1	10	1	0	1
Furfural	3	1	1	2	0	0	0
Glycerine, high gravity...	4	2	1	3	1	0	1
Phenolics, general purpose	10	3	3	6	2	1	3
Passenger tires..........	13	4	5	9	2	3	5
Sulfuric acid............	8	5	2	7	0	0	0
Passenger car tubes......	12	4	5	9	2	2	4
Tractor and implement tires	8	3	1	4	3	1	4
Gum, No. 2 common.....	7	2	2	4	2	1	3
Waste paper, No. 1 mixed	18	4	5	9	5	6	11
Pig lead................	24	7	15	22	3	10	13
Platinum	18	6	9	15	3	5	8
Mercury, 76-lb. flask......	30	10	12	22	6	17	23
Steel barrel, 55 gal.......	7	4	0	4	3	1	4
Welding electrodes......	4	2	0	2	1	0	1
Storage battery, automotive	33	7	19	26	5	2	7
Portland cement.........	14	5	6	11	4	3	7
Sulfur	5	0	4	4	0	0	0
Sodium hydroxide........	5	0	3	3	1	0	1
Pentaerythritol	4	1	2	3	1	1	2
Styrene	13	8	2	10	2	3	5
Glycerine, natural........	5	2	2	4	1	0	1
Total	325	113	123	236	60	67	127

Source: McAllister, *op. cit.*, pp. 395, 417, with several additions from worksheets.

the frequency of price changes, and—it may be added—the amplitude of price changes.

The second study, by John Flueck, utilizes the bids on government purchase contracts; a summary of his data is presented in Table 19–3.[18]

(see V. A. Mund, "Identical Bid Prices," *Journal of Political Economy*, Vol. LXVIII [February 1960], pp. 156).

[18] John Flueck, Staff Paper No. 9 in "Price Statistics of the Federal Government," *op. cit.*

TABLE 19–3
FREQUENCY OF PRICE CHANGES IN BIDS OF GOVERNMENT
CONTRACTS COMPARED WITH BLS PRICE QUOTATIONS

		Number of Obser-	Number of Price Changes*	
Commodity	Period Covered	vations	BLS	Bids
Aluminum sulfate...............	7/49–11/56	16	15	2
Calcium carbide...............	4/51– 9/54	14	13	1
Calcium hypochlorite............	2/49– 3/56	11	6	2
Sulfuric acid...................	11/48– 2/54	7	4	3
Xylene	12/54– 2/57	5	4	0
Acetylene	11/53–10/57	4	3	2
Carbon dioxide (gas)............	11/54–10/57	4	3	0
Oxygen	11/54–10/57	3	2	2
Oxygen	7/54– 7/60	3	2	1
Laundry soap (bar).............	7/54–12/59	21	20	7
Laundry soap (powder)..........	3/49–12/55	18	17	15
Paint, interior.................	3/51– 2/59	19	18	12
Enamel	12/56– 6/57	4	3	1
Gasoline	4/54– 4/58	10	9	3
Anthracite, buckwheat No. 1......	4/51– 4/59	17	16	16
Anthracite, chestnut............	4/51– 4/59	19	18	18
Anthracite, pea...............	4/53– 5/55	3	2	2
Bituminous coal, egg...........	3/53– 6/60	7	6	6
Coke (Birmingham).............	7/57– 6/60	3	1	2
Aluminum alloy sheet...........	1/55– 6/59	12	10	5
Aluminum ingot................	12/53– 5/56	5	4	4
Brass bar....................	1/54– 9/59	12	11	9
Steel sheet...................	2/49– 8/54	14	13	5
Steel sheet...................	7/54– 4/55	3	2	1
Steel plate...................	5/55– 6/57	3	2	1
Plywood A–C.................	1/52– 5/57	17	16	13
Plywood A–D.................	12/51– 8/55	16	15	8
Gummed tape.................	9/51– 1/59	22	21	9
Auto tubes...................	4/56–12/59	6	4	4
Storage batteries..............	2/49– 2/59	6	5	5
Linoleum	8/50–11/59	16	15	10
Glass, plate..................	7/49– 2/59	15	14	10
Golf balls....................	6/49– 2/60	17	16	12
Total	....	352	310	191

* Possible number of price changes, 319.
Source: Flueck, *op. cit.*, pp. 429, 437.

The government bid prices show a change whenever two successive contracts are compared: there were 310 out of 319 possible price changes. The BLS price quotations, on the other hand, showed only 191 changes. Flueck also shows that the amplitude of price fluctuations is on the order of three times as large as the BLS reports.

Both studies, then, confirm our suspicion that the quoted prices are not transaction prices. Even if we could ignore the fact that the classification of prices as administered or market-controlled rests upon the number of reporters, we would have to reject the distinction as resting upon prices which simply do not represent the changing terms on which commodities are actually sold.

Economists have long struggled to find a rational explanation for prolonged price rigidity, which is in general as inadvisable for profit-maximizing monopolists as it is impossible for competitive industries. Putting aside minor or special circumstances (the cost of a price change; the procedural delays in cartel or public regulation), they have failed to discover any such explanation. It appears that the real world has been equally remiss in supplying the phenomena they were seeking to explain.

II. OLIGOPOLY AND INFLATION

If administered prices are prices that are collected from one or two sellers rather than from several buyers, they offer a flimsy basis for any classification of prices as administered or market-determined. The limitations of this approach, however, do not bear on the different thesis that oligopolistic industries have paced an inflationary period.

The traditional economic theory argues that oligopoly and monopoly prices have no special relevance to inflation. A monopolist (to take the simpler case) sets a profit-maximizing price for given demand-and-cost conditions. If inflation leads to a rise in either demand or costs, a new and usually higher price will be set. The price will usually be above the competitive level at any given time, but its pattern over time will not be other than passively responsive to monetary conditions.

One could attack this position by arguing that monopolists and oligopolists want higher prices per se, rather than maximum profits. But no one, so far as I know, has proposed this peculiar theory of motivation for entrepreneurs (although it has been advanced with respect to labor unions).

A second, more sophisticated, version argues that the important industries are *becoming* concentrated and acting more monopolistically. As they raise their prices relative to what they had been under competition, a corresponding fall of absolute prices would be necessary in the remaining competitive industries unless the monetary authorities increased the quantity of money. In this scheme, the active agent of inflation is increasing monopoly, the passive agent the adaptation of the monetary authorities.

This version requires that the economy become increasingly concentrated, and—in the particular context of our problem—that the increase has taken place since 1953. I know of no evidence that this is the case; and I suspect that the 1958 Census will offer a refutation of it. But if it were true, the Kefauver Hearings should have been directed toward newly concentrated industries, not such old stand-bys as steel, automobiles, and drugs.

The Galbraithian version, quoted above, asserts that oligopolists' prices lag behind the prices which would maximize profits. It seems implausible to me, for it assumes that oligopolists cannot recognize a trend and adjust to it either currently or by anticipation. But the basic objection is that his theory really is not directed to the problem of inflation: in a period of stable prices, it offers no explanation as to why oligopoly prices should rise. At most it contains the implicit doctrine that the way to eliminate monopoly profits is to have an inflation and then by some device freeze monopoly prices before they can adjust to the new structure of flexible competitive prices. To state such a position clearly is enough to dismiss it.

The association between concentration of production and the amplitude of price increases during the 1950's has been investigated by Richard Selden and Horace J. dePodwin.[19] Their comparison of price changes from 1953 to 1959 with 1954 concentration yields two results: only 1 percent of price changes is "explained" by concentration ($r = .12$); and within two-digit industry categories there is no relationship between concentration and price movements.[20]

The attribution of inflation to monopoly power of enterprises is therefore lacking both a theoretical rationale and an empirical basis.

III. THE INDUSTRY HEARINGS

Inflation is a characteristic of price levels, not of the movements of prices of individual industries, so what relevance did the Committee hearings on steel, automobiles, and a few other industries have for administered-price inflations? The answer is not explicit in the Hearings, but apparently they were to demonstrate (if it were true) that in important oligopolistic industries prices were, within wide limits, not responsive to market conditions, and that prices were rising more rapidly than cost conditions would have justified. No survey of individual cases within the

---

[19] R. Selden and H. dePodwin, "Business Pricing Policies and Inflation," *Journal of Political Economy*, April, 1963.

[20] The one significant correlation had a negative sign.

powers of a committee could demonstrate the cause of a general inflation, but no general statistical study could lay the basis for legislation.

On this explanation of the industry hearings, steel was the logical candidate. Not only is it a bellwether,[21] but there was strong tradition for the choice: virtually every important price increase in steel since 1948 has been reviewed by a congressional committee.

The Hearings on the steel industry (which run to four volumes plus a committee report) were devoted to proving three points:

1. That price changes of all sellers were approximately simultaneous and identical;
2. That this price behavior indicated the absence of independent, competitive behavior by the various firms;
3. That the price increases were not necessary to compensate for increases in costs.

Strictly speaking, the third point is not sufficient: it is also necessary to show that monopoly profits are increasing over time relative to prices, and this extension raises problems we shall notice later.

The Hearings give the chronology of price increases, and in general the movements of quoted prices are identical and nearly simultaneous.[22] Kefauver found this behavior suspicious: "The point I was asking, why wouldn't it be more competitive if one of these companies at any time didn't increase price as much as you do? . . . Wouldn't it be more competitive if there were at least some slight differences in these prices?"[23] The implied position is that competitive quoted prices will differ a little. But if there are few sellers, so each can easily learn his rival's quoted prices, any persistent difference in quoted prices would be inconceivable unless the buyers were extremely poorly informed (which is not likely in the major steel products).[24]

Roger Blough, to whom the questions were addressed, answered that identical prices (to the buyer) and only such prices were competitive: "What I am trying to state is that, if we offer to sell steel to a customer at the same price as a competitor offers it to the customer, that is very definitely a competitive price."[25] The identity of quoted prices, however, does not prove competition is present—colluding firms would

[21] The phrase is Kefauver's, but this belief is as general as it is dubious, and it is very general.

[22] *Hearings*, Part II, p. 309; Part III, pp. 952 ff.

[23] *Hearings*, Part II, pp. 310, 312. But slight differences in prices were also found unsatisfactory in the automobile hearings, Part VI, pp. 2515 ff.

[24] This problem is discussed at length in my article, "The Economics of Information," *Journal of Political Economy*, Vol. LXIX (June, 1961), pp. 213–25.

[25] *Hearings*, Part II, p. 310.

be at least as likely as competitors to quote a single price. Price identity depends upon the existence of good information by buyers and sellers, not on the presence or absence of independent price policies by various sellers.

And here we must pause to note that actual transaction prices, in contrast to publicly quoted prices, need not be identical even with few sellers. The quantities buyers take are very different, and the conditions of sale are numerous and variable as are the costs of supplying an order. Identity of transaction prices is not at all likely. Unfortunately, the Committee never sought or even conjectured the existence of transaction prices.

Yet Kefauver was obviously correct in his suspicions of the competitiveness of a set of identical sealed bids. The argument that widespread information on prices leads to identical quoted prices is irrelevant to price identity when information is incomplete. Information is obviously incomplete on *future* supply-and-demand conditions. No set of truly independent producers will make the same estimate of market prices for the next month or the next quarter. When a sealed bid pertains to the future deliveries, it, therefore, rests on incomplete knowledge (unless there is an organized futures market). Price identity under these conditions is highly inconsistent with independent, competitive behavior.

Sealed bids on government purchase contracts frequently display price identity.[26] The extent of identical sealed bids was not established in the Hearings. Blough offered in evidence a summary of two periods. In 40 invitations for bids on 619 items in November and December, 1954, there were 3,000 individual bids; 200 of 2,400 competitive bids were identical with those of United States Steel (which made 600 bids). In the second quarter of 1957, there were 26 invitations on 90 items. Here 22 rival bids (out of 400) were identical with those of United States Steel (which made 90 bids).[27] This tabulation is unfortunately too incomplete to be of much value. The extent of identity among bidders other than United States Steel, the amounts involved, the firms that match United States Steel, etc., and the time span between submission of bids and the time when deliveries were to be made would have to be known in order to form a definite conclusion as to the importance of the practice.

The proposition that competition is not wholly effective in the steel industry was not demonstrated nearly so strongly as it could be because the Committee did not look closely at the structure of prices by products

[26] See V. A. Mund, *op. cit.*
[27] *Hearings*, Part III, p. 957.

and geographical areas. But if the proposition is (as I believe) true, did the industry use its concentrated structure to obtain increasing profits in the past decade?

The demonstration that the 1957 rise in steel prices was not necessary to maintain "adequate" profits is interesting chiefly for the level of argument used. The direct costs of wage increases for employees (union and nonunion) were estimated to call for a price increase of $2.50 to $4.00 a ton, depending on the wage increase and output per man-hour employed.[28] In addition, Dr. John Blair estimated that scrap prices had fallen from 1956 to September, 1957, by about $4.00 per ton of steel produced.[29] All other costs were submitted to the most desultory discussion. United States Steel refused to give these costs, on grounds of confidentiality, and emphasized only that depreciation allowances were insufficient because they were reckoned on historical costs—a notion Kefauver believed unacceptable on accounting grounds.[30]

Aside from the fact that the cost analysis was on a deplorable level of superficiality, the whole discussion was up in the air because there was no criterion of reasonable profits. The only test of reasonable profits that the Committee proposed was profits similar to those in the past, or similar to those in other industries (varying with the industry).

The ambiguity found clear expression in the dispute between Kefauver and A. B. Homer, of Bethlehem Steel, over whether the low- or high-cost producers should set the price.[31] Kefauver wished the low-cost producers to cut prices and remove the umbrella over high-cost producers. Homer said, "We have it today, Senator," and although the Senator did not believe it, he could give no argument that they did not have it that day.

But even a showing of monopoly profits would not prove that oligopoly prices were the source of a new kind of inflation: what was needed was a demonstration that profits were rising over time. John Blair skirted such a position with a chart displaying the rate of return on net worth as a function of the operating rate (as a per cent of capacity). It appeared to show that even before the 1957 price increase, the

---

[28] *Hearings*, Part II, p. 389.

[29] *Hearings*, Part II, p. 664. The time periods seem more appropriate to a criticism of inflexibility than of level of price.

[30] *Ibid.*, p. 386. Kefauver also believed that stock splits have an inflationary effect (p. 370), and that the cost of capital to a company is less if it earns less (by reducing prices), with a consequent fall in its corporate income tax, and floats new securities (p. 407).

[31] *Ibid.*, p. 631. The economist would, of course, say that both should and do set the price.

rate of profit was at a historically unprecedented level in the first half of 1957.[32]

Even accepting this, all it would show is that beginning in January, 1957, profit rates (which had actually fallen in the early 1950's) suddenly rose to new levels.[33] Did a current six-month episode show the presence of the new inflation?

On the question of why, on certain occasions in recent years, the steel industry raised prices while operating at relatively low outputs, no light was shed. How real this phenomenon is I do not know; there are no adequate transaction prices on steel products. The presence of congressional investigations such as this is a very strong reason for the steel industry to raise quoted prices whenever a suitable occasion (cost increase) occurs: if it reduced quoted prices in depression, it would have the usual congressional hearings when they were restored in prosperity.[34]

While Means and others were testifying that the rise of administered prices was the cause of the current inflation, another set of economists was testifying before another committee that the failure of administered prices to fall was the cause of the inflation.[35] It must have been reassuring

[32] *Ibid.*, p. 270. The data are not corrected for price-level changes and there is an obvious non-linearity in the scatter, but the details of the analysis need not be discussed here.

[33] In my study of capital and rates of return in manufacturing industries, the following rates of return after taxes for the metal industries are given (*Capital and Rates of Return in Manufacturing Industries* [Princeton, 1963]):

Year	Blast Furnaces Rate of Return (Book Value)	Iron and Steel Foundries Rate of Return (Book Value)	All Primary Metals	
			Book Value	Stable (1947) Prices
1950	10.24%	9.53%	10.08%	7.27%
1951	7.84	8.84	7.90	5.27
1953	6.78	6.27	6.23	3.16
1954	4.86	4.92	4.75	4.15
1955	8.35	7.74	7.85	3.44
1956	7.59	8.83	7.52	5.91
1957	7.49	6.69	6.33	5.41

[34] This was written before President Kennedy's recent intervention in the pricing of steel—a striking example of the growing political concern with individual prices of conspicuous companies.

[35] See, e.g., Charles L. Schultze, *Recent Inflation in the United States* ("Study Paper" No. 1, Joint Economic Committee [September, 1959], pp. 54 ff., 132); and, in a related variant, O. Eckstein and G. Fromm, *Steel and the Postwar Inflation* ("Study Paper" No. 2, Joint Economic Committee [November, 1959]).

to Congress to know that the steel industry was guilty, even if what it was guilty of was in dispute.

I have not gone through all the other industry hearings, but those I have sampled were usually even less relevant to oligopoly inflation. In the automobile hearings, the focus was on the level of profits, with no attention to the inflation thesis. In bread the interest was in local price-cutting, oriented chiefly to the Robinson-Patman Act. In drugs it was on monopoly, quite independent of inflation. Some of this material will no doubt be useful for the study of traditional problems, but it is not germane to the main theme.

IV. CONCLUSION

The price notification bill (S. 215) of Senator O'Mahoney was the logical culmination of the doctrine of administered price inflations. Its major provisions were:

1. The act applied to the largest eight firms in any industry if
   (*a*) they made 50 percent or more of national sales of a product, and
   (*b*) had assets in excess of $10 million.
2. Such companies must notify the FTC of any price increase 30 days in advance of the increase.
3. The FTC and the Anti-trust Division are to hold public hearings on the reasons for and effects of the price increase and report their opinion on its justifiability.[36]

Only O'Mahoney of the members of the committee explicitly supported the bill, although it also received support from J. K. Galbraith, Ben Lewis, and Means, as well as from miscellaneous organizations (the UAW being the most important) and individuals. In addition to much industry opposition, it was opposed by the FTC, the Anti-trust Division, and various economists (Ruggles, Dean, Fackler, etc.).

The details of the bill hardly merit discussion; indeed, one can say the bill had no details. Senator O'Mahoney's "answer," when asked if a company with thousands of prices must appear whenever a single price was increased, is a sufficient commentary on the care with which the bill was formulated.[37]

The merits of the bill hardly deserve comment. To turn a governmental body loose on an immense area without even primitive criteria for

---

[36] *Hearings,* Part XI, pp. 5183–85.
[37] *Hearings,* Part XI, pp. 5655 ff.

judgment would be the most reckless of ventures. Its judgments on the justifiability of price increases would eventually be rejected by some prominent company, and then compulsory price fixing would follow. Neither Means's irrelevant numbers nor Galbraith's dark suspicions seem an adequate basis for such a radical step.

The entire performance of the Kefauver Committee over the past four years has been a highly unsatisfactory one. The Committee has lacked focus—flitting from administered prices to the "fancification" of automobiles to local price discrimination to the accuracy of advertisements for drugs, and where not. Vulgar digressions into the stock options of witnesses are symptomatic of the fishing expedition the Committee had turned into. The levels of evidence have been low, and the selection of academic economists has been somewhat less than representative.

The American economy still has a good deal of monopoly power, and much of it is within the reach of the Sherman Act. The Committee, by drawing attention to the drug industry and to identical bids on contracts, has made a contribution in this area. But its chief results were to popularize the erroneous beliefs that there is an important phenomenon called administered prices, and that if such prices existed they would have something to do with inflation.

PART IV

Antitrust Policy

Two essays on policy deal with recommendations of policy and the effects of past policies. As usual, the recommendations were written well before the study of effects of previous policies. The essays are preceded by a theoretical examination of the economic effects of several ancillary restraints of trade permitted in the common law.

CHAPTER 20
Restraints on Trade in Common Law, or if Justice Taft had been an economist.

CHAPTER 21
The Economic Effects of the Antitrust Laws (*Journal of Law and Economics*, 1966).

CHAPTER 22
Mergers and Preventive Antitrust Policy (*University of Pennsylvania Law Review*, November 1955).

RESTRAINTS ON TRADE

IN THE COMMON LAW

Contracts in restraint of trade were unenforcible under the common law, but restraints which were ancillary to a contract might be allowed if the primary purpose contract was deemed desirable. The law was restated in a famous decision by the then Circuit Court Judge William H. Taft:

The inhibition against restraints of trade at common law seems at first to have had no exception. See language of Justice Hull, Year Book, 2 Hen. V., folio 5, pl. 26. After a time it became apparent to the people and the courts that it was in the interest of trade that certain covenants in restraint of trade should be enforced. It was of importance, as an incentive to industry and honest dealing in trade, that, after a man had built up a business with an extensive good will, he should be able to sell his business and good will to the best advantage, and he could not do so unless he could bind himself by an enforceable contract not to engage in the same business in such a way as to prevent injury to that which he was about to sell. It was equally for the good of the public and trade, when partners dissolved, and one took the business, or they divided the business, that each partner might bind himself not to do anything in trade thereafter which would derogate from his grant of the interest conveyed to his former partner. Again, when two men became partners in a business, although their union might reduce competition, this effect was only an incident to the main purpose of a union of their capital, enterprise, and energy to carry on a successful business, and one useful to the community. Restrictions in the articles of partnership upon the business activity of the members, with a view of securing their entire effort in the common enterprise, were, of course, only ancillary to the main end of the union, and were to be encouraged. Again, when one in business sold property with which the buyer might set up a rival business, it was certainly reasonable that the seller should be able to restrain the buyer from doing him an injury which, but for the sale, the buyer would be unable to inflict. This was not reducing competition, but was only securing the seller against an increase of competition of his own creating. Such an exception was necessary to promote the free purchase and sale of property. Again, it was of importance that business men and professional men should have every motive to employ the ablest assistants, and to instruct them thoroughly; but they would naturally be reluctant to do so unless such assistants were able to bind themselves not to set up a rival business in the vicinity after learning the details and secrets of the business of their employers, ...

For the reasons given, then, covenants in partial restraint of trade are generally upheld as valid when they are agreements (1) by the seller of property or business not to compete with the buyer in such a way as to derogate from the value of the property or business sold; (2) by a retiring partner not to compete with the firm; (3) by a partner pending the partnership not to do anything to interfere, by competition or otherwise, with the business of the firm; (4) by the buyer of property not to use the same in competition with the business retained by the seller; and (5) by an assistant, servant, or agent not to compete with his master or employer after the expiration of his time of service.[1]

Two of these classes of restrictions are analyzed below. The analyses will, at a minimum, display the difference in viewpoint of an economist and a noneconomist, and at a maximum they will suggest what the effects of the partial restraints were.

1. LAND SALES

Landowner A sells or leases land subject to the covenant that the land not be used to enter into competition with A in the business of (say) selling groceries.

If there are many sites which are equally good for a rival grocery to establish itself, the covenant is without consequence. Rivals will appear if it is profitable, and the covenant on A's land would affect neither the competition in grocery retailing nor—if the land has other uses—the value of the land.

So suppose that A owns a large plot about his store, so no one could enter as a close rival in the grocery business except on his land.

1. With the covenant, he will sell or lease land at its value in non-grocery uses. If someone wishes to use a plot of A's land to open a rival shop, A will charge the sum:
   i) the value of the land in other uses, plus
   ii) the value of the share of A's monopoly profits which the buyer will obtain.

2. Without a covenant, A might wish to charge the sum:
   i) the value of the land in other uses
   ii) the value of the share of A's monopoly profit *times* the probability that the buyer will enter the grocery business.

[1] *United States* v. *Addyston Pipe & Steel Co.*, 85 Fed. 271 (1898).

For this latter case, I assume that the land has only a fixed competitive value except for grocery stores. (If the plot is so large that there are also monopoly values in service stations, restaurants, etc., the analysis is merely duplicated for each such use.) Then no buyer will (or can) pay more than the alternative use value if he is a nongrocer. Absent the covenant, therefore, the landowner must choose between

a) Selling the land at a competitive price and seeing one or more rivals enter the grocery business.
b) Utilizing the land himself, say, through tenant farmers.

The latter option may not be feasible because of diseconomies of scale. If it is not feasible, the prohibition of the covenant amounts to a prohibition of price discrimination.

2. APPRENTICES

An apprentice covenants not to compete with his master for a period of seven years after the completion of the apprenticeship.

In a regime of competition among masters, the covenant would be ambiguous. If 100 masters in London train a total of 100 apprentices, does the participation in the London trade by the graduate apprentice (journeyman) of Master A increase the competition A faces? Economically the answer is no. If legally the answer were yes, then the covenant would be an undue burden on the apprentice without any reward to the master: the apprentice would have to move to another market once his training was completed, even though his ex-master did not benefit by any reduced competition (100 rival masters and their apprentices being quite enough).[2] If the ex-apprentices of other London masters were not deemed by the law to compete with a given master, then his competition from former apprentices would be completely beyond his control. Under competition, the masters benefit from the covenant in no case.

Suppose then, that the masters have monopoly earnings in their market. With the covenant, apprentices earn the usual pay of apprentices in competitive labor markets, *plus* a return for the cost of moving after the apprenticeship, and migrate after completing their training.[3] Abolish now the covenant. An apprentice now expects to share a portion of the

---

[2] Hence, apprentices would be fewer than would otherwise be forthcoming, so apprentices' expected earnings after allowance for pointless migration would equal earnings in alternative callings.

[3] There is a possible return to London after seven years of working elsewhere, which could be handled as below in the absence of a covenant. But if the masters cannot prevent immigration of workers, whence comes their monopoly?

monopoly return after he completes his apprenticeship, so the apprenticeship becomes more attractive than alternative callings. The candidates for apprenticeship will bid (through lower wage offers) for admission until their expected earnings, including future monopolistic earnings, equal in present value the expected earnings in other fields. The masters earn more during the apprenticeship and less thereafter; by amounts that have equal present values if apprentices bid correctly. Hence, they will be indifferent to the covenant.

Why, then, did a covenant appear? The simplest answer appears to be as follows: Some apprentices intended to work elsewhere, some did not. A monopolistic master would pay different wages to the two if he could distinguish them. He could not (because obviously the potential rival could misrepresent his intentions). The covenant insured noncompetition. Apprentices not working under the covenant would pay for their sharing of monopoly profits. Permitting the covenant was simply permitting price (wage) discrimination by monopolistic masters. This explanation is readily tested by comparing the wages of apprentices who were not required to migrate with the wages of those who were required to migrate.

Chapter

21

THE ECONOMIC EFFECTS
OF THE ANTITRUST LAWS*

The task I have set is to form a quantitative notion of the effects of the antitrust laws. The task is formidable. A Congress which had goodwill toward scholars would have exempted from the Sherman Act not a collection of special pleaders, as has been our historical practice, but a random sample of industries. A world more favorable to scholars would have had many United States, some of which had antitrust policies. (Our federal nation could have been almost that favorable, but the state antitrust laws have been pushed nearly into oblivion by the federal laws.) In our statistically inefficient world, the investigator must somehow disentangle the effects of one battalion of an army of forces that have been influencing the American economy in the past 75 years.

Many students have undertaken our task, and diverse estimates of the effects of our antitrust laws may be found in the literature. These estimates have invariably been made by one procedure. The scholar studies the history of our policy and in the light of his knowledge of our economy—and perhaps of other economies—he makes a summary judgment. The defect of the procedure is that the link between the survey of experience and the conclusion is not explicit, so different scholars reach different conclusions. Yet it should be the fundamental attribute of a measurement procedure that different men can use it to achieve similar results. Until such procedures are available, there is no tendency for the measurements to improve—each man's work remains independent of all other's work. The main purpose of this paper is to seek improvable procedures.

I. SIMPLE ANTITRUST LAWS

Let us begin with an antitrust law that seems easy to assess: it is the provision of the Panama Canal Act that no company violating the Sher-

* Reprinted from *Journal of Law and Economics*, Vol. IX, October 1966. I wish

man Act be permitted to ship goods through the canal.[1] This act, we assume, has not had any effect upon the methods of shipments used by monopolists, let alone upon the extent of competition, and for several reasons:

1. An instance of enforcement would surely have received much publicity, so presumably none has occurred.
2. It is inconceivable that none of the many violators of the Sherman Act ever used the canal.
3. The Attorney-General gave to the canal authorities an interpretation of the provision which implied that it could be ignored.[2]

I do not wish to quarrel with this universal presumption that the provision never influenced the movement of monopolized goods. I do wish to emphasize the fact that this presumption is a poor substitute for evidence. The provision could have frightened monopolists into using the railroads, and the only way we can eliminate this possibility is by studying the comparative shipments of firms which were and were not prosecuted under the antitrust laws. Perhaps the problem is too small to justify the extensive labor such research would entail, but until this research is done, we possess a presumption, not a finding. The central weakness of the antitrust literature has been its reliance on presumptions—and in cases vastly more important and uncertain than the trifling question with which I begin.

A slightly more significant antitrust law is that no man may serve as director of two companies if at least one has assets of $1 million or more and the two companies compete with one another.[3] The logic of the law is that joint directors could effect collusive schemes between two companies more easily than conspiring officers or directors.

As a matter of history, the law has been invoked in formal complaints on 23 occasions up to January 1965.[4] The one instance leading to court decision concerned Sidney Weinberg who was a director of Sears, Roebuck & Co. and B.F. Goodrich Co., both of which sold a variety of similar consumer goods at retail.[5] The economic merits of the case were negligible.

---

to express my gratitude to Claire Friedland for much of the statistical work; and important contributions were made by Mrs. Belle Cole, Ruth Westheimer, and Barry Herman.

[1] 37 Stat. 567 (1912), 15 U.S.C. § 31 (1964).

[2] 30 Ops. Att'y Gen. 355 (1915).

[3] 38 Stat. 732 (1914), 15 U.S.C. § 19 (1964).

[4] Staff of Subcomm. No. 5, House Comm. on the Judiciary, 89th Cong., 1st Sess., Interlocks in Corporate Management 57 (Comm. Print 1965).

[5] *United States* v. *Sears, Roebuck & Co.*, 111 F. Supp. 614 (D.C.N.Y. 1953).

Let me now begin the empirical study of the effects of antitrust laws. England has no such law. The number of joint directors of companies in the same industry is extraordinarily small, however (see Table 21-1).

TABLE 21-1
INTERLOCKING DIRECTORATES, GREAT BRITAIN, 1964

Industry	Companies	Number of Directors	Number of Overlapping Directors
Aircraft	13	130	1
Boots and shoes.............	50	290	0
Rubber products: Tires.......	8	63	0
Cement	29	194	1

Source: *The Stock Exchange Official Year-Book* (1964).

I am prepared to conclude that our prohibition of interlocking directorships has not had a noticeable effect upon corporate directorates. It therefore is unnecessary to examine the more basic question: Would the existence of many interlocking directorates lead to a decrease of competition?[6]

II. THE EFFECTS UPON CONCENTRATION

We turn now to the first main purpose of the antitrust laws, the prevention of monopoly. This goal was sought by two routes: the prohibition of attempts to monopolize in Section 2 of the Sherman Act; and the prohibition of mergers that tend to reduce competition.

We require both a measure of concentration and—when we consider mergers—a measure of the effects of mergers on concentration. We adopt the Herfindahl index—the sum of the squares of the shares of industry output possessed by each firm. It is a comprehensible measure of firm sizes (with a maximum value of 1 for the index with monopoly and a minimum of $1/n$ with n firms of equal size). That the Herfindahl index is suited to the study of mergers deserves a fuller explanation.

Let us consider a simple way in which the impact of a merger upon the concentration of an industry can be measured.[7] Take, for example, the largest firm and calculate its growth, as a share of the industry, by the

[6] Interlocking directorates are a clumsy technique, even when one desires to coordinate the activities of two firms, so I would not expect their presence or absence to have a significant relationship to the extent of competition among firms.

[7] See George J. Stigler, "The Statistics of Monopoly and Merger," *Journal of Political Economy*, Vol. LXIV (1956), p. 33.

percentages of industry output acquired by merger at different dates. If we assume that the acquired firms would have maintained their shares of industry output in the absence of merger, we may directly calculate the contribution of internal growth and mergers to the growth of the leading firm. For example, the leading English cement producer, the Associated Portland Cement Companies, Ltd., acquired, between 1900 and 1960, approximately 125 percent of industry capacity, but had a market share of 70 percent in 1960. Internal growth would then be reckoned at —55 percent of industry output.

The sum of shares acquired by merger by all firms is unfortunately a meaningless number. There is a problem of duplication: let A have 40 percent, B, 20 percent and C, 10 percent of industry output. If B acquired C (10 percent) and then A acquires B (30 percent), the sum (40 percent) is greater than if A acquired B and C directly. This duplication can of course be avoided by counting each constituent firm only once. More important, the numbers have no scale. If there are 1000 identical firms, and each of 100 acquires 9, the sum of merged shares is 90 percent, although concentration is negligible (4 percent for the largest 4 firms). Or if two firms with shares of 10 percent and 90 percent, respectively, each acquires a firm with 10 percent, the measure of the effect of merger would be the same.

The Herfindahl index, which can be derived from general arguments on the probability of successful collusion,[8] is a more appropriate measure of the sum of merger activity in the industry. If firms with shares p_1 and p_2 combine, the Herfindahl index rises by

$$(p_1 + p_2)^2 - p_1{}^2 - p_2{}^2 = 2p_1 p_2.$$

In the 1000 firms industry above, the Herfindahl index would rise, after the 900 firms were acquired, to .01 from its previous level of .001. If a firm with 90 percent of output acquires a firm with 10 percent, the Herfindahl index rises .18 from .82 to 1, whereas a merger of two firms each with 10 percent raises the index by only .02.

The basic test of the effectiveness of our policies to prevent monopoly and high concentration must of course be: has it made concentration in American industry lower than it would otherwise be? An answer is sought along three lines: comparisons of the United States with other countries which have no antitrust law; comparisons of periods before and

---

[8] See my article, "A Theory of Oligopoly," *Journal of Political Economy*, Vol. LXXII (1964), pp. 54 f.

after passage of antitrust laws; and comparisons of industries exempt from and subject to the antitrust laws.

1. The Comparison with England

The English economy is one source of information about an economy in which there is no public policy against concentration of control. The English economy operates in an otherwise similar legal environment and in approximately the same state of technology. Its smaller size in general tends to lead to higher concentration than we observe in the United States because the optimum size of enterprise is roughly the same in the two countries.[9] Since our economy has grown from perhaps twice the size of the British economy in 1900 to four times the British size in 1965, we should expect *national* concentration in America to be lower and to be declining relative to British concentration. However, for cement and steel, where regional data are available, we compare a region in the United States with England to reduce the bias. More work is required in this area.[10]

Comparisons have been made of the history of concentration in seven industries in the United States and England since approximately 1900. Seven industries will scarcely support any general conclusion, and the comparison is presented primarily for methodological purposes. The reason the sample is so small is that it has proven to be rather difficult to piece out tolerably reliable estimates for all the British and some American industries. The output of each American automobile company has long been reported by weeks, for example, but even approximate outputs began to be reported on a regular basis in England less than twenty years ago.

The data for these industries (automobiles, cement, cigarettes, flat glass, soap and detergents, steel, tires) are given in the appendix; they are summarized graphically in Figure 21–1.

1. The automobile industry has been more highly concentrated in the United States than in the United Kingdom for the entire period studied.
2. The cement industry has been much more highly concentrated in the United Kingdom than in the United States (Lehigh Valley). Concentration has not risen over time in the United States.
3. The cigarette industry is concentrated in the United States, but at

[9] So, at least, argues P. S. Florence, *The Logic of British and American Industry* (1953), pp. 22–29, as to relative optimum sizes in the two countries.
[10] The 1954 ratios of U.S. to U.K. industry size are: automobiles, 8.8 (1955); cement, 1.0; cigarettes, 3.6; glass, 7.0; soap, 8.9; steel, 5.1; tires, 6.0.

FIGURE 21–1

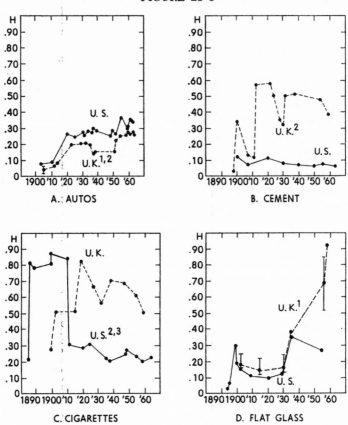

A. AUTOS

B. CEMENT

C. CIGARETTES

D. FLAT GLASS

a much lower level since the dissolution of American Tobacco. Since 1911 the concentration in Great Britain has been much higher than in the United States.

4. The American glass industry in the 1950's was less concentrated than the British industry (which is a monopoly). Concentration has risen in the United States since the 1920's, however, to a high level.

5. The soap industry is substantially more highly concentrated in the United Kingdom than in the United States, but concentration is fairly high in the United States.

6. The steel industry (ingots) was fairly highly concentrated in the United States after U.S. Steel was formed, but it has declined steadily and substantially. Nevertheless, it is above the level in the United Kingdom.

7. The rubber tire industry is highly concentrated in the United Kingdom but concentration is declining somewhat; concentration is substantially lower in the United States, and has had no trend since the 1930's.

FIGURE 21–1 (*Continued*)

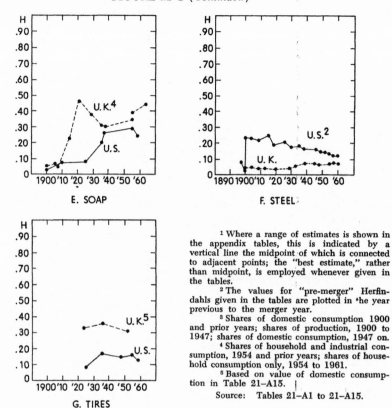

E. SOAP

F. STEEL

G. TIRES

[1] Where a range of estimates is shown in the appendix tables, this is indicated by a vertical line the midpoint of which is connected to adjacent points; the "best estimate," rather than midpoint, is employed whenever given in the tables.

[2] The values for "pre-merger" Herfindahls given in the tables are plotted in the year previous to the merger year.

[3] Shares of domestic consumption 1900 and prior years; shares of production, 1900 to 1947; shares of domestic consumption, 1947 on.

[4] Shares of household and industrial consumption, 1954 and prior years; shares of household consumption only, 1954 to 1961.

[5] Based on value of domestic consumption in Table 21–A15.

Source: Tables 21–A1 to 21–A15.

These instances are compatible with the hypothesis (which I presently favor) that the Sherman Act was a modest deterrent to high concentration.[11] The underlying statistical tables (see Appendix) suggest that mergers to achieve very high concentration ($H > .3$) were more common in England than in the United States. These hypotheses can, of course, eventually be tested against a much larger body of data: the test is improvable.

2. The Decline of Horizontal Mergers

A second and more comprehensive set of data look to the impact of the 1950 anti-merger amendment to the Clayton Act. These data concern

[11] The industries favorable to the hypothesis that the Sherman Act has served to keep down concentration are cement and cigarettes, with glass, soap and tires pointing more weakly the same way. The automobile and steel industries support the opposite interpretation. Since 1911, merger has not been a major source of high concentration in the United States.

the number of horizontal mergers engaged in by the 200 leading companies in manufacturing and mining. The basic data are presented in Table 21–2.

TABLE 21–2
DISTRIBUTION OF LARGE MANUFACTURING AND MINING ACQUISITIONS
BY TYPE AND BY PERIOD OF ACQUISITION

	1948–1953		1954–1959		1960–1964	
Type of Merger	*Number*	*Percentage*	*Number*	*Percentage*	*Number*	*Percentage*
Horizontal	18	31.0	78	24.8	42	12.0
Vertical	6	10.3	43	13.7	59	17.0
Conglomerate:						
Market Extension.......	4	6.9	20	6.4	24	6.9
Product Extension......	27	46.6	145	46.2	184	52.9
Other	3	5.2	28	8.9	39	11.2
Total	58	100.0	314	100.0	348	100.0

Source: Bureau of Economics, Federal Trade Commission.

These merger data suggest that the 1950 anti-merger statute has been a powerful discouragement to horizontal mergers. The fraction of horizontal mergers by large companies has fallen to low levels. Even this Federal Trade Commission count of horizontal mergers is heavily biased toward this type of merger: two companies were considered in the same industry and market if even a small fraction of their sales overlapped. There are also no important mergers recorded since 1950 in the seven American industries in Tables 21–A1 to 21–A14.

Unfortunately, the extent of horizontal mergers in earlier times has not been measured—it seems incredible but it is true that all forms of merger are combined in the standard merger series. (In our seven industries horizontal mergers were more frequent and important before than after 1950; see Table 21A–17.) The deficiency in the statistical history of mergers is of course remediable.

3. The Exempt Areas

The industries exempt from the antitrust laws are still another potential source of information, but a reluctant source. Most exempt industries are subjected to regulation of other sorts, and presumably have economic characteristics which distinguish them from non-exempt unregulated industries.

The insurance industry (or industries) are a fairly simple example of exempt industries. The exemption is not unqualified, but no merger cases have been brought against insurance companies, and the impact of the 1950 merger statute is presumably negligible.[12] Nevertheless, the level of concentration is low in the life and fire-and-casualty branches of the industry, and merger activity has been quite minor. The data for fire and casualty insurance companies is given in Table 21–A18; they may be summarized:

Year	Herfindahl Index	Contributions of Mergers from Previous Date
1945	.0163	
1953	.0164	.0000
1963	.0189	.0024

Almost as low concentration is found in a typical industrial state.[13]

The ambiguity in such evidence is that we have no standard of comparable nonexempt industries. Still, the levels of concentration and of mergers in insurance have been so low that it is virtually impossible to conceive of a pattern (of sharply falling concentration) in nonexempt industries, such that the insurance industry would corroborate our previous finding on the substantial effects of the 1950 merger act.

III. THE EFFECTS UPON COLLUSION

The main thrust of the Sherman Act was against conspiracies in restraint of trade, and the judgment of its success must rest largely on its achievements in this direction. No type of legislative endeavor, however, is harder to measure in its effects than a prohibition of actions which can be concealed.

Through 1963, there were some 957 completed antitrust cases reported in the Commerce Clearing House (CCH) Bluebooks in which

---

[12] The industry is exempt to the extent (1) that states regulate the industry, and (2) certain forbidden acts, such as concerted boycotts, are not engaged in. The Antitrust Division believes mergers of insurance companies are exempt if the states have so-called Little Clayton Acts; see Hearings Pursuant to S. Res. 57 Before the Subcommittee on Antitrust and Monopoly of the Senate Committee on the Judiciary, *The Insurance Industry*, 86th Cong., 1st sess., pt. 2, at 931 (1960).

[13] Thus the Herfindahl ratio in Illinois in 1963 was .0232 for fire and casualty insurance.

some element of conspiracy was charged.[14] Of these cases, the Department of Justice won exactly 756, or slightly over three quarters of the total. In addition, a large number of Federal Trade Commission cases involving collusion have been brought. We can equally well hail the numerous cases (and equally the victories) as evidence of the beneficial effect of the Sherman Act, or as evidence of its failure. What we want, of course, is a census of collusion, detected and undetected, and a census with and without an antitrust law.

Our difficulty rests on one fundamental fact: we do not have a generally acceptable theory of oligopoly. If we had such a theory, it would tell us what the determinants of successful collusion are, and we could then investigate the effects of the Sherman Act upon these determinants. When the event we wish to study is clandestine, we cannot rely upon direct observation.

I believe that my theory of oligopoly is a useful tool for this study, precisely because it seeks to isolate the determinants and forms of successful collusion—or rather, the determinants of successful cheating and hence unsuccessful collusion. The argument turns on the problem of getting reliable information on the observance of collusive agreements: invoices and sellers and buyers, and even physical shipments, may lie. And where an agreement cannot be enforced, it will not be obeyed.

On this view, certain methods of collusion are highly efficient. The most efficient is the joint sales agency, for then price cutting is impossible and any large, hidden movement of goods is also virtually impossible. This plausible position is supported by European cartel experience:

This method (by which the cartel has access to the records of each member), no matter how rigorously it is administered, nevertheless does not give a complete guarantee against evasions of the cartel policy. Rather, it is a popular, recurring complaint that one cannot detect clever violations, especially concealed price reductions. This leads the cartels in ever rising numbers to the establishment of a *common selling agency* as the only wholly reliable protection against evasion. It is not an individual incident, but rather wholly typical, that one of the oldest and best organized Austrian cartels, the plate glass syndicate, explained when a common selling bureau was established that without this device even the severest controls would not prevent price-cutting or the exceeding of quotas.[15]

It is relevant to observe that marine insurance was exempted from the antitrust laws by the Merchant Marine Act of 1920. A syndicate of

[14] The tabulation of cases has been made by Michael Marks in an unpublished study.

[15] Kestner, *Die Organizationszwang* (1912), p. 153.

domestic and some foreign companies was formed, and their business was assigned to the syndicate, in which each of the member insurance companies had a quota of participation. No member may deal directly in this market except by permission of, and at rates set by, the syndicate—a strict joint sales agency system.[16]

Somewhat less efficient collusion is achieved by the assignment of customers, whether individually or by geographic area or otherwise. There is still a possible inducement to secret price cutting: in the long run, the favored customers may grow relative to their rivals who purchase from another seller who abides by the cartel price. Actual shipments to non-assigned customers are usually detectable, as in the case of joint sales agencies.

Both the joint sales agency and the assignment of customers are obvious to the buyers and therefore they are likely to be called to the attention of the antitrust division and, once suspected, their existence is easily proven. No such ease of detection exists with the lesser forms of collusion, such as price agreements, but these lesser forms also are much less easily enforced.[17]

The types of collusion I call efficient (joint sales agencies and assignment of customers) are more likely found to be in violation of the antitrust laws than the other types of collusion. This is almost necessarily true, since the efficient types of collusion are *per se* offenses, whereas the inefficient types of collusion include a fair number of innocuous trade association activities and other uncertain extensions of the law. The hypothesis is, in fact, readily tested: in an analysis of a small sample of the two types of cases, we obtain the results in Table 21–3. The sample is small so that the test is weak (the results could arise by chance with probability .2) but the sample could readily be enlarged.

This line of argument may be, and I hope is, plausible, but it is not yet persuasive. Two things are needed. The first is a substantial testing of the oligopoly theory that underlies this argument. A systematic empirical test has so far eluded me. The second omission is a showing that the "nonefficient" forms of collusion are substantially less efficient than the "efficient" forms. This latter defect can be partially remedied, I believe, by the following procedure.

A series of cartel cases have been brought for a variety of reasons,

[16] Hearings Pursuant to S. Res. 57, *supra* note 12, at pts. 2 and 9. The cartel agreement is reprinted in pt. 9 at 5555 to 5633.

[17] With one important exception. The government as buyer usually uses bidding techniques which make secret price cuts impossible. Hence, collusive systems usually work best against governmental buyers.

TABLE 21–3
ANALYSIS OF COLLUSION CASES BY TYPE AND OUTCOME*

Type	Government Wins	Defendant Wins	Total
Efficient	9	4	13
Inefficient	9	8	17
Total	18	12	

* Cases identified by Commerce Clearing House (CCH) number are as follows (only one of a group of closely related cases is included): "Efficient" cases, Nos. 14, 18, 24, 34, 83, 239, 240, 254, 277, 282, 348, 349, and 355; "Inefficient" cases, Nos. 21, 66, 76, 215, 218, 227, 241, 243, 244, 246, 248, 265, 273, 274, 284, 331, and 343.

Source: The Federal Anti-Trust Laws, with summary of cases instituted by the United States (1951); supplementary information necessary for assigning cartels to "efficient" and "inefficient" classes was obtained from U.S. Courts, *Federal Anti-Trust Decisions* (Vols. 1-12).

including the contagious property of a prominent case in a large industry of eliciting parallel complaints. I hypothesize that the interval between inception of a scheme and its detection will be shorter for the more efficient techniques. If so, the act has reduced the comparative gain, and hence the comparative frequency, of these forms of collusion. A small number of cases has been analyzed, and the pattern is in keeping with the hypothesis.[18]

Types of Collusion	Number	Period from Inception of Alleged Collusion to Complaint
Efficient	7	21.6 (± 3.9) months
Inefficient	10	56.7 (± 2.4) months

The accumulation of more such cases (many are available) and more fundamentally the rigorous testing of the underlying oligopoly theory would greatly strengthen this argument.

IV. CONCLUSION

The substantive findings of this study are meager and undogmatic:

1. The Sherman Act appears to have had only a very modest effect in reducing concentration.
2. The 1950 Merger Act has had a strongly adverse effect upon horizontal mergers by large companies.

[18] The cases analyzed have Commerce Clearing House (CCH) case numbers: 18, 24, 34, 83, 277, 348, and 349 in the efficient class; 66, 76, 215, 218, 244, 265, 273, 274, 284, and 343 in the inefficient class.

3. The Sherman Act has reduced the availability of the most efficient methods of collusion and thereby reduced the amount and effects of collusion.

Discussions of methodology are usually offered as a substitute when an author has lacked the imagination to devise strong tests and the diligence to compile a large body of evidence, and I apologetically follow this tradition. I do not claim that any reasonable man must accept the above conclusions, for even the strongest (on the effects of the antimerger statute) is not overpowering in the volume or pointedness of the evidence. I do claim that each of the findings is improvable, and the extension of this work will shrink the range of defensible conclusions.

Appendix

The concentration data in the following tables are based upon a variety of industry histories, trade journals, the financial press, etc. The references which are given after Table 21–A18 are only to the main sources. Especially in the earlier years a considerable amount of indirect estimation is necessary, so the figures are only approximate. The estimates of the shares of medium-size and small companies are especially rough; however, variations in the estimated shares of these companies have an almost negligible effect on an industry's Herfindahl index. The share of the largest company in the terminal year is included in the tables beginning with the earliest Herfindahl year in which its share exceeded 25 percent.

Mergers are defined here to include the acquisition of 50 percent or more of the common stock of one company by another and the creation of formal joint sales arrangements. Unless otherwise indicated, the Herfindahl index shown for a given year is based on company shares after all mergers taking place in that year.

With the exception of cement and steel, for which capacity shares were employed, wherever possible the Herfindahl indexes are based on company shares of domestic consumption (as approximated by production plus imports, less exports). Where it was necessary to employ some other basis (for example, production shares) the magnitude of exports or imports is indicated in the footnotes if either was considerable.

TABLE 21–A1
U.S. AUTO INDUSTRY; CONTRIBUTIONS OF MERGERS AND
CONCENTRATION MEASURES FOR SELECTED DATES*

Selected Dates	H	GM Share 1931–1964	Contributions of Mergers to ΔH	Remarks
1904	.076			
1908			.0179	GM formed
1909–10	.090		.0022	U.S. Motors formed
1912			.0001	Chevrolet-Little
1916			.0090	GM-Chevrolet
1917			.0001	Maxwell-Chalmers
1918			.0020	GM-Scripps Booth
1920	.279			
1922			.0018	Ford-Lincoln
1925	.243			
1928			.0059	Dodge-Chrysler
			.0002	Hupp-Chandler
1929	†			
1931	.284	.433		
1932	.261	.412		
1935	.292	.384		
1937	.283	.406		
1938	.307	.448		
1939	.297	.437		
1948	.253	.406		
1950	.298	.454		
1952	.275†	.418		
1953			.0004	Kaiser-Willys
1954			.0006	Hudson-Nash
			.0008	Studebaker-Packard
1955	.363	.508		
1960	.286	.436		
1961	.315	.466		
1962	.352†	.519		
1963	.342	.510		
1964	.331	.491		

* Based on production shares prior to 1925; based on shares of new car registrations, including imports, 1925 and after.
† Herfindahl indexes based on production shares, and hence comparable with U.K. figures, are as follows: 1929 = .218 (exports = 10% of production, imports negligible); 1952 = .278 (exports and imports = 4% and 1%, respectively, of production); 1962 = .383 (exports and imports = 3% and 5%, respectively, of production).

TABLE 21–A2
U.K. AUTO INDUSTRY; CONTRIBUTIONS OF MERGERS AND CONCENTRATION
MEASURES FOR SELECTED DATES, BASED ON SHARES OF PRODUCTION*

Selected Dates	H	Morris-BMC Share 1924–1964	Contributions of Mergers to ΔH	Remarks
1905	.02–.05			
1910			.0012 max.	BSA-Daimler
1912	.065			
1913	.084			
1919			.0008 max.	Talbot & Darracq
1921			.0018	form STD
1924	.202	.305		
1926–27			.0133	Morris-Wolseley
1928			.0006	Humber-Hillman
1929	.212	.350		
1931			.0002 max.	Rolls-Royce—Bentley
1932	.208	.334		
1935	.198	.315	.0026 max.	Rootes-STD
1937	.147	.233	.0016	Morris-Riley
1938	.160	.235		
1945			.0030	Standard-Triumph
1947			.0002 max.	Aston Martin-Lagonda
1952	.158 pre-merger	.197		
	.235 post-merger	.394	.0776 max.	Austin & Morris form BMC
1955	.253	.390	.0007	Rootes-Singer
1960	.253†	.365		
1961	.275	.385		
1962	.261	.377		
1963	.273	.385		
1964	.253	.368		
1966			.0168‡	BMC-Jaguar

* Exports as per cent of production were as follows: 1913, 6%; 1924, 10%; 1929, 13%; 1932, 16%; 1935 and 1937, 14%; 1938, 13%; 1952, 61%; 1955, 38%; 1960, 40%; 1961, 36%; 1962, 43%; 1963, 38%; 1964, 36%. Retained imports as percent of production were 16% in 1913, 9% in 1924 and 12% in 1929; in every later year for which a Herfindahl index is given above, retained imports were less than 5%.

† In 1960, shares of domestic sales for the top 2 and top 5 companies were 70% and 90% respectively; production shares employed above for the top 2 and top 5 were 67% and 96%, respectively.

‡ Based on shares of domestic market. Source: *Wall Street Journal*, July 12, 1966, p. 1.

Max. = Maximum estimate, i.e., companies taken as equal in size when no other information is available.

TABLE 21–A3
U.S. CEMENT INDUSTRY (LEHIGH VALLEY*); CONTRIBUTIONS OF MERGERS AND
CONCENTRATION MEASURES FOR SELECTED DATES, BASED ON PLANT CAPACITY

Selected Dates	H	Contributions of Mergers to ΔH	Remarks
1900†	.132		
1902		.0203	Lehigh-Saylor
1904		.0083	Atlas-Keystone
1905		.0025	Alpha-National
1907	.092		
1912		.0019	Alpha-Catskill
1920	.118		
1924		.0058	Lehigh-Tidewater
1925		.0004	North American (Security)-Helderberg
		.0008	Dexter - Penn-Allen
1926		.0057	Lehigh-Bath
		.0040	Penn. Dixie-Penn. Cem.
		.0007	North American (Security)-Acme
1928‡		.0022	International-Phoenix
1929	.086		
1939	.079		
1948	.072		
1954		.0025	Martin-Lawrence
1955	.080	.0024	Allentown-Valley Forge
1963	.072		

* Eastern Pennsylvania, New York east of Buffalo, New Jersey, Maryland and extreme eastern West Virginia.
† In most cases, capacities interpolated between dates of first shipments and 1907.
‡ FTC dates control beginning 1925 for International-Phoenix.

TABLE 21–A4

U.K. CEMENT INDUSTRY; CONTRIBUTIONS OF MERGERS AND CONCENTRATION
MEASURES FOR SELECTED DATES, BASED ON PLANT CAPACITY

Selected Dates	H	APCM Share 1900 to 1959	Contribution of Mergers to ΔH	Remarks
1900	.028 pre-merger	.088 (White)		Before APCM formed
	.359 post-merger	.594	.3317	After APCM formed
1907	.142	.361		
1912	.119 pre-merger	.322		Before BPCM formed
	.565 post-merger	.750	.4446	BPCM formed and acquired by APCM
1922	.576	.753	.0475	APCM-Kent
1924	.501	.700	.0466	APCM-Humber
1928	.368	.580	.0199	Red Δ formed
			.0004	East-Lewes
1931	.331 pre-merger	.549		Before Red Δ acquisition
	.498 post-merger	.701	.1673	After Red Δ acquisition (and Tunnell-Clyde merger, contribution = .0004)
1933-34†			.0147	Formation of Alpha
1936†			.0002	Rugby-Bachelor
1938	.512	.700	.1650	APCM-Alpha
1955	.480	.667	.0022	Rugby-Nelson
1959	.395	.598		

† Employs 1938 shares.

TABLE 21–A5

U.S. CIGARETTE INDUSTRY; CONTRIBUTIONS OF MERGERS AND CONCENTRATION MEASURES FOR SELECTED DATES, BASED ON NUMBER OF CIGARETTES CONSUMED DOMESTICALLY*

Selected Dates	H	Reynolds Tob. Co. Share 1921– 1963†	Contribu- tions of Mergers to ΔH	Remarks
1890	.207 pre-merger		.6050	Allen & Ginter,
	.234* pre-merger		.6911*	W. S. Kimball, Good-
	.812 post-merger			win, Kinney, W. Duke
	.925* post-merger			form Amer. Tob. Co.
				and acquire S. F. Hess
1891	.779			
1892			.0906	S. Hernsheim-Amer.
1894			.0391	H. Ellis-Amer.
1898			.0912	Drummond-Amer.
1899			.1482	Amer. acquisition of
				Monopol, National,
				W.R. Irby, and
				Liggett & Myers
1900	.809		.0082	S. Anargyros-Amer.
	.860*		.0121	J. Bollman-Amer.
1901			.0230	Brown-Amer.
			.0109	C. V. Winfree-Amer.
1903			.0338	Wells, Whitehead-Am.
			.0104	Craft-American
1911*	.831		—.5292	Break-up of Am. Tob.
1912*	.302		.0003	Formation of Tob.
				Products Corp.
1916*			.0004	Schinasi-Tob. Products
				Corp.
1917*			.0004	Prudential-Tob. Prod-
				ucts Corp.
1918*			.0004	Falk-Tob. Products
1921*	.286	.354		
1923*			.0186	Tob. Products Corp.-
				American
1925*	.318	.416		
1935*	.212	.282		
1937*	.197	.281		
1944*			.0021	Axton-Fisher-
				Phillip Morris
1947	.242*	.283		
	.256	.301		
1954	.216*	.247	.0011	Benson & Hedges-
	.221	.251		Phillip Morris
1958	.198*	.281		
	.202	.287		
1963	.221	.344		

* For 1911 through 1944 figures are based on shares of total output. In other years, alternative figures given based on total output wherever indicated by "*"; Exports as percent of total output for selected years are as follows: 1890, 11%; 1900, 31%; 1912, 14%; 1921, 14%; 1935, 3%; 1947, 9%.
† The American Tobacco Co. share slightly exceeded that of the Reynolds Tobacco Co. in 1947 and 1954 and varied between 80 and 96 percent of production from 1890 (post-merger) to 1911 (pre-dissolution).

TABLE 21–A6
U.K. CIGARETTE INDUSTRY; CONTRIBUTIONS OF MERGERS AND
CONCENTRATION MEASURES FOR SELECTED DATES, BASED
ON SHARES OF DOMESTIC CONSUMPTION*

Selected Dates	H	Imperial Share 1900 to 1959	Contribution of Mergers to ΔH	Remarks
1900†	.281	.516 (Wills)		Before formation of Imperial Tobacco Co.
1901–02†			.2259	Formation of Imperial and acquisition of Ogden
1903†,‡	.507	.710		After formation of Imperial
1915‡	.507	.710		
1920	.830	.910		
1926			.0235	Imperial-Ardath
1928	.670	.814		
1932§			.0494	Imperial-Gallaher
1933§	.565	.738		
1934§			.0398	Jackson group to Imperial via Gallaher
1937§			.0034	Robinson to Imperial via Gallaher
1938§	.712	.841	.0336	Imperial-Walters
1946§			—.0857	Imperial interest in Gallaher reduced to less than 50%
1947	.690	.824		
1952			.0001 max.	Carreras-Dunhill
1952–53			.0136 max.	Imperial-John Wood, Charlesworth & Austin, Express Tobacco (via Ardath)
1954	.612	.772		
1955			.0003 max.	Gallaher-Benson & Hedges
1958			.0002	Carreras-Rothmans
1959	.496	.652		
1960			.0044	Imperial-Phillips (via Ardath)
1961			.0168	Gallaher-Wix

* 1947 and prior year shares are based primarily on consumption in lbs; later year shares are based on consumption in value terms; in 1954 cigarettes were 84.0% of all U.K. manufactured tobacco production by weight and 86.7% of production in value terms.

† Based on estimated shares in 1903, hence entire difference between H for 1900 and H for 1903 is necessarily due to 1901–02 merger contribution.

‡ Identical 1903 and 1915 estimates for H reflect unchanged Imperial share as estimates for smaller companies are only approximate.

§ From 1932 to 1946 Imperial owned 51% of the equity of Gallaher, whereas after 1946 Imperial owned less than 50% (42.5% in 1956), hence Imperial is considered above as having acquired Gallaher in 1932 and divested itself of Gallaher in 1946; if Imperial and Gallaher are considered independent throughout, H for 1933 = .516, H for 1938 = .641 and the *only* entries in the merger contribution column from 1932 through 1946 would read as follows: .0019 Jackson-Gallaher; .0002 Robinson-Gallaher; and .0318 Imperial-Walters.

Max. = employs maximum estimates of acquired company shares where no exact information available.

TABLE 21–A7

U.S. FLAT GLASS INDUSTRY*; CONTRIBUTIONS OF MERGERS AND
CONCENTRATION MEASURES FOR SELECTED DATES, BASED
ON SHARES OF VALUE OF PRODUCTION†

Selected Dates	H	L-O-F Share‡ 1935– 1954	PPG Share‡ 1900– 1954	Contribu- tions of Mergers to ΔH	Remarks
1895	.035 pre-merger .066 post-merger			.0306	After PPG joined with 4 other plate companies but before formation of American Glass Co.
1895–99				.2376	American Glass Co. formed
1899	.304				
1900	.192		.242	−.0545	Break-up of Amer. Glass into Amer. Window Glass Co. and independent companies
1901				.0182§	Independent Glass Co. formed
1902	.158‖		.225	.0056§	Federation (Coop) formed
1904				§	Break-up of Indep. & Federation (Coop)
				.0006	Mississippi Glass Co.-Appert Glass and Rolland Glass
1909	.106		.234		
1910				**	
1912				.0119	Formation of John- ston Brokerage Agency
1913				.0059	Formation of U.S. Window & sales contract with PPG
1919	.094		.229		
1920				.0027	Formation of National Plate
1925				.0003	Libbey-Owens— Fairfield

TABLE 21–A7 (Continued)

Selected Dates	H	L-O-F Share‡ 1935–1954	PPG Share‡ 1900–1954	Contributions of Mergers to ΔH	Remarks
1928				.0027	Libbey-Owens— Adamston
1929	.136		.298		
1930				.0104	L-O and Edw. Ford form L-O-F
				.0109	PPG-Standard
1931				.0138	L-O-F acquires Ottawa, Ill. plants of Nat'l Plate
1932				.0017	Mississippi—Highland-Western
1933				—.0049	L-O-F divestiture of Adamston
1935††	.346	.424	.399	.0024	Formation of Fourco
				.0131††	L-O-F acquisition of Vitrolite and sales contract with Blue Ridge
1936				.0005	Amer.-Baker Bros.
1948				—.0006	Blackford split-off from Fourco
1954	.280	.380	.340		

* Sheet, plate, and rolled glass; excludes laminated glass and products of purchased glass.

† Prior to 1935 a complex and indirect procedure was necessary. Company capacities were used to estimate company shares of plate, sheet, and rolled glass, which in turn were estimated separately by production processes (hand v. machine, Colburn v. Fourcault machine, etc.) from production data.

The Herfindahl index for 1902 calculated directly from production is estimated to be between .164 and .176.

In 1935, when there was considerable idle capacity in sheet and plate, the Herfindahl index on the basis employed in earlier years is estimated to be approximately .260.

Imports as percent of production were as follows: 1895, approx. = 17%; 1899 = 8.4%; 1909 = 5.0%; 1919, negligible; 1929 = 5.0%; 1935, negligible; 1954 ≠ 5.5%. Exports were 5.0% in 1919 and less than 5% in other Herfindahl years.

‡ As shares of L-O-F and PPG are almost identical in 1935 and 1954, both companies' shares are shown here for those years. Shares of the American (Window) Glass Co. in the period when it was the dominant firm are as follows: 1899 = .499; 1900 = .359 (after split-off of independent companies); 1902 = .256.

§ Contributions of 1901 and 1902 mergers are excluded from Table 21–A17 calculations as inadequate information is available to estimate effect of dissolution of both companies in 1904.

‖ See note † above.

** Formation of Imperial Window Glass Co. in April 1909 omitted as company was dissolved in Nov. 1910 and hence operated only in the 1909–10 blast.

†† Exact date of L-O-F sales contract with Blue Ridge is not available; 1935 is earliest year when contract known to be in operation.

TABLE 21–A8

U.K. FLAT GLASS; CONTRIBUTIONS OF MERGERS AND CONCENTRATION MEASURES
FOR SELECTED DATES, BASED ON SHARES OF DOMESTIC CONSUMPTION

Selected Dates	H		Pilkington Share 1904 to 1955	Contributions of Mergers to ΔH	Remarks
1901				.0051	Pilkington-Ravenhead
1904	best est.	.190	.288		
	range*‡	.170–.232	.216–.360		Includes cartel of continental companies exporting plate to U.K. as one company§
1913	best est.	.154	.364		
	range*‡	.121–.221	.273–.455		Cartel above ended§
1930	best est.	.168	.373		
	range*	.135–.256	.255–.492		Includes Belgian sheet & plate cartels and German sheet & plate cartels and Czech sheet cartel each as one company§
1935		.370†	.584		ditto§
1954	range*†				
	max. est.	.725–.834	.844–.912		§
	range*‡				
	min. est.	.533–.748	.699–.859		§
1955‖		.904	.950	.1793–.0699*†	Pilkington-Chance
				.3512–.1557*‡	

* Employs extreme estimates of company shares of rolled glass, for which no information is available.
† Evaluates output at export prices.
‡ Evaluates output at import prices, including tariff.
§ Imports as percent of consumption were as follows: 1904, 75%; 1913, 68%; 1930, 33%; 1935, 30%; 1954, negligible.
‖ Pilkington began purchase of Chance stock in 1936; complete ownership was achieved in 1955. Exact year when majority interest achieved is not available; Pilkington directors appear on the Chance Board of Directors for the first time in 1951.

TABLE 21–A9

U.S. SOAP INDUSTRY;* CONTRIBUTIONS OF MERGERS AND CONCENTRATION MEASURES
FOR SELECTED DATES, BASED ON SHARES OF VALUE OF OUTPUT

Selected Dates	H	P & G Share 1935 to 1958	Contribution of Mergers to ΔH	Remarks
1900	.030			
1903			.0046	P & G-Schultz & Co.
1909	.068			
1910			.0049	P & G-D. S. Brown
1919			.0002	Palmolive-Crystal
			.0002	B. T. Babbitt-Mendelson
1925	.088			
1926			.0051	Palmolive-Peet
1927			.0124	P & G-Wm. Waltke
			.0019	P & G—Rub-No-More
1928			.0290	Colgate-Palmolive Peet
			.0033	P & G—Globe
1929			.0043	P & G—Duz Co.
1930			.0082	Colgate-Palm-Peet—Kirkman
			.0106	P & G—James S. Kirk
1933			.0007	P & G—Hewitt Brothers
1935	.198	.357		
1936			.0024	P & G—Cincinnati Soap Co.
1937	.259†	.432		
1939			.0112	Lever—Gold Dust
1951	†			
1954	.288	.500		
1955			.0002	Purex-Old Dutch
1956			.0004	Purex-Manhattan
1957			.0088	Lever-Monsanto's "All" division
1958	.253	.452	.0002	Purex-Wrisley
1964			.0008	Purex-Fels

* 1957 SIC definition, but excludes alkaline detergents and glycerine. 1937 and before includes shaving preparations. 1909 and before includes glycerine and 1900 includes candles, to the extent produced in soap establishments of large companies.

† 1951 H based on shares of household soap and detergent output (i.e. excluding industrial) = .314; comparable figure for 1937 = .245.

TABLE 21–A10

U.K. SOAP INDUSTRY; CONTRIBUTIONS OF MERGERS AND CONCENTRATION
MEASURES FOR SELECTED DATES, BASED ON SHARES
OF DOMESTIC CONSUMPTION IN TONS*

Selected Dates	H	Lever Share 1915– 1961	Contribu- tions of Mergers to ΔH	Remarks
1899			.0024	Lever-Benj. Brooks
1900	.057			
1905	.063			
1906			.0040	Lever-Vinolia
			.0040	Lever-Hodgson & Simpson
1907	.045			
1908			.0142	Lever-Hudson
1910–12†			.0459	Lever-Thomas, Cook & Others
1911			.0027	Crosfield & Gossage form Crossage
1913‡			.0896	Lever-Crossage
1915‡	.228	.460		
1917			.0603	Lever-Watson
1919‡			.0128	Lever-Price (Gibbs)
1920			.0384	Lever-Knight
1921	.462	.670		
1925			.0922	Lever-BOCM
1929	.376	.600		
1935	.308	.535		
1938	.300	.515		
1954§	.350	.523		
	.391‖	.543		
1961§	.432‖	.594	.0044	Lever-Pinoya

* See Table 21–A11 for 1900 through 1921 on production shares basis, in tons, for selected years.

† Excludes Knight and Watson as Lever had obtained less than 50% interest in 1910–1912.

‡ De facto merger of Lever and Crossage dated 1913, year in which Lever acquired 50% interest; 1915 H = .170 and merger contribution = .1378 if merger dated 1919, year Lever acquired full control.

§ Estimated H based on the value shares in 1954 and 1961 = .384 and .430 resp. (synthetic detergents weighted 1.5, following Edwards and Puplett "soap equivalent" concept).

‖ In terms of shares of household consumption only, that is, excludes industrial.

TABLE 21–A11

U.K. SOAP INDUSTRY—CONTRIBUTIONS OF MERGERS AND CONCENTRATION
MEASURES FOR SELECTED DATES, BASED ON SHARES
OF PRODUCTION IN TONS 1900–1921

Selected Dates		H	Lever Share 1915 and 1921	Contributions of Mergers to ΔH*	Remarks
1900		.059			
1905		.078			
1907		.056			
1911				.0130	Crosfield & Gossage form Crossage
1913†				.1729†	Lever-Crossage
1915	max. est.	.364	.593		
	min. est.	.313	.548		
1921		.535	.725		

* Computed on production shares basis only for mergers involving Crosfield & Gossage (Crossage), i.e., companies other than Lever with large export trade. See Table 21–A10 for other merger contributions.

† Merger contribution = .2112 if merger dated 1919. See Table 21–A10, footnote ‡.

TABLE 21–A12

U.S. STEEL INDUSTRY; CLEVELAND-DETROIT, CHICAGO, PITTSBURGH-YOUNGSTOWN
& EASTERN DISTRICTS*—CONTRIBUTIONS OF MERGERS AND CONCENTRATION
MEASURES FOR SELECTED DATES BASED ON INGOT CAPACITY†

Selected Dates‡	H	U.S. Steel Share 1901 to 1960	Contributions of Mergers to ΔH§	Remarks
1899	.084‖		.0001	Formation of Republic
1900			.0003	Formation of Crucible
1901	.021 pre-merger	.206 (Carnegie)		
	.233 post-merger	.472	.2117	Formation of U.S. Steel**
1902			.0248	U.S. Steel-Union Steel
1903			.0010	U.S. Steel-Troy Steel
1904	.232	.471	.0130	U.S. Steel-Clairton Steel
1908	.225	.463		
1911			.0003	Crucible-Midland
1916	.240	.475	.0017	Bethlehem-Pennsylvania
1917			.0002	Bethlehem-American
1919			.0002	Wheeling Steel & Iron-LaBelle Iron Works Whitaker Glessner
1920	.178	.405		
1922			.0043	Bethlehem-Lackawanna
1923			.0077	Bethlehem-Midvale Steel & Ordnance (Coatesville & Johnston plants)
			.0018	Youngstown Sheet & Tube-Brier Hill Steel-Steel & Tube Co. of Amer.
1926	.206	.419		
1927			.0002	American Rolling Mill-Forged Steel Wheel
1928			.0004	Republic Iron & Trumbell Steel
1929			.0002	Amer. Rolling-Ashland
			.0004	Formation of Nat'l Steel: Weirton Steel, Great Lakes
1930	.177	.377	.0038	Formation of Republic Steel: Republic Steel & Iron, Central Alloy Steel, Donner Steel & Bourne Fuller
			.0003	Amer. Rolling Mill-Sheffield Steel

TABLE 21–A12 (Continued)

Selected Dates‡	H	U.S. Steel Share 1901 to 1960	Contributions of Mergers to ΔH§	Remarks
1934			.0002	Amer. Rolling Mill-Scullin Steel
1935	.183	.382	.0023	Republic-Corrigan-McKinney
1936			.0001	Amer. Rolling Mill-Rustless Iron & Steel
1938	.163	.350		
1942			.0014	Jones & Laughlin-Otis
1944			.0003	Jones & Laughlin-Electric Weld Tube Division
1945	.156	.336		
1946			—.0124	U.S. Steel divestiture of Farrell & Mingo works to Sharon Steel & Wheeling Steel resp.
			.0005	Republic-Defense Plant Corp. So. Chicago plant
1948	.143	.312		
1951	.138	.304		
1954	.130	.291		
1957	.125	.276	.0003	Jones & Laughlin-Rotary Electric
1960	.122	.266		

* The American Iron and Steel Institute in its *Directory of Iron and Steel Works of the United States and Canada* (1954, 1957) divides the United States into six districts according to the principal regional markets which are served by states producing steel. We have excluded steel facilities in the southern and western districts comprising the following states: Alabama, Alaska, Colorado, California, Georgia, Nebraska, North Carolina, Oklahoma, Oregon, South Carolina, Tennessee, Utah, Virginia, and the Canal Zone. The source for capacities by state between 1911-1960 is the American Iron and Steel Institute's *Annual Statistical Report* (1911-1960). The American Iron and Steel Institute's *Directory of Steel Works and Rolling Mills* in the United States and Canada for 1901, 1904, and 1908 provided state totals for these years. Capacity by state was interpolated for the intervening years where necessary.

Company notes re. exclusion of southern and western facilities:

1. U.S. Steel: Excluded are steel ingot capacities of the Tennessee Coal, Iron & Railway Co. from 1907 on; Columbia Steel Co., 1930 on and the Geneva Steel Co., 1946 on.
2. Bethlehem: Excluded are ingot capacities of the Pacific Coast Steel Corp. and the Southern California Iron and Steel Manufacturing Co. from 1930 on.
3. Republic: Excluded are plant at Birmingham, Ala. in 1901 & 1904 and the Gulf States Steel Co. from 1937 on.
4. Armco: Since 1945, firm total excludes plants of Sheffield Steel Corp. in Sand Springs, Okla. and Houston, Texas.

† That is, based on shares of productive capacity in tons.

‡ Herfindahls were computed for all years between 1900 and 1960 in which the AISI published directories.

§ Mergers are recorded for the following largest firms in the industry: United States Steel, Bethlehem, Republic, Youngstown Sheet and Tube, Jones and Laughlin, National, Inland, Wheeling, Crucible, Pittsburgh, Armco and Sharon.

‖ The Herfindahl for 1899 is based on capacities included in the 1901 directory but reflects the size of firms prior to the formation of the U.S. Steel Corporation (1901), the Crucible Steel Co. (1900), and Republic Iron and Steel Co. (1899), and after the incorporation of the Federal Steel Co. (1898), the National Steel Co. (1899), and the American Steel & Wire Co. of N.J. (1899).

** Incorporating the following steel-producing companies: Carnegie, Federal Steel, National Steel, American Steel and Wire Co., National Tube, American Steel Hoop Co., American Sheet and Steel Co., American Bridge Co.

TABLE 21–A13

U.K. Steel Industry—Contributions of Mergers and Concentration Measures for Selected Dates, Based on Ingot Capacity*

Selected Dates	H	Contributions of Mergers to ΔH	Remarks
1900	.036		
1902		.0022	Guest Keen-Nettlefords
			Alfred Baldwin-Wright Butler
			John Brown-Thomas Firth
1903	.040	.0030	Dorman Long-Northeastern Steel
			Formation of Stewarts & Lloyds
1905		.0060	Beardmore-Mossend Steel Works
			South Durham-Cargo Fleet
1908	.035		
1910		.0056	South Durham-Palmers Shipbuilding & Iron
1913	.032		
1915		.0026	David Colville-Clydebridge Steel &
			Glengarnock Iron & Steel
1916		.0007	Steel, Peech & Tozer-Samuel Fox
1917		.0021	Steel, Peech & Tozer-Frodingham
			Richard Thomas-Cwmfelin Iron & Steel
1918		.0034	Formation of United Steel Cos.
			Baldwins-Brymbo Steel
1920	.037	.0012	John Summers-Shelton Iron & Steel
			Guest, Keen & Nettlefords-John Lysaght
			Stewarts & Lloyds-Alfred Hickman
1925		.0017	Richard Thomas-Grovesend Steel & Tinplate
1928	.042		
1929		.0015	Formation of English Steel
1930		.0061	Formation of Lancashire Steel
			Formation of Colvilles
			Formation of British (Guest, Keen &
			Baldwins) Iron & Steel
			Dorman Long-Bolchow Vaughan
1932	.051		
1936		.0070	Colvilles-Lanarkshire Steel & Steel Co. of
			Scotland
1938	.067		
1944	.068	.0030	Formations of Richard Thomas & Baldwins
1947†	.070	—.0033	Formation of Steel Co. of Wales through
			Guest, Keen & Baldwins divestiture of
			Margum & Port Talbot
1953		.0003	Firth Brown-Beardmore
1954†	.068	.0005	Tube Investments-Parkgate Iron & Steel
1957	.067		
1960	.065		

* Except for 1900 and 1913, when shares of output in tons were employed, company shares are based on furnace capacity per heat without adjustment for differences in heats per week or number of operating weeks in the year.

† 1947 figures are pre-nationalization. 1954 figures are based on 1954 shares of companies denationalized between 1935 and 1957.

TABLE 21–A14
U.S. RUBBER TIRES AND TUBES INDUSTRY; CONTRIBUTIONS OF MERGERS AND
CONCENTRATION MEASURES FOR SELECTED DATES, BASED ON
VALUE OF DOMESTIC CONSUMPTION PLUS EXPORTS*

Selected Dates	H	Contributions of Mergers to ΔH	Remarks
1912		.0226	Goodrich-Diamond
1915		.0061	Fisk-Federal
1923		.0007	Lee-Republic
1925	.089		
1926		.0002	Seiberling-Portage
1929		.0030	Goodrich-Hood
1930		.0096	Goodrich-Miller
1931		.0373	U.S. Rubber-Gillette
			U.S. Rubber-Samson
1935	.168	.0119	Goodyear—Kelly-Springfield
1939		.0116	U.S. Rubber-Fisk
1945		.0007	General-Penna
1947	.163		
1954	.165		
1958	.141		

* Exports as % value of production were as follows: 1925, 3.7%; 1935, 3.5%; 1947, 8.3%; 1954, 4.4%; 1958, 3.7%.

TABLE 21–A15

U.K. Rubber Tires and Tubes Industry; Contributions of Mergers and Concentration Measures for Selected Dates, Based on Value of Domestic Consumption plus Exports*

Selected Dates	H	Dunlop Share 1924 to 1952	Contributions of Mergers to ΔH	Remarks
1912				Large-scale tire output begins
1924	.363	.584		Before import tariff
1925			.0899	Dunlop-Macintosh
1927				Import tariff imposed
1933			.0070	BTR-IRGP&T (Palmer)
			.0171	Dunlop-India
			.0009	BTR-Stepney
1935	.355	.571		
1938			.0001	North British-U.S. Rubber (Dominion)
1947			.0007	Dunlop-Tyres (Scotland)
1952	.271	.465		
1953			.0056	Dunlop-Simons (Tyresoles)

* That is, imports plus U.K. production. Exports as % of production plus imports were as follows: 1924, 16%; 1935, 22%; 1952, 25%—see Table 21–A16 for alternative figures based on domestic consumption.

TABLE 21–A16
U.K. RUBBER TIRES AND TUBES INDUSTRY; CONTRIBUTIONS OF MERGERS
AND CONCENTRATION MEASURES FOR SELECTED DATES, BASED ON
VALUE OF DOMESTIC CONSUMPTION*

Selected Dates	H	Dunlop Share 1924 to 1952	Contributions of Mergers to ΔH	Remarks
1924	.334†	.557		
1925			.0813	Dunlop-Macintosh
1933			.0095	BTR-IRGP&T (Palmer)
			.0121	Dunlop-India
			.0014	BTR-Stepney
1935	.355†§	.571		
1938			.0001	North British-U.S. Rubber (Dominion)
1947			.0004	Dunlop-Tyres (Scotland)
1952	.301‡	.497		
1953			.0070	Dunlop-Simons (Tyresoles)

* That is, imports and production less estimated exports.

† Exports assumed to be in proportion to production for U.K. companies in 1924 and 1935.

‡ 1952 figures are for actual supply to home market, that is, exports not estimated as in other years; 1952 figure comparable with 1935 and 1924 is .271.

§ Same as H based on share of imports plus U.K. production in Table 21–A15 as imports negligible in this year.

TABLE 21–A17
CONTRIBUTIONS OF MERGERS AND INTERNAL GROWTH TO CHANGES IN
CONCENTRATION FOR SELECTED PERIODS, U.S. &. U.K.

	(1) Period*	(2) ΔH	(3) Contribution of Mergers to ΔH	(4) Contribution of Internal Growth to ΔH = Col. (2) less Col. (3)
Autos, U.S.	1904–20	.203	.031	.172
	1920–39†	.018	.008	.010
	1939–52	—.022	.000	—.022
	1952–64	.056	.002	.054
U.K.	1905–24‡	.167	.003	.164
	1924–38	—.042	.018	—.060
	1938–52	.075	.081	—.006
	1952–64	.018	.001	.017
Cement, U.S.	1900–20	—.014	.033	—.047
	1920–39	—.039	.020	—.059
	1939–55	.001	.005	—.004
	1955–63	—.008	.000	—.008
U.K.	1900–22§	.548	.824	—.276
	1922–38	—.064	.414	—.478
	1938–55	—.032	.002	—.034
	1955–59	—.085	.000	—.085
Cigarettes, U.S.	1890–1921‖	.052	.631††	—.579
	1921–37‖	—.089	.019	—.108
	1937–54‖	.019	.003	.016
	1954–63**	.000	.000	.000
U.K.	1900–20	.549	.226	.323
	1920–38	—.118	.150	—.268
	1938–54‡‡	—.100	—.072	—.028
	1954–59	—.116	.000	—.116
Flat Glass, U.S.	1895–1919§	.059	.232	—.173
	1919–35	.252	.053	.199
	1935–54	—.066	.000	—.066
U.K.	1904–35§§	.180	.000	.180
	1935–55‖‖	.534	.070-.351	.183-.464
Soap, U.S.	1900–25	.058	.010	.048
	1925–37	.171	.078	.093
	1937–54	.029	.011	.018
	1954–58	—.035	.010	—.045

TABLE 21–A17 (Continued)

	(1) Period*	(2) ΔH	(3) Contribu- tion of Mergers to ΔH	(4) Contribu- tion of Internal Growth to ΔH = Col. (2) less Col. (3)
U.K.	1900–21	.405	.272	.133
	1921–38	−.162	.092	−.254
	1938–54	.050	.000	.050
	1954–61***	.037	.004	.033
Steel, U.S.	1899–1920	.094	.253	−.159
	1920–38	−.015	.022	−.037
	1938–54	−.033	−.010	−.023
	1954–60	−.008	.000	−.008
U.K.	1900–20†††	.001	.027	−.026
	1920–38	.030	.016	.014
	1938–54	.001	.000	.001
	1954–60	−.003	.000	−.003
Tires, U.S.	1925–35	.079	.062	.017
	1935–54	−.003	.012	−.015
	1954–58	−.024	.000	−.024
U.K.‡‡‡	1924–35	−.008	.115	−.123
	1935–52	−.084	.001	−.085

* The dates below were chosen to break the data, so far as possible, into the following four periods:

1. Initial Herfindahl year to earliest post-World War I year. With the exception of industries in which important mergers took place in the 1890's, the initial year is 1900, or the earliest year thereafter for which it was possible to compute a Herfindahl index.
2. Earliest post-World War I year to latest pre-World War II year.
3. Latest pre-World War II year to mid-1950's.
4. Mid-1950's to terminal Herfindahl year.

† See note *, Table 21–A1.
‡ Employs average of minimum and maximum estimates for H in 1905.
§ Employs pre-merger figure in initial year.
‖ Based on shares of cigarette production.
** Based on shares of cigarettes consumed domestically.
†† Production share figure employed for 1890 formation of American Tobacco.
‡‡ See note *, Table 21–A6.
§§ Employs "best estimate" in Table 21–A8 for 1904.
‖‖ Employs extreme estimates in Table 21–A8 for 1955 merger.
*** 1961 adjusted to basis of earlier years by 1954 ratio of H including industrial to H excluding industrial.
††† See note *, Table 21–A13.
‡‡‡ Based on value of domestic consumption plus exports in Table 21–A15.

Source: Tables 21–A1 to 21–A16.

TABLE 21–A18
U.S. Fire and Casualty Insurance Companies, Stock and Mutual,
Contributions of Mergers and Concentration Measures for
Selected Dates, 1945–1963, Based on Net Premiums Written*

Selected Dates	H	Contributions of Mergers to ΔH	Remarks
1945	.0163		
1947		.000002	Employers Mutual of Wausau—Hudson Mohawk
1951		.00003	Nationwide—National Casualty
1953	.0164		
1954		.000002	Employers Group—Halifax Insurance
		.00011	Fireman's Fund—National Surety
		.000006	Fire Ass'n of Phila.—Eureka Cas.
1956		.00027†	Continental Cas.—Nat'l Fire of Hartford
		.00012	Amer. Ins. of Newark—Amer. Auto Insurance
		.000007	Fire Ass'n of Phila.—Gen'l Cas. of Wisc.
1957		.00063	America Fore—Fireman's (Loyalty) Group
1958		.00010	America Fore-Loyalty—Yorkshire
		.000005	Fire Ass'n of Phila.—Hoosier Cas.
1959		.00004	Commercial Union—North British
		.000002	Northern Ins.—Maine Bonding and Casualty
1960		.00001	Employers—Northern Assurance
		.000004	Springfield-Monarch—Standard Ins. of Tulsa
		.000006	Springfield-Monarch—Freeport Ins.
1961	.0154‡	.000002	Reliance—Standard Fire of New York
		.00006	Reliance—Standard Accident
		.00008	Royal-Globe—London and Lancashire
1962		.00003	General Accident—Camden Fire
		.000005	St. Paul F & M—Birmingham Fire and Cas.
		.00007	U.S. Fidel. & Guar.—Merchants Fire Assurance
		.00003	Nationwide—Commercial Standard
1963	.0189§	.00003	James S. Kemper—Economy Fire and Cas.
		.00025†	Cont'l-Nat'l Fire—American Casualty
		.00047	Fireman's Fund—Amer. Ins. of Newark
		.000007	Great Amer.—First Ins. of Hawaii
		.00007	Maryland Casualty—Northern Insurance

* Excludes factory mutuals, reciprocal and Lloyds companies.
† If accident and health excluded = .00012.
‡ 1961 H, excluding accident and health = .0168.
§ Comparable figure for state of Illinois, 1963 = .0232.

TABLES 21–A1 TO 21–A18

PRINCIPAL SOURCES

U.S. Automobile Industry:

Automotive Industries (periodical).
Automotive News and Automotive News Almanac (periodicals).
Edwards, Dynamics of the United States Automobile Industry (1965).
Epstein, The Automobile Industry: its Economic and Commercial Development (1928).
Federal Trade Commission, Report on Motor Vehicle Industry (1939).
Kennedy, The Automobile Industry: the Coming of Age of Capitalism's Favorite Child (1941).
Seltzer, A Financial History of the American Automobile Industry (1928).
Temporary National Economic Committee, Investigation of Concentration of Economic Power, Monograph No. 27, The Structure of Industry (1941).
Ward's Automotive Year Book (various years).

U.K. Automobile Industry:

Andrews and Brunner, The Life of Lord Nuffield (1955).
Buchanan, Mixed Blessing: the Motor in Britain (1958).
Maxcy and Silberston, The Motor Industry (1959).
Silberston, The Motor Industry 1955–1964, 27 Bulletin-Oxford University Institute of Economics and Statistics 253 (1965).
Society of Motor Manufacturers and Traders, Ltd., The Motor Industry of Great Britain (various years).
Youngson, The British Economy, 1920–1957 (1960).

U.S. Cement Industry:

American Portland Cement Association, Directory of Portland Cement Manufacturers in the U.S.
Federal Trade Commission, Report of Federal Trade Commission on price bases inquiry: Basing point formula and cement prices (1932).
Lesley, History of the Portland Cement Industry in the United States (1924).
Pit and Quarry (periodical).
Federal Trade Commission, Cement Industry (1933).

U.K. Cement Industry:

Davis, Portland Cement (1909).
Cembureau, World Cement Directory (1961).

U.S. Cigarette Industry:

Cox, Competition in the American Tobacco Industry, 1911–32 (1933).
Jacobstein, The Tobacco Industry in the United States (1907).
Jones, The Trust Problem in the United States (1924).
Nicholls, Price Policies in the Cigarette Industry (1951).
Printer's Ink: Jan. 28, 1944; Feb. 2, 1945; Feb. 1, 1946; Jan. 31, 1947; Jan. 23, 1948; Apr. 1, 1949; Jan. 13, 1950; Jan. 5, 1951; Nov. 18, 1952; Jan. 9, 1953; Jan. 15, 1954; Dec. 31, 1954; Dec. 30, 1955; Dec. 28, 1956; Dec. 27, 1957; Dec. 26, 1958; Dec. 25, 1959; Dec. 23, 1960.
Bureau of Corporations, Report of the Commissioner of Corporations on the Tobacco Industry pts. I, II and III (1909, 1911 and 1915).

U.K. Cigarette Industry:

Gt. Brit. Monopolies Commission, Report on the Supply of Cigarettes and Tobacco and of Cigarette and Tobacco Machinery, Cmd. No. 218 (1961).

Gt. Brit. Board of Trade, Standing Committee on Trusts, Tobacco Industry, Cmd. No. 558 (in vol. 23 of Parliamentary Papers) (1920).

U.S. Flat Glass:

Glass Factory Year Book and Directory (1927, 1930, 1963, 1965).
American Glass Trade Directory (1909–1913).
Davis, The Development of the American Glass Industry (1949).
Fortune, May, 1955 and May, 1956.
National Glass Budget, Nov. 11, 1899; Oct. 19, 1901; Oct. 26, 1901; Jan. 25, 1902; Mar. 22, 1902.
Glass Factory Directory (1916, 1919, 1939, 1943).
Stocking and Watkins, Monopoly and Free Enterprise (1951).
Tariff Commission, Flat Glass and Related Glass Products (1937).

U.K. Flat Glass:

Barker, Pilkington Brothers and the Glass Industry (1960), and correspondence with Professor Barker.
Pilkington Brothers Ltd., correspondence.

U.S. Soap Industry:

1925 and prior years:
Bureau of the Census, Census of Manufactures 1910 and 1925. Establishment data adjusted to company basis employing information on establishment locations from various industrial manuals and company histories.

1935 and after:
A. C. Nielsen Co. data—Advertising Age, Mar. 30, 1964; Oct. 24, 1963; Nov. 30, 1963; Jan. 28, 1963; Dec. 26, 1960.
Lief, It Floats (1958).
Procter and Gamble Company, Into a Second Century with Procter and Gamble (1955).

U.K. Soap Industry:

Corlett, The Economic Development of Detergents (1958).
Gt. Brit. Parliament, Standing Committee on Trusts, Report on the soap industry, Cmd. No. 1126 (in vol. 16 of Parliamentary Papers) (1921).
Puplett, Synthetic Detergents (1957).
Redfern, The Story of the C.W.S. (1913).
Wilson, The History of Unilever (1954).

U.S. Steel Industry:

American Iron and Steel Institute, Directory of Iron and Steel Works in the United States and Canada, (various years).

U.K. Steel Industry:

1938 and prior years:
Burn, Economic History of Steelmaking, 1867–1939 (1940).
Iron and Coal Trades Review, Supplement, Mar. 30, 1900 and Feb. 12, 1904.
Ryland's Directory of Ironmongers of Great Britain (various years).

1939 and later years:
British Iron and Steel Federation, Statistical Year Book. After 1954 the title changed to Iron and Steel: Annual Statistics.

U.S. Tire Industry:

Allen, The House of Goodyear (1936).
Gaffey, The Productivity of Labor in the Rubber Tire Manufacturing Industry (1940).
Lief, The Firestone Story (1951).
Sobel, Economic Impact of Collective Bargaining Upon the Rubber Tire Industry (1951) (unpublished dissertation in University of Chicago Library).
Wolf and Wolf, Rubber; A Story of Glory and Greed (1936).
Ziegler, Current Cases in Business (1964).

U.K. Tire Industry:

Allen, The Industrial Development of Birmingham and the Black Country, 1860–1927 (1929).
Allen, The House of Goodyear (1936).
Donnithorne, British Rubber Manufacturing (1958).
Dunning, American Investment in British Manufacturing Industry (1958).
Gt. Brit. Monopolies Commission, Report on the Supply and Export of Pneumatic Tyres (1955).
History of the Rubber Industry (Schidrowitz and Dawson, eds., 1952).
Palmerton, Market for Rubber Products in the United Kingdom (1922).

U.S. Fire and Casualty Insurance Industry:

Best's insurance reports, fire, marine and miscellaneous (various years).
Insurance year book (various years up to 1955); Insurance by states of fire and marine, casualty, surety and miscellaneous lines (after 1955).
The Spectator Desk Directory of Insurance (1964).

GENERAL REFERENCES

United States

The Structure of American Industry (Adams ed., 3d edition, 1961).
Federal Trade Commission, Report on Corporate Mergers and Acquisitions (1955).
Bureau of the Census, Census of Manufactures (various years).
Department of Commerce, Foreign Commerce and Navigation of the United States (various years).
Commerce Clearing House, records of antitrust cases. [Record in United States v. Procter and Gamble Co., 356 U.S. 677 (1957).]
Temporary National Economic Committee and Bureau of the Census, various concentration studies.

United Kingdom

Allen, British Industries and Their Organization (3d ed. 1951).
National Institute of Economic and Social Research, Economic and Social Study No. 15 (Burn ed. 1958).
Cook, Effects of Mergers (1958).
Evely and Little, Concentration in British Industry (1960).
Fitzgerald, Industrial Combination in England (1927).
Gt. Brit. Board of Trade, The Report on the Census of Production (various years).
Gt. Brit. Customs and Excise Dept. Statistical Office, Annual Statement of Trade of the United Kingdom with foreign countries and British possessions (various years).
Macrosty, The Trust Movement in British Industry (1907).
Maizels and Leak, The Structure of British Industry, 108 J. Royal Statistical Soc'y (Series A) 142 (1945).
Mennell, Takeover; The Growth of Monopoly in Britain, 1951–61 (1962).
Rees, Trusts in British Industry, 1914–1921 (1922).

Chapter

22

MERGERS AND PREVENTIVE
ANTITRUST POLICY*

A distinction may be drawn between two kinds of antitrust law, the preventive and the corrective. The preventive seeks to outlaw those forms of behavior which, if pursued far enough, reduce or eliminate competition. The corrective seeks to eliminate monopolistic power already in existence, or at least to curb certain exercises of this power. Undoubtedly, there are policies that fall on the borderline between these categories, but in general, the distinction can be made with tolerable certainty.

Almost all of the American antitrust law is corrective. This need not be argued for the Sherman Act, and I think that it is almost as true of the Clayton Act. The latter's prohibitions upon price discrimination and tying-clauses apparently were adopted in part to prevent the appearance or spread of monopoly, but it is evident that both types of policies can arise only when monopoly power is already possessed. No competitive seller will continually accept a lower price from some buyers than he can get by diverting his goods to other buyers;[1] and no buyer with adequate alternative supply sources will accept the limitations imposed by tie-in sales or total requirements contracts without an offsetting reduction in price. Section 7 of the Clayton Act,[2] the antimerger

---

* Reprinted from *University of Pennsylvania Law Review,* Vol. 104, No. 2 (November 1955).

[1] The widespread opposition to this view even among disinterested students has impressed itself upon me in the course of the deliberations of the Attorney General's National Committee to Study the Antitrust Laws. A good deal of the opposition is due to the fact that non-economists look only at the nominal price, whereas the economist uses "price" to denote all the conditions of sale, including, *e.g.,* the credit rating of the buyer. Part of the opposition arises also from the perennial, and at times perhaps deliberate, confusion between sporadic and systematic price discrimination. The *Report of the Attorney General's National Committee to Study the Antitrust Laws* (1955) (hereinafter cited as *Report*) is not free from this latter confusion. See *Report* at 218, 336.

[2] 38 Stat. 731 (1914), as amended, 15 U.S.C. § 18 (1952).

section, is the only important instance of preventive antitrust legislation.[3] I shall discuss this section after briefly discussing the general problem of preventive antitrust policy.

PREVENTIVE ANTITRUST POLICY IN GENERAL

In the nature of things, a preventive antitrust policy cannot be wide-flung. An antitrust policy is employed by a society which wishes to use the competitive market, rather than powerful private or public bodies, to regulate most economic activity. Many business activities could lead to monopoly. Some, like innovation, are generally applauded; some, like advertising, have more equivocal reputations; and some, like moving to low wage sections, are all too widely deplored. If a society were to intervene in every activity which might possibly lead to a reduction of competition, regulation would be ubiquitous and the whole purpose of a public policy of competition would be frustrated.

The policy of competition rests upon the assumption that economic forces will go far toward preserving a competitive economy, so that only a moderate amount of preventive (and corrective) antitrust action is necessary to achieve a tolerably satisfactory level of competition. This assumption is today almost an American monopoly; most Europeans believe that competition is self-destructive, and their confidence in this belief has not been diminished by the enormous efforts they expend in suppressing competition. But I accept the assumption as a fundamental empirical truth; the history of the American economy in the twentieth century testifies that a modest program of combatting monopoly is enough to prevent any considerable decline in competition.

A preventive antitrust policy, therefore, should be directed at activities which on their face have a general and important tendency to reduce competition, and only at such activities. Mergers of business rivals are unique in the degree to which they meet this requirement. By definition, they involve at least a temporary reduction in the number of independent enterprises in the industry. This is, indeed, their chief purpose; historically the other purposes of mergers (of large firms) have been incidental and unimportant.[4] The control of mergers since 1890 would have given us an

---

[3] Perhaps the FTC's mandate to eliminate unfair methods of competition works in the same direction; but unfair methods of competition are probably at least as pervasive among small businesses as large, and the common types of FTC cases have only modest relevance to monopoly.

[4] In recent times, the avoidance of taxes has become a significant force in bringing about mergers. See Butters, Lintner, and Cary, *Effects of Taxation: Cor-*

industrial structure substantially less concentrated than that we now possess.

The only other type of business activity that seems to invite preventive antitrust policy is the cooperation of firms within an industry —which is economically only an incomplete form of merger. But here, in contrast with mergers, the difficulty is that there are many justifiable as well as many unjustifiable forms of cooperation. When an industry seeks to standardize its products or engages in joint research or defends itself against attacks by other industries (*e.g.*, margarine v. butter), no antitrust questions need be raised. In fact, such cooperation is almost identical from an economic viewpoint with purchase of the activity from an outsider: the industry may collect its own market information, or it may buy the information from a McGraw-Hill publication. There appears to be no feasible distinction, from the standpoint of preventive antitrust policy, between forms of cooperation which may reduce competition if pursued far enough, and those which will leave competition unimpaired.[5] The Attorney General's Committee is probably right in believing that each class, although not each instance, of trade association activities should be judged separately.[6]

In addition to these general types of preventive antitrust policy, there are many ad hoc policies, most of which stem from the economic activities of government. Thus the government plant disposal programs, the licensing of sequestered foreign patents, armed forces procurement policy and sundry other government policies have paid some attention to the preservation of competition. Very possibly the list of such policies should be lengthened; for example, the vast research expenditures of the Federal Government now go chiefly to large business enterprises which are allowed to own the patents resulting from the government-financed research, and it is not obvious that this scheme pays adequate attention to competition and other social goals. But these ad hoc policies raise fewer questions of principle than of fact, and we shall not examine them here.

MERGERS

The amended section 7 of the Clayton Act is an untested part of the antitrust laws, and thus poses an especially troublesome problem to

---

porate Mergers (1951). Taxes, while often an inducement to sell a flourishing enterprise, are not the reason why the sale is made to a business rival.

[5] Of course, one can distinguish certain forms of cooperation which immediately reduce competition, but their control is part of corrective antitrust policy.

[6] *Report* at 19-24.

the antitrust agencies. They naturally fear to spell out in a concrete and meaningful fashion the specific criteria of mergers which reduce competition to an illegal extent. Lacking extensive experience in enforcement, they could easily devise criteria which have large and embarrassing loopholes, or alternatively, the criteria might prove obstructive of innocent and even desirable mergers. Considerations such as these presumably explain, and possibly even justify in part, the evasive action taken by the enforcement agencies when asked for criteria.

But such considerations do not dictate an equal measure of evasiveness by the Attorney General's Committee which, after all, was not burdened with judicial authority or administrative powers. Yet the *Report* lists several pages of "factors" which should be taken into account in judging the legality of a merger; the following is a distressingly representative sample of this listing:

"(a) What companies buy or sell in the market, how many, and what are the significant differences among them: (i) large, medium, and small (market shares, or rank of large companies, etc.); (ii) degrees of vertical integration; (iii) uses of the product; and (iv) the significance of the product under study in the output or in the purchases of different companies."[7]

Ignoring the naked ambiguity of some phrases such as (iii), it will be observed that nothing is said of how these factors work. For example, there is no hint as to whether the presence of large buyers or the existence of vertical integration serves to make an otherwise debatable merger more or less objectionable.

It is one thing to recognize that there will necessarily be some difficult and puzzling borderline cases in the enforcement of the new section 7; it is another and very different thing to assume that one must approach the interpretation and enforcement of the section in a purely ad hoc manner. We should not entrust the administration of general statutes to enforcement agencies with the lonesome admonition that they should act in the public interest. I propose to discuss some possible criteria and problems in the enforcement of the anti-merger section.

Horizontal Mergers

Much discussion of section 7 implicitly seems to assume that its chief applicability will be to the firm that engages in a succession of mergers, each raising its share of the industry's output by a fairly small percentage. The question of the effect of any one merger on competition

[7] *Id.* at 126.

then becomes: Which straw breaks a camel's back? This is a real problem,[8] but surely its importance is much exaggerated. Often a single
merger will substantially reduce competition: some camels try to haul
pianos.

The elimination of mergers which certainly or almost certainly
reduce competition by a very substantial amount may, in fact, prove to
be the chief contribution of the new section 7. Many of these mergers
would be within the reach of the Sherman Act, it is true, but the less
exacting standards of the Clayton Act will greatly simplify the task of
prohibiting such mergers. Moreover the amended section 7 will serve
as a prod to the Department of Justice, which has almost completely ignored the task of enforcing the Sherman Act prohibitions of unconsum-
mated *attempts* to monopolize.[9]

The most difficult task in devising criteria of the applicability of
section 7, however, arises for the mergers which are not sufficiently large
relative to their industries as to become probable or palpable Sherman
Act cases. Here one can proceed along two very different, but not inconsistent, lines.

The first line employs a legal criterion. If, in the industry, there have
been significant instances of conspiracy or attempted conspiracy in restraint of trade, then any merger of two or more firms of substantial size
should be forbidden. A conspiracy to restrain trade is easier to form, and
more effective in its operation, if the firms in an industry are fewer and
the leading firms are larger. A past record of conspiracy shows that the
number is already too small, or the relative size of some firms is already
too great, to allow a further weakening of the forces of competition.

This criterion of monopolistic history is very powerful; it dictates,
for example, that there should be no mergers by the larger companies in
steel and cement which have records of conspiracy through basing point
price systems. It dictates that there should be no mergers in industries
characterized by frequent antitrust violations, such as various kinds of
electric lamps and lights, movie exhibition and abrasives. Only if the
attempts at conspiracy were absurd and unrealistic gestures, condemned
in advance by market realities, could one dismiss this sort of proof of
present or incipient overconcentration within an industry.

The second line of analysis is more directly economic. The basic
test of an undesirable merger is that, if the merging firm continues this

---

[8] See p. 301 *infra.*
[9] 26 Stat. 209 (1890), 15 U.S.C. § 2 (1952).

type of merger activity, competition will be appreciably reduced. It requires only a moment's thought to reveal that this basic test is not easily translated into objective and manageable criteria. Even a low rate of merger, if continued long enough, may lead to high concentration and reduce competition substantially. If the merging firm begins to raise prices, often other firms will be attracted to the industry, so should one not also predict the rate of entry of new firms? Aside from questions of fact about the history of mergers and entry of firms—which can be troublesome enough, of course—we must make decisions as to (i) what a critical level of concentration may be; (ii) the time horizon we employ; and (iii) what may be the costs of excessive zeal in combatting mergers.

The level of concentration which seriously threatens competition still eludes precise determination by the economist. We all recognize that in a properly defined industry, if the largest firm has less than 10 percent of the output, competition will be effective—in the absence of collusion which itself generally will be less probable and effective when concentration is low. And when one firm has 40 or 50 percent or more, or two to five firms have 75 percent or more of the industry's output, competition will seldom plague the industry. Between such widely separated limits, the level of concentration which poses a serious threat to competition will vary with the ease with which new firms can enter the industry, the rate of growth of the industry, the closeness of substitute products made by other industries and their competitive organization and other factors.

To this area of uncertainty, one must add that of the time period over which we should extrapolate the recent trends of concentration. If we use a very long period, almost all mergers are suspect; if we use a very short period, we are simply discussing a single merger and thus ignoring the possibility that the reduction of competition may be a process as well as an event. But this is really a minor problem, I conjecture. Firms which are seeking a commanding position in their industry move swiftly as a rule, and a very few years—say five—should usually be sufficient to reveal their plans.

We cannot prohibit all classes of mergers which might conceivably reduce competition without interfering with legitimate and desirable mergers which have no adverse effect, or only a negligible effect, upon competition. Moreover, it is necessary to recognize the possibility that some mergers which raise concentration or reduce an already small number of firms will increase competition. This situation may arise when the small firms in an industry are relatively inefficient and cannot survive as independent enterprises; if they can survive by merging, the number of effective competitors in the industry is increased.[10] The recent mergers of the small firms in the automobile industry were presumably tacitly approved by the antitrust agencies on this line of thinking, and conceivably properly so.

Those mergers which increase both concentration and competition are most uncommon, however. In industries where one must produce a fifth or more of the nation's output in order to achieve an efficient or profitable productive technique, competition will be weak whether one does or does not allow mergers. If the economies of scale are not substantial, the proper social policy would be to dissolve the giant firms rather than to allow mergers of the small; if the economies of scale are substantial, then competition cannot be used to regulate the industry.

Proposals for the enforcement of the antimerger statute should also take into account the practical limitations on the investigations that the enforcement agencies can make. It would be absurd to expect a thorough investigation of each of the hundreds or thousands of mergers of interstate commerce dimensions that occur each year. One must eliminate the vast majority of mergers from review, but the elimination should be made on the basis of presumptive legality and economic unimportance, and not—presumably, as at present—on the basis of the caprice of notoriety.

I should think that the foregoing considerations are best met by a set of rules such as these:

1. There should be a presumption that every firm with less than 5 to 10 percent of an industry's output (after merger) may engage in the merger. Within this range, the percentage should be lower, the larger the industry.
2. Every merger by a firm which possesses one fifth or more of an industry's output after the merger shall be presumed to violate the statute.[11]
3. In the situations that lie between these limits, the merger should

---

[10] The *Report* mentions two other types of mergers which may serve desirable ends. First, ". . . mergers may ease from the market companies which have failed in the competitive struggle and thus prevent potential bankruptcies." *Report* at 124. It is not explained why the acquiring firm should pay more than a bankruptcy price, unless it is also acquiring some market control. Second, ". . . [mergers] may spur operating economies by spreading overhead costs. . . ." *Id.* at 125. This is simply inaccurate arithmetic; the merged firm has the sum of the overhead costs of the constituent firms and presumably no greater output. In any case, spreading—or piling up—overhead costs is no spur—or bridle—to operating economies.

[11] It is interesting to notice that in the recent complaint against Schenley Industries, Inc., for acquiring control of Park & Tilford, the merged firm is near this borderline of one-fifth. The merged firm would have 20.5% of productive capacity, 26% of production, 17% of bottled whiskey, 19% of storage capacity, 22% of inventories and 19% of dollar volume of sales, according to the complaint. *United States v. Schenley Industries, Inc.*, Civil No. 1686, D. Del., Feb. 14, 1955.

be investigated by the enforcement agencies if the aggregate annual sales of the merging firms will exceed some absolute level—say five million dollars—after merger.[12] Its legality should be judged along the lines discussed above.

A set of rules such as these would serve the double purpose of giving the business community some advance knowledge of public policy toward most mergers, and of achieving the important goals of the legislation.

Vertical Integration

The foregoing discussion pertains only to horizontal mergers, *i.e.*, mergers of firms within the same industrial category. Both the *Report* and the literature of antitrust have devoted considerable attention to two other categories of mergers: the vertical integration of enterprises, and the conglomerate firm.

It is not obvious that the vertical merger has any direct antitrust relevance. Suppose that there are one hundred firms (of reasonably similar sizes) in each of the consecutive processes of spinning, weaving and dyeing a particular textile. Each process will be competitively organized. Suppose that there is universal vertical integration, so that instead of 300 firms, one hundred in each process, we now have one hundred firms, each operating in all three stages. Why should not all the processes still be competitive?—we have just finished saying that one hundred firms in any industry are sufficient for competition. Except in empirically unimportant cases, there is no reason to expect that vertical integration has any monopolistic implications so long as every stage of production is competitive.[13]

Of course vertical integration loses its innocence if there is an appreciable degree of market control at even one stage of the production process. It becomes a possible weapon for the exclusion of new rivals by increasing the capital requirements for entry into the combined integrated production processes, or it becomes a possible vehicle of price discrimination.[14] In these cases new vertical mergers are not desirable, and one should supplement our rules with an additional one:

[12] Such a cut-off point has economic as well as administrative justification. A monopolist of small absolute size will normally be encroached upon by new rivals much sooner than a monopolist of large absolute size. See my introduction to *Business Concentration and Price Policy* (1955).

[13] The one probable effect upon competition is indirect. It may be true of certain industries that the firms most likely to enter them are firms which sell to or buy from them. Then vertical integration would reduce the number of potential entrants, and in borderline cases (hence the empirical unimportance of the exceptions) decrease somewhat the competition within a given stage of production.

[14] See George J. Stigler, "The Division of Labor Is Limited by the Extent of the Market," *Journal of Political Economy*, Vol. LIX (1951), pp. 190–91.

4. Where a firm has a fifth or more of an industry's output, its acquisition of more than five to ten percent of the output capacity of industries to which it sells or from which it buys in appreciable quantities shall be presumed to violate the statute.

This rule is simply an adaptation of rules 1 and 2.

Conglomerate Mergers

Conglomerate mergers owe much of their current interest, and perhaps their intellectual parentage, to Corwin Edwards, who has portrayed them as a menacing but elusive form of organization.[15] The essence of this type of firm, as I understand it, is that although the firm need not have an appreciable degree of market control in any one market, yet because of the many markets in which it operates and the large resources it possesses, a power is acquired to sell and buy at preferential terms. I must confess that the exact mechanics by which the total power possessed by the firm gets to be larger than the sum of the parts (in individual markets) escape me, and I am not sure that there are any companies that meet the specifications of the conglomerate firm. There is a certain resemblance between Edwards' concept and the structure of, *e.g.*, duPont, but duPont has monopoly power in many markets, and therefore one does not have to resort to conglomerateness to explain its power and prosperity.

If there are conglomerate firms, I suspect that their chief sins are associated with their amassing of wealth. But the antitrust laws are not the weapons with which to deal with non-monopolistic concentrations of wealth.

Patent Acquisition as Merger

The *Report* fails to mention in either the Merger or Patent Chapters whether the acquisition of patents from a rival may be prevented under section 7 of the Clayton Act. The control of mergers should extend, of course, to the accumulation by one firm of any form of property whose concentration of ownership will reduce competition in an important market, and therefore it should extend to the accumulation of patents. The *Report* mentions the Sherman Act as limiting the accumulation of patents with intent to monopolize,[16] but patents of a rival are part of his "assets" and presumably subject also to the Clayton Act's mandate against acqui-

[15] See Corwin Edwards, "Conglomerate Bigness as a Source of Power," in *Business Concentration and Price Policy* (1955).
[16] *Report* at 227 n.21.

sition of "any part of the assets." The ambiguous language of the *Report* seems to ask for a clearer showing of impairment of competition in the case of patent acquisition than in the case of ordinary mergers, but no justification is given for this priority of patent rights over antitrust objectives (which pervades section v of the *Report*), and I doubt that one can be given.

The antimerger statute, it is evident, is the fundamental element of our preventive antitrust policy. It seems a conservative estimate that fully one half of the major cases which have been brought under the Sherman Act have been necessary simply because we did not have an effective antimerger policy in the past. The antitrust agencies should take this lesson to heart; the new statute deserves a place of high priority in the antitrust policy of the United States.

APPENDIX

Monopolistic Competition in Retrospect*

Before the Great Depression, that chasm between dark-ness and light, economists had generally looked upon the economy as a mixture of industries that approximated conditions of perfect competition and industries that were "monopolies." The competitive industries, it was believed, were satisfactorily analyzed by the theory of competition, and although the "monopolies" were diverse in structure and power, they could be informatively analyzed by a discriminating use of the theory of monopoly. Individual economists varied considerably in the relative im-portance they attached to these two groups of industries, of course, but they varied surprisingly little in the type of analytical system they deemed appropriate to the analysis of economic events. This is not to say that the details of the analytical system were, or were thought to be, definitive: indeed certain portions of the system, such as duopoly, admittedly were (and are) in wretched shape.

Then came the works of Mrs. Robinson and Professor Chamberlin, who criticized this viewpoint and demanded a new orientation of our thought. Because of the high quality of their volumes, and because it was the "'thirties," they were enthusiastically received. Then too, their mes-sages seemed to reinforce one another, but this was a confusion that was quickly detected by, and almost only by, Professor Chamberlin.

Of Mrs. Robinson's work I need say little. It is amply clear, on a re-reading at this distant date, that her message was in no sense revolu-tionary, although at times her language was rebellious. Her two basic theses were: (1) that price theory is capable of great improvements in elegance and significant improvements in logic; and (2) that the theory of monopoly is the appropriate instrument of analysis of all real situa-tions in which the assumptions of perfect competition are not completely and exactly fulfilled. If she gave no evidence for her second thesis, to which I shall return later, she contributed much to the fulfillment of the first. Her volume marks no break with the tradition of neo-classical eco-

* Reprinted from *Five Lectures on Economic Problems* (London School of Economics, 1949).

nomics; indeed it contains, I think, too uncritical an acceptance of the substantive content of orthodoxy.

Professor Chamberlin was a true revolutionary. Instead of assimilating observed market structures into exclusive classes such as competition and monopoly, he told us, we must throw off our theoretical heritage and look at the world with clear and candid eyes. Then we shall find that no simple dichotomy does justice to the rich variety of industrial organization. True, there are (a very few) industries that closely resemble those studied by the economist of perfect competition. True, there are (perhaps more) firms that partake of the nature of monopoly as this concept was used in neo-classical economics. But vastly more often the firm displays a mixture of insulation from other rivals, by means of real or fancied product differences, and of indirect rivalry by way of (1) the willingness of some consumers to shift among products and (2) the ability of firms to change their products. As a result, there are important—in fact, typical —phenomena which cannot be explained, or can be explained only with serious error, if economic reality is forced into the neo-classical categories.

Let us spell out Professor Chamberlin's *Weltanschauung* in a bit more detail. Suppose our primary interest is (or perhaps I should say, begins with) the housing of the people who work in New York City. Even casual observation indicates the prominence of two characteristics in this housing market: (1) a great variety of products; and (2) a certain "unsystematism" or irregularity or randomness in the interrelationships among these products. (1) The housing facilities range from incredible estates to unbelievable slums. Every unit is unique in a rigorous technological sense and, more relevant, there are thousands of classes of dwellings whose rents need not move in strict proportion on threat of wholesale vacancy or queuing up. Our housing facilities, moreover, roam far afield. They extend to several states directly, and—through summer and winter places and other channels—ultimately to the whole world. They very probably extend also to automobiles, fur coats, and trips abroad, for the competition may well be stronger between these products and various classes of housing than the competition between some classes of housing. (2) Nor is there any systematic arrangement of this assemblage of products. The barriers between products are not of uniform height or thickness, nor is there any discernible order in their occurrence. It is not impossible that apartments A and B do not compete directly and yet are both in close rivalry with automobiles. The existence of many similar and closely situated apartments is compatible with pervasive duopoly.

This picture of economic life was not fundamentally new, but Professor Chamberlin's reaction was. Customarily the picture had led to some sort of "institutional" economics, that strange mixture of magnificent methodological pronouncements and skinny, *ad hoc* analyses. Chamberlin, however, persevered to construct an analytical system of recognizable type to deal with the picture: the co-ordinates of his diagrams would be price and quantity, not Church and State.

Chamberlin's vision was clearly a legitimate way of looking at economic life. One may even argue that it was more congruent with untutored observation, and in this sense more "realistic." But these are points, not of unimportance, but of complete irrelevance, despite the part they played in securing popularity for his theory. There is a question of minor interest: Did Chamberlin develop from this viewpoint a logically consistent theory of economic events? And there is a question of paramount importance: Does a theory incorporating this viewpoint contain more accurate or more comprehensive implications than the neoclassical theory? I wish to emphasize this second question because it is not true that a theory which is realistic in its assumptions—if any meaning can be attached to this—is necessarily realistic in its implications, a theme to which I shall return.

But let us return to Chamberlin's picture. How does he reduce this stupendous diversity and complexity to a manageable system without assuming away its essential characteristics?

1. THE FIRST ATTEMPT: CHAMBERLIN

One cannot long talk sensibly and simultaneously about a Connecticut estate, a Brooklyn walk-up, and a New Jersey hotel—to say very little of the fur coats and trips to Europe. And so Professor Chamberlin introduced the "group":

> The group contemplated is one which would *ordinarily* be regarded as composing one imperfectly competitive market: a number of automobile manufacturers, of producers of pots and pans, of magazine publishers, or of retail shoe dealers.[1]

The ambiguity of the concept of a group is not removed by this enumeration or the references to competing monopolists; we are left with the strong impression that the Marshallian industry has reappeared and we

[1] *Theory of Monopolistic Competition*, 5th edition, p. 81. Our interest at this point is in the early editions, but with two exceptions the quotations are identical in content and pagination in the first and fifth editions. The first exception is in the above quotation: "ordinarily" is not italicized in the early editions.

do not understand its new rôle, for our new picture is one of diversity. But then our picture is not an analytical system; it is therefore necessary to turn to Chamberlin's use of the concept in order to discover its rôle in his analytical system.

The subsequent analysis indicates that the group is a collection of (producers of?) fairly close substitutes; and at least once Chamberlin refers to "groups of products that are close substitutes for each other" (p. 140). More formally, the group may be defined as the collection of firms whose cross-elasticities of demand exceed some pre-assigned value. We must suspend judgment on the usefulness of the concept until we see the results to which it permits Chamberlin to arrive, but several direct implications of the definition should be noticed at once:

1. It is perfectly possible, on Chamberlin's picture of economic life, that the group contain only one firm, or, on the contrary, that it include all of the firms in the economy. This latter possibility can readily follow from the asymmetry of substitution relationships among firms: taking any one product as our point of departure, each substitute has in turn its substitutes, so that the adjacent cross-elasticities may not diminish, and even increase, as we move farther away from the "base" firm in some technological or geographical sense.¹

2. The picture of diversity and unsystematism also makes it very likely, if the group contains several firms, that the products be heterogeneous from the technological viewpoint.

3. The picture also dictates that often, and perhaps usually, a large or dominant rôle is played by firms outside the group in determining prices and profits within the group.

The importance of the group concept for the theory of monopolistic competition must be emphasized. Chamberlin asks the reader: can not the conventional theory of monopoly cope with the problems of monopolistic competition? And he answers: No. "Monopolistic competition, then, concerns itself not only with the problem of an *individual* equilibrium (the ordinary theory of monopoly), but also with that of a *group* equilibrium (the adjustment of economic forces within a group of competing monopolists, ordinarily regarded merely as a group of competitors)" (p. 69). The group is no mere expedient to get the analysis started, it is the vehicle of Chamberlin's theory of interdependence of products.

What, then, can we say of the (perhaps) 100 products—dwellings and limousines—in the group? Further simplification is obviously necessary, and Chamberlin introduces what he calls the "uniformity" assumption:

We therefore proceed under the heroic assumption that both demand and cost curves for all the "products" are uniform throughout the group (p. 82).

Again we must pause: the uniformity assumption is only temporary, we are promised, but even a temporary assumption should be meaningful. How can different products have uniform costs and demands? The quantity axes of the various product diagrams are simply not the same: one measures three-room apartments, another four-room houses, and perhaps still another, restaurant meals (an excellent substitute for a kitchen). We cannot translate one into another by the ratio of their prices, for we are constructing the apparatus to explain prices. We do not wish to say that two physically similar apartments are "really" the same. They are not the same if their prices differ, and perhaps even if they do not differ[2] —this is the fundamental picture. And we do wish to say that restaurant meals plus a bedroom may form a better substitute for a Manhattan apartment than does a Brooklyn apartment—this is also part of the picture.

And yet, by the uniformity assumption Chamberlin has implicitly defined the group as a collection of physically homogeneous products. The identity of costs and demands is otherwise meaningless, and so also is the demand curve he proceeds to draw for a firm on the assumption that "competitors' prices are always identical" (p. 90). We simply cannot attach meaning to the statement that physically diverse things have the same price. This physical homogeneity possibly destroys, at least temporarily, Chamberlin's monopolistic competition (except for spatially distributed firms), for he has also assumed that buyers have perfect knowledge (p. 73), in order further to simplify the analysis. With perfect knowledge and homogeneous products, must not the demand curve confronting each firm be infinitely elastic? But the uniformity assumption is only temporary, we recall.

So we have 100 products of various sorts (blinking the inconsistency) or of one sort, but with negatively sloping demand curves (dropping the assumption of perfect knowledge), what then? Our vision tells us that we are unlikely to find symmetry, continuity, or any sort of smoothness in the relationships among these products. To meet this problem, Chamberlin introduces what I shall term the "symmetry" assumption:

---

[2] ". . . general uniformity of price proves nothing as to the freedom of competition from monopoly elements" (p. 88).

Specifically, we assume for the present that any adjustment of price or of "product" by a single producer spreads its influence over so many of his competitors that the impact felt by any one is negligible and does not lead him to any readjustment of his own situation (p. 83).

It is now an anti-climax to notice that Chamberlin further assumes, throughout his entire volume, that (1) the only relationship between products is that of substitution—complementarity "is beyond the scope of our problem" (p. 39 n.), and (2) the Marshallian cost apparatus is acceptable *in toto*: the vision of diversity and unsystematism does not extend to the resources market.[3]

But now we have utterly abandoned the picture with which our analytical technique was designed to deal: there is no variety and there is only one possible type of interrelationship between products. We probably have a Marshallian industry. We appear also to have negatively sloping demand curves for individual products, because our picture and our group are inconsistent with our uniformity assumption. The tangency of average cost and demand curves which we now deduce is of little importance to us: this familiar result of competitive theory, I will argue later, is not enriched. Possibly of more importance is the finding that even under these extreme conditions our new variable, "product," cannot be "measured along an axis" (p. 79)—that is, cannot be measured. Each time "product" appears in the discussion, we are told to choose it to maximize profits, and nothing more.[4] As a result, for practical purposes the theory of monopolistic competition concerns only consumers moving among products, and ignores products moving among consumers.

We hasten on to the sections in which the uniformity and symmetry assumptions are separately (but, oddly, never jointly) lifted. Oligopoly may, and perhaps usually will, enter if the symmetry assumption fails, and then we are reduced to the familiar uncertainty over assumptions and results (pp. 100–4), from which we salvage only the conclusion that prices may be higher than under competition (p. 104). The effect of diversity of demand and cost conditions is even more devastating: there may be monopoly profits throughout the group at equilibrium—and then

[3] Although, in strict logic, it must: there are no consumer goods that are purchased exclusively by consumers.

[4] "The difficulties of representing graphically the variation of 'product' render hazardous any attempt to define with precision the exact point of equilibrium. It would seem that the most that can be said is that it will be characterized by (1) the equation of cost and price, and (2) the impossibility of a 'product' adjustment by anyone which would increase his profits" (p. 97). This, of course, is a statement of the problem, not of its solution.

again, there may not. Indeed, although Professor Chamberlin does not state the possibility, it is not even clear that equilibrium is attainable: under these vague conditions prices may continue to change, and new firms may continue to enter and old firms continue to leave the "group." This indeterminacy is especially likely if we recognize variety through time—the consumers' liking for novelty, which Professor Chamberlin should surely add to his picture. He sums up the effects of diversity:

> To sum up this phase of the matter, our statement of the group problem must be modified by recognizing that the demand curves are not adjusted uniformly to a position tangent to the cost curves. In so far as profits are higher than the general competitive level in the field as a whole or in any portion of it, new competitors will, *if possible*, invade the field and reduce them. If this were always possible, as hitherto assumed, the curves would always be tangent and monopoly profits would be eliminated. In fact it is only partially possible. As a result some (or all) of the curves may lie at various distances to the right of the point of tangency, leaving monopoly profits scattered throughout the group—and throughout the price system (p. 113).

It will be observed that the theory of monopolistic competition now contains no conditions of equilibrium, only a definition of equilibrium.

As a result, in the general case we cannot make a single statement about economic events in the world we sought to analyze. It is true that many such statements are made by Chamberlin, but none follows rigorously from the ambiguous apparatus. All of the definite comparisons with competition, for example, are made when there is uniformity and symmetry.[5] Indeed even these comparisons rest upon the further and technically inadmissible assumption that the cost curves of a firm will be the same under competition and monopolistic competition, although there is no presumption that the size of the "group" will be the same in the two situations if they really differ.[6]

---

[5] This is recognized in a footnote (p. 78 n.), where it is said that if there is not tangency, the monopolistically competitive output of the firm may exceed the competitive output. This is held to be an unimportant exception because of "considerations introduced below in connection with the group problem." In the group discussion, under symmetry and uniformity, the footnote is recalled (p. 88.) but not elaborated. The exception is forgotten when diversity of costs and demands is reached, although tangency of cost and demand curves has now vanished, and with it the improbability of the exception.

[6] The neglect of cost differences is justified on two grounds. (1) Many industries are constant cost industries—a result borrowed from Marshallian analysis, for which there is no presumption in the Chamberlin group. (2) The belief that even with increasing or decreasing cost industries, "the divergences from the norms of purely competitive theory are always of the same sort" (p. 87). This belief is without foundation.

And so the first attempt has failed.[7] Professor Chamberlin did not reduce his picture of reality to a manageable analytical system.

2. THE SECOND ATTEMPT: CHAMBERLIN-TRIFFIN

In the course of time and controversy, Professor Chamberlin indicated the probable desirability of abandoning the concept of the group, which in his system was, after all, an anachronistic vestige of neo-classical economics. When discussing the closely related concept of entry of new firms (into a group), he said:

> The upshot of the matter seems to be that the concept is not very useful and is even seriously misleading in connection with monopolistic competition. It is, in reality, a concept usually related to a market for a definite commodity, and the fundamental difficulty is that there is no such commodity under monopolistic competition beyond that produced by an individual firm (p. 201).

But he does not follow this line of thought to its conclusion:

> It is not meant by this argument to discard completely the concept of an "industry." In many connections, it is obviously useful to delimit a portion of the economic system and study it in some degree of isolation from the rest. And if this can be done, although entry is never "free," it is not wholly without meaning to speak of the *relative* ease with which this particular field may be entered, in the sense of the relative ease with which substitutes for the particular products which compose the "industry" may be produced. One emerges from any attempt to classify industries, however, with a feeling that it is all exceedingly arbitrary. The "common sense" definitions of industries in terms of which practical problems are likely to be studied seem to be based much more upon technological criteria than upon the possibility of market substitution (p. 202 n.).

Except for the last sentence, which is an indirect admission of the entire Marshallian system,[8] the tenor of the argument is that the group must go.

---

[7] I pass over the theory of selling costs because my subject is monopolistic competition, not the economics of Professor Chamberlin. Selling costs played only one rôle in the discussion that we need notice: their existence was adduced as a criticism of the theory of perfect competition, for none would be needed with perfect knowledge. Professor Chamberlin was right in concluding that perfect competition is a poor instrument in analyzing selling costs. His results might have been more informative, however, if he had chosen to drop the assumption that the economy was stationary, rather than the assumption that the economy was competitive.

[8] This last sentence is even more remarkable in the original article of which the above quotations are revisions: "It seems much easier and more defensible to set up classifications based upon technological criteria than upon the possibility of market substitution." ("Monopolistic or Imperfect Competition?" *Quarterly Journal of Economics,* Vol. LI [1937], 568n.)

This is a most baffling state in which to leave the theory of monopolistic competition, for we recall that the theory differs from that of monopoly only in containing a group equilibrium. "As for monopoly, *as ordinarily conceived and defined,* monopolistic competition embraces it and takes it as a starting point" (p. 68, not in first edition). But if the group is suspect, if at best it is a notion "not wholly without meaning," the theory of monopoly seems to be also the final destination.

It was left for an able disciple, Dr. Robert Triffin, to carry the purification of the technique a step farther, in his *Monopolistic Competition and General Equilibrium Theory* (1940). He succeeds in making the analytical apparatus portray faithfully the original picture of variety and unsystematism. Costs, demands, and hence profits of each firm are functions of all prices in the economy, i.e. profits of firm $i = \phi$ ($p_1, p_2, \ldots, p_n$), where n is very large. The firm will maximize profits, subject to the usual uncertainties of oligopolistic situations—that is, it will equate marginal revenue and marginal cost.

And what of the group? It must go, for it is inconsistent with the fundamental vision. "In the general pure theory of value, the group and the industry are useless concepts" (p. 89). "Product differentiation robs the concept of industry of both its definiteness and its serviceability" (p. 188). How, then, are we to analyze the inter-relationships among firms? Apparently we cannot; Dr. Triffin's chapter (III) on the theory of external interdependence consists only of an elegant classification of types of interdependence.

Dr. Triffin does not fail to draw the conclusion that monopolistic competition has nothing to say of the interdependence of firms; this silence is indeed hailed as an advance over the Marshallian theory (p. 189). The basis for this claim deserves our attention. Dr. Triffin visualizes the discipline as composed of two very different types of studies: the "general pure theory of value"; and the investigation of concrete economic problems—for example, the New York housing problem:

Is anything gained by limiting the investigation to a group of close competitors, which we would call a group or industry? In an empirical, statistical study, yes: we can, in this way, reduce to a manageable size the research work involved, without any serious loss in precision or exhaustiveness. In the general statement of value theory, no: when competition is discussed in general abstract terms, we may just as well make the group (or industry) coextensive with the whole economic collectivity. The problems are the same, and the complexity is no greater.

In other words, the value of these groupings is only a concrete, empirical one: it is never useful to speak of "industries" or "groups" in a general, abstract way, but it may be very helpful to speak of the oil industry, the coal industry, the steel industry, etc. (p. 88).

And in his conclusion, Dr. Triffin goes on:

Instead of drawing its substance from arbitrary assumptions, chosen for their simplicity and unduly extended to the whole field of economic activity, our theory may turn to more pedestrian, but more fruitful methods. It will recognize the richness and variety of all concrete cases, and tackle each problem with due respect for its individual aspects. More advantage will be taken of all relevant factual information, and less reliance will be placed on a mere resort to the pass-key of general theoretical assumptions (p. 189).

I would emphasize the separateness of these two types of economic analysis in Triffin's view of economics: there is neither substitution nor complementarity between the general theory and the specific economic investigation. The theory has nothing to learn from the study of specific problems because these problems are so diverse that no single inductive generalization is possible.[9] Conversely the study of specific problems has nothing to gain from the general theory, for the theory can provide no apparatus to raise relevant questions, to indicate relevant types of facts, or to guide the economist in handling the facts to reach useful conclusions.

This is a fundamentally mistaken rôle to assign to general theory. The study of economic theory is not defensible on aesthetic grounds—it hardly rivals in elegance the mathematics or physics our sophomores learn. The theory is studied only as an aid in solving real problems, and it is good only in the measure that it performs this function. Dr. Triffin's advice is fundamentally to give up theory, "to tackle each problem with due respect for its individual aspects." Chamberlin's picture of reality has finally led, when consistently followed, to the familiar reaction: *ad hoc* empiricism.

3. THE REASONS FOR FAILURE

Professor Chamberlin's failure to construct an analytical system capable of dealing informatively with his picture of reality is not hard to explain. The fundamental fact is that, although Chamberlin could throw

---

[9] Thus, after Dr. Triffin examines freedom of entry, he concludes, "Which type of entry prevails in any particular case is to be ascertained and 'explained' by an investigation of the facts. Analytical reasoning is powerless to deduce the answer from general, universally valid assumptions" (p. 123).

off the shackles of Marshall's view of economic life, he could not throw off the shackles of Marshall's view of economic analysis. Marshall's technique was appropriate to the problem set to it: it deals informatively and with tolerable logic with the world of competitive industries and monopolies. But it is lost in the sea of diversity and unsystematism, and Chamberlin is lost with it.

Dr. Triffin's failure, on the other hand, seems to me attributable to his attempt to make the general theory an accurate description of all reality. It is as if an artist is commissioned to paint the picture of a typical skyscraper: and since skyscrapers are thick and thin, of variable height, of differing colours, with various architectural designs, his painting must be blank because it would violate reality if it contained a single identifiable detail. Dr. Triffin should have been warned by the Walrasian theory of general equilibrium he sought to generalize. This theory proved to be relatively uninformative, even when it had as many equations as unknowns; it was not likely to gain in usefulness when the unknowns were multiplied and the equations reduced.

4. CONCLUDING OBSERVATIONS

I wish to close by offering an estimate of the net contribution of the attempt to construct a theory of monopolistic competition. Before undertaking this appraisal, however, it is necessary to set forth certain methodological principles.[10]

The purpose of the study of economics is to permit us to make predictions about the behavior of economic phenomena under specified conditions. The sole test of the usefulness of an economic theory is the concordance between its predictions and the observable course of events. Often a theory is criticized or rejected because its assumptions are "unrealistic." Granting for a moment that this charge has meaning, it burdens theory with an additional function, that of description. This is a most unreasonable burden to place upon a theory: the rôle of description is to particularize, while the rôle of theory is to generalize—to disregard an infinite number of differences and capture the important common element in different phenomena.

But this line of argument grants the ungrantable: it is often impossible to determine whether assumption A is more or less realistic than assumption B, except by comparing the agreement between their im-

---

[10] The present interpretation of these principles is due to Professor Milton Friedman; see Talcott Parsons, *The Structure of Social Action*.

plications and the observable course of events. One can but show that a theory is unrealistic in essentials by demonstrating that its predictions are wrong.

Should monopoly or competition be used to analyze the New York housing market? The answer is: both. If we are interested in the effects of rent ceilings and inflation, the theory of competition provides informative predictions. If we are interested in why one location rents for more than another, the theory of monopoly may be an informative guide. Different theories, each with its particular assumptions, can be applied to the same phenomena to answer different questions.

These remarks are especially relevant to the theory of monopolistic competition. A good deal of the support for this theory stems from the mistaken demand for correspondence between "reality" and premises. The theory is further supported by the erroneous view, for which Professor Chamberlin bears some responsibility, that if the premises of competitive theory depart (in a descriptive sense) from the facts, the implications of that theory must be wrong.[11]

This leads me to the specific contribution of the theory of monopolistic competition: the analysis of the many-firm industry producing a single (technological) product under uniformity and symmetry conditions, but with a falling demand curve for each firm. Chamberlin's analysis of this particular situation is essentially correct, and many economists appear to wish to incorporate it into neo-classical theory. It should be incorporated, not if it is a more "realistic" description of industries, but if it contains different or more accurate predictions (as tested by observation) than the theory of competition. I personally think that the predictions of this standard model of monopolistic competition differ only in unimportant respects from those of the theory of competition because the underlying conditions will usually be accompanied by very high demand elasticities for the individual firms. But this is a question of fact, and it must be resolved by empirical tests of the implications of the two theories (a task the supporters of the theory of monopolistic competition have not yet undertaken).

The general contribution of the theory of monopolistic competition, on the other hand, seems to me indisputable: it has led to reorientation and refinement of our thinking on monopoly. We are now more careful to pay attention to the logical niceties of definitions of industries and com-

---

[11] "In all of the fields where individual products have even the slightest element of uniqueness, competition bears but faint resemblance to the pure competition of a highly organized market for a homogeneous product" (p. 9).

modities. We are now more careful to apply monopoly theory where it is appropriate. The importance of the trade mark and of advertising, and the need for study of product structure and evolution, have become more generally recognized. These and other improvements may seem disappointing to the hopeful proposers of a proud new theory, but they should not be. This is the way sciences grow. One of the prominent lessons of the history of human thought is that new ideas do not lead to the abandonment of the previous heritage; the new ideas are swallowed up by the existing corpus, which is thereafter a little different. And sometimes a little better.

Index

INDEX